BLACK ENTERPRISE
GUIDE TO
STARTING YOUR
OWN BUSINESS

Black Enterprise books provide useful information on a broad spectrum of business and general-interest topics, including entrepreneurship, personal and business finance, and career development. They are designed to meet the needs of the vital and growing African American business market and to provide the information and resources that will help African Americans achieve their goals. The books are written by and about African American professionals and entrepreneurs, and they have been developed with the assistance of the staff of *Black Enterprise,* the premier African American business magazine.

The series currently includes the following books:

Titans of the B.E. 100s:
Black CEOs Who Redefined and Conquered American Business
by Derek T. Dingle

Black Enterprise Guide to Starting Your Own Business
by Wendy Beech

BLACK ENTERPRISE
GUIDE TO
STARTING YOUR
OWN BUSINESS

Wendy Beech

John Wiley & Sons, Inc.

New York • Chichester • Weinheim • Brisbane • Singapore • Toronto

To my father, Wallace Beech.
Thanks for letting me take over your entire home office
to complete this project.
I couldn't have done it without your love and support.
I love you Daddy.

This book is printed on acid-free paper. ∞

Copyright © 1999 by Black Enterprise. All rights reserved.

Published by John Wiley & Sons, Inc.

Published simultaneously in Canada.

This publication is designed to provide accurate and authoritative information in regard to the subject matter covered. It is sold with the understanding that the publisher is not engaged in rendering professional services. If professional advice or other expert assistance is required, the services of a competent professional person should be sought.

Library of Congress Cataloging-in-Publication Data:

Beech, Wendy.
   Black enterprise guide to starting your own business / by
Wendy Beech.
       p.   cm. — (Black enterprise series)
   Includes bibliographical references and index.
   ISBN 0-471-32454-X (pbk. : alk. paper)
   1. New business enterprises.   2. Black business enterprises.
I. Title. II. Series.
HD62.5.B43   1999
658.1' 141' 08996073—dc21   98-55275

Printed in the United States of America.

10   9   8   7   6

CONTENTS

PREFACE

Have you ever considered what it would be like to be in business for yourself? If you're like most people, the thought has crossed your mind. After all, you did pick up this book. But what does it take to be a successful black business owner? Capital? A solid business plan? A knowledgeable staff? A good location?

When Earl G. Graves launched *Black Enterprise* magazine in 1970, he found that being an African American entrepreneur required all of these things, and then some. In his best-selling book, *How to Succeed in Business Without Being White*, Graves warns black business owners that, to successfully sell their products and services, they will need more than a captivating advertising campaign, an executive suite of offices, and Harvard MBA graduates as employees. He insists that African American entrepreneurs will also need "a junkyard dog mentality." He writes, "If you don't know what that means, you've never climbed a junkyard fence and encountered a guard dog trained to get a grip on you and not let go. True entrepreneurs don't let go. If one venture fails, they try another. If one product doesn't sell, they look for a better idea. If one company official isn't buying, they look for another who will. Like the junkyard dog, they hang on no matter how much they are shaken, cursed, beaten, and kicked. . . . "

Undoubtedly, as a new entrepreneur you will face a number of challenges that will test your commitment to the American dream called entrepreneurship. Securing start-up capital is just one of the many challenges that may make you question your decision to try business ownership.

When Deborah Sawyer, president and CEO of Environmental Design International Inc., decided to launch her company in 1991, she had only $20,000 in start-up capital, but needed about $300,000. After three months in operation, she approached area banks for financing, but suffered 23 rejections. "Banks were not eager to lend to service businesses, particularly to women- or minority-owned high-tech companies," says Sawyer, who operates a full-service environmental consulting firm. But Sawyer didn't give up. She continued making a pitch for the dollars she needed to grow her business. As a result of her unyielding persistence, she secured additional monies from the twenty-fourth bank she visited. Today, her company earns about $10 million in revenues.

Even the largest of today's black business owners faced what seemed to be unbeatable odds, but persevered. John H. Johnson, CEO of Johnson Publishing Company, Inc., had a dream to start a magazine geared toward black

America. But it was the early 1940s, and a publication aimed at "Negroes" was unheard of. "The first 25 years were difficult, trying to get circulation and to break through in advertising to get large companies to recognize that black consumers had money and would respond to advertising directed to them," says Johnson, who initially borrowed against his mother's furniture to launch the first magazine targeted toward African Americans. But Johnson did not waver in his efforts and now Johnson Publishing Company, which has spawned *Ebony, Jet, Ebony Man,* and *Ebony South Africa* magazines has earned more than $360 million in sales.

There are many success stories among black business owners. For more than a quarter century, *Black Enterprise* has chronicled these tales while simultaneously giving its readers the tools they need to build a successful business. We've witnessed the phenomenal and diverse successes of such companies as TLC Beatrice, BET Holdings, Karl Kani Infinity, Pro-Line Corporation, and Essence Communications. But, to our dismay, we've also observed the downfall of Daniels & Bell and the sale of Johnson Products. Through it all, however, we have upheld our commitment to educate, inspire, and uplift those who have ever thought about starting their own business, and those currently traveling the path of entrepreneurship.

The *Black Enterprise Guide to Starting Your Own Business* is an extension of our mission to promote and support black entrepreneurs. Nearly 30 years ago, when Earl Graves launched *Black Enterprise,* now an award-winning publication, there were only 45,000 black businessowners in the nation. According to the Small Business Administration's Office of Advocacy, today more than 621,000 black-owned businesses are operating in industries ranging from agriculture and construction to transportation and finance.

Increasingly, African Americans from all social classes and backgrounds are seizing the opportunity to run their own shops. African American men and women sit as founders, presidents, and CEOs of some of the largest black-owned businesses in the nation, as evidenced by *Black Enterprise's* annual B.E. Industrial/Service 100, B.E. Auto Dealer 100, and B.E. Insurance, Investment, Financial, and Advertising Companies. But many blacks are still floundering on the sidelines, scared to take that first step. Others, who have begun the journey and hit roadblocks along the way, have given up because they did not know how to overcome the obstacles or were too proud to ask for help.

Throughout this book, we will provide you with a comprehensive and motivating blueprint to achieve business success. The information and advice in each chapter are supported by true stories of real entrepreneurs. We'll describe the problems they faced and tell you how they handled them. Each chapter concludes with a summary checklist of recommendations and a list of resources for more information, with addresses, phone numbers, and Web sites.

The *Black Enterprise Guide to Starting Your Own Business* is meant to be a reference tool to give you the energy, the resources, the motivation, and the urge to follow your dreams and make them come true. This text will also give you a competitive advantage in the business world, which will be extremely important as you go toe-to-toe with both small and large businesses competing for consumer dollars. It is written with the African American entrepreneur in mind, but we also encourage nonminority business owners to benefit from the discussion of the critical start-up issues that affect all entrepreneurs, whether black or white, Asian or Native American, Latino or European.

We realize that it's very easy to get overwhelmed when starting your own business. There's so much to learn, and even more to do. You have employees to pay, inventory to order, customers to attract, advertising dollars to net, and then you have to eat and sleep too. But if you are passionate about your business and walk carefully and slowly as you begin to build, you *can* succeed. Think of entrepreneurship as a journey of a thousand miles. As an eastern philosopher once said, it begins with a single step.

Step One: Turn the page.

1

BEING YOUR OWN BOSS: ARE YOU READY?

Three gold cards. An annual salary towering over $100,000. A company car. Most people working a grueling 9-to-5 day would give their eyeteeth for these rewards. Wanda James had them all when she was the regional marketing manager for Avery Dennison, an office products company based in Pasadena, California. Still, she gave them up to become an entrepreneur. Why?

"I wasn't growing anymore, and I realized that I had gotten all I could get from corporate America," says James, who worked in marketing for six years. "I did well in my job, but there came a point when the lack of promotions and limited job responsibilities said, 'Little black girl, you're not going any further.'"[1]

Determined to find fulfillment in life, James decided to purchase the Jamaican Café, a Caribbean-style restaurant located in Santa Monica, California. Scott Durrah, her fiancé, was a good friend of the former owner, so when the three were casually talking one night at the restaurant, James discovered that it was up for sale. It didn't take James long to determine that she wanted to become the new owner, so, after partnering with Durrah, the two began writing a business plan and crunching numbers to figure the start-up costs. Emptying out their savings account and borrowing from family members and credit cards, they raised the $50,000 they needed for the closing costs. In August 1996, the Jamaican Café opened its doors under new ownership.

Today, the restaurant serves a wide variety of Caribbean dishes as well as some American specialties. It has attracted a loyal following, including such celebrities as the Wayans Brothers, Michael Keaton, and Roseanne, and has earned nearly $800,000 in revenues.

Looking back on her decision to leave the security of a full-time job to swim in the unsure waters of entrepreneurship, James says she holds no regrets. "Sure it was tough to give up the paycheck and the perks, but I don't feel like I gave up anything that was of any huge importance," she says. "Plus, what I have gained is so much more. I work for myself, and one day I hope to own many different businesses." For James, becoming an entrepreneur filled a need for self-fulfillment.

If someone were to ask you why *you* want to start a business, what would be your answer? Financial freedom? Independence? Creative license? A retirement nest egg? Compared to other start-up queries—how to price a product or service, how to secure financing, or how to find the right location—this is a simple question. But it is one of the most important issues you will have to consider when taking your first few steps toward entrepreneurship.

The goals you set for your business will impact every decision you make in getting your company off the ground. It will affect the type of business you choose to pursue, how you evaluate your chances for success, and how you assess whether you have what it takes to become an entrepreneur.

In this chapter, we will discuss some of the more common reasons why individuals decide to start their own businesses, and will provide an overview of how you can set yourself on the path toward ownership. You might think that a hefty loan from your neighborhood bank is all you will need for the journey, but capital is not nearly enough to help you make a successful start. Among other things, you will need leadership skills, a competitive attitude, and a healthy dose of patience.

WHY TRY OWNERSHIP?

Take a moment to ask yourself why you would like to become an entrepreneur. Perhaps you have dreams of taking over the family business, or aspirations to build an empire from the ground up. Whatever your reasons, it's important that you identify them before you get started. Your goals will guide your operation and steer you toward success.

Here are some of the common reasons why people decide to hang out their shingle:

Money
Many people—particularly those working in a corporate setting—feel shortchanged when all their efforts go toward doing a good job "for the team," but the bonuses go only to the "captains." The thought of starting a business in which they can create riches for themselves rather than for someone else is

enticing. But, how much they stand to make, and how quickly they're likely to make it, will depend on the type of business, the competition, the market saturation, and a host of other factors. Still, becoming an entrepreneur can be very rewarding financially. Just keep in mind that you may not have a positive cash flow during your first few years in operation. In fact, it may take several years for you to make a profit. But with proper planning and a healthy dose of patience, entrepreneurship can be a pot of gold at the end of the rainbow.

Being Your Own Boss
How many times have you stormed out of your manager's office uttering beneath your breath, "If I were the boss, I would. . . . " Many people opt for business ownership because along with the title comes a license to "call the shots" in every area such as naming the business, hiring employees, setting policies, and developing advertising campaigns. For many people, becoming an *employer* is a sure-fire way to assume certain leadership positions that are not available to an *employee*. Realize, however, that if you're the type of person who enjoys total autonomy, you will have to seriously consider how you will handle certain management responsibilities, especially if you decide to take on a partner or two.

Developing Your Own Idea
Some people seek ownership so that they can explore an idea(s) that has been rejected or ignored by former employers. That's what Rachael Lewis did when she opened Rachael's Totz 'n' Teenz Model Management Inc. from her Manhattan apartment in 1993. Lewis was bitten by the entrepreneurial bug while working as a receptionist/messenger for an adult modeling agency in Miami. Sitting at her desk, she conceived an idea to develop a kids' division and began pursuing it. "I was tired of answering the phones. It was boring to me," says Lewis. "So I started working with some kids, but when I went to the owners of the agency about starting a kids' division and offered to run it, they said no. They said it was not a good idea, so that's when I spoke to my parents about borrowing money to start my own agency." Lewis's agency now works with over 150 teen models, many of whom have signed contracts with major clients, including Ralph Lauren, Tommy Hilfiger, Avon, and Toys 'R' Us. Like Lewis, many individuals simply want to develop a concept in a way that they see fit and not according to how others suggest it should be approached. Entrepreneurship gives them the breathing room to follow their dreams.

Establishing Job Security
Working in corporate America has become no more secure than placing your money on a blackjack table. That's why many people have chosen to make the transition from employee to employer. Entrepreneurship is also risky (according to the Small Business Administration, half of all new businesses

fail within the first four years of operation), but it offers a sense of security that cannot be found in the cubed environments within a city skyscraper. Entrepreneurship gives people a chance to build toward retirement for themselves and their families without the fear of being downsized or right-sized. When you're running your own shop, no one can fire you—except your customers. And as long as they're happy, you're open for business.

Creating a Different Lifestyle

Do you ever feel like your typical workweek is a scene from the movie *Ground Hog Day* (Bill Murray, as the main character, relives the same day over and over and over)? Many people who start their own businesses are not just looking to change jobs; they're in search of a different lifestyle. Depending on the type of business you choose to start, you could travel internationally, appear on television and/or radio, or speak in front of large organizations. For those seriously bothered by tedium, entrepreneurship is a way to take on new challenges and feel valued and important.

To Shatter a Glass Ceiling

Some individuals—particularly women and minorities—feel they can only go so far when they're working for someone else. However, when they're working for themselves, the sky is the limit. Business ownership also gives them the respect and recognition they feel they're entitled to.

Feeding Your Ego

Some people start a business because of how it looks and how it makes them feel. People like saying "I own a supper club" or "I own a computer company" or "I own a clothing boutique," and then seeing the reaction that follows. A word of caution: If ego-gratification is one of your main reasons for pursuing ownership, think seriously about how important it is to you and how much it will impact certain decisions you make regarding the business. Don't invest valuable time and money in starting a company only to please or impress someone. That person may not even care whether you succeed or fail.

Whatever your purpose for starting a business, a key decision is whether you will pursue it full-time or part-time. Many entrepreneurs start a business part-time to reduce their financial risk and give them time to learn the industry and the potential market for the business before they decide to devote all of their energy and resources to it. Operating a part-time business can mean taking on just one client or customer as opposed to 10 or 20, or working for family or friends in your spare time.

If you are concerned about business failure, consider launching a part-time operation. If the business folds, you will still have your full-time job to fall back on. Even as a part-time entrepreneur, you will be required to put in long hours if you hope to be successful. Also, even though you may operate your business part-time, some of the start-up costs will not necessarily go down. For example, the price of a computer will remain the same whether you use it 20 hours per week or 40 hours per week.

For any venture, part-time or full-time, you will need to set short-term as well as long-term goals. The primary long-term goal is evident: build a successful business. But, in doing so, you may very easily get overwhelmed and feel that you're not getting anything done. To avoid feeling inadequate, set realistic and achievable milestones along the way. They will give you peace of mind and assurance that you are forging ahead. Here are some of the short-term goals you can establish:

1. Choose a business name.
2. Apply for a business license or permit (if one is required for your operation).
3. Set up a business bank account.
4. Trademark your product's name.
5. Find a commercial real estate broker.
6. Locate a good tax attorney.

To stay on track, create a timetable showing the target date for completion of each task. Each small victory will prove inspiring and invigorating during the first few months of your new business.

DO YOU HAVE WHAT IT TAKES?

Your reasons for wanting to go into business for yourself may be legitimate. You may have a life-changing product that no one else has ever conceived, or a unique twist to a service that makes all others pale by comparison. But do you have what it takes to make that product or service a success?

At the very least, becoming an entrepreneur requires guts. Effie Booker, co-owner of Cabana Car Wash and senior vice president at Wells Fargo Bank in Houston, Texas, will be the first to tell you that it takes more than courage to keep a business afloat. Thinking back to when she opened her second location, she says it also takes commitment.

"On the day we opened up the second car wash, I happened to go down on my lunch hour to see how things were going and when I got there the guys had cars lined up. They said to me, 'Ms. Booker, we have all these cars that we have to have ready. Some customers want them by noon and some by five o'clock, but there's no way we can do it because we've only got three people,'" she recalls.

"So I called my office and told them that I was taking the rest of the day off. Well, I didn't have time to change my clothes and although I was dressed in a spring suit, with pearls and high heels, all I could do was stand there, swing the pearls behind my neck, grab a high-speed bus and go at it. By the time I finished, my hair was all over my head, my pearls were behind my neck, and I had ripped my pantyhose from one end to the other, but you do what you have to do to run your business. And there's not one role within my company that I won't get out there and do if I need to do it, high heels and all, from cashiering to being in the pit changing plugs, because I love my business and I'm committed to making it a success."

Guts and dedication are two traits that you must possess in order to become a successful business owner. In addition, you need the right mix of skills and personal qualities. One of the more common reasons why businesses fail is because the owner does not have business experience in or knowledge of the field he or she wants to enter. Before you get started, assess whether you have the right talents and attributes to run your own shop.

Here is the ideal mix of skills and personal qualities that entrepreneurs should possess:

1. *Leadership skills.* It's one thing to be a good manager, but another to be a strong leader. Managers know how to do things right, but leaders always do the right things. As an entrepreneur, you will be called on to do both. You will have to solve a myriad of problems, both big and small. Your employees will look to you for guidance and direction on how to grow the business, and you must be able to deliver. If you feel more comfortable having others tell you what to do, entrepreneurship is not for you.

2. *Business experience.* Whether it's in bookkeeping, market research, advertising, or customer service, most soon-to-be entrepreneurs have some *knowledge* about what it takes to start a business, and some *experience* in the field they hope to enter. If you have neither, don't panic. Having business experience is not a prerequisite to starting your own company. To compensate for any skills you lack, you can take business courses at a local university or college, talk with professional consultants about particular issues, or volunteer to work at an existing business in your chosen field.

3. *A sacrificial attitude.* One of the first things that you will be forced to give up, particularly during the fledgling years of the business, is the 9-to-5, Monday-through-Friday work schedule. Becoming an entrepreneur can require working ten to twelve hours, seven days a week. You could also end up working on holidays (particularly if your business is in the retail industry). So say goodbye to much of your free time, as well as those coveted three-week vacations you had grown accustomed to. You will also have to sacrifice a regular paycheck. Many business professionals advise paying yourself first, but this may not be the best move. Your employees and suppliers are important to the survival of your business. Without them, you would not have a business, so you may want to pay them first.

4. *Strong interpersonal skills.* As an entrepreneur, you will have to deal with customers, employees, suppliers, accountants, lawyers, advertising executives, technicians—the list goes on and on. To be successful in business, you must be able to work with a variety of people and personalities.

5. *Intelligence.* Forget about what you scored on your SATs and business college entrance exams. To be a successful entrepreneur, you will need more than just "book smarts." You will need good old-fashioned "street smarts" and common sense. Successful entrepreneurs can effectively deal with real-world business experiences. They can foresee problems before they occur and have the ability to devise workable solutions.

6. *Strong management skills.* You will have to manage a series of relationships with your banker, clients, customers, and any family members who may decide to join you in running the business. However, one of your most important managerial duties is overseeing your employees. Can you deal with firing as well as hiring workers? Are you able to handle reprimanding staff when they are consistently late, or are stealing from the company, or are insubordinate? If you cannot deal with personnel problems, are you comfortable with assigning that authority to someone else? Successful entrepreneurs can control employee–employer relationships and delegate authority where needed.

7. *Good organizational skills.* When you start your own business, organization is essential. You must keep track of everything that goes on in your operation, or face doom. Don't get caught beneath a stack of papers a mile high when Uncle Sam comes calling.

8. *Competitive attitude.* No matter what type of business you start, you're bound to face competition, either directly or indirectly. You can't give up when several similar stores open just a few miles away. You have to come out fighting and find ways to promote your product or service as *the* best, not one of the best.

9. *High energy and optimism.* Starting your own business requires long hours and a lot of hard work, so you must be energetic. People who are starting a business while they are maintaining a full-time job must develop ways to muster a few extra ounces of strength. If you find yourself getting run down, look into changing your diet or starting an exercise program. Successful entrepreneurs are upbeat and always able to go that extra mile.

10. *Self-confidence.* Many people make the mistake of starting a particular type of business only because of its profit potential. You must like and believe in what you're doing, or it will be impossible to convince customers and other clients to use your product or service. If you don't like kids, don't start a toy store. If you can't stand

working around food, don't open a restaurant. Make sure that you have a passion for your business.

Assessing your skills for entrepreneurship is not an elaborate process. Begin by simply making a checklist of your strengths and weaknesses and your likes and dislikes. Then match them against typical entrepreneurial qualities like those listed above. Be honest in determining what you can and cannot do. You will only hurt yourself if you fake your abilities. Don't worry if you lack some of the characteristics of an entrepreneur. No one is perfect. Besides, good business owners accept their shortcomings and find ways to compensate for them.

Here are a few ways in which you can offset your weaknesses.

Hire Help

You will first have to determine whether you can afford to hire employees. Most new business owners are on a limited budget and can't afford to hire a full staff right away. Only you can determine whether the convenience of paying someone to do some of your chores outweighs the cost. Bear in mind that hiring an individual(s) whose skills complement yours can save you from making mistakes that could kill your business. For example, if maintaining orderly income-and-expense records is not your strong suit, you may want to hire a bookkeeper. In the most extreme case, inaccurate books and files could mean handing over the keys to your business to the IRS.

Develop a Partnership

Some entrepreneurs choose to take on a partner or two who possess the skills they are lacking. This route means giving up total control of your business and sharing all the decision making with your partner (see Chapter 4). Finding a good partner is not easy. Many people choose a friend or family member, but such close ties could kill your business if you're not careful. For example, sibling rivalry is a major reason why only one-third of family-owned firms survive past the first generation. Before handing over a piece of your business to *anyone* else, make sure there is a good match in qualifications and personality traits.

Learn Additional Skills Yourself

You're never too old to learn. If hiring employees or choosing a partner is not right for you, consider acquiring some skills yourself. You can do this in one of three ways:

1. *Trial-and-error.* You can develop skills by learning from your mistakes. The only disadvantage to this approach is that, as a new business owner, you can afford to make only so many faux pas. Trial-and-error is usually beneficial to entrepreneurs who are working on their third or fourth new business. However, if you find yourself making

blunders during the early phases of your new operation, don't panic. You can still come out on top. Eric Marshall, founder and president of Clique Creative Services, is living proof. Marshall, a trained photojournalist and graduate of Indiana University, started his business in 1987 in a 450-square-foot portrait studio. Using old photography equipment, he conducted shoots for weddings and high schools. However, Marshall soon grew tired of taking sophomoric photos and branched out into the commercial design arena. Having had little experience in the design field and even less in the business world, he lost valuable contracts. "I used to share my ideas with potential clients before signing a contract," says the self-taught businessman. "They would either change their minds or steal my ideas. I soon realized that wasn't how business is conducted and began charging clients up front for half of the job's cost." Through trial-and-error, Marshall has been able to build a strong client base, which has earned him nearly $500,000 in sales. "I'm just beginning to truly understand what it takes to be successful."[2]

2. *College courses.* A business class or seminar at a local college or university may help you acquire the knowledge you need, but be aware that courses can be expensive and time-consuming. Also, they rarely offer much help in dealing with real-life business situations.

3. *Business incubator.* These business assistance programs nurture start-ups by providing expert advice on such issues as business planning, technology, and marketing. They also offer access to office space, supplies, and equipment. About 1,100 business incubators are operating worldwide; roughly half are located in the United States (see Chapter 5). For the incubator nearest you, call the National Business Incubation Association at 740-593-4331.

When you are assessing your skills, keep in mind that entrepreneurship is not like changing jobs. There will be new responsibilities, new challenges, and a chance to meet new people, but you're responsible for an entire operation, not just one or two tasks. You will have to create benefits plans, meet with suppliers and advertising executives, keep the books, calculate and pay taxes, and do anything and everything in between.

Entrepreneurs play many roles. Among those you can expect to play are:

- *Business planner.* Whatever you decide to do within your business—add a new product, hire additional staff, or switch employee benefits packages—you will be required to do all of the planning. It is also your responsibility to execute plans in a way that satisfies those who will be affected by them.

- *Bill collector.* Unless you hire a collection agency (most new businesses cannot afford the service fees), it will be your responsibility to keep track of customers who are not paying their bills. You must understand the legal issues surrounding collection and the best methods for trying to get clients to pay up.

- *Tax collector.* If you hire employees, you will be responsible for deducting federal, state, and local taxes from their paychecks. In many states, retail businesses are required to collect sales tax from customers who purchase merchandise and other personal property (see Chapter 13).

- *Market researcher.* One of your biggest hurdles will be defining your target audience. Who are your customers? Where are they located? What are their demographics (age, income, occupation, education)? You will be responsible for gathering all the information that will tell you whether your business is going to fly.

- *Sales and marketing guru.* Few start-ups can afford to hire a top salesperson or advertising agency to pitch their product or service. You will be required to devise catchy phrases, write ad copy, visit potential customers, and do the necessary market research to uncover how to succeed in your industry.

- *Secretary.* As the business grows, you will do less and less typing, filing, hole punching, and the like. A receptionist will share the load or take it over entirely. When starting out, however, you may have to answer phones, send and open your own mail, and acknowledge e-mail messages or orders. The benefit of these small tasks is that they enable you to stay on top of every aspect of running your business.

- *High-tech expert.* Successful entrepreneurs know about the latest changes in information technology and are able to adapt their businesses accordingly. As a new business owner, research the high-tech purchases that make sense for your operation. Although the newest computer hardware and software will be expensive, you can find low-cost equipment that will effectively meet the needs of your company. In addition to purchasing a computer you should also sign up with an Internet Service Provider (ISP) to obtain access to the World Wide Web (see Chapter 10).

- *Clinical therapist.* Entrepreneurs often find themselves embroiled in the personal problems of their employees. Issues such as domestic abuse and inadequate child care can impact the workplace and may affect the success of your operation. In anticipation of these problems, devise general strategies for dealing with them. Simply firing an employee may land you in court as a defendant. Besides, certain skills are difficult to find. Consider establishing programs that will bring distressed workers back on track. For example, if many of your employees are single mothers, find out the local rules (zoning, supervisers' qualifications) for setting up a day care program on or near your premises, to cut down on absenteeism.

- *Accountant.* Many entrepreneurs say they are too busy to crunch numbers. But unless you enlist the help of a professional accountant, you're risking disaster. Find out which records, receipts, and supporting documents you need to keep, and how to maintain them (see Chapter 12). Ask the accountant to walk you through preparing tax forms and keeping accurate financial statements. Use the services of a professional, but study each financial statement carefully.
- *Lawyer.* You will never have to argue a case before the Supreme Court. However, as an owner of a business, you will need to gain an understanding of certain regulations regarding tax and employment law. You may also be required to prepare legal documents such as work orders for independent contractors.

WEIGHING THE COST OF YOUR VENTURE

Do you know how much money it will take to get your business off the ground? If you can answer "Yes," you're one step closer to entrepreneurship. But if your answer is "No," stop right here. You have some serious thinking to do.

Determining what financial resources will be required to launch your business is critical to its survival. Too often, business owners underestimate their money needs and end up closing their doors before celebrating their first anniversary.

Many entrepreneurs think that because they have a unique product or service, the money will just roll in. But what if it doesn't? Will you be financially prepared to weather the storm? You cannot assume that lively sales during your first year in operation will compensate for inadequate financing. When determining the cash you will need to get started, you should assume that no sales will be made the first year and that you will be operating at a loss.

There are many sources of financing (for example, bank loans, family and friends, and venture capital firms); we will discuss them in Chapter 8. One of the most common sources is personal savings. If, like many entrepreneurs, you can use your own money to start your business, you are tapping the most ideal financial resource. By using your personal reserves, you will not have to worry about paying back any loans. But if you fail to accurately assess your personal assets from the start, you could end up losing more than just the business.

Before you decide to empty out your bank account, make a list of *all* of your assets and liabilities. The process may seem a bit elementary, but it will help you to see clearly what you have and what you don't have, which translates into what you can and cannot afford.

If your debt is extensive, you may want to reconsider starting a business right now. Becoming an entrepreneur requires serious financial risk.

Can you afford to fail? If you cannot, do not take the plunge. You may have a great idea, an optimistic attitude, and the enthusiasm of a powerball lottery winner, but without the proper financing, you're sunk.

The amount of money you will need to get started hinges on several factors: the type of business you open, where you choose to locate, the number of employees you intend to hire, the types of equipment you will require, whether you will commission professional consultants, and so forth. For example, if you plan to open a home-based basket-making business, your start-up costs will be far lower than if you were to open a computer software company situated in the center of town.

Each business's costs are different, but several basic start-up costs are on virtually all entrepreneurs' expense lists. These include the following:

- *Rent.* Most entrepreneurs rent or lease office space to house a new business. Rental prices vary according to location and class or type of building; rates can range anywhere from $10 to $50 or more per square foot. For example, a 500-square-foot, Class A office in midtown Manhattan (New York) will cost much more to lease than a 1,000-square-foot, Class C suite in the central business district of New Orleans (Louisiana). Most lessors (landlords or owners of the property) will require that you pay the first month's rent plus a security deposit before moving in. (Leasing is covered in detail in Chapter 5.)

- *Business license and/or permit.* Most local, city, and state governments require that you obtain a general business license to operate in their jurisdiction. Licensing costs vary according to locale and the type of business you operate. Some businesses have to secure a special *state occupational license,* which is issued to any professional who offers products or services that require regulation. For example, a doctor, dentist, or lawyer would be required to obtain a special license to open a practice. Permits may also be required to sell certain products. (Licenses are covered in detail in Chapter 6.)

- *Business insurance.* The amount you will need to spend on insurance depends on the type of business you open and where you operate it. For example, both a home-based public relations firm and a cookie manufacturing company will need to obtain property and general liability insurance. But the cookie company will also need to secure product liability insurance, which would cover the costs if someone gets sick from eating the product and sues the company. Each business has different insurance needs, so consult your insurance agent for individual packages and specific premiums. (Insurance is covered in detail in Chapter 6.)

- *Equipment and inventory.* Some businesses are more equipment-intensive than others, but these are the basic items that virtually every operation will use: a two-way telephone system, an answering machine, a facsimile (fax) machine, a standard personal computer and modem, and signage. Make a list of all the materials you will need. To figure out the costs for each, visit several vendors for price quotes, and, based on your research, calculate how much you will have to allocate for each item. Take the same approach with your inventory. Make a list of all necessary supplies, then comparison shop at wholesale or outlet stores for the best prices. When stocking up on office and cleaning supplies, remember that it's cheaper to buy in bulk.

- *Phone and utilities.* Deposits may be required by the local telephone and utility companies. The exact amount of your telephone deposit will depend on the number of lines you need and the type of service you choose. Estimate the deposit as at least $100. The amounts of your gas and electric deposits will depend on your projected usage.

- *Professional consultation.* You're bound to work with all sorts of business experts throughout the life of your business. But during the infant stages of your operation, two professionals you are almost guaranteed to consult are an accountant and a lawyer. An accountant can assist you in preparing your books and taxes; a lawyer will provide legal advice and help you complete and file any necessary legal documents. Fees vary; most accountants and lawyers charge by the hour. Some lawyers, however, will require a retainer fee, to be paid up front before services are rendered. This fee can run as much as $2,000 to $3,000, so you'll want to shop around.

- *Marketing budget.* As a new business owner, you will need to initiate an advertising campaign to let people know that you exist. How much money you allocate for your marketing needs (advertising, public relations, and/or promotions) will depend on your industry as well as your competition. Some businesses start with very little advertising; others spend a sizable amount to launch their operation. Plan to set aside a certain percentage of your projected gross sales (anywhere from 2 to 5 percent) for your advertising budget (see Chapter 9).

- *Employee payroll.* Whether you have a full-time or a part-time business, you will need to set aside preopening payroll or salaries for yourself as well as any additional staff you intend to hire. A good rule of thumb is to earmark one month's salary plus a three-month reserve for all employees.

- *Transportation.* Your need to shell out money for the use of a car, truck, or van will depend on the type of business you operate. For example, if you start a pizza delivery business, you are going to need some form of transportation. When searching for a vehicle, consider leasing or buying a used car or truck to save money. Vehicle insurance will be an added transportation expense. Contact your insurance agent for premiums.

- *Special considerations (remodeling, fixtures, and so on).* Some new businesses will require cosmetic surgery. For example, most retail spaces, like those found in a shopping mall, come as a plain vanilla shell. If you start a retail clothing store, you may need to build-out or renovate your space (build shelves, install lighting and rack fixtures, add carpeting and other decorative items to support your business). To figure the cost of your build-out—in real estate terms, your *leasehold improvements*—secure bids from a contractor. A construction company will generally provide you with a free bid after you create a design. Your lessor can do the build-out for you, but, if you go this route, plan to spend anywhere from $35 to $40 per square foot (depending on the location) for the build-out itself.

- *Miscellaneous costs.* On your first day in business, you're going to need cash for the register. How much should you have? There's no fixed amount, but a few hundred dollars (maybe $200 or $300) should do it. You may incur some unanticipated expenses. Perhaps a pipe bursts and threatens to flood the business your first day in operation, or robust sales wipe out your inventory and you must purchase additional items to satisfy customers. Just in case Murphy's Law goes into effect, allocate about 10 percent of the total cost of your start-up expenses to cover any unforeseen circumstances.

PLANNING FOR THE LONG HAUL

As you can see, there are many factors to consider when starting a business. It requires more than printing up business cards, hanging out a shingle, and tacking an "Open for Business" sign in the window. A lot of planning must go into that first day, to ensure that there is a second day, a third, fourth, fifth, and so on.

There are no shortcuts to becoming a successful entrepreneur. The process is long and sometimes tedious, but the steps you take will lead to prosperity if you walk slowly and carefully. Some people want to fly by the seat of their pants into entrepreneurship. "I'll figure it out as I go along," they say. But this attitude will kill a business before it even gets off the ground. Ask yourself: Do you want to be in it for the long haul? Are you willing to sacrifice short-term gain for long-term success? Remember, anyone can whip up a storefront for a day. The question is: Will it be around tomorrow?

No business is failure-proof. Among the factors that contribute to the downfall of businesses, large and small, are the following:

- Undercapitalization.
- Lack of skilled personnel.

- Inability to deal with the competition.
- Failure to accurately assess the market potential.
- Delinquent bank loans.
- Inadequate amount of working capital.
- Bad relationships with vendors and suppliers.
- Internal strife (particularly in family-owned businesses).
- Death of key owners and/or personnel.
- Inability to keep good financial records.
- Failure to collect receivables.
- Pricing goods or services too low or too high.
- Shunning professional consultation.
- Failure to obtain the proper insurance.

When launching your business, don't put off *any* aspect that will impact your progress. Bookkeeping is a classic example of an area that causes owners to shudder. "I'll get to it later," they insist. But later gets later and later and later, until it's too late. Treat each aspect of starting a new business with care. Devote as much attention to figuring out your reasons for wanting to start a business as you do to searching for a location for that business. Becoming an entrepreneur is a lot of hard work, but it's also a lot of fun. The pride and accomplishment you will feel that first day in business will be well worth the time, effort, and money you invest.

CHECKLIST

HOW YOU CAN PREPARE FOR OWNERSHIP

✓ **Define your reasons for wanting to become a business owner.** Are you interested in achieving independence, financial freedom, creative license, or a retirement nest egg? State your goals.

✓ **Measure your personal traits and professional experience.** Entrepreneurship is not for the lighthearted. To run a business for the long haul, you must be committed, gutsy, intelligent, competitive, and self-confident. Whatever skills or traits you are lacking, you must devise ways to compensate for them.

✓ **Understand the varied roles of the business owner.** As an entrepreneur, you are the boss, but you are also the bill collector, market researcher, sales representative, secretary, and accountant. Determine whether you can handle those roles.

✓ **Weigh the costs of your new venture.** No new business can get off the ground without money. Determine how much capital it will take for you to launch your firm, and where you will obtain the funding.

✓ **Settle in for the long haul.** Business ownership is not easy. To be successful, you must have a plan. Forget about flying by the seat of your pants into entrepreneurship. Pay careful attention to every aspect of starting your venture, and walk slowly and carefully as you begin to build.

RESOURCES FOR MORE INFORMATION

ASSOCIATIONS

- *American Association of Minority Businesses (AAMB), Inc.,* 537 W. Sugar Creek Road, Suite 104, Charlotte, NC 28213; 704-376-2262; www.website1.com/aamb. The AAMB is a national benefits services association that assists minority business owners in building their managerial and technical skills. The organization gives minority business owners access to a number of resources, including business equipment, financial services, insurance products, and business supplies. The AAMB also sponsors educational and motivational business development seminars and programs throughout the year.

- *American Institute of Small Business (AISB),* 7515 Wayzata Boulevard, Suite 201, Minneapolis, MN 55426; 1-800-328-2906 or 612-545-7001; www.aisbofmn.com. The American Institute of Small Business is considered to be the leading publisher of educational materials designed for the small business owner and the self-employed. The organization's publications can be reviewed in over 2,000 libraries, 2,500 high schools, and 525 colleges and universities. The organization conducts seminars and workshops on a variety of topics, including how to set up a small business.

- *American Management Association International (AMA),* 1601 Broadway, New York, NY 10019; 212-586-8100; www.amanet.org. The AMA operates management centers and offices in some of the major American cities, including New York, Washington (DC), Boston, Atlanta, and Chicago, and provides business-related seminars in 300 additional metropolitan areas. For its members, this organization provides information concerning all disciplines of management, including financial, human resources, purchasing, insurance and risk management, research and development, and sales and marketing.

- *National Black Chamber of Commerce (NBCC),* 2000 L Street, NW, Suite 200, Washington, DC 20036; 202-416-1622; www.nbcc-e-train.org. The NBCC is an umbrella organization for hundreds of affiliates scattered throughout the country. This organization offers, to the start-up and existing entrepreneur, useful information concerning such things as finances, management, procurement, and advertising.

2

BIRTHING YOUR
BUSINESS IDEA

Do you have an idea for a business that you've always wanted to explore? Perhaps a series of cultural toys, a dessert delivery service, or a clothing line for pedigree pooches? Starting a business based on your own idea is one of the most gratifying things you could ever do. If the business is a success, you will earn hefty revenues, as well as win praise from your peers and the consumers you serve.

But what type of business should you start? Most people who want to open their own shop have a specific business idea. Others have only a general idea, or no idea at all. Business experts often suggest choosing something that you love. For example, if you like to cook, you may want to consider opening a catering business. If you love children, you may want to try your hand at a day care center or a toy store. Frank Mercado-Valdes turned his love and passion for old black movies into a film production and syndication company. You've probably heard of it—the African Heritage Movie Network.

"I loved watching old black movies, but I could never find any of them on local television," says Mercado-Valdes of his reasons for starting the company. With a $25,000 investment and $350,000 loan from the Pro-Line Corporation, Mercados-Valdes launched the New-York-based business in 1993. The company has purchased 30-day syndication rights to many black classics, including *Cotton Comes to Harlem, Car Wash, Coffy* and *Shaft*, and more recent pictures such as *Glory* and *Crooklyn*. The films are distributed and aired through the company's "Movie of the Month" series, hosted by film legends Ossie Davis and Ruby Dee, and "Primetime Presentations," a quarterly special. Both appear in 125 markets nationwide.

Choose a business idea that you know you will enjoy developing. You don't want to spend thousands of dollars and work night and day building a business that you don't like. But liking it should not be your sole criterion for selecting a venture. You should also consider several other factors that will impact your chances for success, such as the competition and market saturation.

In this chapter, we will discuss some factors you should weigh before starting a business and will indicate several resources you can use to find an idea that's right for you. We will also show you how to protect your idea with a patent or a trademark in case an unscrupulous colleague tries to pull the rug out from under you.

FACTORS FOR FINDING A BUSINESS THAT FITS

When deciding what type of product or service you are going to offer, there are several things you should consider. Never assume that just because you have a novel idea and a bubbly "Go get 'em!" attitude, you will automatically find success. Give careful thought to the following factors before you take the plunge.

Market Potential

Most successful business ideas have found a market niche. Part of choosing a good business is defining what consumers *need* and what they *want*. In 1992, a mere stone's throw from the famous Apollo Theater in New York, many people wanted Sylvia Woods' homemade barbecue sauce. Since 1962, Woods and her husband Herbert have operated Sylvia's Restaurant, a famous Harlem soul food eatery. For more than three decades, customers have enjoyed fried chicken, candied yams, black-eyed peas, and other southern dishes. But patrons have been particularly taken with Sylvia's homemade barbecue sauce, so when enough customers told Sylvia that they'd buy her sauce by the gallon, she realized the potential success of bottling this product. "For the holidays, people would bring bottles and jars and ask us to sell them the barbecue sauce," Woods remembers. "Then, one night, firemen came in with their gallon jugs and said, 'Can you give us gallons of your sauce because it's *sooooooo* good,' and that's when I knew we were on to something." In response to the consumer appeal, Woods and her son Van, president of Sylvia Woods Enterprises, started developing a line of products using Sylvia's down-home southern recipes. Taking customer favorites from the restaurant menu and packaging them for sale, Woods launched her Queen of Soul Food Line in 1992. "We first started with the barbecue sauce, and from there, Van said, 'Well, why not the hot sauce?' Some people liked the collard greens, so he said, 'Let's put the greens in the can,' and then, there was the beans," Woods explains. The retail food line contains some 17 items, including Sylvia's Specially Cut Yams, Kicking Hot Sauce, and Mild & Sassy Original Sauce. Now available nationwide, the products are sold in such stores as Pathmark and D'Agostino's in New York, and Stop, Shop and Save in Baltimore. "The people asked for our product and we simply gave it to them," says Woods. As Woods did, you must ask yourself if there is a demand for your product or service.

Competition
No matter what type of business you choose, you're bound to face competition, and some businesses are more competitive than others. For example, you can expect computer supply companies to have more rivals than, say, pet stores. How many competitors will your business be forced to deal with? Can your idea compete successfully? Conducting market research will identify your competitors, define their strengths and weaknesses, and suggest the measures you should take to ensure that your business stays afloat (see Chapter 3).

Resources Required to Penetrate the Market
What seems like a good idea on paper may not be a good idea in practice. Some business ideas may be too costly to pursue, particularly for small shopkeepers with limited budgets. When deciding on a particular business, consider how much money you will need to get started, and what other resources will be required to make your idea a "go." Will you need a special research and development team to gather information about producing your product (particularly if it's a new invention)? Will you have to extensively train your staff to operate special machinery and other equipment? Don't get in over your head just because your idea sounds like a winner. Make sure it is doable and won't break you financially.

Uniqueness of Product or Service
Your product or service should offer customers something they cannot get anywhere else, but you need not develop an original idea or invention when deciding on the type of business you want to own. You can create a product or service by improving an existing one. For example, maybe you can build a better mousetrap or a safer baby car seat. Effie Booker, the very committed owner of Cabana Car Wash, created an innovative atmosphere where customers can pamper their cars *and* experience a 15-to-20-minute vacation to the Caribbean islands. Walk onto the premises of Cabana Car Wash and you will find palm trees swaying in the wind. Step inside and you will find floral patio seating beneath a huge umbrella, attendants dressed in tropical uniforms, and Caribbean music wafting overhead. "When we opened, the whole idea of having a theme took off. In fact, I think we were probably the first car wash to come out with the whole Caribbean theme," says Booker, whose business also includes a detailing center and lube facility. "At our car wash, we invite customers to come in, sit down, relax, and eat some yogurt, while we pamper their cars. People really like it. In fact, sometimes our customers get so relaxed

they forget about their cars and we end up telling them, 'Your car has been ready for 20 minutes.'" Like Booker, you too can overcome the competition by offering better service, better support, or a new approach to an old idea.

Market Saturation

How many fast-food restaurants, shoe shops, and video stores are in your area? Probably too many to count. When selecting your company, consider market saturation. You may have a great idea, but there may not be enough room in the industry for you because 10,000 other people are producing a similar product or service. A good example of a market-saturated product is chocolate chip cookies. Virtually everyone loves the tasty snack, but walk the aisles of your favorite supermarket and you'll find more than enough of the chip-cookie makers: Toll House, Keebler, Famous Amos, and the list goes on and on. A small-time cookie maker—unless he or she has a unique brand (perhaps a gourmet recipe)—will find it very difficult to obtain market share in this industry. Before you spend valuable time and money producing your product or service, find out whether there is room for another entry in the market.

Although it is much more difficult to start a business from an original idea than from one that has already been established, most entrepreneurs prefer to launch their businesses from scratch. Some others prefer options that do not require having to build a business from the ground up. If you prefer having a head start, consider purchasing an existing company or buying into a franchise (see Chapters 14 and 15, respectively). Keep in mind that if you buy a business, you may have to deal with a number of inherent issues such as previous brand or product imaging, and obsolete equipment. If you opt to buy a franchise, you may have to pay royalties—depending on which franchise you choose—for the use of the brand name and abide by strict operational guidelines.

Selecting a business that meets your budget and tastes, *and* has consumer appeal, can be a daunting task. Here are a few tips to help you choose one that's right for you:

- *Make a list of your likes.* Start by identifying the things you enjoy doing: your hobbies, extracurricular activities, and any particular skills or work experience you may have acquired. For example, if you are good with flowers and plants, and have a greenhouse that the whole neighborhood admires, bear this in mind. A landscaping business could be the right outlet for you. Match your list against a list of the types of businesses that can utilize your skills and talents. This is not a foolproof system for choosing a business that's right for you, but it's a good start. As an entrepreneur, you will be living, sleeping, and breathing your business. It's important that you enjoy what you're doing and have a passion for your product or service.

- *Look for low start-up fees.* Chances are, as a new business owner, you will have limited funds. If this is the case, you may want to choose a business that requires a minimal amount of start-up capital and brings you up-front payment. For example, suppose you love to write and would like to start a magazine. You would need to purchase several computers, hire reporters, contract with a printer, and rent office space, at the very least. The up-front cost can be tens of thousands of dollars (depending on the size and type of magazine you launch), and you may not see any profit for years. But if you hire yourself out as a freelance writer, prepare articles for several different publications, and operate from your home, you can save lots of money and get paid immediately for your work.

- *Stay away from seasonal businesses.* Unless you can and are willing to ride out the slow sales periods of businesses such as Christmas decoration stores, ski shops, and beachwear boutiques, do not start a seasonal business. However, if you are capable of weathering the off-season financial drought, operating a seasonal shop will afford you a lot of time off. This is a plus factor if you are raising a family and could use some down time in a business venture.

- *Consider service-oriented rather than product-oriented businesses.* Service businesses are often easier and cheaper to launch than those that offer a product. Service businesses don't require the purchase of much equipment, nor do they demand that you hire employees immediately. For example, if you operate a home cleaning service, you need only a few bottles of household cleaner; a broom, a mop, and a bucket; and one employee—you.

- *Avoid stiff competition.* We appear to be living in an age of factory outlet stores and discount warehouses. When choosing a business, consider whether your product or service will be in direct competition with these sources. For example, you may want to start a small neighborhood stationery store, and you have all the skills required to do so. But major competition from large discount providers such as Staples and Office Max may not allow you to compete, at least not in price. In this instance you would have to weigh competing in personalized service.

- *Look for businesses with repeat customers.* Successful businesses keep customers coming back for more. Choose a business that will generate a consistent and steady flow of consumers. Among these types of operations are pool, pet, and computer supplies stores.

Whatever business idea you choose, know that it is yours to develop. Taking a business idea from conception to production and then to a successful market can be exciting, so don't be afraid to use your imagination and have some fun along the way.

FINDING A BUSINESS THAT'S RIGHT FOR YOU

How many times have you witnessed the introduction of a new product and said, "I could've thought of that?" New products and product ideas hit the marketplace virtually every day. Some are original inventions; others are niche products and services: similar to the products and services that already exist, but innovative because they satisfy some unmet need. For example, Federal Express is a niche idea for postal delivery services. The multimillion-dollar business delivers mail and other packages, but it has carved a niche in the market by guaranteeing overnight delivery of these items to any destination in the country.

The world is full of business ideas just waiting to be tapped, but they're not going to fall right into your lap. You have to go out and find them. Knowing where to look is the key to your chances for success.

One of the first places you can look is in the mirror. Yes, the mirror. Play the role of the consumer. Is there a particular product or service that you wish were available but can't find anywhere? If *you* feel there is a need for a particular item, others may feel the same way as well. What skills and talents do you have that could be applied to some of today's businesses? For example, can you style hair and give manicures, pedicures, and killer massages? If so, a beauty spa may be just the right business for you. If you have a flair for colors, textures, and design, you may want to try opening an interior decorating firm. Or perhaps you talk a mile a minute and know sports better than the alphabet. If these are your skills, a sports agency or sporting goods store may be calling out your name.

As you take inventory of your experience, match your skills against the types of businesses that the market demands. You may be a great cook who can prepare meals for 500 people, but you may not be able to obtain a profitable market share in the highly saturated catering industry. Instead, try to develop a niche in that market. For example, your catering business could target children's parties or focus on weddings and holiday events only.

Another way to find new business ideas is to talk with other business owners. Some entrepreneurs will not be willing to share their insights and experiences with you—particularly if you're going to be a direct competitor—but others will offer helpful advice on the day-to-day operations of a business. Just don't expect to get any trade secrets.

You can also consider working on a part-time basis in a business that you would like to own. This will give you the opportunity to learn the ropes of a particular operation, build your skills base, and acquire any knowledge that you may be lacking—all without the financial and personal commitment of being a full-time entrepreneur. Perhaps more importantly, becoming an employee in a business that you think you would *like to own* will give you a chance to see whether it is really what you *should own*. Although there are laundry lists of reasons why businesses fail, one of the more frequent reasons involves choosing a business. Some entrepreneurs simply make the wrong choice.

Conducting extensive market research will provide you with a wealth of information about possible business opportunities. If money is no object, you can hire a market research firm to locate potential business ideas for you. But if you're like most new business owners, your budget will not allow such a luxury. This means you will have to conduct the research yourself.

Begin with the mainstream press. At your library, read copies of the leading newspapers and news magazines: *The New York Times, The Philadelphia Inquirer, The Los Angeles Times, The Wall Street Journal, U.S. News & World Report, TIME,* and *Newsweek.* Also, look through business publications such as *Black Enterprise, Forbes, Fortune, Business Week,* and any others you can find. Consider subscribing to two or three business publications so that you can keep up with any changes in the economy that may affect your operation once it gets off the ground.

When thumbing through these resources, look for emerging trends—whether business, social, or cultural—that you could parlay into a successful business venture. Here are several examples of the types of trends you might encounter:

1. *Increase in dual-income families.* The days when, typically, the husband worked at a 9–5 job while the wife stayed home to take care of the house and children are virtually gone. Dual-income families are ruling the workplace, and couples have little time for a number of household tasks, especially those traditionally performed by the wife. Opportunities for businesses could include house-cleaning, lawn care, carpet cleaning, and pool cleaning services, as well as a day care center or an interior decorating firm.

2. *Computer technology on the rise.* Who doesn't have a computer these days? Whether laptop or desktop, PC or Macintosh, there has been phenomenal growth in computer technology. Because many people do not have the expertise or skills to maintain their systems themselves, they will hire professionals to service their equipment. This affords an opportunity for a number of business ideas: computer technician, computer consultant, Web site designer, desktop publisher, and graphic designer.

3. *Baby boomers with bucks.* Men and women who are now entering their fifties have a larger amount of disposable income than perhaps any segment of the population. Many are readying themselves for retirement by putting their hard-earned dollars into mutual funds, stocks, and other investment opportunities, but, as a group, they are spending a little as well. Their desire to pamper themselves can translate into a number of different business opportunities associated with travel, recreation, retailing, food, and clothing.

4. *Globalization of business marketplace.* Doing business globally is no longer a luxury reserved for large corporations. Many smaller

business organizations are finding opportunities in Latin America, Asia, and Africa. Rural countries are in need of products and services that are commonplace in the United States. Some business ideas you may want to pursue to fill consumer needs overseas include: laundromats, plumbing services, or computer supply stores.

5. *A more health-conscious nation.* More Americans are working hard at living healthy. Nutritional food stores are common in every city and mall. And even if you don't carry a membership card for a local gym, you probably know someone who does. To tap into this emerging trend, you could consider opening a day spa, an aromatherapy store, or a fruit juice bar. Any of these ideas could become profitable business ventures.

6. *Company downsizing.* Unfortunately, companies ranging from private hospitals to public technology giants have made significant cuts in staff to save money. However, to keep production at its peak, the same companies are "outsourcing" certain services—hiring outside professionals and businesses to perform tasks once completed in-house. An upside to downsizing can be found in these business opportunities: legal and paralegal services, billing services, public relations, and meeting planning.

Business Conferences

If you are about to embark on a path toward entrepreneurship, you would do well to attend at least one business conference. Business conferences are large meetings, seminars, or symposia at which business owners congregate to gather information about how to start, run, and grow a successful company. These meetings give entrepreneurs an opportunity to meet and network with other business owners and share real-world experiences. By attending, you'll be visiting a candyland of new business ideas.

Most business conferences are sponsored and/or held by large corporations, professional associations, and major business publications. For example, each year *Black Enterprise* magazine holds its Black Enterprise/NationsBank Entrepreneurs Conference. The five-day event attracts chief executives from some of the largest black-owned businesses in the nation (such as Robert Johnson, CEO of BET Holdings Inc., and Roy D. Terry, president of Terry Manufacturing Company, an apparel manufacturing firm in Roanoke, Alabama) as well as small shopkeepers working in industries ranging from architecture to computers to catering.

Business conferences schedule a number of sessions and workshops that cover specific aspects of running a successful business. For example, there may be discussions about writing a business plan, securing start-up capital, doing business abroad, selecting strategic partners, and using technology to grow a company. But, like the BE Entrepreneurs Conference, many gatherings also have business expos at which a variety of companies set up booths to promote their operations and talk with interested consumers about their products and services. If you're looking for information on ideas that may interest you, spend some time walking the aisles of a business expo. You can talk with experienced owners (who may have businesses similar to the one you would like to start) about the feasibility of your idea, how to get started, and the day-to-day operations of a company.

To find out about upcoming business conferences in your area, contact your local chamber of commerce or visitors' and convention center. A registration fee will be required. Costs vary, but you can expect to pay at least $100 as an attendee.

Business conferences cater to the needs of entrepreneurs, but non-business-owners are still welcome. A host of professionals—accountants, lawyers, motivational speakers, authors, financial experts, and the like—also attend such events to gather information about how they can better serve the business community and to lend support to individual owners.

A business conference is a watering hole for virtually anyone interested in entrepreneurship. Whether you are a banker, a rookie business owner, or a veteran with 30 years of experience under your belt, attending these events can be rewarding, both professionally and personally.

Trade Shows

Trade shows provide a great forum for the exchange and introduction of business ideas. By attending, you can also:

- View the latest trends, products, and services.
- Network with peers and customers.
- Attend educational seminars.
- Experience the latest technology.
- Consult with experts about potential ideas.
- Learn about your competitors.
- Generate sales.
- Promote your business.

Trade shows are usually sponsored by associations in a variety of industries: jewelry, apparel, food, computers, toys, architecture—the list goes on and on.

Finding the best trade shows, as an attendee or an exhibitor, can be challenging and very time-consuming. To locate one that will serve you well, consider the following:

- *Trade Show News Network.* The source for the Commercial News USA Tradeshow Information Services, a summary of leading trade shows that includes event descriptions, locations, dates, histories, exhibitor lists, attendee demographics, and other conference information. Information on trade shows covers 106 industries. To find out more about Trade Show News Network and the Commercial News USA Tradeshow Information Services, visit the Web at www.tsnn.com /cmnewsusa/.

- *Tradeshows Online.* If you've ever wanted to attend a trade show without the hassle of the crowds, the worry over expenses, or the time spent in making travel arrangements, you may want to try this service. Its cyberspace shows are designed to reflect an actual trade show. As long as you have a computer and Internet access, you can tap into a number of events and get the same experience as if you were attending in person: exhibitor booths, product displays, business information, seminars, professional resources, and other data that you can use to help you find a new business idea. You can sign up by visiting the Tradeshows Online Web site at http:// tradeshows-online.com/html/about.html.

- *Trade Show Central (TSC).* This free Internet service provides easy access to information on more than 50,000 trade shows, conferences, and seminars. By visiting the Web site (www.tscentral.com/html /what6.html), you can search a comprehensive directory of international shows. Just set the criteria (trade show name, industry category, location, and date of show) and you can get a personalized list of shows that fit your specifications. From that list, you can select events about which you would like more information.

If you do not have Internet access, contact your local chamber of commerce about upcoming trade shows.

Professional Business Consultants

One of the biggest mistakes new business owners make when choosing a business is: they don't seek the advice of a professional consultant. Some are reluctant to seek assistance because they are too proud; others simply don't know where to find a helping hand. Whether you live in a remote area of Montana or in the center of a bustling metropolis, help is available and much of it is cheap, if not free-of-charge.

A number of professional consultants work in or donate time to small business centers, chambers of commerce, and civic groups throughout the nation. They can help you make a wise business choice. The Service Corps of Retired Executives (SCORE), one of the more notable organizations, provides free counseling and training to new and existing small businesses.

SCORE is a national nonprofit organization sponsored by the U.S. Small Business Administration (SBA). It is made up of more than 13,000 volunteer business counselors enrolled in 389 SCORE chapters nationwide. In addition to counseling, SCORE offers low-cost workshops and seminars (ranging in price from $20 to $75, depending on the program) covering a number of business topics, including the basics of business accounting, marketing your firm, financing your start-up, and leasing a location.

If you're worried about revealing your prized idea to a stranger, don't be. There are several ways in which you can protect your product or service; we'll discuss them later in this chapter. SCORE business counselors, in particular, honor the association's Code of Ethics, which states that all information discussed between you (the client) and the SCORE adviser is classified as proprietary and confidential.

Since its founding in 1964, more than 3.5 million Americans have used services provided by SCORE. To locate the chapter nearest you, call 1-800-634-0245.

Business Associations

Business and trade associations are good resources to tap when searching for a business idea. The *Encyclopedia of Associations,* published by Gale Research Inc., Detroit, Michigan, lists descriptions of over 140,000 national, international, regional, state, and local associations. These include trade and professional associations, social welfare and public affairs organizations, and religious, sports, and hobby groups.

You can find the *Encyclopedia of Associations* in the reference section of your local library. If you have an idea you would like to pursue, thumb through the index to find an association that caters to the industry in which you are interested, then call to speak with a representative. Once you open for business, you may want to consider taking out a membership in one or two associations related to your industry. This will give you access to additional resources such as organization newsletters, discounts, and other business-related materials.

PERFORMING YOUR LITMUS TEST FOR SUCCESS

You've determined that you have what it takes to become your own boss. You've chosen an idea that matches your skills and your tastes. Now you're ready to pour your life savings into producing a business idea that is nothing less than a sure winner. Right? Wrong.

All too often, entrepreneurs rush into ownership with what they think is a good idea, but it turns out to be a bad idea on which they have wasted valuable time and money. The entrepreneurs also suffer public humiliation, which could have been avoided had they taken the time to evaluate the idea's chances for success.

To some business owners, measuring the potential success of an idea may seem like a tedious task, but, if done correctly, it can make the difference between earning big bucks and filing for bankruptcy. You may be a hardworking individual who earned an MBA in finance from Harvard, but if your idea has no potential for profitability, you're sunk.

Some business owners overlook this important task because they do not know how to determine whether their idea will succeed in the marketplace. The following criteria will help you establish whether your idea is a winner:

Marketability

To accurately calculate your business idea's chances for success, you must know as much as possible about your potential market. The whole purpose of market research—which we will discuss in greater detail in the next chapter—is to thoroughly investigate and examine the environment in which you intend to promote and sell your product or service. As part of your litmus test for success, you need to determine the demographics of your potential market. For example: What is the size of your target audience? What is the average age of your consumer? Average income? Social class? When you perform your research, you should be looking for answers to these questions:

1. *Who are your competitors?* Remember that you can have both direct and indirect competition. If you operate an ice cream parlor, you will compete with Baskin & Robbins (direct competitor), but you will also share the market with alternative dessert vendors such as pastry and candy shops (indirect competitors).

2. *Who are your potential customers?* Where do they live and how will their location influence where you situate your business? For example, if your customers are military men and women, you may need to set up shop near naval, army, and air bases, or universities that have Reserve Officers' Training Corps (ROTC) units.

3. *How much is your target audience willing to pay for your product or service?* Research what your competitors are charging, and use that amount as a measuring rod for the prices that you may need to set. You don't want to charge too much *or* too little. Either extreme will eventually drive you out of business (see Chapter 11).

4. *How will you reach your customers?* What marketing techniques are most effective for reaching your audience? What methods will you use to let your target audience know that you exist? How much will those methods cost? (See Chapter 9.)

5. *What is your positioning in the marketplace?* Will you fill a special niche, or will your product or service be very similar to those that already exist?

Profit Potential

A large determinant of your business idea's success is the profitability of your product or service. Start by determining how much it will cost to get your business off the ground. Create a business budget that accounts for each expense. More often than not, you will find that things cost more than you had anticipated, so cushion your budget to cover additional costs. Any extra cash will help to carry you through the periodic lulls in cash flow that you may experience during the infant stage of your business. Establish how much income you can expect from your business, and compare it with the amount you must spend to meet the market's demands. If your idea is not likely to generate the presale costs plus a profit, the product or service you intend to sell may not be worth the time, energy, and money you planned to invest.

Financial Means

Determining how much money you will need to launch your business is relatively easy. Finding ways to finance your venture is the hard part. Many commercial financial institutions are skittish about loaning money to new small businesses because they consider them to be bad risks. Rather than a new entrepreneur just starting out, most bankers want an owner who has a track record. Your idea is not going to fly unless you have the means to fund its development and its successful launch, so consider how you will secure financing. Among the available options are: a Small Business Administration loan, backing given by a venture capital firm, and funds borrowed from family and friends (see Chapter 8).

Legal Ramifications

One role you do not want after starting a new business is defendant in a lawsuit. Litigation is a surefire way to create a negative reputation for yourself and your product or service. When determining your idea's success quotient, consider what legal problems might be encountered in the type of business you want to start. For example, if you plan to operate a business that will sell food, you could be exposed to product liability if consumers claim they got sick after eating your product. Consult your insurance agent or lawyer about any potential liabilities, and take steps to protect yourself and your business (see Chapter 6). Then decide whether the possible exposure to lawsuits is worth the risk of opening the type of business you had in mind.

PROTECTING YOUR BUSINESS IDEA

After spending countless days or months—or even years—conceiving and then developing an idea, the last thing you want is to have someone steal it. Protect yourself and your business idea by using a patent, trademark, or copyright.

Patents, trademarks, and copyrights are protections for intellectual properties; they refer to the rights associated with intangible knowledge or concepts. Copyrights generally reserve the right to sell, distribute, and/or reproduce written material. For example, authors or publishers copyright articles, books, and other printed material. As an entrepreneur, you will need to secure a patent or trademark to keep others from infringing on your ideas. Obtaining a patent or trademark for intellectual property will afford you protection, but the onus will be on you to prove any violation of your ideas. This can be very time-consuming and costly, but in the long run you will find that the energy and money are well spent.

To prevent any mishaps in the process of getting a patent or trademark, you may want to have your attorney handle all the paperwork involved, as well as any legal proceedings that may develop. Delegating the task to a professional will give you the peace of mind that comes when everything is being handled in a timely and orderly fashion. It will also allow you to focus on the day-to-day operation of your business.

The next two sections will give you an overview of patents and trademarks. You need this information to protect your business.

Patent Protection

A patent is a right granted by the U.S. Government to an inventor to exclusively make, use, or sell an invention for a specified period of time, usually 17 years. Applying for a patent can be a very expensive and time-consuming process. Obtaining a patent can take years.

For starters, you must conduct a search to make sure that the product or invention you intend to market isn't similar to, or the same as, one that already exists. You can conduct a search of your product at the Search Room of the U.S. Patent and Trademark Office (PTO) in Arlington, Virginia. If you are unable to make a trip to Arlington to conduct the search, you can hire local researchers to do it for you. Their fees will usually cost you from $250 to $500. You can also use the Patent and Trademark Depository Libraries (PTDLs), which can be found in just about every state. They contain patent and trademark information issued from the U.S. Patent and Trademark Office. Most PTDLs have, on record, all full-text patents published since 1790, and all trademarks published since 1872. A selection of foreign patents issued is also available. For the PTDL nearest you, call the U.S. Patent and Trademark Office at 703-308-9000. Use of the library facilities is free. However, there is a fee for making copies of any patent and trademark information.

Your next step in the patent filing process is to write a concise description of your invention and attach any supportive materials. You must also fill out an application form and create a scale drawing of your proposed product. When all of these elements have been accounted for, the approval process begins. Remember: It can take months, and even years, for a patent to be granted, and not every patent will receive a stamp of approval. According to the U.S. Patent and Trademark Office, more than 100,000 applications are received yearly, and only about 50 percent are granted patents. When so many queries are being turned down, the whole process may seem futile, but there are several reasons (other than exclusivity) why you should obtain a patent:

- It protects your claim to the ownership of your idea. Without that protection, it's virtually your word against the alleged offender if a lawsuit should occur.
- Having a patent signifies that you are serious about your product and that you are willing to invest the time and money to see it through. Financial institutions look favorably on patent holders. Having a patent could increase your chances to obtain financing, if needed.
- Securing a patent may give you a jump on the competition and discourage rivals, particularly those who are unaware of how the patent process works.

How much will the entire process cost? The patent search, application filing fee, maintenance expenses, and attorney fees will cost you in excess of $10,000 ($3,000 to $5,000 will most likely go toward legal fees alone). If this is too steep for your pocketbook, realize that you don't have to go through the patent process to protect your product. Under the U.S. "first to invent" law, you can claim the rights to your invention even if someone has already filed a patent application for a similar product with the U.S. Patent and Trademark Office. However, you must provide documentation that indicates you were the first person to invent the idea. The Patent and Trademark Office publishes guidelines on how to protect your idea for up to one year before you officially file for a patent. Prepatent protection (1) allows you to reduce the costs of securing the intellectual property and (2) gives you the opportunity to develop your idea further before introducing it into the marketplace.

You can also file a disclosure statement with the federal government. This document will protect your idea for up to two years, and your product for one year after it is introduced to the public. After the first year of public knowledge, you must file for a patent if you want full protection for your invention.

If none of these options is to your liking, you can move full speed ahead with your idea and ditch the patent approval process altogether. Burnett Nelson, president of The 101 Group, did just that. Nelson's company, which is located in Houston, Texas, designs and manufactures instructional classroom furniture. Among the pieces offered are tables with pop-out CD storage racks, and desks with reversible panels that allow students to build blocks on one side and review a map of the United States on the other. Nelson created a prototype for his multifunctional classroom table in 1991, but rather than head for the Patent and Trademark Office in Washington to secure intellectual protection for his innovation, he took his prototype to a national Head Start conference in Indianapolis, Indiana.

"I did conduct patent research. But after looking at the expense of securing the patent and realizing that it does not necessarily prevent someone from trying to knock you off, I determined that my biggest protection was to get the product out to the market as fast as possible, make sure that it was well-designed and maintained, and continue to modify it and stay ahead of the competition," he explains. Nelson seems to be meeting his goals. His client base now includes the TSU/HISD Laboratory School in Houston, a slew of schools in the Houston Independent School District, Head Start, and educational facilities throughout Florida and Illinois.

If, like Nelson, you choose to invest your time and money in readying your invention for the marketplace, you may want to use a nondisclosure agreement. This document is a confidentiality contract between you and any person with whom you share your invention. For example, if you make details of your product available to a manufacturer, the nondisclosure agreement would state that all parties involved agree to keep all information about the invention private and confidential.

This document is extremely important if you forgo the patent process. Without it, you run the risk of giving away your invention and having no legal way to retrieve it. If you want to share your idea with corporations and other organizations, know that they should be willing to sign a nondisclosure agreement. If a particular company is not comfortable with such a contract, move on to the next one.

To speed the process of getting your invention to the public market, you can license your product to an outside entity. Under a licensing agreement, you grant a company the right to manufacture your product in return for cash and/or royalties. This process is simple and ideal for an entrepreneur who wants to profit from his or her idea without having to give up total control of it.

Mark Your Territory with a Trademark

What do Coke, Pepsi, the Nike swoosh symbol, and the NBC network chimes all have in common? They're all trademarks. A trademark is a word, phrase, symbol, design, sound, or color, or some combination of these elements, that identifies and distinguishes a product or service from others in the marketplace.

Like patents, trademarks or "brand names" safeguard your product or service from infringement, and grant you "offensive" or exclusive rights to its use. Technically, by using the name in commerce, you have established "common law rights" to the mark. But to ensure the fullest protection, especially in the event of a lawsuit, you should register a state or federal trademark.

Trademarks are commonly used in connection with several other marks, including:

- *Service mark.* A name or abbreviation that identifies a source of services and distinguishes that source from other services found in the marketplace. For example, the letters CBS represent the service mark of a major broadcast network.
- *Certification mark.* A symbol or name of an independent group, board, or commission that judges the quality of goods or services. The Good Housekeeping seal of approval is a certification mark.
- *Collective mark.* An identifying name or symbol that shows membership in an organization. A police badge, indicating affiliation with law enforcement, is an example.
- *Trade name.* A word or words under which a company conducts business. A trademark, in contrast, represents a word or symbol under which a company sells a product or service. For example, *Procter & Gamble* is a trade name. *Ivory* is a trademark, or brand name, for one of Procter & Gamble's soaps.

When choosing a mark, consider whether it is generic or descriptive. A generic mark is a word or symbol that is already used in the public domain to identify goods or services. A descriptive mark is found on a product or service that has not yet entered the public marketplace on a large scale. If your mark is either generic or descriptive, you will not be granted offensive rights to its use.

Once you've labeled your product or service, you can begin the trademark filing procedure by conducting a name search of both registered and unregistered marks. Be forewarned that the U.S. Patent and Trademark Office does not conduct searches to determine whether a mark has already been registered or an application is pending, unless the office is acting on an application. If you simply want to check the status of a mark, you will either have to conduct the search yourself or have someone complete the task for you.

If you go it alone, you can search for registered marks in the *Trademark Register of the U.S.* or *CompuMark Directory of the U.S. Trademarks.* You should be able to find both resources in your local library or through computer databases such as CompuServe or Dialog. You can also comb the records of your state office or visit a patent and trademark depository library, which will have CD-ROMS containing a trademark database of registered and pending marks. Unregistered marks can be found in the *Thomas Register, McRae's Blue Book,* and the *Gale Trade Names Register.*

If you would like a professional to conduct a search for you, you can contact a trademark search firm such as the Trademark Service Corporation (1-800-872-6275) or Thomson and Thomson (1-800-692-8833). On average, a nationwide search can take as long as four business days and will cost you up to $350.

When your search is complete, you can file your application for a trademark (see Figure 2.1). You are not required to conduct a search before filing an application, but if you choose a mark that already exists, you may face a lawsuit. Know that if two similar marks come into question, your mark need not be identical, or your goods or services the same as another, for your application to be rejected. The PTO will consider whether there is a likelihood of confusion when consumers try to distinguish one set of goods or services from another. Other factors that may hinder your registration include:

- Having lengthy written material. For this type of original matter, you should seek a copyright.
- Using surnames or geographical destinations as your trademark.
- Using immoral, deceptive, or scandalous material.
- Using a slogan that is simply informational or flattering in nature.

You can file for a trademark at either the state or federal level. If you plan to conduct business only locally, you can get a state registration through the office of your Secretary of State. This will cost you anywhere from $50 to $120. If you plan to use the mark nationwide, you will need to register a federal trademark through the PTO. There are three ways in which you can qualify to file for federal registration:

1. If you have already used a mark in commerce, you may file based on that use. In this instance, you would fill out a "use" application.
2. If you have not used the mark, you may file an "intent-to-use" application (see Figure 2.2), which states that you will use the mark in commerce.
3. If you live outside the United States but would like to file an application in this country, certain international agreements allow you to do so, based on an application or registration in another country. A U.S. registration provides protection only in the United States. If you wish to protect a mark in other parts of the world, you will need to seek protection in each country separately, according to that country's laws. For more information about securing trademarks abroad, consult with your attorney or the U.S. offices in the country of your interest.

A federal application must be filed in the name of the owner of the mark and must be accompanied by: a drawing of the mark on a separate sheet of paper, and a fee of $245 per class (i.e., for each individual product/service used in connection with the mark). If you wish to register more than one mark, or to submit more than one version of the same mark, you will need to file a separate application for each mark or version.

When submitting your application, indicate your telephone number on the form and include a stamped, self-addressed postcard on which you have listed each item in your mailing. The PTO will stamp the filing date and the

Figure 2.1   Trademark/Service Mark Application

TRADEMARK/SERVICE MARK APPLICATION, PRINCIPAL REGISTER, WITH DECLARATION	MARK (Word(s) and/or Design)	CLASS NO. (If known)

TO THE ASSISTANT COMMISSIONER FOR TRADEMARKS:

APPLICANT'S NAME:

APPLICANT'S MAILING ADDRESS:

(Display address exactly as it should appear on registration)

APPLICANT'S ENTITY TYPE: (**Check one** and supply requested information)

	Individual - Citizen of (Country):
	Partnership - State where organized (Country, if appropriate): _____ Names and Citizenship (Country) of General Partners: _____
	Corporation - State (Country, if appropriate) of Incorporation:
	Other (Specify Nature of Entity and Domicile):

GOODS AND/OR SERVICES:

Applicant requests registration of the trademark/service mark shown in the accompanying drawing in the United States Patent and Trademark Office on the Principal Register established by the Act of July 5, 1946 (15 U.S.C. 1051 et. seq., as amended) for the following goods/services (**SPECIFIC GOODS AND/OR SERVICES MUST BE INSERTED HERE**):

BASIS FOR APPLICATION: (Check boxes which apply, **but never both the first AND second boxes**, and supply requested information related to each box checked.)

[ ]	Applicant is using the mark in commerce on or in connection with the above identified goods/services. (15 U.S.C. 1051(a), as amended.) Three specimens showing the mark as used in commerce are submitted with this application. • Date of first use of the mark in commerce which the U.S. Congress may regulate (for example, interstate or between the U.S. and a foreign country): _____ • Specify the type of commerce: _____ (for example, interstate or between the U.S. and a specified foreign country) • Date of first use anywhere (the same as or before use in commerce date): _____ • Specify intended manner or mode of use of mark on or in connection with the goods/services: _____ (for example, trademark is applied to labels, service mark is used in advertisements)
[ ]	Applicant has a bona fide intention to use the mark in commerce on or in connection with the above identified goods/services. (15 U.S.C. 1051(b), as amended.) • Specify manner or mode of use of mark on or in connection with the goods/services: _____ (for example, trademark will be applied to labels, service mark will be used in advertisements)
[ ]	Applicant has a bona fide intention to use the mark in commerce on or in connection with the above identified goods/services, and asserts a claim of priority based upon a foreign application in accordance with 15 U.S.C. 1126(d), as amended. • Country of foreign filing: _____ • Date of foreign filing: _____
[ ]	Applicant has a bona fide intention to use the mark in commerce on or in connection with the above identified goods/services and, accompanying this application, submits a certification or certified copy of a foreign registration in accordance with 15 U.S.C 1126(e), as amended • Country of registration: _____ • Registration number: _____

NOTE: Declaration, on Reverse Side, MUST be Signed

PTO Form 1478 (REV 6/96)
OMB No. 0651-0009 (Exp. 06/30/98)   U.S. DEPARTMENT OF COMMERCE/Patent and Trademark Office

Figure 2.1   *(continued)*

DECLARATION

The undersigned being hereby warned that willful false statements and the like so made are punishable by fine or imprisonment, or both, under 18 U.S.C. 1001, and that such willful false statements may jeopardize the validity of the application or any resulting registration, declares that he/she is properly authorized to execute this application on behalf of the applicant; he/she believes the applicant to be the owner of the trademark/service mark sought to be registered, or if the application is being filed under 15 U.S.C. 1051(b), he/she believes the applicant to be entitled to use such mark in commerce; to the best of his/her knowledge and belief no other person, firm, corporation, or association has the right to use the above identified mark in commerce, either in the identical form thereof or in such near resemblance thereto as to be likely, when used on or in connection with the goods/services of such other person, to cause confusion, or to cause mistake, or to deceive; and that all statements made of his/her own knowledge are true and that all statements made on information and belief are believed to be true.

_____   _____
DATE   SIGNATURE

_____   _____
TELEPHONE NUMBER   PRINT OR TYPE NAME AND POSITION

INSTRUCTIONS AND INFORMATION FOR APPLICANT

TO RECEIVE A FILING DATE, THE APPLICATION <u>MUST</u> BE COMPLETED AND SIGNED BY THE APPLICANT AND SUBMITTED ALONG WITH:

1. The prescribed **FEE ($245.00)** for each class of goods/services listed in the application;
2. A **DRAWING PAGE** displaying the mark in conformance with 37 CFR 2.52;
3. If the application is based on use of the mark in commerce, **THREE (3) SPECIMENS** (evidence) of the mark as used in commerce for each class of goods/services listed in the application. All three specimens may be the same. Examples of good specimens include: (a) labels showing the mark which are placed on the goods; (b) photographs of the mark as it appears on the goods, (c) brochures or advertisements showing the mark as used in connection with the services.
4. An **APPLICATION WITH DECLARATION** (this form) - The application must be signed in order for the application to receive a filing date. Only the following persons may sign the declaration, depending on the applicant's legal entity: (a) the individual applicant; (b) an officer of the corporate applicant; (c) one general partner of a partnership applicant; (d) all joint applicants.

SEND APPLICATION FORM, DRAWING PAGE, FEE, AND SPECIMENS (IF APPROPRIATE) TO:

Assistant Commissioner for Trademarks
Box New App/Fee
2900 Crystal Drive
Arlington, VA 22202-3513

Additional information concerning the requirements for filing an application is available in a booklet entitled **Basic Facts About Registering a Trademark**, which may be obtained by writing to the above address or by calling: (703) 308-HELP.

This form is estimated to take an average of 1 hour to complete, including time required for reading and understanding instructions, gathering necessary information, recordkeeping, and actually providing the information. Any comments on this form including the amount of time required to complete this form, should be sent to the Office of Management and Organization, U.S. Patent and Trademark Office, U.S. Department of Commerce, Washington, D.C. 20231. Do NOT send completed forms to this address.

Figure 2.2 Allegation of Use for Intent-to-Use Application

ALLEGATION OF USE FOR INTENT-TO-USE APPLICATION,WITH DECLARATION (Amendment To Allege Use/Statement Use)	MARK (Identify the mark)
	SERIAL NO.

TO THE ASSISTANT COMMISSIONER FOR TRADEMARKS:

APPLICANT NAME:

Applicant requests registration of the above-identified trademark/service mark in the United States Patent and Trademark Office on the Principal Register established by the Act of July 5, 1946 (15 U.S.C. §1051 *et seq.*, as amended). Three specimens per class showing the mark as used in commerce and the prescribed fees are submitted with this statement.

Applicant is using the mark in commerce on or in connection with the following goods/services (CHECK ONLY ONE):

☐ (a) those in the application or Notice of Allowance; **OR**

☐ (b) those in the application or Notice of Allowance **except** (if goods/services are to be deleted, list the goods/services to be **deleted**): _____

_____

_____

Date of first use in commerce which the U.S. Congress may regulate: _____

Specify type of commerce: _____
              (for example, interstate and/or commerce between the U.S. and a foreign country)

Date of first use anywhere: _____

Specify manner or mode of use of mark on or in connection with the goods/services: (for example, trademark is applied to labels, service mark is used in advertisements): _____

_____

_____

The undersigned, being hereby warned that willful false statements and the like so made are punishable by fine or imprisonment, or both, under 18 U.S.C. §1001, and that such willful false statements may jeopardize the validity of the application or any resulting registration, declares that he/she is properly authorized to execute this Amendment to Allege Use or Statement of Use on behalf of the applicant; he/she believes the applicant to be the owner of the trademark/service mark sought to be registered; the trademark /service mark is now in use in commerce; and all statements made of his/her own knowledge are true and all statements made on information and belief are believed to be true.

_____   _____
Date   Signature

_____   _____
Telephone Number   Type or Print Name and Position

☐   **Check here if Request to Divide is being submitted with this statement** (if Applicant wishes to proceed to publication or registration with certain goods/services on or in connection with which it has used the mark in commerce and retain an active application for any remaining goods/services, a divisional application and fee are required. 37 C.F.R. §2.87)

PLEASE SEE REVERSE FOR MORE INFORMATION

PTO Form 1553   U.S. Department of Commerce/Patent and Trademark Office
OMB No. 0651-000 (Exp. 06/30/98)

Figure 2.2   *(continued)*

INSTRUCTIONS AND INFORMATION FOR APPLICANT

In an application based upon a bona fide intention to use a mark in commerce, **the Applicant must use its mark in commerce before a registration will be issued.** After use begins, the applicant must file the Allegation of Use. If the Allegation of Use is filed before the mark is approved for publication in the *Official Gazette* it is treated under the statute as **an Amendment to Allege Use (AAU).** If it is filed after the Notice of Allowance is issued, it is treated under the statute as **a Statement of Use (SOU).** The Allegation of Use cannot be filed during the time period between approval of the mark for publication in the *Official Gazette* and the issuance of the Notice of Allowance. The difference between the AAU and SOU is the time at which each is filed during the process.

Additional requirements for filing this Allegation of Use:

1) the fee of $100.00 per class of goods/services (**please note that fees are subject to change, usually on October 1 of each year**): and
2) three (3) specimens of the mark as used in commerce for each class of goods/services (for example, photographs of the mark as it appears on the goods, labels for affixation on goods, advertisements showing the mark as used in connection with services).

•   The Applicant may list dates of use for one item in each class of goods/services identified in the Allegation of Use. The Applicant must have used the mark in commerce on all the goods/services in the class, however, it is only necessary to list the dates of use for one item in each class.

•   Only the following persons may sign the verification on this form: (a) the individual applicant; (b) an officer of a corporate applicant; (c) one general partner of a partnership applicant; (d) all joint applicants.

•   The goods/services in the Allegation of Use must be the same as those specified in the application or Notice of Allowance. The Applicant may limit or clarify the goods/services, but cannot add to or otherwise expand the identification specified in the application or Notice of Allowance. If goods/services are deleted, they may **not** be reinserted at a later time.

•   Amendments to Allege Use are governed by Trademark Act §1(c), 15 U.S.C. §1051(c) and Trademark Rule 2.76, 37 C.F.R. §2.76. Statements of Use are governed by Trademark Act §1(d), 15 U.S.C. §1051(d) and Trademark Rule 2.88, 37 C.F.R. §2.88.

> **MAIL COMPLETED FORM TO:**
>
> **ASSISTANT COMMISSIONER FOR TRADEMARKS**
> **BOX AAU/SOU**
> **2900 CRYSTAL DRIVE**
> **ARLINGTON, VIRGINIA 22202-3513**

Please note that the filing date of a document in the Patent and Trademarks Office is the date of receipt in the Office, not the date of deposit of the mail. 37 C.F.R. §1.6. To avoid lateness due to mail delay, use of the certificate of mailing set forth below, is encouraged.

COMBINED CERTIFICATE OF MAILING/CHECKLIST

Before filing this form, please make sure to complete the following:

☐   three specimens, per class have been enclosed;
☐   the filing fee of $100 (subject to change as noted above), per class has been enclosed; and
☐   the declaration has been signed by the appropriate party

CERTIFICATE OF MAILING

I do hereby certify that the foregoing are being **deposited** with the United States Postal Service as first class mail, postage prepaid, in an envelope addressed to the Assistant Commissioner for Trademarks, 2900 Crystal Drive, Arlington, VA 22202-3513, on _____ (date).

_____   _____
Signature   Date of Deposit

_____
Print or Type Name of Person Signing Certificate

This form is estimated to take 15 minutes to complete including time required for reading and understanding instructions, gathering necessary information, record keeping and actually providing the information. Any comments on the amount of time you require to complete this form should be sent to the Office of Management and Organization, U.S. Patent and Trademark Office, U.S. Department of Commerce, Washington, D.C. 20231. Do not send forms to this address.

application's serial number on the postcard and will send it to you to acknowledge that your application was received. The application evaluation process can take anywhere from four to five months. A PTO examining attorney will review your mark to see if it can be registered. If not, the attorney will issue a letter of refusal indicating the grounds for its rejection, or any corrections that may be needed on the application. You must respond to any objections within six months of the mailing date of the refusal letter, or your application will be terminated. For an application, contact the PTO at 1-800-PTO-9199.

Compared to the patent process, obtaining a trademark is not as time-consuming or expensive. A trademark can last indefinitely if you continue to use it to identify your product or service. A federal trademark is good for 10 years and has 10-year renewal terms. Between the fifth and sixth years following the initial registration date, you must file an affidavit revealing certain information to keep your registration active. If you do not, your registration will be canceled.

Use of Trademark Symbols

If you have decided to use a trademark as your brand name, it is important that you use it properly. There are three symbols that you can acquire to notify the public about your rights to the mark. The first two are "TM" (trademark) and "SM" (service mark). Anyone who claims the rights to a trademark can use the TM symbol on proprietary goods or the SM symbol after the name of a service business. Your mark does not have to be registered, nor do you have to have an application pending, before you can begin using those two symbols.

The third mark is "R," which indicates that your mark has been registered with the PTO. You can begin placing this mark on your products *only after* registration of the mark has been secured.

Reasons for Registering a Trademark

Some people are comfortable with having just common-law rights to a product or service name, so they don't bother to engage in the trademark procedure. But registration is important to the success of your business. Here are some typical reasons why you should file an application:

- *Nationwide priority.* You may start by using the mark in only one area, but registering a trademark gives you the right to use it anywhere in the nation. If your business spreads, you're prepared for that growth.

- *Benefit of "constructive notice."* Registering your trademark informs the public that you are using a particular brand name and discourages others from trying to use it for themselves. If your mark is registered, no one who attempts to use the mark can say, "Oh, I didn't know."

- *Benefit of "prima facie."* This legal term means that if you ever must go to court to defend your mark, you need not waste time or money proving that ownership and exclusive rights belong to you. A trademark gives validity to your case and presents immediate, clear, and plain evidence that the mark is yours.

- *Licensing.* By registering your trademark, you make it an asset that can be licensed, sold, or transferred. This can translate into even greater profits for you.

- *Court protection.* A trademark gives you the right to sue in federal district courts if someone infringes on your ownership.

- *Penalty for offenders.* If your mark is copied, you are assured that swift and stiff legal action will be taken. The penalty for copying a mark is up to $250,000 in fines or five years in jail for the first offense, or $1,000,000 in fines or fifteen years in prison for the second offense and any thereafter.

The trademark process can be a daunting task. There is a lot of complex language surrounding it and enough information to compile into a book of its own. To get more details about the filing process, as well as trademark rights and their limitations, consult an attorney who deals with trademark law, contact the PTO office, or visit their Web site at www.uspto.gov/. There you will find a number of supplementary materials including a booklet called the *Basic Facts About Trademarks.*

CHECKLIST

HOW TO BEGIN BUILDING YOUR BUSINESS IDEA

✓ **Comb available resources for a captivating concept.** Your best ideas for a new business may very well come from you. As a consumer, what kind of product or service would you like to have, or what type do you need that is not already available in the marketplace? In addition to looking inward, search outward. Pore over the newspaper and business publications for trends that you can transform into a unique start-up. Also, attend business conferences and talk with professional consultants about potential ideas.

✓ **Weigh your chances for success.** Having a good idea is not nearly enough to build a successful business, especially because 10,000 other people could have the same "good idea." You must consider other elements that could impact your chances for success: the competition, a market saturation, and the uniqueness of your product or service.

✓ **Safeguard your prized possession.** Don't give unscrupulous people a chance to pilfer your idea before you introduce it to the marketplace. Protect your product or service by securing a patent or trademark.

RESOURCES FOR MORE INFORMATION

ASSOCIATIONS

- *Service Corps of Retired Executives (SCORE),* 409 3rd St. SW, 4th Floor, Washington, DC 20024; 800-634-0245; www.score.org. SCORE, a national organization sponsored by the U.S. Small Business Administration, provides free counseling to new and existing small business owners. The organization provides workshops that discuss a number of business-related issues: writing a business plan, financing, tax planning, cash flow, and advertising. SCORE chapters are scattered throughout the United States.

- *The Society of American Inventors (SAI),* 202 Delaware Building, 137 South Main Street, Akron, Ohio 44308; 1-800-USA-IDEA (1-888-872-4332); www.inventorshelp.com. SAI was formed to protect the rights of small inventors and give them the resources to move their idea from the patent stage to the marketplace. The organization provides a number of services directed toward business and intellectual property; a technical department for engineering and drafting assistance; a graphics department for layout and illustration; and a marketing/licensing department for help in commercializing inventors' concepts. When working with inventors, SAI does not demand ownership, decision-making authority, or a profit percentage.

- *U.S. Patent and Trademark Office, Trademark Assistance Center,* 2900 Crystal Drive, Room 4B10, Arlington, VA 22202-3513; 703-308-9000; www.uspto.gov. This center provides general information about the trademark and patent registration process and answers queries regarding the status of pending applications and registrations. Online, you can access information regarding the Patent and Trademark Depository Libraries (PTDLs) located throughout the nation.

3

MARKET RESEARCH 101

When you are starting your own business, it is impossible to have too much information. Whether you are launching a new baby oil product or starting a meals-on-wheels delivery service, you will want to gather as many details as possible about your customers, your competition, your resources, and the industry in general. Some entrepreneurs think that if they have the right amount of money, equipment, and skills, their business will automatically succeed. However, without the right types and amount of information, none of these will save an operation from ruin. By conducting market research, you can gather the data you need to successfully launch your venture and, in the process, weed out any ideas that may not be feasible.

In this chapter, we will discuss the basic methods of market research and explain how you can best evaluate your customers, your competition, and your industry.

DEFINING MARKET RESEARCH

According to the Marketing Research Association (MRA), market research is a process used to define the size, location, and/or makeup of the market for a product or service.[1] Essentially, market research is a means by which you can (1) pinpoint what consumers want and need, and (2) identify the *s*trengths, *w*eaknesses, *o*pportunities, and *t*hreats of your product or service (this is known as conducting SWOT analysis). You can also use market research to answer questions relating to the four Ps of marketing:

1. *Product.* What do consumers want, and what will you offer? Market research helps you to determine what types of products or services consumers buy, and why they buy them. You must also identify why customers will choose your items over the competition's.

2. *Price.* How much do you intend to charge for your product or service? Is your price comparable to that of other suppliers of similar goods and services? Is it too high or too low? Research what consumers are willing to pay for particular items, and what the competition is charging.

3. *Place.* What sales channel will you use to promote your product or service? By conducting market research, you may discover that consumers prefer to purchase certain types of products in certain types of places. For example, if you decide to launch a custom swimwear line, you may find that customers favor buying their outfits at a retail store rather than through a mail-order catalog.

4. *Promotion.* How will you position your product or service in the marketplace? Will it be considered a high-end product or a discount item? Market research will help you find a comfortable fit in the marketplace for your product or service, and will define advertising media to which consumers are most receptive. For example, if you operate a fast-food restaurant, you may find that customers are more responsive to a 30-second television commercial that shows people eating burgers and fries than to a newspaper ad picturing a Coke and a hamburger.

Getting into the minds of potential consumers is not easy. It involves analyzing a number of issues ranging from product appeal to packaging preferences. Still, to increase your chances of success, it is a process you must endure.

Many companies invest a lot of time and money in market research. For example, Coke and Pepsi know virtually everything imaginable about beverage drinkers. They know at what temperature the average person likes to drink a soda. They know how many of their commercials customers see on an annual basis, and, believe it or not, how many ice cubes most people put into a glass.

As a new business owner, you may not have the financial means to be highly sophisticated in your research efforts; nonetheless, you must know your market well. Look closely at what types of products and services consumers buy. Find out where, when, and how they buy them. More importantly, determine *why* consumers purchase the goods and services that they do.

No matter what type of business you decide to start, you must begin your market research by defining your information needs. Ask yourself what you are trying to find out about your potential market. Do you want specifics about how your product or service will fare among your target audience? Or, to gauge your profit potential, do you want general sales information? How you define your information needs will dictate the market research method you'll use to collect data. However, your budget will also be a factor. The costs to conduct market research vary according to the type of method used; prices can range from as little as $2,000 to as much as $30,000 or more. Carefully weigh your options before choosing any one method. Once you make a selection, start collecting your data and begin analyzing your findings. But don't expect to finish in a matter of days. Performing market research can be a very time-consuming task. Depending on how much information you need, and the market research method you adopt, it can take anywhere from two to four months to complete.

You can perform the research yourself or hire an outside consultant. Besides locating the information you need, a market research consultant can analyze and interpret the materials for you. Several directories are available to find one of these experts in your area. The MRA publishes *The Blue Book Research Services Directory.* This three-volume resource lists market research services nationwide, according to methodology (services that provide telephone interviews, focus groups, mail surveys, and so on). The directory costs $110, but you should be able to find a copy in the reference section of your local library. The American Marketing Association publishes a similar resource called *The Green Book,* which is also available in most libraries.

If you choose to do your own research, you may want to consider taking a market research course to bolster your knowledge of the process. The MRA, in conjunction with the University of Georgia, offers a program called "Principles of Marketing Research." The course basically provides a general understanding of what is required to effectively collect data using different market research techniques. Check your local colleges and universities for similar programs.

The amount of work that goes into conducting thorough and effective market research keeps many business owners at bay. However, it is imperative that you test the waters of entrepreneurship before plunging in. It could make the difference between whether you sink or swim.

METHODS OF MARKET RESEARCH

Whether you decide to conduct your market research solo or to solicit a consultant to help with the process, here are the five market research methods that you may use:

1. *Historical.* Involves studying old records, files, and other materials to help define existing market conditions.
2. *Observational.* Requires using current data to forecast future conditions.

3. *Survey.* Perhaps the most popular method used. Administers, to a defined group of people, via telephone, mail, fax, or the Internet, a questionnaire that gauges the potential success of a product or service.

4. *Experimental.* Involves using controlled tests to determine whether your goods or services are needed or wanted. A litmus test for your product or service.

5. *Nonexperimental.* Yields data in an uncontrolled environment. Research is done during the normal course of business activity.

Whichever method you choose, the data you collect will represent either primary market research or secondary market research.

Primary Market Research

Primary market research is "original research" that involves collecting data directly from the source. To use a simple example, let's say you are a city beat reporter covering a three-alarm house fire. If you ask the surviving victims of the house fire how the blaze ignited, technically you are collecting primary research. If you use the firefighters' report to gather details about the fire, you are performing secondary research. We will discuss secondary research later in this chapter.

As a new business owner, you should place a lot of emphasis on performing primary research. A key benefit from conducting this type of market research is that you are able to get information that is specific to your needs, not just general data about your industry or the type of business that you operate. Conducting primary research allows you to ask specific questions of sources and receive immediate answers that can be applied to running your operation.

Primary research consists of experimental research and nonexperimental research. Experimental research involves the use of test subjects (people who serve as guinea pigs for a project) in a controlled environment to gauge the impact of each factor or variable involved. For example, a group of potential customers, aged 18 to 25 years, who are drivers of sports cars, may be shown various automobile commercials. Each subject is then asked specific questions designed to measure the possibility that he or she would purchase the cars advertised.

The data collection techniques typically used to perform experimental research include laboratory studies and field studies. These tests are quite effective in gauging actual market performance of a product or service, but they can be expensive. The field study is the less expensive method of the two. A field study uses real-world tests in a controlled group of stores. Two types of tests can be used when conducting a field study:

1. *Controlled store testing.* If you cannot afford to hire consultants or researchers to create a product development program for you, test your product by placing it in selected stores. Many small business owners will solicit a willing store owner(s) (often at a small fee) to carry their products. By using this type of testing, you can determine weaknesses and make changes before you mass distribute your product. Controlled store testing can also provide results that duplicate real-market conditions. The pitfall is that by singling out certain sites, you may not get results that are representative of your entire target buyer population.

2. *City/regional market testing.* This type of testing provides more reliable feedback about how well a product will do in the marketplace. However, small businesses don't typically conduct this type of testing as part of a field study because of cost. A city or regional test requires that you work with a market research company that will match clusters of stores and will manage distribution, advertising, and in-store merchandising. These services can cost you up to tens of thousands of dollars.

Even more expensive than a city or regional market field test is a laboratory study. Conducting this kind of experimental research can cost you anywhere from $50,000 to $100,000. However, you can still use these tests without spending a small fortune. Simply check with your local or national trade and business associations. These groups often gather the findings from laboratory tests performed by other companies. You should be able to find industry-specific organizations in the *Encyclopedia of Associations* at your local library.

Experimental research occurs in a controlled setting. Nonexperimental research takes place in a real-world setting: the variables and environment are not controlled. In other words, the product is placed in the normal course of business activity. This approach is less expensive than experimental research, and its reliability is very high.

Nonexperimental research is used by businesses to test a number of factors. Among them are:

- How buyers respond to new products and to improvements in existing products.
- How price hikes will affect buyers' purchasing.
- How a new product can compete with competitors' new products.
- How buyers evaluate the advertising, design/packaging, and positioning of a product.

The two types of nonexperimental research are:

1. *Qualitative research,* which gathers subjective reactions from only a limited number of test subjects.

2. *Quantitative research,* which uses a limited number of questions to collect responses from several test subjects.

Qualitative Research

Qualitative research is primary research (original research) of a particular subject that is conducted as part of normal business activity (nonexperimental research). Business owners who perform this type of research are more concerned with how subjects *feel* about their product or service, rather than gathering numerical data that can be measured.

In laypersons' terms, qualitative research can be equated to simply sitting down with a potential consumer and conducting an in-depth interview or discussion about your product or service. Keep in mind that the results of qualitative research depend on the topic, the demographics of the targeted buyers, and the researcher's professional experience. The findings, therefore, may not accurately represent an entire market.

Generally speaking, qualitative research involves holding focus groups or personal interviews. A focus group is basically a group interview or survey in which a certain number of target buyers are gathered together to discuss a new product idea. They are asked their opinions about the product, and they share their thoughts, concerns, criticisms, likes, and dislikes with one another and with the researcher. You can hire a market research company to conduct a focus group for you, but it is less expensive if you hold one yourself. A focus group can be created by simply assembling a few friends, family members, coworkers, and neighbors. You can also find potential consumers through the phone book's business pages.

More than likely, you will have to pay focus group participants anywhere from $30 to $100 (or more) per participant. You can offer to provide free food, but most group members will expect some monetary compensation for their time. You can hold a focus group at little or no cost by recruiting college or university students (particularly those involved in an entrepreneurship or a marketing program) to work with you. That's what Vivian Gibson, president of The MillCreek Company, did to investigate the potential success of her hot sauce—Vib's Caribbean Heat.

Like many new business owners, Gibson did not have a huge market research budget to pay for laboratory tests and extensive surveys. To save money, she approached a professor in the graduate program at the Washington University School of Business about using her product as a market research project. "I asked him if he could assign me a couple of graduate students to conduct the research as a class project, and fortunately, at that time, many business schools like the one at Washington University were beginning to develop a curriculum in which they were giving students more realistic experiences, so he jumped at my offer," explains Gibson.

"In fact, his students competed for many businesses that were presented to them, and I was lucky enough to get four graduate students who actually liked hot sauce. Essentially, I became their class project, and they conducted a full-scale market research campaign with statistics, focus groups, surveys, and all the other things that I could not afford to do and could not have done in such a sophisticated manner. The research took about 10 weeks. After the students finished, they furnished me with an actual report with statistics and data. I thought it was a pretty worthwhile effort and an economical way to get my research done."

If you are short on cash, consider enlisting the help of college students to head your focus group and other aspects of your market research efforts. Contact the administration or marketing department of a university near you, and inquire about any entrepreneurial programs.

The second type of qualitative research is the individual interview. In this more personalized method, the researcher goes one-on-one with a target buyer via the telephone or in person. Telephone interviews can be costly, but the results are quick and the method is able to reach a large number of people in a target audience. Face-to-face interviews require that you prepare questionnaires and travel to and from specified destinations. This method, besides being very costly and time-consuming, decreases your chances of getting a sample that is representative of your entire target population. Exercise caution when using this research technique.

Quantitative Research

Like qualitative research, quantitative research is primary research that is conducted during normal business activity. However, because it provides numerical data that can be measured, it is more reliable than qualitative research and more representative of the total target buyer population.

In essence, conducting quantitative research is like conducting a survey. It uses large numbers of people ("sample respondents") and a specific set of questions. To accurately perform quantitative research, you will need the following items:

A Sound Questionnaire. Whether you conduct your questionnaires by phone, fax, mail, e-mail, or written response, you need a well-crafted blueprint for gaining results that are accurate and statistically reliable. If you plan to use a telemarketer, prepare a script to ensure that each interviewee (target buyer) is responding to the same questions. Your questions should be based on common sense and designed to gather information that is critical to the development of your product or service. Prepare questions that the respondents can easily understand and answer. It is not uncommon for researchers to prepare closed-ended or "yes/no" questionnaires. Avoid the following in preparing your list:

- Questions that elicit background information that is not useful to your market research efforts.
- Questions that go over the interviewee's head. Don't solicit answers to questions that require a specific core base of knowledge that the sample respondents may not have.

- Vague questions.
- Trick questions.

A typical questionnaire can include queries designed to obtain the following information:

- Demographic details such as age, gender, economic status, residence, and occupation of the target buyer.
- The product brands that sample respondents use.
- The frequency at which certain brands are purchased.
- The reasons for sample respondents' use of particular products.
- What respondents like and dislike about certain brands.
- How respondents rank certain product brands.
- Whether price is a determining factor when a respondent purchases particular product brands.

A Random Sample of People.   When selecting sample respondents, you can choose either a probability sample or a nonprobability sample. In a probability sample, each respondent has an equal chance of being chosen. This type of random sample creates better representation of the entire target buyer population. A nonprobability sample is more biased because it limits sample respondents to a particular group of people. To illustrate the difference between the two samples, let's say you want to gauge whether potential consumers will purchase your new line of babies' toys. If you arbitrarily select parents by mail or telephone, you've created a probability sample. If you stand outside a Toys 'R Us or Babies 'R Us store and canvass parents as they are leaving, you've formed a nonprobability sample. Many small business owners use nonprobability sampling because it is less expensive.

A Proper Sample Size.   The larger the sample, the greater the accuracy of actual market performance. Your budget and the "confidence level" (degree of accuracy) that you are willing to accept will dictate your sample size. If you are unsure about how many people to include in your sample, consult a market research professional. Typically, at least 100 sample respondents should be used for a probability sample.

Secondary Market Research

If you have ever written a research paper for school, you have conducted secondary research. Secondary research involves using information that other entities—organizations, industry and trade associations, businesses, chambers of commerce, and the media—have compiled. It is the least expensive form of market research, but it may not be as reliable as some of the other methods we have discussed thus far, because the information you receive may not have been created with your specific needs in mind.

There are two types of secondary research: internal research and external research. Internal research involves studying information created by your own company. When using this method, you are gathering data that were generated for purposes other than marketing—perhaps for financial reasons. Examples of internal research include:

- Information drawn from accounting records.
- Information taken from daily, weekly, monthly, or annual sales reports created for products or locations.
- Information about the competition.

External research involves studying information gathered by industry professionals, organizations, or companies that specialize in compiling data about particular businesses. Two companies that track consumer sales information could prove useful in your market research efforts: (1) Information Resources, Inc. (IRI) and (2) AC Nielsen Company. However, to obtain either IRI or Nielsen data can cost thousands of dollars each month. For free or more low-cost secondary research resources, consider the following alternate sources.

The Library
The business section of your local library is a great place to start searching for information about your target buyers, competition, and industry. A wealth of resources is at your fingertips, and experienced library personnel can point you in the right direction. Among the references you can use are publications provided by the U.S. Census Bureau and the U.S. Department of Commerce. Your librarian can also provide you with the *Editor and Publisher Marketing Guide,* which contains demographic information about household income and retail sales for the readership of over 1,500 newspapers nationwide.

Media Outlets
Your local newspaper, network and cable television, radio stations, and local and national business-related magazines are great resources for gathering demographic information about potential target audiences. Each of these media prepares reports indicating specific details about their viewership or readership: age, income, product brand preferences, occupation, and other key attributes. They can also provide information about economic trends, technological trends, tax issues, financing, advertising, and other business concerns. Among the media resources you can use are: *Black Enterprise, The Wall Street Journal* and its Dow Jones News/Retrieval Service, and Dun & Bradstreet (D&B) Information Services. D&B publishes a number of regional and global directories that list company demographics (sales, number of

employees, and public vs. private businesses). D&B tracks about 40 million companies worldwide; of these, 19.7 million are U.S. businesses.

The Internet

By taking a trip through cyberspace you can obtain tons of information critical to your business. There are several Internet services that you can use: America Online Inc., CompuServe, Yahoo Inc., Lycos, and Prodigy Services Company. These Internet services give you access to many business databases. For example, Nexis, the business unit of Lexis-Nexis, provides a news and business online information service, plus company, financial, demographic, market research, and industry reports. You can subscribe to several of these online services for a monthly fee of about $20.

Barter Organizations/Civic Clubs

A number of civic organizations can assist you in your market research efforts. As an African-American entrepreneur who may be faced with special challenges and business needs, you may want to contact your local African American Chamber of Commerce. In addition to providing you with information about your target audience, your competition, and your industry, this organization can give you advice and supply resources for overcoming potential barriers associated with financing, licensing, or procurement. Special sources available include black business directories; workshops and seminars tailored to black business owners; regional and national conventions for power networking; health benefit plans; and monthly news publications. Black Chambers of Commerce are not only resource outlets, they are advocacy groups for black entrepreneurs. Membership fees can range from $50 to $500. These organizations exist in virtually every part of the country. The National Black Chamber of Commerce, an umbrella for more than 170 affiliate chapters, is located in Washington, DC. Call 202–416-1622 to find a chapter in your area.

Local, State, and Federal Government Agencies

State and local agencies can supply information relative to the area that they serve. For example, your local Bureau of Census publishes the *County and City Data Book*, which provides information on the population, income, retail sales, health, education, employment, and housing for a particular area. If you want more broadly based or national data, contact the Small Business Administration (SBA) in Washington, DC. The SBA sponsors a number of resource outlets, including the Service Corps of Retired Executives (SCORE) and Small Business Development Centers (SBDCs), each of which can suggest the type of research you need to compile, and where you can gather the best information. The U.S. Department of Commerce is another great governmental resource. It sponsors the Minority Business Development Agency (MBDA), the only federal agency created specifically to encourage the growth of minority-owned businesses. The MBDA operates a nationwide network of business development centers. Look for one when you need assistance in market research or other business services, such as financial planning and management.

Trade and Professional Associations

Trade associations typically provide industry-specific information, but access to data is granted to members only. Professional associations (which also require a membership fee) generally offer a broader base of industry data. Among the associations you should consider joining is the American Marketing Association (AMA). Its personnel and publications will explain the various methods of market research, suggest the types you should use, and offer ways to obtain the necessary data. The Marketing Science Institute is another source for various research studies on particular topics. There are about fifteen associations within the marketing research industry.

Colleges and Universities

Using educational institutions in your market research efforts may be the cheapest way for you to gather the information that you need. You could start in the college library, where a number of faculty and student theses and business-related projects may be stored. You can also contact the administrator of the marketing or management department for information about any ongoing market research efforts. In many instances, students will volunteer to assist you in exchange for college credit and professional experience. Many universities also have entrepreneurial programs that can prove advantageous to your market research needs.

RESEARCHING YOUR CUSTOMERS

When you have assembled the appropriate market research tools, you can put them to good use. First, identify your target audience. To whom do you want to market your products or services? Next, determine whether your product or service matches what your potential customers may want or need.

By accurately defining your customer base, you will be able to successfully position your product or service in the marketplace.

There are two groups of customers whom you will end up targeting whether you wish to sell to 16-year-old high school students or major suppliers: (1) end users and (2) channel users.

End Users

These customers are the ultimate users of your product or service. To identify them, you must consider both demographic and lifestyle characteristics. Demographic data are tangible and measurable pieces of information that separate one group of people from another. Examples are:

- Age.
- Income.
- Education.
- Ethnicity.
- Gender.
- Occupation.
- Geographic location.
- Household size.
- City size.
- Marital status.

Lifestyle information represents the intangible aspects of buyers. These include:

- Religious beliefs.
- Cultural habits.
- Political beliefs.
- Entertainment/recreation activities.
- Travel selections.
- Music and literature favorites.
- Food preferences.
- Values/moral systems.

You can gather information about end users by performing primary or secondary research.

Channel Users

These customers serve as intermediaries between end users and business owners. Consumer goods (e.g., health and beauty aids, or food products) may be packaged and sold to a large distributor, who resells them to a local distributor, who resells them to a wholesale buyer, who then resells them to individual business owners. Ultimately, the owner or manager of each store places the products on the store shelves for purchase by individual customers (the end users). Channel buyers are influenced by a number of factors when they are making purchases. Their age or location is only the beginning. When targeting this group of potential customers, consider the following elements:

- *The item's profit potential.* No buyer wants a product or service that has no profit potential. The higher the profit margin, the greater the chance that a potential channel user will purchase your goods.

- *Strong buyer–seller relationships.* Every business owner needs to develop a sound business relationship with his or her channel buyer. A good relationship will foster repeat business, help to establish a good track record, and secure additional customers.
- *Advertising programs.* Many buyers are swayed heavily toward products or services that are promoted on television, on radio, and in local newspapers. Carefully consider how you will advertise your products or services to get the greatest impact (see Chapter 9).

To get a better handle on who your customers might be, you can develop a market niche, or segment your market environment. Niche marketing is a process whereby you identify heavy users of your type of product or service. Market segmentation involves carving up the entire market into several sections. For example, you may divide your customers up according to age, income, or occupation. Perhaps you will sell your goods and services to those age 18 to 35, individuals who earn annual salaries over $100,000, or people who work in the medical field.

Whether you decide to develop a niche or to segment your market as a way of defining your customer base, be aggressive and detailed in your research efforts. Remember, the closer you are to pinpointing your target audience, the more efficient your marketing strategy will become.

RESEARCHING THE COMPETITION

No matter what type of business you own, you are going to experience some competition. The first step, in researching your competitors, is to define who they are. Many competitors may not seem to be rivals, but they are. Be alert to any company that may pose a potential threat to your business. To give you a clearer picture of who your competitors might be, consider the following three tiers of competition:

- *First tier.* These direct competitors, in consumers' eyes, have a product or service that is similar to or interchangeable with yours. For example, if you operate a shoe shop, your first-tier competitor may be another shoe store that is five miles down the road.
- *Second tier.* These competitors offer products that are similar but are in a different business category. Let's say you own a small flower shop. Your competitors are: major garden centers, home improvement stores, professional landscapers, and anyone who can provide customized and personalized service. Second-tier competitors do not offer the exact same product, but their goods or services could hurt your profit potential.
- *Third tier.* This most remote form of competitors hopes to gain a share of the dollars derived from the entire industry. To illustrate: If you

operate a gourmet popcorn store, you are providing a snack item. Your competitors may include such businesses as candy stores, wholesale outlets, and even supermarkets, which carry several brands of chips, cookies, peanuts, and pretzels.

It is crucial that you consider all three tiers when researching your competition. If you understand *all* those who may be potential competitors, you have an opportunity to create changes in your products or services that could make them more advantageous or beneficial to your target buyers.

After you identify your competitors, determine their strengths and weaknesses. Pay special attention to your first-tier competitors; they will be the ones with whom you'll go head-to-head in the contest for consumer dollars. Find out as much about them as possible. You can start by simply driving past their stores and taking some mental notes. How does the store look from the outside? Is there a steady flow of foot traffic in and out of the business? If your competitor is a retail outlet, go in and buy a few things so that you have a chance to survey the size of the staff, the experience of management, the range of prices, and any other information you deem necessary. You may want to do this fact finding undercover.

Study your competitors' advertisements, brochures, and promotional materials. Talk with their customers (off site, of course). Ask them what they like or dislike about the business, and what they want that is presently not provided. Use your competitors' shortcomings as an opportunity to carve a niche for your own business. Also, contact the competitors' suppliers. They can be a great source of information when researching rivals, but don't expect them to share proprietary information with you.

You can also find out a lot about the competition by attending trade shows or by simply asking industry experts the right questions. By conducting secondary research, you should be able to find information about the competition's strengths and weaknesses. Depending on the type of business you own, you may need to consider a number of different factors. The general information you should know about your rivals includes:

- Their financial strength.
- Their market share versus yours.
- Their ability to develop new products, and the pace at which they can market them.
- How consumers perceive their products or services.

By defining your competitors' strengths and weaknesses, you can learn ways to make your product or service more attractive.

Another important goal when you are researching your rivals is to determine what their next moves will be. This information will give you an opportunity to beat them to the market or to do better whatever they had planned to do. Anticipating their moves will not be an easy task. Your competitors' future activities hinge largely on their objectives, and until you clearly understand their purpose and business goals you will not be able to predict their next move. By observing their current strategies, you may be able to get a sense of your rivals' future intentions. Aggressive pricing and promotion may indicate a planned attempt to monopolize the market or to develop the power to penetrate the global marketplace.

To identify your competitors' next tactics, gather secondary information from sales reports, outside consultants, market surveys, and trade associations. Follow the progress of competitors' products, keeping careful watch for any improvements, flaws, or trends.

SIZING UP YOUR INDUSTRY

In your research, try to determine the present size of your industry, its potential for future growth, and any trends that may affect your business. You could spend months, even years, tracking down every little detail about your field. Instead, focus your research and gather only the information that is critical to your company's success.

As previously mentioned, a variety of resources can be used in your market research efforts. When determining the size of your industry, you may want to use secondary market research. Trade associations, as well as federal information resources, publish statistics on industry size. Here are just a few U.S. Census Bureau publications (available in most libraries) that can assist you in sizing up your market:

- *Census of Retail Trade.* Documents data for over 100 types of retail facilities, grouped by community (with population over 2,500), city, county, and state. Supplies information on the employment, payroll, and total sales of retail outlets. Published every five years; updated with monthly supplements.
- *Census of Manufacturers.* Lists statistics for 450 different classes of manufacturing industries. Includes information on the number of facilities, assets, rent, and inventories. Published every five years (the years ending in 2 and 7); updated with yearly supplements.
- *County Business Patterns.* Published annually; includes statistical summaries on the number and type of businesses in a particular county, as well as their taxable payroll and employment. All information is segmented by industry and county.
- *Census of Selected Services.* Like the *Census of Retail Trade*, this publication lists more than 100 types of service establishments, such as hotels and restaurants. Published every five years (years ending in 2 and 7) and updated monthly.

To determine how your business will fare in the future, you must go back to the past. That means using historical data. After all, to coin an old adage, "You won't know where you're going until you know where you've been." By accurately analyzing and interpreting information from past markets, you will have a clearer picture of how your operation may progress.

Forecasting future market growth is not an easy task; you might consider seeking professional help in this area. Start by checking out the *Statistical Abstract of the United States*, published by the U.S. Census Bureau. This publication lists both current and historical information about a number of topics: income, prices, education, employment, local government, manufacturing, and more. This resource is in most libraries.

Next, identify the trends (social, economical, political, or cultural) that exist in your industry, and determine how they may affect your business's moving forward. For example, suppose you own a retro 1970s apparel shop, but the trend in clothes is moving toward more of an urban contemporary, hip-hop look. You will need to adjust your business accordingly, if you plan to compete. You might establish a hip-hop section in your store, or reposition your product line so that it meets the needs of a specific audience—costume party-goers, for example.

Identifying industry trends can be a fairly simple task. As we discussed in Chapter 2, you can begin by reading the mainstream press (*The Wall Street Journal* and *The New York Times*), business publications, and industry trade publications. Watching television can help; certain TV programs, and commercials, can give you insight into how your industry may progress in the future. We're not suggesting you become a couch potato during all prime-time hours, but unless your TV time is given entirely to *Star Trek, Hercules,* and *Xena,* you can pick up details that may pertain to your type of business. For example, if you operate a cellular phone services company, something as subtle as cell phone use in virtually every 30-something sitcom could indicate an emerging trend in personal communication systems. This is an unscientific method of researching industry trends, but it will give you some sense of what products or services are taken for granted, or how their use may grow in the future.

CHECKLIST

FACTORS TO CONSIDER WHEN SIZING
UP YOUR MARKET

✓ **The four Ps of marketing.** Product, price, place, and promotion. When conducting your market research efforts, you should identify what product or service you will provide, how much you will charge, what distribution channels you will use, and how you will advertise or promote your goods or services.

✓ **The basic methods of market research.** Several research tools can be used to collect data about your product or service and the industry you intend to serve. You can use a historical, observational, survey, experimental, or nonexperimental method, as long as it yields either primary or secondary market research data.

✓ **Your customers.** Who is your target audience? When conducting market research, you must identify the public to whom you will sell your products or services. Are your customers end users or channel users? How old are they? What types of jobs do they have? Where do they live? What are their religious, cultural, or political beliefs? These are some of the questions you must ask when you're researching your potential customers.

✓ **Your competition.** Identify your rivals and their strengths and weaknesses. Make sure you define your first-, second-, and third-tier competitors. **All** your competitors should be considered contenders. Pay close attention to any company that may pose a potential threat to your business.

✓ **Your industry.** How large is your industry, and what trends may affect your operation? Gather detailed information on your field from industry-specific publications. The U.S. Census Bureau publishes a variety of texts that outline the demographics of retail and manufacturing firms. You should also check out business magazines and the mainstream press.

RESOURCES FOR MORE INFORMATION

ASSOCIATIONS

- *American Marketing Association (AMA),* 250 South Wacker Drive, Suite 200, Chicago, IL 60606; 312-648-0536; www.ama.org. AMA is the world's largest and most comprehensive professional society of marketers. Through seminars, workshops, and more than 25 national conferences, this organization bolsters the knowledge and skills of its members. Program topics include customer satisfaction, research, promotion, and business-to-business marketing.

- *Marketing Research Association (MRA),* 1344 Silas Deane Highway, Suite 306, Rocky Hill, CT 06067-0230; 860-257-4008; www.mra-net.org. The MRA is a professional association that supports the marketing and opinion research industry by providing its members with opportunities to expand their marketing research and other business-related skills. This organization publishes a number of publications including *Alert!,* the official newsletter of the MRA, which informs readers about current industry news, management techniques, research technology and trends, and association events.

- *Marketing Science Institute (MSI),* 1000 Massachusetts Avenue, Cambridge, MA 02138; 617-491-2060; www.msi.org. MSI is a nonprofit institute that creates and disseminates leading-edge market research studies by academic scholars. Among other activities, the organization circulates various publications and news items relevant to the market research field.

- *Minority Business Development Agency (MBDA),* 14th & Constitution Avenue, NW, Washington, DC 20230; 202-482-5061; www.mbda.gov. The MBDA is the only federal agency created specifically to encourage the growth of minority-owned businesses. Through its business development centers, this organization provides a wide range of services to new and existing business owners, including market research, business plan development, and financial assistance.

- *U.S. Small Business Administration (SBA),* 409 3rd Street, SW, Washington, DC 20416; 202-606-4000 or SBA Answer Desk, 1-800-827-5722; www.sba.gov. The SBA is dedicated to providing customer-oriented information and full-service programs to the business community. This federal organization gives new and existing business owners access to a wealth of information, including market research, financial resources, business plan writing, procurement opportunities, and technology trends.

(continued)

RESOURCES FOR MORE INFORMATION *(continued)*

INTERNET SERVICES

- *America Online Incorporated*, 8619 Westwood Center Drive, Vienna, VA 22182; 703-448-8700.

- *CompuServe*, 5000 Arlington Centre Boulevard, Columbus, OH 43220; 1-800-336-3330.

- *NEXIS*, Meade Data Central, P.O. Box 933, Dayton, OH 45401; 800-227-9597.

- *Prodigy Services Company*, 445 Hamilton Avenue, White Plains, NY 10601; 1-800-776-0845.

- *Yahoo!*, 3420 Central Expressway, 2nd Floor, Santa Clara, CA 95051; 408-731-3300.

Minority Business Development Centers scattered throughout the country can assist you with your market research efforts. To find a facility in your area, call the regional center closest to you.

- **Atlanta, GA:** 401 Peachtree Street, Suite 1715, Atlanta, GA 30308-3516; 404-730-3300.

- **Boston, MA:** 10 Causeway Street, Room 418, Boston, MA 02222; 617-565-6850.

- **Chicago, IL:** 55 East Monroe Street, Suite 1406, Chicago, IL 60603-5792; 312-353-0182.

- **Dallas, TX:** 1100 Commerce Street, Suite 7B23, Dallas, TX 75242; 214-767-8001.

- **Miami, FL:** 51 SW 1st Avenue, Suite 928, Miami, FL 33130; 305-536-5054.

- **Philadelphia, PA:** 600 Arch Street, Room 10128, Philadelphia, PA 19106; 215-861-3597.

- **San Francisco, CA:** 221 Main Street, Room 1280, San Francisco, CA 94105; 415-744-3001.

4

CHOOSING A BUSINESS FORM

MillCreek. It sounds more like the name of a community than a company. Over 30 years ago, it was. However, in 1994, Vivian Gibson adopted the name for her specialty food business. Unlike many entrepreneurs who search for titles for their firms, Gibson didn't label her company with her first or last name. She chose a company name that would help her remember a piece of her own history.

"MillCreek is a community that doesn't exist anymore," says Gibson, as she proudly begins telling her story. "It was a community in St. Louis where working-class blacks lived until it was destroyed in the late 1950s, early 1960s. The city razed the whole community and put in industrial parks and a highway, but years later, when people would refer to St. Louis and the black community, nobody said anything about it. They only mentioned an area of black professionals that survived the urban renewal, so I started doing some research with a high school class and we called it 'Where is MillCreek Anyway?' We went back to look up MillCreek, find out who lived there, and what kinds of businesses were there. Well, it turned out that a lot of people knew about MillCreek, but nobody talked about it, so it was a personal crusade for me to get people to talk about this community. This was around 1994, when I started my business, so I thought what better way to spark conversation and give honor and recognition to a place that I was once a part of, so I named my business 'The MillCreek Company.' Now, whenever someone asks me how I came up with the name—and people often do—I can give them a little piece of history."

No matter what type of business you start, you will have to choose a name for your venture. Like Gibson, you can reach back into history when branding your business, or you can simply use your first name, your last name, or a variation of both. But the labeling doesn't stop there. After deciding on a title for your business, you must choose the legal form under which you will operate: sole proprietorship, general partnership, limited partnership, corporation, subchapter S corporation, or limited liability company. It may sound simple, but it requires serious decision making if you are to run your operation effectively.

In this chapter, we will discuss how you can choose a name for your business. You may shrug off the task as inconsequential, but it is important that you give careful consideration to what you will call your company. The name you give your operation will carry the reputation of your business for years to come and will help customers identify your products or services from those of your competitors, so do not take this start-up task lightly. We will also examine the six legal forms of business and discuss how you can select an entity that's right for you.

NAMING YOUR BUSINESS

Perhaps one of your easiest decisions when you start a new business is choosing its name. Many entrepreneurs simply use their own name (typically, their last name) when branding their company; for example, Earl G. Graves Ltd., Johnson Publishing Company, or Terry Manufacturing. Others go for a bit more creativity: Karl Kani Infinity Inc., Soft Sheen Products, and Community Pride Inc. (All are members of the B.E. Industrial/Service 100, a listing of the nation's largest black-owned businesses, published annually by *Black Enterprise* magazine.)

The two types of business names you will need to consider in your search are:

1. *Fictitious.* This is a name other than your own. For example, if Jane Doe owns a beauty supply store, she may choose to call it House of Beauty rather than Jane Doe's Beauty Supply Store. Fictitious names generally apply to sole proprietorships and partnerships, which we will discuss later in this chapter. They are also known as "assumed names" or DBAs (Doing Business As).

2. *Nonfictitious.* This name *is* your own. For example, as stated above, Earl G. Graves Ltd. (of which the owner is Earl G. Graves) would be considered a nonfictitious business name. Corporations typically use nonfictitious names.

If you are well known and well respected in your community, you may want to use your own name. The reputation you may have acquired in other activities, such as neighborhood associations and other civic groups, could reflect well on your business and serve as a wonderful advertising and marketing tool. However, if your business fails, or you get into legal trouble, the name could taint any future ventures you may try to launch. Give careful thought to which type of name you will use.

If you select a fictitious business name, you will be required to do a little more legwork than if you select a nonfictitious name. For example, if you choose a name other than your own, you may be required to register it with the city, county, or state. Some states will require that you file the name in the office of the county recorder of deeds, fill out a fictitious name statement, and pay a modest fee. Other areas will instruct you to advertise your business's name in the local newspaper, to inform the public that you are the carrier of the name. In addition to your filing fee, which may range from $10 to $100, allow for some advertising costs.

Registering a fictitious name will take about two to three weeks. The process varies from state to state, so ask the office of your county recorder of deeds for specific details.

If you choose a nonfictitious name, you will not be required to file a "name statement" nor to pay any advertising costs to prove that you represent the business.

Choosing a name can be fun, but don't get too involved in your brainstorming session or spend months on this start-up task. Here are a few guidelines for your search for that perfect name:

- Make the name short.
- Be creative.
- Choose a name that's easy to remember.
- Select a name that describes the type of business you own.
- Make the name attractive and appealing to potential customers.
- Avoid using names that are misleading. In other words, if you are not a licensed electrician, then your business name should not suggest or state that you are.

After you decide on a name, select the legal form of your business. Whether you start a business from the ground up or buy an existing firm, you will need to choose the business entity that is right for you. The six forms from which you can choose are: (1) sole proprietorship, (2) general partnership, (3) limited partnership, (4) corporation, (5) subchapter S corporation, and (6) limited liability company (see Table 4.1). The form you select will depend on your financial goals and how much liability you are willing to shoulder.

Each legal form has its advantages and disadvantages, so consult your attorney and a tax adviser or accountant before making your final selection. Know that whatever choice you make, it is not written in stone. You can start

Table 4.1   Business Types—Characteristics

TYPE	LIABILITY	TAX CONSEQUENCES	ADVANTAGES	DRAWBACKS
SOLE PROPRIETORSHIP				
One owner, who maintains complete control of the operation.	All obligations of the business rest with the owner. In the event of a lawsuit, the owner's personal assets can be accessed.	Considered a "nontaxable" entity; business assets and liabilities are not separate from owner. Owner files all income and expenses on his or her personal income tax return.	Easiest and cheapest legal business form to start. Requires little, if any, paperwork.	Owner is totally liable for all obligations of the business. Business ends with the owner's death or departure.
GENERAL PARTNERSHIP				
Has two or more members, who share in the management responsibilities, profits, and losses of the business.	Each partner is responsible for all business obligations.	Each partner reports income and expenses on individual tax returns. The business is not viewed as a separate taxable entity.	Relatively inexpensive and easy to start and operate.	Unless a partnership agreement is put in place, the partnership ends with the death or withdrawal of one of the partners. All partners are held liable for all business debts.
LIMITED PARTNERSHIP				
Has two classes of partners: general partners and limited partners. General partners control operation of the business.	General partners are held responsible for all business obligations. Limited partners are only liable for the amount they've invested in the business.	Annual tax return filings. Both general and limited partners report their income and expense on individual tax returns.	Limited partners' liability for business debts is limited, as long as they do not engage in daily operations of the business.	General partners are held liable for all business debts. Partnership could end with the death of a general partner if a partnership agreement is not in place.

out as a sole proprietorship, but, as the needs of your business change and the operation grows, you can transform your company into a partnership or a corporation.

SETTING UP A SOLE PROPRIETORSHIP

Most new small businesses are sole proprietorships: they begin with a single owner. A sole proprietorship is the easiest and cheapest legal business form to establish. It requires no paperwork or documents unless you choose a fictitious name, and the tax consequences are less burdensome than for a partnership or corporation.

If you set up a sole proprietorship under a fictitious name, most regions will require that you file a fictitious owner affidavit (see Figure 4.1). This document indicates that you are the owner of the business and notifies the

Table 4.1   *(continued)*

TYPE	LIABILITY	TAX CONSEQUENCES	ADVANTAGES	DRAWBACKS
CORPORATION				
Owned by shareholders. Structure includes a board of directors and corporate officers.	Shareholders held liable for only the amount of their stock investment.	Considered a separate business entity, a corporation pays its own taxes. Shareholders pay taxes on their individual dividends.	Members have limited liability for business debts. A corporation has perpetual life since it can survive the deaths or withdrawals of shareholders, owners, and partners.	More expensive and complex to start than a general partnership or sole proprietorship. A separate taxable entity subject to both state and federal taxes.
SUBCHAPTER S CORPORATION				
Has no more than 75 shareholders. Includes a board of directors and corporate officers.	Shareholders are responsible for the amount of their investment.	Each shareholder pays taxes and reports profits and losses on individual tax returns.	Owners have limited liability. Does not suffer from double taxation. Can survive the deaths or withdrawals of shareholders, owners, and partners.	All shareholder profits and losses are allocated based on the number of stock shares. More expensive to launch than a sole proprietorship or partnership. Owners must meet certain criteria to file under this form.
LIMITED LIABILITY COMPANY				
Has two or more partners, who all have authority within the business.	Members are not responsible for business debts.	Partners' income and expenses are reported on individual tax returns.	Partners can participate in daily activities of business and still sustain their limited liability status. Profit or loss is not distributed according to stock shares.	Rules governing limited liability companies differ according to each state. Generally, the consent of all partners or owners is needed before transferring the business.

public and the local government that your company is operating under an "assumed" name. The requirements for filing a fictitious affidavit vary according to the location, so ask your county recorder of deeds for information about the proper filing procedure and the necessary forms. If you intend to operate in several locations, you will have to file a fictitious affidavit in each county or city where you plan to conduct business. After filing for this deposition, make a copy and keep it on file with the rest of your business records. You will need it later on, particularly when you open a business bank account under your fictitious name.

Depending on where you live, you may also be required to obtain a business license from the county or city (see Chapter 6). If you eventually open several other branches to your original store, you may have to obtain a business license in each area where a store is located. For more information, you should contact the county registrar or the licensing department in your

Figure 4.1   Legal Business Forms

TRADE NAME CERTIFICATE

N.J.S.A. 56:1-1 et seq.

Filing Fee $32.00 - includes a certified true copy

To: Gloucester County Clerk

I _____
(give name in full)

hereby CERTIFY that the business conducted under the FIRM name of:

_____
(give name in full)

was established for the purpose of carrying on the business of:

_____
(state nature of business)

located at _____ Phone _____

Town _____ State _____ Zip Code _____

and the firm is composed of the following individuals:

NAME	No. & Street	MUNICIPALITY

STATE OF NEW JERSEY   ⎫
COUNTY OF GLOUCESTER ⎬ SS
                       ⎭

_____, of full age, being duly

sworn according to law, on his oath, says that he is the person who made out the foregoing certificate, and

that the statements therein made are true and correct in each and every particular.

Sworn   and   Subscribed   to   Signature of Deponent _____

before me this _____ day

of _____ 19

_____
Notary Public or Attorney
GC-7423

Figure 4.1   *(continued)*

To be executed by all non-resident registrants

AUTHORIZATION TO ACCEPT SERVICE OF PROCESS

The undersigned non-resident of New Jersey registering to do business within New Jersey in accordance with the provisions of Chapter 255 of the Laws of 1951, do hereby constitute the County Clerk of the County of Gloucester my true and lawful attorney upon whom on original process in any action at law against me to be served. It is agreed that any original process so served upon the County Clerk shall be of the same force and effect as if duly served on me within this state.

X_____

Signed, Sealed, and Delivered
in the Presence of:

X_____

_____
Notary Public or Attorney

area. The fee to obtain a business license will vary according to your locale and the type of business that you operate.

If you plan to hire employees, you will need to obtain a federal Employer Identification Number. This can be secured by filing Form SS-4, Application for Employer Identification Number (see Figure 4.2). Call the Internal Revenue Service at 1-800-TAX-FORM to receive a copy of the form.

No matter what business entity you choose, you are going to assume some liability. As a sole proprietor, you are responsible for *everything* that happens in or as a result of the business. In other words, if an employee is stealing the profits and you are unable to pay your suppliers, you're held responsible. If creditors are knocking on the door because your accounts are delinquent, all fingers point to you. Even if someone slips and falls on the premises of your business, you can be held liable. As a sole proprietor, you must keep in mind that personal liability gives business creditors the right to attack your personal assets for monies due from the business. In turn, personal creditors can pounce on your business assets to cover personal debt.

Because all obligations of the business will rest with you, you should carefully consider what legal actions could be taken if something were to go wrong. If your type of business presents a potential for lawsuits, consider purchasing business insurance to protect you and your prized asset.

The types of insurance you may want to consider buying include general insurance and product liability insurance (see Chapter 6). (Malpractice insurance, another option, is typically purchased by professional business owners such as doctors or dentists and will protect them if a patient is injured.)

Figure 4.2   Form SS-4, Application for Employer Identification

Form **SS-4** (Rev. February 1998) Department of the Treasury Internal Revenue Service	**Application for Employer Identification Number** (For use by employers, corporations, partnerships, trusts, estates, churches, government agencies, certain individuals, and others. See instructions.) ▶ **Keep a copy for your records.**	EIN OMB No. 1545-0003

<table>
<tr><td rowspan="12" style="writing-mode:vertical-lr">Please type or print clearly.</td><td colspan="2">1   Name of applicant (legal name) (see instructions)</td></tr>
<tr><td>2   Trade name of business (if different from name on line 1)</td><td>3   Executor, trustee, "care of" name</td></tr>
<tr><td>4a   Mailing address (street address) (room, apt., or suite no.)</td><td>5a   Business address (if different from address on lines 4a and 4b)</td></tr>
<tr><td>4b   City, state, and ZIP code</td><td>5b   City, state, and ZIP code</td></tr>
<tr><td colspan="2">6   County and state where principal business is located</td></tr>
<tr><td colspan="2">7   Name of principal officer, general partner, grantor, owner, or trustor—SSN or ITIN may be required (see instructions) ▶</td></tr>
</table>

8a   Type of entity (Check only one box.) (see instructions)

Caution: *If applicant is a limited liability company, see the instructions for line 8a.*

☐ Sole proprietor (SSN) _____   ☐ Estate (SSN of decedent) _____
☐ Partnership   ☐ Personal service corp.   ☐ Plan administrator (SSN) _____
☐ REMIC   ☐ National Guard   ☐ Other corporation (specify) ▶ _____
☐ State/local government   ☐ Farmers' cooperative   ☐ Trust
☐ Church or church-controlled organization   ☐ Federal government/military
☐ Other nonprofit organization (specify) ▶ _____   (enter GEN if applicable) _____
☐ Other (specify) ▶

8b If a corporation, name the state or foreign country (if applicable) where incorporated	State	Foreign country

9   Reason for applying (Check only one box.) (see instructions)   ☐ Banking purpose (specify purpose) ▶ _____
☐ Started new business (specify type) ▶_____   ☐ Changed type of organization (specify new type) ▶ _____
☐ Purchased going business
☐ Hired employees (Check the box and see line 12.)   ☐ Created a trust (specify type) ▶ _____
☐ Created a pension plan (specify type) ▶   ☐ Other (specify) ▶

10 Date business started or acquired (month, day, year) (see instructions)	**11** Closing month of accounting year (see instructions)

12   First date wages or annuities were paid or will be paid (month, day, year). **Note:** *If applicant is a withholding agent, enter date income will first be paid to nonresident alien. (month, day, year)* . . . . ▶

13 Highest number of employees expected in the next 12 months. **Note:** *If the applicant does not expect to have any employees during the period, enter -0-. (see instructions)* . . . . ▶	Nonagricultural	Agricultural	Household

14   Principal activity (see instructions) ▶

15   Is the principal business activity manufacturing? . . . . ☐ **Yes**   ☐ **No**
If "Yes," principal product and raw material used ▶

16   To whom are most of the products or services sold? Please check one box.   ☐ Business (wholesale)
☐ Public (retail)   ☐ Other (specify) ▶   ☐ N/A

17a   Has the applicant ever applied for an employer identification number for this or any other business? . . . . ☐ **Yes**   ☐ **No**
Note: *If "Yes," please complete lines 17b and 17c.*

17b   If you checked "Yes" on line 17a, give applicant's legal name and trade name shown on prior application, if different from line 1 or 2 above.
Legal name ▶   Trade name ▶

17c   Approximate date when and city and state where the application was filed. Enter previous employer identification number if known.

Approximate date when filed (mo., day, year)	City and state where filed	Previous EIN

Under penalties of perjury, I declare that I have examined this application, and to the best of my knowledge and belief, it is true, correct, and complete.	Business telephone number (include area code)
Name and title (Please type or print clearly.) ▶	Fax telephone number (include area code)

Signature ▶   Date ▶

Note: *Do not write below this line. For official use only.*

Please leave blank ▶	Geo.	Ind.	Class	Size	Reason for applying

For Paperwork Reduction Act Notice, see page 4.   Cat. No. 16055N   Form **SS-4** (Rev. 2-98)

General liability insurance will protect you if someone is injured on your business premises. Product liability insurance will safeguard your business against lawsuits if someone gets sick or has other adverse effects from using your product.

Assuming all responsibility for a business can be a bit frightening for a new entrepreneur, who must also worry about such start-up issues as financing, advertising, and choosing a location. But if the business you start is virtually risk-free, a sole proprietorship may be the best choice for you. If personal liability is more than you are willing to bear, choose a different legal form that provides greater protection, such as a corporation.

A sole proprietorship requires the least amount of paperwork, which translates into less stress for the owner when tax time rolls around. The Internal Revenue Service (IRS) defines a sole proprietorship as a "nontaxable" entity in which the business assets and liabilities are not separate from, but are considered to belong to, the business owner.

As a sole proprietor, you will be required to list your business income and expenses on the IRS's Schedule C (which indicates profit or loss from a business), or Schedule C-EZ (which indicates net profit from a business but is restricted to owners who fulfill a list of requirements). (See Figures 4.3 and 4.4 for examples of these forms. Because of space constraints, entire forms are not included here.)

The net profit or loss listed on Schedule C is transferred to page one of Form 1040, U.S. Individual Income Tax Return (see Figure 4.5). This simply means that no separate tax rate schedule is applied to you as a sole proprietorship. Your individual tax rate will determine how much tax will be due on the earnings of your business.

In addition to income tax, you could also be responsible for paying self-employment tax on business profits, and payroll tax (if you have employees). Self-employment tax is recorded using Schedule SE (see Figure 4.6). We will discuss business taxes in greater detail in Chapter 13.

As a sole proprietor, you will have complete control over your business; you will make all the decisions. Complete autonomy may sound like music to your ears, but setting up a sole proprietorship does have drawbacks. Consider the following advantages and disadvantages of sole proprietorships before making your final decision.

The advantages include:

- *Simplicity.* This type of business entity is easy to start and operate. Once you decide to operate your business as a sole proprietorship, much of your legwork has already been done.
- *Minimal start-up cost.* When starting a sole proprietorship, your expenses will be minimal because very few documents will have to be filed.
- *Single taxation.* The IRS does not treat a sole proprietorship as a separate business entity, so you will not be taxed twice.

Figure 4.3   Form 1040, Schedule C, Profit or Loss from Business

SCHEDULE C (Form 1040)	**Profit or Loss From Business** (Sole Proprietorship) ▶ **Partnerships, joint ventures, etc., must file Form 1065.**	OMB No. 1545-0074
Department of the Treasury Internal Revenue Service (O)	▶ **Attach to Form 1040 or Form 1041.** ▶ **See Instructions for Schedule C (Form 1040).**	**19 97** Attachment Sequence No. **09**

Name of proprietor | Social security number (SSN)

A Principal business or profession, including product or service (see page C-1) | **B** Enter principal business code (see page C-6) ▶

C Business name. If no separate business name, leave blank. | **D** Employer ID number (EIN), if any

E Business address (including suite or room no.) ▶ ....
City, town or post office, state, and ZIP code

F Accounting method: (1) ☐ Cash   (2) ☐ Accrual   (3) ☐ Other (specify) ▶ ....

G Did you "materially participate" in the operation of this business during 1997? If "No," see page C-2 for limit on losses. ☐ Yes ☐ No

H If you started or acquired this business during 1997, check here . . . . ▶ ☐

Part I   Income

1	Gross receipts or sales. **Caution:** *If this income was reported to you on Form W-2 and the "Statutory employee" box on that form was checked, see page C-2 and check here* . . . . ▶ ☐	**1**
2	Returns and allowances	**2**
3	Subtract line 2 from line 1	**3**
4	Cost of goods sold (from line 42 on page 2)	**4**
5	**Gross profit.** Subtract line 4 from line 3	**5**
6	Other income, including Federal and state gasoline or fuel tax credit or refund (see page C-2) . . .	**6**
7	**Gross income.** Add lines 5 and 6 . . . . ▶	**7**

Part II   Expenses. Enter expenses for business use of your home **only** on line 30.

8	Advertising	**8**	19	Pension and profit-sharing plans	**19**
9	Bad debts from sales or services (see page C-3) . .	**9**	20	Rent or lease (see page C-4):	
10	Car and truck expenses (see page C-3)	**10**		a Vehicles, machinery, and equipment .	**20a**
				b Other business property . .	**20b**
11	Commissions and fees . .	**11**	21	Repairs and maintenance . .	**21**
12	Depletion	**12**	22	Supplies (not included in Part III) .	**22**
13	Depreciation and section 179 expense deduction (not included in Part III) (see page C-3) . .	**13**	23	Taxes and licenses	**23**
			24	Travel, meals, and entertainment:	
				a Travel	**24a**
14	Employee benefit programs (other than on line 19) . . .	**14**		b Meals and en-tertainment .	
15	Insurance (other than health) .	**15**		c Enter 50% of line 24b subject to limitations (see page C-4) .	
16	Interest:				
	a Mortgage (paid to banks, etc.) .	**16a**		d Subtract line 24c from line 24b .	**24d**
	b Other	**16b**	25	Utilities	**25**
17	Legal and professional services	**17**	26	Wages (less employment credits) .	**26**
			27	Other expenses (from line 48 on page 2)	**27**
18	Office expense	**18**			

28	**Total expenses** before expenses for business use of home. Add lines 8 through 27 in columns . ▶	**28**
29	Tentative profit (loss). Subtract line 28 from line 7	**29**
30	Expenses for business use of your home. Attach **Form 8829**	**30**
31	**Net profit or (loss).** Subtract line 30 from line 29.	
	• If a profit, enter on **Form 1040, line 12,** and ALSO on **Schedule SE, line 2** (statutory employees, see page C-5). Estates and trusts, enter on Form 1041, line 3.	**31**
	• If a loss, you MUST go on to line 32.	
32	If you have a loss, check the box that describes your investment in this activity (see page C-5).	
	• If you checked 32a, enter the loss on **Form 1040, line 12,** and ALSO on **Schedule SE, line 2** (statutory employees, see page C-5). Estates and trusts, enter on Form 1041, line 3.	**32a** ☐ All investment is at risk.
	• If you checked 32b, you MUST attach **Form 6198.**	**32b** ☐ Some investment is not at risk.

For Paperwork Reduction Act Notice, see Form 1040 instructions.   Cat. No. 11334P   Schedule C (Form 1040) 1997

Figure 4.4   Form 1040, Schedule C-EZ, Net Profit from Business

SCHEDULE C-EZ (Form 1040) Department of the Treasury (O) Internal Revenue Service	**Net Profit From Business** (Sole Proprietorship) ▶ Partnerships, joint ventures, etc., must file Form 1065. ▶ Attach to Form 1040 or Form 1041. ▶ See instructions on back.	OMB No. 1545-0074 19**97** Attachment Sequence No. **09A**

Name of proprietor	Social security number (SSN)

Part I   **General Information**

You May Use This Schedule Only If You:	▶	• Had business expenses of $2,500 or less. • Use the cash method of accounting. • Did not have an inventory at any time during the year. • Did not have a net loss from your business. • Had only one business as a sole proprietor.	▶	**And You:**	• Had no employees during the year. • Are not required to file **Form 4562**, Depreciation and Amortization, for this business. See the instructions for Schedule C, line 13, on page C-3 to find out if you must file. • Do not deduct expenses for business use of your home. • Do not have prior year unallowed passive activity losses from this business.

A	Principal business or profession, including product or service	**B Enter principal business code** (see page C-6) ▶
C	Business name. If no separate business name, leave blank.	**D Employer ID number (EIN), if any**

E   Business address (including suite or room no.). Address not required if same as on Form 1040, page 1.

City, town or post office, state, and ZIP code

Part II   **Figure Your Net Profit**

1	**Gross receipts.** Caution: *If this income was reported to you on Form W-2 and the "Statutory employee" box on that form was checked, see **Statutory Employees** in the instructions for Schedule C, line 1, on page C-2 and check here* . . . . ▶ ☐	**1**	
2	**Total expenses.** If more than $2,500, you **must** use Schedule C. See instructions	**2**	
3	**Net profit.** Subtract line 2 from line 1. If less than zero, you **must** use Schedule C. Enter on **Form 1040, line 12,** and ALSO on **Schedule SE, line 2.** (Statutory employees **do not** report this amount on Schedule SE, line 2. Estates and trusts, enter on Form 1041, line 3.)	**3**	

Part III   **Information on Your Vehicle.** Complete this part **ONLY** if you are claiming car or truck expenses on line 2.

4   When did you place your vehicle in service for business purposes? (month, day, year) ▶ ..... / ..... / ..... .

5   Of the total number of miles you drove your vehicle during 1997, enter the number of miles you used your vehicle for:

a Business .... **b** Commuting .... **c** Other ....

6   Do you (or your spouse) have another vehicle available for personal use? . . . . ☐ **Yes**   ☐ **No**

7   Was your vehicle available for use during off-duty hours? . . . . ☐ **Yes**   ☐ **No**

8a Do you have evidence to support your deduction? . . . . ☐ **Yes**   ☐ **No**

b If "Yes," is the evidence written? . . . . ☐ **Yes**   ☐ **No**

For Paperwork Reduction Act Notice, see Form 1040 instructions.	Cat. No. 14374D	Schedule C-EZ (Form 1040) 1997

Figure 4.5   Form 1040, U.S. Individual Income Tax Return

Form **1040**

Department of the Treasury—Internal Revenue Service
U.S. Individual Income Tax Return (O) **1997**

For the year Jan. 1–Dec. 31, 1997, or other tax year beginning   , 1997, ending   , 19   OMB No. 1545-0074

IRS Use Only—Do not write or staple in this space.

Label

(See instructions on page 10.)

Use the IRS label. Otherwise, please print or type.

L A B E L   H E R E

Your first name and initial   Last name

Your social security number

If a joint return, spouse's first name and initial   Last name

Spouse's social security number

Home address (number and street). If you have a P.O. box, see page 10.   Apt. no.

City, town or post office, state, and ZIP code. If you have a foreign address, see page 10.

For help in finding line instructions, see pages 2 and 3 in the booklet.

Presidential Election Campaign (See page 10.)

Do you want $3 to go to this fund? . . . .
If a joint return, does your spouse want $3 to go to this fund? . . . .

	Yes	No	Note: Checking "Yes" will not change your tax or reduce your refund.

Filing Status

Check only one box.

1 ☐ Single
2 ☐ Married filing joint return (even if only one had income)
3 ☐ Married filing separate return. Enter spouse's social security no. above and full name here. ▶ _____
4 ☐ Head of household (with qualifying person). (See page 10.) If the qualifying person is a child but not your dependent, enter this child's name here. ▶
5 ☐ Qualifying widow(er) with dependent child (year spouse died ▶ 19   ). (See page 10.)

Exemptions

If more than six dependents, see page 10.

6a ☐ **Yourself.** If your parent (or someone else) can claim you as a dependent on his or her tax return, **do not** check box 6a. . . . .

b ☐ **Spouse** . . . .

c **Dependents:**

(1) First name Last name	(2) Dependent's social security number	(3) Dependent's relationship to you	(4) No. of months lived in your home in 1997

No. of boxes checked on 6a and 6b ____

No. of your children on 6c who:
• lived with you
• did not live with you due to divorce or separation (see page 11)

Dependents on 6c not entered above ____

Add numbers entered on lines above ▶ ☐

d Total number of exemptions claimed . . . .

Income

Attach Copy B of your Forms W-2, W-2G, and 1099-R here.

If you did not get a W-2, see page 12.

Enclose but do not attach any payment. Also, please use Form 1040-V.

7	Wages, salaries, tips, etc. Attach Form(s) W-2	7
8a	**Taxable** interest. Attach Schedule B if required	8a
b	**Tax-exempt** interest. DO NOT include on line 8a . . . [8b]	
9	Dividends. Attach Schedule B if required	9
10	Taxable refunds, credits, or offsets of state and local income taxes (see page 12) . .	10
11	Alimony received	11
12	Business income or (loss). Attach Schedule C or C-EZ	12
13	Capital gain or (loss). Attach Schedule D	13
14	Other gains or (losses). Attach Form 4797	14
15a	Total IRA distributions . [15a] b Taxable amount (see page 13)	15b
16a	Total pensions and annuities [16a] b Taxable amount (see page 13)	16b
17	Rental real estate, royalties, partnerships, S corporations, trusts, etc. Attach Schedule E	17
18	Farm income or (loss). Attach Schedule F	18
19	Unemployment compensation	19
20a	Social security benefits . [20a] b Taxable amount (see page 14)	20b
21	Other income. List type and amount—see page 15	21
22	Add the amounts in the far right column for lines 7 through 21. This is your **total income** ▶	22

Adjusted Gross Income

If line 32 is under $29,290 (under $9,770 if a child did not live with you), see EIC inst. on page 21.

23	IRA deduction (see page 16)	23
24	Medical savings account deduction. Attach Form 8853 .	24
25	Moving expenses. Attach Form 3903 or 3903-F . . .	25
26	One-half of self-employment tax. Attach Schedule SE .	26
27	Self-employed health insurance deduction (see page 17)	27
28	Keogh and self-employed SEP and SIMPLE plans . .	28
29	Penalty on early withdrawal of savings	29
30a	Alimony paid b Recipient's SSN ▶	30a
31	Add lines 23 through 30a . . . . ▶	31
32	Subtract line 31 from line 22. This is your **adjusted gross income** . . . . . ▶	32

For Privacy Act and Paperwork Reduction Act Notice, see page 38.   Cat. No. 11320B   Form **1040** (1997)

Figure 4.6   Form 1040, Schedule SE, Self-Employment Tax

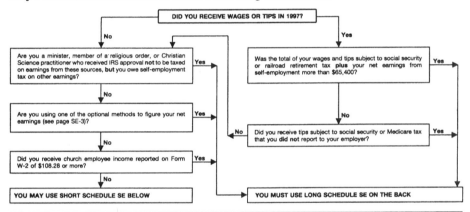

SCHEDULE SE	**Self-Employment Tax**	OMB No. 1545-0074
(Form 1040)	▶ See Instructions for Schedule SE (Form 1040).	1997
Department of the Treasury Internal Revenue Service (O)	▶ Attach to Form 1040.	Attachment Sequence No. **17**
Name of person with **self-employment** income (as shown on Form 1040)	Social security number of person with **self-employment** income ▶	

Who Must File Schedule SE

You must file Schedule SE if:

- You had net earnings from self-employment from **other than** church employee income (line 4 of Short Schedule SE or line 4c of Long Schedule SE) of $400 or more, **OR**
- You had church employee income of $108.28 or more. Income from services you performed as a minister or a member of a religious order **is not** church employee income. See page SE-1.

Note: *Even if you had a loss or a small amount of income from self-employment, it may be to your benefit to file Schedule SE and use either "optional method" in Part II of Long Schedule SE. See page SE-3.*

Exception. If your only self-employment income was from earnings as a minister, member of a religious order, or Christian Science practitioner **and** you filed Form 4361 and received IRS approval not to be taxed on those earnings, **do not** file Schedule SE. Instead, write "Exempt–Form 4361" on Form 1040, line 47.

May I Use Short Schedule SE or MUST I Use Long Schedule SE?

DID YOU RECEIVE WAGES OR TIPS IN 1997?

	No		Yes	

Are you a minister, member of a religious order, or Christian Science practitioner who received IRS approval **not** to be taxed on earnings from these sources, **but** you owe self-employment tax on other earnings? →Yes→

Was the total of your wages and tips subject to social security or railroad retirement tax **plus** your net earnings from self-employment more than $65,400? →Yes→

↓No

↓No

Are you using one of the optional methods to figure your net earnings (see page SE-3)? →Yes→

←No Did you receive tips subject to social security or Medicare tax that you **did not** report to your employer? →Yes→

↓No

Did you receive church employee income reported on Form W-2 of $108.28 or more? →Yes→

↓No

YOU MAY USE SHORT SCHEDULE SE BELOW	→	**YOU MUST USE LONG SCHEDULE SE ON THE BACK**

Section A—Short Schedule SE. Caution: *Read above to see if you can use Short Schedule SE.*

1	Net farm profit or (loss) from Schedule F, line 36, and farm partnerships, Schedule K-1 (Form 1065), line 15a	**1**	
2	Net profit or (loss) from Schedule C, line 31; Schedule C-EZ, line 3; and Schedule K-1 (Form 1065), line 15a (other than farming). Ministers and members of religious orders, see page SE-1 for amounts to report on this line. See page SE-2 for other income to report	**2**	
3	Combine lines 1 and 2	**3**	
4	**Net earnings from self-employment.** Multiply line 3 by 92.35% (.9235). If less than $400, **do not** file this schedule; you do not owe self-employment tax . . . . ▶	**4**	
5	**Self-employment tax.** If the amount on line 4 is: • $65,400 or less, multiply line 4 by 15.3% (.153). Enter the result here and on **Form 1040, line 47.** • More than $65,400, multiply line 4 by 2.9% (.029). Then, add $8,109.60 to the result. Enter the total here and on **Form 1040, line 47.**	**5**	
6	**Deduction for one-half of self-employment tax.** Multiply line 5 by 50% (.5). Enter the result here and on **Form 1040, line 26**	**6**	

For Paperwork Reduction Act Notice, see Form 1040 instructions.   Cat. No. 11358Z   Schedule SE (Form 1040) 1997

The disadvantages include:

- *Full liability.* You are personally held responsible for all obligations of the business.
- *Limited ownership.* By definition, a sole proprietorship is limited to one individual. You can always bring in other people later, but the sole proprietorship would have to be dissolved and a new business form would have to be created.

ESTABLISHING A PARTNERSHIP

A partnership is a business entity that involves two or more business owners who share management responsibilities, profits, and all liability. Two types of partnerships can be formed: (1) a general partnership or (2) a limited partnership.

To set up a general partnership, the first step is to choose a partner. Just about anyone can become a cohort: a friend, family member, limited liability company, or corporation. No matter whom you select, be sure you know that partner well. Many partnerships split after only a few years of operation because the individuals lack the right chemistry to succeed. That was not true for Cynthia R. Jones and Barry K. Worley. They have been partners in their graphic design company, Jones–Worley Inc., for nearly 10 years. They credit their solid union to proper planning.

Jones, who owns 65 percent of the business, started her company as a freelance graphic design firm. She worked with Worley on several assignments, but decided in 1990 that she wanted to invite her long-time colleague into the business. Jones knew Worley's work well. She recognized that his strong background in signage could complement her skills and help strengthen her company's competitiveness. She was comfortable working with Worley and saw that their personalities didn't clash. Still, she asked Worley a lot of questions before the two wed their resources. For example, Jones, an African American businessperson, anticipated obtaining business as a woman- and minority-owned design firm. She thought this might be a sensitive area for Worley, who is white, so she asked the tough question to gauge his feelings. Worley was comfortable with his role. He agreed that Jones should be the more visible partner so that they could get the types of contracts they were looking for.

The two also questioned each other about their personal lives (their marital status and kids, both of which might affect how much time they could spend on the business) and work styles, to see if they made a good match. They did. "Cynthia is impatient to see results and I'm more laissez faire," says Worley. "But it works because if we were both the same I think our employees would have a difficult time with us, which might have a negative effect on our ability to satisfy clients," he says.

Jones, as president, solicits business for the Atlanta-based firm and manages the finances. Worley, as vice president, oversees signage work projects. Together, they have secured some major design contracts, including one for the 1996 Summer Olympics. Jones-Worley was recognized for being the only woman- and black-owned graphics firm on the design team that created the "Quilt of Leaves" theme for the summer games. Other clients of the partnership have included AT&T, Delta Air Lines, Coca-Cola, and Turner Broadcasting.[1]

Picking the right person to be a partner can make the difference between success or failure, so make your choices carefully. You should consider the following factors when you are selecting a partner.

1. *Financial history.* Starting a business is stressful enough without having to worry about debt that a partner may bring into the operation. Perform a background check on your potential partner's credit history, and don't play favorites. Even if the possible partner is a longtime friend or family member, investigate his or her financial past as thoroughly as you would someone you've known for only a couple of years. No matter what the relationship, if the person has a poor credit history, it could affect your chances of securing financing for your business. Ask yourself these questions as you conduct your search:

- Is the potential partner responsible with money?
- Has he or she ever filed for bankruptcy?
- Does he or she owe back taxes?
- Are there any liens on his or her personal property?
- Has the individual been involved in past business activities? If so, how did he or she manage the finances?

Ask your potential partner for permission to look into his or her financial history before proceeding; this would include securing a credit report from Equifax or any of the other major credit reporting companies. If the person says no, be wary. You probably will not want to do business with this individual.

2. *Professional strengths.* Many business owners form a partnership to combine not only capital but skills and experience. If you are a creative person who hates to keep the business's books, you may choose a partner who is a financial whiz. Or, if you dislike making presentations or schmoozing with clients, you might partner with an individual who is more extroverted and likes being out front. When choosing a partner, consider what professional skills he or she will bring to the table, and decide whether they would complement what you have to offer. That's what Bob Adams did when launching Adams-McClure Inc., a promotional printing company based in

Denver, Colorado. When Adams, now president of the company, discovered that a small printing business was up for sale, he knew he had the deal-making experience to make it work. He even had a client to get the ball rolling—Coors Brewing Company, his former employer. But he needed a few partners who could help get the presses up and running. For this expertise, he turned to three former business associates, Randy McClure, Bob Knappe Sr., and Joe Frink. "I needed partners who knew the printing business, could think fast, and keep up," says Adams, whose company is on the 1998 B.E. Industrial/Service 100 list. "Frink's experience in prepress, plus Knappe's and McClure's knowledge of sales, production, and finishing, covered the business from A to Z," he says. Knappe had successfully operated his own finishing company for 5 years, which added to the partnership's arsenal of skills. In addition to brainpower, the partners added capital to the mix. With Adams's investment of $25,000, he acquired a 51 percent ownership in the business. The other three partners threw in $25,000 and split the remaining shares of the business. The partners' strong mixture of talent has gained accounts with clients such as the Miller Brewing Company and Coca-Cola.[2]

3. *Personal life.* The condition or events of one's personal life can greatly affect the livelihood of a business, so ask about such personal factors as a potential partner's arrest record and marital status. If a partner has a criminal record, it could keep you from obtaining bank loans and securing business from suppliers and vendors. A spouse can also significantly affect how much time and money a person will invest in a business. Find out whether his or her spouse supports the efforts of your potential partner before putting anything in writing. Also, consider the stability of your partner's marriage. In any divorce proceedings, your personal assets could be investigated, to determine the partner's true worth. Or, as part of a divorce settlement, your partner's shares could be transferred, making the spouse an unwelcome partner in your business.

4. *Health history.* It is important that prospective partners have a clean bill of health. Be sure you're not making plans with someone who may not be able to see them through because of chronic health problems. Ask potential partners about their health history and insurance coverage. If their well-being is unstable, it could bring financial hardship to your business in the form of large medical expenses.

5. *Value system.* Do you and your potential partners share the same values? Are you in sync on particular social, cultural, or economic issues that may impact your business success? When choosing a partner, it is important that you get along and that you share a common sense of values or morals; otherwise, the union will not work. Discuss business goals with potential partners, to be sure everyone is on the same page. If you have any doubts or misgivings, keep looking until you find someone who fits more comfortably.

Forming a perfect partnership is not easy. Often, it is hard to determine whether a partnership will work until you've begun working with a person on a day-to-day basis. Gather as much preliminary information as possible about prospective cohorts. This will increase your chances for success and spare you the headaches of having to dissolve one partnership and start another.

Besides combing through financial and other records for information about potential partners, talk with their friends, family members, former coworkers, clients, and other associates, about their personal habits. A simple attribute such as personal hygiene may not appear to be a significant concern, but it could make the difference between landing clients and having them turn away. As a business owner, you will be working with a number of important professionals. You need someone who is well groomed and well mannered.

Find out how the person behaves in social and professional settings. Does he or she have any habits that could prove embarrassing as well as costly to your business?

Determine how efficiently this person manages time and projects. Is he or she capable of handling multiple assignments? If so, how quickly can they be turned around, and what is the quality of the work? Perhaps most important, probe the person's integrity. Can you trust this person to run the business in your absence, or to make important decisions when you are unable to do so? Some of these questions may be tough to ask, but it is better to find out about potential problems before you enter a partnership than to discover, years later, that you've made the wrong choice.

After you select a partner, you need to set up a partnership agreement, a document that spells out the responsibilities of each partner. Your agreement can be oral or sealed with a handshake, but it would be best to put it in writing to prevent future conflicts. A partnership agreement is a complex document that should be created and/or reviewed by an attorney. A typical partnership agreement includes the following items:

1. Financial contribution of partners.
2. Management and control by partners.
3. Profit and loss sharing.
4. Responsibilities and duties of partners.
5. Life of the partnership.
6. Partnership continuation (criteria that will enable the partnership to continue in the event of a situation that would otherwise cause it to dissolve).
7. Guidelines for admission of a new partner.
8. Right of first refusal (other partners have the right to purchase a withdrawing partner's interest in the business before the partner can offer it to someone outside the company).
9. A stated policy on how a deceased partner's interest will be handled.

10. A stated policy on how a partner's interest will be handled if he or she decides to withdraw from the company.

11. Voting rights of partners.

A partnership agreement is like a prenuptial agreement: it protects the assets of an individual(s) in case the partners part. Other measures you can take to protect yourself include:

1. *A buy/sell agreement,* which explains how the value of a partner's interest in the business will be handled if the partner dies or decides to leave the company. A buy/sell agreement prevents disputes that may arise over who will purchase a withdrawing partner's interest. For example, the agreement might indicate that the partner's stock can be purchased only by members of the partnership and not by outside entities. This type of agreement is widely used among family-owned firms, where the owners wish to keep the business in the family. When a partnership has not drawn up this document, most states will dictate a 50–50 split of business assets and debts upon the dissolution of a partnership.

2. *Key person life insurance.* A life insurance policy should be taken out on key members within the business, to provide immediate cash in the event that one of them dies while he or she is an active partner. This type of insurance can be purchased for each partner, or limited to certain individuals (e.g., senior partners). The beneficiaries of this policy are the organization or its members. The cash it provides can be used by the surviving partners to keep the business fully operational in the absence of a key partner, or to buy out the deceased partner's interest via a buy/sell agreement.

If you establish a general partnership, you may have to obtain a business license in the area where you intend to conduct business. If you will be operating in multiple locations, you will have to secure a business license in each of those areas.

If your partnership has a fictitious name, you will be required to file a fictitious name affidavit. Forms can be obtained from your local county clerk's office. Filing requirements vary according to jurisdiction, so call or visit your local county seat to find out about the proper filing procedure.

If you plan to hire helpers, you must file for a federal Employer Identification Number (Form SS-4; see Figure 4.2). Call 1-800-TAX-FORM to order a copy of the form.

At tax time, all partnerships must report income and expenses on IRS Form 1065, U.S. Partnership Return of Income (see Figure 4.7). Partnership profits and losses "pass through" to your personal income and are taxed at your personal rate. Each partner is responsible for reporting his or her partnership (not personal) income on Form 1065, using Schedule K-1. Any taxes due are paid individually by the partners.

Figure 4.7 Form 1065, U.S. Partnership Return of Income

Form **1065**	**U.S. Partnership Return of Income**	OMB No. 1545-0099
Department of the Treasury Internal Revenue Service	For calendar year 1997, or tax year beginning ...., 1997, and ending ...., 19 ..... ► **See separate instructions.**	**1997**

A Principal business activity	Use the IRS label. Other- wise, please print or type.	Name of partnership	D Employer Identification number
B Principal product or service		Number, street, and room or suite no. If a P.O. box, see page 10 of the instructions.	E Date business started
C Business code number		City or town, state, and ZIP code	F Total assets (see page 10 of the instructions) $

G Check applicable boxes: **(1)** ☐ Initial return **(2)** ☐ Final return **(3)** ☐ Change in address **(4)** ☐ Amended return
H Check accounting method: **(1)** ☐ Cash **(2)** ☐ Accrual **(3)** ☐ Other (specify) ► ....
I Number of Schedules K-1. Attach one for each person who was a partner at any time during the tax year ► ....

Caution: *Include only trade or business income and expenses on lines 1a through 22 below. See the instructions for more information.*

Income

1a Gross receipts or sales	**1a**		
b Less returns and allowances	**1b**		**1c**
2 Cost of goods sold (Schedule A, line 8)			**2**
3 Gross profit. Subtract line 2 from line 1c			**3**
4 Ordinary income (loss) from other partnerships, estates, and trusts *(attach schedule)*			**4**
5 Net farm profit (loss) *(attach Schedule F (Form 1040))*			**5**
6 Net gain (loss) from Form 4797, Part II, line 18			**6**
7 Other income (loss) *(attach schedule)*			**7**
8 **Total income (loss).** Combine lines 3 through 7			**8**

Deductions (see page 11 of the instructions for limitations)

9 Salaries and wages (other than to partners) (less employment credits)		**9**
10 Guaranteed payments to partners		**10**
11 Repairs and maintenance		**11**
12 Bad debts		**12**
13 Rent		**13**
14 Taxes and licenses		**14**
15 Interest		**15**
16a Depreciation (if required, attach Form 4562)	**16a**	
b Less depreciation reported on Schedule A and elsewhere on return	**16b**	**16c**
17 Depletion **(Do not deduct oil and gas depletion.)**		**17**
18 Retirement plans, etc.		**18**
19 Employee benefit programs		**19**
20 Other deductions *(attach schedule)*		**20**
21 **Total deductions.** Add the amounts shown in the far right column for lines 9 through 20		**21**

22 **Ordinary income (loss)** from trade or business activities. Subtract line 21 from line 8		**22**

Please Sign Here

Under penalties of perjury, I declare that I have examined this return, including accompanying schedules and statements, and to the best of my knowledge and belief, it is true, correct, and complete. Declaration of preparer (other than general partner or limited liability company member) is based on all information of which preparer has any knowledge.

► Signature of general partner or limited liability company member   ► Date

Paid Preparer's Use Only	Preparer's signature ►	Date	Check if self-employed ► ☐	Preparer's social security no.
	Firm's name (or yours if self-employed) and address ►		EIN ►	
			ZIP code ►	

For Paperwork Reduction Act Notice, see separate instructions.   Cat. No. 11390Z   Form **1065** (1997)

Limited Partnership

A limited partnership consists of two classes of partners: (1) general partners, who are responsible for managing and operating the business, and are held personally liable for all obligations to the partnership; and (2) limited partners, who have no control over the partnership and are not permitted to engage in its management or daily operations. (They do share in the profits of the business, but their losses are limited to how much they have contributed to the partnership.)

To establish a limited partnership, you must obtain and file a certificate of limited partnership with your secretary of state's office. This document contains information about the limited partnership, including its name, address, and purpose, and the names of the general partners. The requirements for filing a limited partnership certificate vary in each state.

In some jurisdictions, a limited partnership agreement, not unlike the one used in general partnerships, may be required.

Like a general partnership, a limited partnership is required to file its taxes annually, using Form 1065. Limited and general partners of a limited partnership are required to report their income and expenses on their individual tax returns and to pay any taxes that are due.

FORMING A CORPORATION

A corporation, one of the best known forms of business entities, is perhaps the most preferred among entrepreneurs. However, it is also the most complex. Unlike a sole proprietorship, which is owned by only one individual, a corporation is owned by several shareholders—individuals to whom stock in the business has been issued. They do not have direct control over the day-to-day operations of the company, but they are responsible for electing and removing directors of the corporation.

The corporate board of directors oversees the business operations and makes major decisions regarding the corporation's personnel, salaries, dividends, and policies. The directors are responsible for meeting at least once each year to discuss past and present business performance, as well as to make plans for the future. Their duties also include appointing the corporate officers who actually carry out the daily activities of the company—typically, a president, vice president, secretary, and treasurer.

Corporations offer many advantages not afforded by other legal business forms. Unlike a partnership, which can dissolve at the death or withdrawal of one of the partners, a corporation has a perpetual life. However, to increase the protection of your corporation, you can create a buy/sell agreement (also known as a shareholder's agreement) and purchase key person life insurance for the principals in your company.

Because corporations, by law, are considered to be separate business entities, they have limited liability. All obligations of the business belong to the corporation, not the individual shareholders. If the corporation is unsuccessful or is held liable for any damages or debts, shareholders will lose only their stock investment. Their personal assets cannot be accessed, unless the veil of corporate limited liability is pierced. This can only occur if a person filing a lawsuit can prove that a corporation is not truly a separate entity from its shareholders; that is, corporate formalities—holding annual directors' and shareholders' meetings, recording the minutes of the meetings in the corporate registrar, issuing stock certificates to shareholders, and electing directors—are not performed. If these formalities are not fulfilled and someone files a lawsuit against the corporation, the shareholders will be held liable for the obligations of the business.

Limited liability is generally afforded to corporations that sell stock to a large number of shareholders. If you own a small, closely held corporation, your liability risk becomes greater.

Despite its numerous benefits, forming a corporation is more complicated and expensive than setting up a sole proprietorship or a general partnership.

When establishing a corporation, you must first choose a name. The name should be unique, but it should also include one of these terms: "Corporation" (or "Corp."), "Incorporated" (or "Inc."), "Limited" (or "Ltd."), "Company," or "Chartered," or some phrase indicating that your entity is truly a corporation. It cannot duplicate or resemble a corporate name that is already in use. To determine whether the name you've chosen for your corporation is available, you can call your secretary of state's office. You can also search the Internet. Visit Lexis-Nexis, a legal research database, and search its corporate name database for the state where you will incorporate. If you find an available name but are not yet ready to incorporate and would like to reserve the name, you can file an application with your secretary of state's office. Most states will allow you to reserve a corporate name for at least 100 days. Once you're ready to incorporate, register the name with the state.

Conducting a name search may seem like a tedious task on your corporate "to-do list," but it is important to take it seriously and perform the search. If you do not and the name you have chosen has already been secured, you will not be able to incorporate your business.

Your next step in forming a corporation is filing for your articles of incorporation at your secretary of state's office. Filing fees vary in each state. After the articles of incorporation have been filed, you will receive a certificate of incorporation. Depending on the state in which your business is located, you may be required to file a copy of your articles of incorporation in the local recorder's office.

You can conduct business in other states after your corporation is formed and registered in your own state. However, you are required to file for qualification in any state where you choose to do business, and a fee will be required as well.

In some states, you can form a closed corporation. This type of corporation appeals to small business owners because it lacks many of the administrative tasks of a regular corporation. It is managed by its shareholders, but directors are not elected and officers are not appointed. Consult your attorney for specific details about a closed corporation if this legal form of business appeals to you.

Professional service providers, such as doctors, lawyers, or dentists, can also form a corporation. The clear advantage to a professional corporation is that the individuals will not be held liable for the malpractice of others in the company. (Each would remain liable for his or her own actions.) Professional corporations adhere generally to the rules that apply to a regular corporation, but they must use the term "Chartered" or "Incorporated," or the letters P.C. (professional corporation) or P.A. (professional association) as part of their name.

Within a professional corporation, only professionals can own shares in the company, and the corporation can offer only one form of service. For example, if you own a law firm and some of the attorneys are also certified public accountants, your firm can provide only legal services, not accounting services. Consult your attorney or accountant about specifics if you plan to form a professional corporation.

The main disadvantage of a corporation is double taxation. Unlike a sole proprietorship, a corporation is considered a separate taxable business entity and is subject to both federal and state taxes. Any income earned by the corporation is taxed at the corporate level and must be recorded on Form 1120 (see Figure 4.8). Income distributions made to shareholders are also taxed as dividends on the shareholders' individual tax returns. As a small business owner, this may be a hard pill to swallow, even though corporations' first $75,000 in income is taxed at a lower rate. Because the tax laws surrounding corporations are complex, consult your accountant and/or attorney about specific tax concerns before deciding whether incorporation is right for you.

SELECTING SUBCHAPTER S STATUS

At first glance, a Subchapter S corporation looks much like a regular corporation. It operates similarly and has basically the same structure (a board of directors, officers, and shareholders). The main difference is that a Subchapter S corporation does not suffer from double taxation. This business entity elects to be taxed similar to a general partnership for federal tax purposes: income, losses, tax credits, and other tax items "pass through" the company to the shareholders. (In a general partnership, they are passed through to individual partners.) A Subchapter S corporation files Form

Figure 4.8   Form 1120, U.S. Corporation Income Tax Return

Form **1120**	**U.S. Corporation Income Tax Return**		OMB No. 1545-0123
Department of the Treasury Internal Revenue Service	For calendar year 1997 or tax year beginning .... , 1997, ending .... , 19 ... ▶ **Instructions are separate. See page 1 for Paperwork Reduction Act Notice.**		**19 97**

A Check if a:	Use IRS label. Other-wise, print or type.	Name	**B** Employer identification number
1 Consolidated return (attach Form 851) ☐			
2 Personal holding co. (attach Sch. PH) ☐		Number, street, and room or suite no. (If a P.O. box, see page 5 of instructions.)	**C** Date incorporated
3 Personal service corp. (as defined in Temporary Regs. sec. 1.441-4T— see instructions) ☐		City or town, state, and ZIP code	**D** Total assets (see page 5 of instruction)

E Check applicable boxes: (1) ☐ Initial return   (2) ☐ Final return   (3) ☐ Change of address $

Income	**1a**	Gross receipts or sales	**b** Less returns and allowances	c Bal ▶	**1c**
	2	Cost of goods sold (Schedule A, line 8)		**2**
	3	Gross profit. Subtract line 2 from line 1c		**3**
	4	Dividends (Schedule C, line 19)		**4**
	5	Interest		**5**
	6	Gross rents		**6**
	7	Gross royalties		**7**
	8	Capital gain net income (attach Schedule D (Form 1120))		**8**
	9	Net gain or (loss) from Form 4797, Part II, line 18 (attach Form 4797)		**9**
	10	Other income (see page 6 of instructions—attach schedule)		**10**
	11	**Total income. Add lines 3 through 10** . . . . ▶		**11**

Deductions (See instructions for limitations on deductions.)	**12**	Compensation of officers (Schedule E, line 4)		**12**
	13	Salaries and wages (less employment credits)		**13**
	14	Repairs and maintenance		**14**
	15	Bad debts		**15**
	16	Rents		**16**
	17	Taxes and licenses		**17**
	18	Interest		**18**
	19	Charitable contributions (see page 8 of instructions for 10% limitation) . . .		**19**
	20	Depreciation (attach Form 4562)	**20**	
	21	Less depreciation claimed on Schedule A and elsewhere on return . .	**21a**	**21b**
	22	Depletion		**22**
	23	Advertising		**23**
	24	Pension, profit-sharing, etc., plans		**24**
	25	Employee benefit programs		**25**
	26	Other deductions (attach schedule)		**26**
	27	**Total deductions. Add lines 12 through 26** . . . . ▶		**27**
	28	Taxable income before net operating loss deduction and special deductions. Subtract line 27 from line 11		**28**
	29	**Less:** **a** Net operating loss deduction (see page 9 of instructions) . . .	**29a**	
		b Special deductions (Schedule C, line 20)	**29b**	**29c**

Tax and Payments	**30**	**Taxable income.** Subtract line 29c from line 28		**30**
	31	Total tax (Schedule J, line 10)		**31**
	32	**Payments: a** 1996 overpayment credited to 1997	**32a**	
	b	1997 estimated tax payments . .	**32b**	
	c	Less 1997 refund applied for on Form 4466	**32c** ( ) d Bal ▶	**32d**
	e	Tax deposited with Form 7004	**32e**	
	f	Credit for tax paid on undistributed capital gains (attach Form 2439) . . .	**32f**	
	g	Credit for Federal tax on fuels (attach Form 4136). See instructions . . .	**32g**	**32h**
	33	Estimated tax penalty (see page 10 of instructions). Check if Form 2220 is attached . . . ▶ ☐		**33**
	34	**Tax due.** If line 32h is smaller than the total of lines 31 and 33, enter amount owed . .		**34**
	35	**Overpayment.** If line 32h is larger than the total of lines 31 and 33, enter amount overpaid		**35**
	36	Enter amount of line 35 you want: **Credited to 1998 estimated tax** ▶ Refunded ▶		**36**

Sign Here	Under penalties of perjury, I declare that I have examined this return, including accompanying schedules and statements, and to the best of my knowledge and belief, it is true, correct, and complete. Declaration of preparer (other than taxpayer) is based on all information of which preparer has any knowledge.		
	▶ Signature of officer	Date	▶ Title

Paid Preparer's Use Only	Preparer's signature ▶	Date	Check if self-employed ☐	Preparer's social security number
	Firm's name (or yours if self-employed) and address ▶		EIN ▶	
			ZIP code ▶	

Cat. No. 11450Q

1120S (not shown here), but the business income is taxed only once, at the shareholder level. Another difference is that, with the Subchapter S corporation, all profits, losses, and other items that "pass through" must be proportionate to the shareholder's shares of stock. In other words, if you own 65 percent of the stock, you must receive 65 percent of the losses, profits, credits, and any other items that pertain.

Subchapter S corporations are more popular among small and medium-size businesses than among larger corporations. With such a major benefit as single taxation, why would any company choose *not* to elect this status? Certain criteria for filing as a Subchapter S corporation make it difficult for a large company to operate as this type of business entity. According to federal income tax law, any company filing as a Subchapter S corporation must meet ALL of the following criteria:

1. The corporation must not have more than 75 shareholders. (Prior to 1997, the number was only 35.)
2. All shareholders must agree to elect the Subchapter S status.
3. The company must be incorporated in the United States.
4. The corporation cannot have more than one class of stock. (Nonvoting stock is not considered a separate class of stock.)
5. The corporation may not be a member of an *affiliated group*, defined as one or more groups of corporations bound by stock ownership with a common parent company that owns at least 80 percent of the voting power.
6. The corporation cannot have shareholders who are nonresidents of the United States, unless the shareholder is an estate or trust authorized to be a Subchapter S corporation stockholder under tax law.

To set up a Subchapter S corporation, you must first incorporate your business. Next, you must file, on a special IRS form, your election to be taxed similar to a partnership. This step will allow you to sustain the limited liability enjoyed by corporations, but avoid being taxed at the corporate level.

LIMITED LIABILITY COMPANIES

The limited liability company (LLC) is a relatively new business form. Until recently, only 38 states recognized this type of business entity. Now, LLCs have become available in all 50 states, but the laws governing these companies differ in each state.

A limited liability company (LLC) has a number of advantages and disadvantages. The advantages are:

1. *Tax flow-through status.* For federal tax purposes, LLCs are, in most cases, treated like general partnerships. The income and losses generated in an LLC "pass through" to personal income and are taxed at the personal rate. Federal tax information is reported on Form 1065. Keep in mind that state tax laws may not recognize an LLC as a partnership. Check your state legislation before filing.

2. *Limited liability.* LLCs enjoy the liability protection of a corporation. Individuals are not responsible for the debts of the business.

3. *Management capabilities.* Members can manage the business themselves, without losing their limited liability status.

4. *Flexible membership.* LLCs can have an unlimited number of people, corporations, or partnerships, unlike a Subchapter S corporation, which is limited to 75 shareholders.

5. *Disproportionate distributions to owners.* LLCs are not required to make all distributions in accordance with the number of shares held by each owner. A member of an LLC can have a 40 percent interest in the company's assets but receive 60 percent of the income that is generated.

6. *Multiple issues of stock.* Unlike a Subchapter S corporation, an LLC can have different classes of stock.

The disadvantages are:

1. *Restriction on transferability of interest.* This is one of four characteristics of the typical corporation (the other three are: continuity of life, centralization of management, and limited liability). Generally, transferability of interest allows any member of a company to easily transfer his or her interest to another person without the permission or consent of the other members. In an LLC, this privilege is restricted.

2. *Cost.* It is more expensive to form an LLC than a sole proprietorship or a general partnership. Some states charge an initial filing fee plus an annual fee. Check with your secretary of state's office for details and the necessary forms.

3. *New entity.* Because LLCs are relatively new, the legislation governing these business entities is still being formed. The ways in which LLCs are treated may differ in each state. For example, in Wyoming, an LLC can end with the death or retirement of a business owner. Check with your attorney about the regulations surrounding LLCs in your area.

To form an LLC, you must file articles of incorporation with your secretary of state's office. Some states also require that you create an operating agreement (similar to a partnership or shareholder's agreement) that spells out how the business will be conducted. Like a partnership agreement, your operating agreement can be oral, but, to prevent future conflicts, it is always best to put it in writing. Seek legal advice when setting up your operating agreement.

Because an LLC is treated like a partnership, you may be subject to self-employment taxes and, if you hire employees, to payroll taxes. If you hire workers, you will need to file Form SS-4 with the IRS to obtain a federal Employer Identification Number.

LIMITED LIABILITY PARTNERSHIPS

Even newer to the realm of business forms is the limited liability partnership. It shares the tax advantages of a limited liability company, but it differs from an LLC because it is open only to certain professions, such as physicians and attorneys. The limited liability partnership is recognized in only about 40 states. Consult your lawyer if you qualify to set up this type of business form.

As you can see, choosing a legal form of business is not as simple as selecting an acronym and getting to work. There are serious issues to be considered before making your selection. Whichever legal form you choose, make sure that you seek legal advice for specifics about: legislation that may impact your business, the proper filing procedure for each entity, and the costs that you will incur.

CHECKLIST

HOW TO LEGALLY SET UP YOUR BUSINESS

✓ **Choose a name.** Choosing a name for your business is relatively easy but extremely important. The name you give your company will carry its reputation for years to come and will help consumers differentiate your product or service from your competitors'. Choose your title carefully.

✓ **Select a legal form of business.** There are six legal structures under which you can operate your business: (1) sole proprietorship, (2) general partnership, (3) limited partnership, (4) corporation, (5) Subchapter S corporation, or (6) limited liability company. Each has its own advantages, disadvantages, and tax consequences. Consider how much liability you are willing to shoulder before making your final selection.

✓ **Consult a professional.** Every new business owner should enlist the help of an attorney and an accountant when choosing a legal form of business. Your attorney can advise you regarding your liability under certain structures of business, and your accountant can help you decipher the language surrounding your tax consequences.

RESOURCES FOR MORE INFORMATION

ASSOCIATIONS

- *American Bar Association (ABA),* 750 North Lake Shore Drive, Chicago, IL 60611; 312-988-5000; www.abanet.org. ABA provides legal assistance to new and existing entrepreneurs. The organization publishes information in a variety of areas, including legal forms of business, employment problems, and public education. It also maintains a Lawyer Referral and Information Services unit, which will help you identify your needs for an attorney and will refer you to a lawyer, community, or governmental agency that handles specific legal issues.

- *Internal Revenue Service (IRS),* 1111 Constitution Avenue, NW, Washington, DC, 20224; 800-829-1040; www.irs.gov. The IRS provides a wealth of tax information for business owners. Using this organization, you can research details about how to legally structure your company and view publications outlining the tax issues of forming a business. The IRS can supply you with every tax form needed to record personal and/or business income. Call the closest regional office of the IRS to request the forms you need.

5

LOCATION, LOCATION, LOCATION

You've given careful thought to the type of business you would like to start. You've researched your potential market and chosen a legal business form. But have you given any consideration to where you would like to hang out your shingle? For example, would you prefer the mall or a business park? A freestanding building or a business incubator? At home or in an office high-rise?

Choosing a location is a critical aspect to starting a new business. Where you locate your enterprise will depend on several factors: the type of business you own, your competition, the makeup of your community, and your budget. But whether you operate a flower shop, a candy store, or a restaurant, you will need a location that contributes to your company's profitability. A poor location can kill even the best planned business idea, but a good location can do more for the success of your operation than any glitzy ad campaign.

Real estate professionals often say that the three most important factors in choosing a business space are location, location, and location. Securing a good site is key to running a successful business, but obtaining a good facility is equally important. You may open a top-of-the-line clothing boutique in the heart of Manhattan, where millions of well-dressed people travel every day, but if your facility is shabby from the inside out, few customers will want to patronize your business.

Choosing an appropriate location and facility for your business takes time and careful planning. Before you schedule an appointment with a downtown realtor, first assess the needs of your business. Itemizing the tools you'll need to operate successfully will help you choose a facility that is right for you. For example, if you want to start a home improvement store, you will need a place where you can load and unload large pieces of inventory. Therefore, in your search for a location and a facility, you would look at sites that support building docks.

Defining your needs in advance of your actual search will keep you from wasting time looking at sites and buildings that don't match your criteria. Don't rush your decision. Many overanxious entrepreneurs will take a spot just because it's cheap or available, but, ultimately, their business suffers. Take your time. Don't expect to find a site within a matter of days or weeks. The length of time needed to find a space will vary according to your requirements. Allow anywhere from 15 to 18 months for the actual search, paperwork, moving, and transition process.

In this chapter, we will discuss several facility options and how to choose one that works best for your business. Most new entrepreneurs will rent or lease office space in a mall, business park, or business incubator. But, to cut costs, many new business owners will set up shop at home. We will provide some guidelines for how you can make your work-at-home environment a successful experience, and will also detail the procedure for leasing space in an outside office.

Keep in mind that your location and facility will make an indelible impression on your customers, employees, suppliers, banker, and competitors. To some degree, your site represents the quality of your product or service. More important, it will impact your bottom line, so walk slowly and carefully in your search for the right business address.

STARTING A HOME-BASED BUSINESS

When surveying facilities to house your business, you've probably thought about choosing an executive suite, a neighborhood mall, or even a loft. But have you considered your home? Increasingly, new entrepreneurs are choosing to launch an operation out of their home. In fact, every 11 seconds, someone starts a new home-based business. According to IDC/LINK, a New York-based market research firm, there are more than 24 million home-based businesses nationwide, with services ranging from computer consulting and house cleaning to medical billing and meetings planning.

Some entrepreneurs choose to work out of their home because it's convenient. This is especially true for a working mom, who must split her time between her kids and the corporate structure. Of all home-based businesses, 37 percent are operated by women. Other new business owners decide to set up shop at home because of the low start-up cost required. How much *you* will need to spend will vary according to the type of business you start, the equipment needed, and the number of employees you hire. Some ventures can be launched for as little as $500.

A home-based business can be a viable choice, but not everyone is cut out to work from home, and not every home will successfully support a business. Before you rearrange the basement or assess that spare bedroom, consider these three factors: (1) the type of business you want to start; (2) local zoning regulations; and (3) your discipline quotient.

1. *The type of business you want to start.* Not all businesses can thrive from a home base, so before you print up business cards and lay out the welcome mat, you must decide the nature of your business and whether you will be able to operate it successfully from your place of residence. Maybe your lifelong dream has been to start a recording studio or a restaurant, but businesses like these will not lend themselves to a residential environment. To determine whether your choice of business can be home-based, ask yourself these questions:

- *Does your business require a lot of customer or client visits?* Many businesses rely on heavy walk-in traffic (an example is a tax preparation store). But this could create a disturbance in your home—and ultimately, in your neighborhood—if the volume is too high. If your business generates many visitors, you may run into problems with local zoning rules. However, if you can find ways to get around a constant flow of traffic in and out of your home, you may be able to operate. For example, perhaps you can set up a separate structure in your backyard. This may actually be more to your advantage than using the basement or spare room because some customers may feel uncomfortable conducting business with you in your home. A separate structure may ease any doubts they have regarding your level of professionalism and your ability to provide a quality product or service. But be aware that local zoning laws may place restrictions on your right to construct a small building on your premises. Check with your city's zoning or planning board before you count on that site.

- *Will your business require large amounts of space?* You may need storage space for huge pieces of equipment or large amounts of inventory. Also, you may need to hire several employees. All of these requirements demand an adequate amount of space for an efficient flow of your goods or services. If you are thinking about starting a large-scale marketing firm with 10 public relations agents and top-notch computer equipment, but you only have a small bedroom from which to work, launching your business in your home may not be feasible. Instead, you would benefit from leasing space in a free-standing building. (We will discuss leasing later in this chapter.)

- *Does your business negatively impact the surrounding community?* As a professional, you would not purposely disturb your neighbors with your business activities, but some operations inevitably produce noise and air pollution or toxic wastes. If your company would produce such undesirable effects, don't set it up in your home. If your neighbors file a complaint, you could be forced to take down your shingle.

After reading these few caveats, you may be asking yourself: "What kind of business *can* I start in my home?" Here are some suggestions:

- *Service businesses.* Residential cleaning, construction, or home repair companies can comfortably operate from a home because they generally require work at the customer's site. Typically, only paperwork and other "undisturbing" back-office duties are completed at the home office.
- *Businesses set up in a traditional 9-to-5 office environment.* Computer programming, graphic design, desktop publishing, accounting, freelance writing, and just about any consulting business would work well in a home.
- *Day care and catering.* Believe it or not, some residential areas will allow these types of businesses. However, you may be required to obtain a home-occupation permit or a business license to satisfy the zoning rules. Entrepreneurs who start these types of businesses often have separate structures or construct additional rooms adjacent to their home.

2. *Zoning regulations.* Even if you would prefer a work-at-home environment, local, state, or federal zoning laws can prevent you from setting up shop in your residence. Some communities prohibit home-based businesses altogether; others impose such heavy restrictions that operating an at-home company could be very difficult. Local zoning laws can restrict:

- *The right of the property owner to build separate structures.* Some areas will not permit the addition of separate buildings, in a backyard or alongside a house, for business activity.
- *The number of employees you are allowed to have.* Some areas forbid having any people, other than domestic servants, working in a home.
- *How much of your home can be used exclusively for your business.* As an example, home-based business owners living in Chicago may not use more than 10 percent of their residence exclusively for their operations.
- *Your ability to advertise.* Some local ordinances prohibit the use of signage for advertising purposes. This law is enforced mainly to sustain a residential "feel and look" to the neighborhood.
- *Parking capabilities.* If you think your customers can park anywhere on your neighborhood street, think again. Laws may enforce no-parking rules or force you to provide off-street parking for those who will visit your business. This could seriously impact the success

of your operation. If customers have to drive around for several minutes to snag a space, they may head straight for the competition's huge parking lot.

- *The amount of vehicular traffic in the neighborhood.* If your street was once a quiet stretch on which children could ride their bikes, and your business has changed it into the Indianapolis 500, zoning laws could shut down your operation.
- *The type of equipment and materials permitted.* Does your business require the use of large pieces of equipment? If your machines create excessive noise and contribute to the production of offensive odors, you may have to dispose of them and find less bothersome alternates.

Granted, some of the limitations that may be applied to your business are strict, but many ensure the safety and preservation of the neighborhood. If you are finding it difficult to see "their" perspective, ask yourself: If someone else's business was causing noise, traffic, odors, pollution, and waste next to your home, how would you feel about it? Would you want this type of business on your block or even in your town?

Ask your local zoning or planning board for information regarding the laws in your area. Search through the local ordinance files at your public library, or obtain the information from your local chamber of commerce or from an industry or trade association.

If you live in an apartment, condominium, or co-op, or if you rent rather than own your home, check your lease or ownership agreement to find out whether operating a business from your residence is permitted. Depending on the laws in your area and the type of business you start, you may have to obtain a home occupation permit or a business license. The licensing process may involve an inspection to determine whether your home meets the local health, building, and fire codes. Any businesses that produce food would most likely be subject to inspection. Fees for permits vary in each city or state but usually range between $25 and $100.

If your area does not support the type of business you would like to start, consider filing a variance with the zoning or planning board in your community. A variance, also referred to as a conditional-use permit, allows you to operate a business in an area not zoned for that purpose. But be forewarned: variances are not easily granted (see Chapter 6). You will have to prove that your livelihood would be destroyed if the variance is not given, and that the business you intend to start would not change the character of your neighborhood.

If you are thinking about forgoing the process of investigating the rules and regulations that govern home-based businesses, and operating on the good graces of your neighbors, think again. For a while, no one may complain about the loud tuba, flute, saxophone, and drum noises coming from your music-lesson studio, but eventually someone will. If you are found in violation of any ordinances, you could be forced to shut down your operation. Do your homework. You do not want to invest a lot of time, energy, and savings into planning a business, hiring employees, and advertising your grand opening, only to find out that your business is labeled an illegal operation.

3. *Your discipline quotient.* Working from home sounds ideal. There's no clock to punch and no boss to peek over your shoulder. Depending on the type of business you run, you might be able to report to work in your favorite pink fuzzy slippers. But are you disciplined enough to focus and be productive when you're home alone? Some people work more efficiently and productively when they're surrounded by coworkers. If a basket of dirty laundry, Oprah's next segment on Denzel Washington, or a sunny day for golf will distract you from your work, a home-based business may not be right for you.

Setting Up Your Home Office

When you've determined the type of business you would like to start from your home, and confirmed that it is permitted in your area, you can begin setting up your home office. This is a very important task. How, and where, you set up your office in your home will greatly impact the success of your operation. Moreover, it will have tax implications for your business.

In a work-at-home environment, it can be very difficult to clearly designate an area that is just for work. Perhaps no one knows that better than Olusola Seriki. Seriki started his real estate development firm, Metro-ventures/USA Inc., from his home in 1992. But, like many home-based business owners, he found it challenging to isolate his home business from his home life.

"We were in a small townhome, so I had a little nook in our guest room where I set up my computer and all the things that I needed to sort of make it feel like a business, but there were some specific challenges to doing this," says Seriki, who worked out of his home for two years before acquiring space in a freestanding office building in Columbia, Maryland. "There was the constant challenge of protecting my paperwork from young children crawling all over the place, and just needing to work until two or three o'-clock in the morning without disturbing anyone else. I was still employed by a major corporation when I launched my home business, so I needed to work at night; but that sometimes caused conflict with the other members of the household," he says.

Before you set up your home office, you will need to define your work area. Your work space should allow you to perform all the necessary tasks to run your business without disturbing the activities of the rest of the household. Most home-based business owners find an isolated part of the home to set up their office (the attic, the basement, a spare bedroom or enclosed porch). Don't set up at the kitchen table or in the family room. The heavy traffic in these areas of the home could disrupt your business activities and create a negative image for your company, particularly if customers and clients must visit your business site.

The kind of product or service that you offer will help you define your work area. For example, if your business requires that customers, suppliers, and employees travel in and out constantly, select an area that is isolated from the rest of your house. You don't want your banker or your food supplier to be stepping over games and other toys in your family room on the way to your office. If feasible, set up a separate entrance. This is particularly recommended if you operate out of your basement. An additional door could give visitors immediate entry, without coming through other areas of the house.

When defining your work space, pay careful attention to cost. A few structural changes—a separate detached building, wood paneling, or carpeting—may satisfy the needs of your business, but can you afford these modifications? Remember, as a new entrepreneur, your capital is limited and your cash flow may not be positive at the outset. Be cautious about how much you spend on items and additions that are not absolutely necessary to the start-up of your operation. Don't scrap your ideas for upgrading; just put them off until profits start to roll in. Use this as an opportunity to accomplish some of the short-term goals we discussed in Chapter 1, and set a target date for their completion. For example, you might say, "When my monthly sales reach x dollars, I will wallpaper the office."

Your next step in setting up your home office is to obtain all the equipment you will need to operate. Each piece should contribute to the profitability and productivity of your business. Many home-based entrepreneurs make the mistake of thinking that just because they will operate out of their home, they need not pay special attention to furnishings such as a desk, tables, computer equipment, and other supplies. These items need not be expensive or state-of the-art, but they should be quality products that add value to your company. Be sure that your equipment will not detract from your business image. If customers will visit your office and you do not look like you "mean business," you will eventually find yourself out of business.

The last issue to consider in putting together your home office is safety. This is particularly important for work-at home moms and dads. Take precautions to ensure that your kids and your clients are protected when they enter your work space. If you have small children, childproof your area by putting safety caps over electrical outlets and keeping sharp objects (such as scissors or letter openers) in hard-to-reach places. To safeguard your clients, make sure that personal items that could be potentially hazardous are removed from your office and from any portions of the house leading to it. For example, if your son loves to skateboard and leaves the board in a hallway leading to your office, a customer may slip and fall—and may sue you. Some hazards may go unnoticed, so be sure you have sufficient liability coverage to protect you from any claims (see Chapter 6).

Getting Your Financial House in Order

When Uncle Sam comes calling for his piece of your home business—on or before April 15—you want to be ready. Set up a detailed record-keeping system, and keep track of all business-related expenses. This is required of every new business owner, whether the venture is set up in the home or in an office outside of the residence (see Chapter 12). If you need some help with record-keeping, consult an accountant. For a less expensive approach, use computer software programs such as Quicken®, which offer easy-to-follow formats for separating business and personal expenses. Never mix the two. Before your first day in business, set up a separate business bank account.

When filing your tax return, keep in mind that several expenses are tax-deductible: office supplies, professional and trade memberships/dues, travel expenses, postage, and employee wages and benefits. Many home-based business owners can also claim a "home office" deduction (part of their rent or utilities costs, or a depreciation amount based on the area of their home that is used for the business). We'll discuss taxes in greater detail in Chapter 13.

SELECTING A BUSINESS COMMUNITY

If setting up a home-based business is not in the cards for you, you may want to consider leasing space in an outside facility. Before you grab the rentals section of your daily newspaper, consider the type of community where you would like to house your business. Not every area will successfully support your business; you must conduct a thorough analysis of any community where you are thinking about setting up shop. For example, retail businesses, which rely on heavy foot and vehicular traffic, must be situated in high-visibility areas where they are exposed to their potential target markets. So, although you may want to locate your antique shop in the quiet, spacious confines of a small suburban town (where rental rates are often cheaper, but population is diminished), this particular type of community may not suit the needs of your business.

The following factors must be considered when you are surveying a potential community: population, economic infrastructure, resident demographics, resident attitude, and zoning ordinances. Each is examined here in detail.

Population

Plainly put, without customers your business is sunk. When you survey a potential community, determine whether the population base will support your business. Are there enough people (who match your target audience, of course) who could become customers? You can obtain information about an area's population by contacting the U.S. Bureau of the Census in Washington, DC. The Bureau publishes reports indicating specific business types and the populations of the areas in which they are located. If you find that the population in a particular town is not sufficient for your type of firm, move on to the next possible location.

Economic Infrastructure

Is the unemployment rate relatively high in your prospective area? What is the average family income? Are most people employed full-time or part-time? These are some of the questions you will need to ask when you are evaluating a community's economic infrastructure. The economic well-being of a community will greatly impact your chances for success because it will dictate the level of income among residents, as well as their employment status. You can garner information about a community's economic picture by studying U.S. Bureau of Census data or by simply taking some mental inventory. For example, if you notice that recent high school and college graduates are migrating from your prospective area because jobs are scarce, this may be a sign that the economic outlook is grim. Or you may notice that few or no chain stores have set up shop, and the handful of boutiques that are scattered about the area are closing within one year or two years of opening. Given these facts, you may want to research another area for your business.

Resident Demographics

Getting to know your potential customers is key to running a successful business. When you are evaluating the population of a particular community, it is important to determine their wants and needs so you can properly position your product or service (see Chapter 3). Another key factor is whether they have particular traits that will help to support your business. Consider the following demographics when you are evaluating the residents of an area:

1. *Occupation.* What types of jobs do the residents have, and where do they work? Are they working in blue-collar or white-collar jobs? Knowing their occupations will give you a sense of their spending patterns and their socioeconomic level.

2. *Disposable income.* What kind of purchasing power do the residents have? If most are living from paycheck to paycheck, there's little chance that they will have the means to make many purchases beyond the necessities. But if they have a fair amount of disposable income, much of it could end up in your cash register.

3. *Hobbies or extracurricular activities.* Do the residents perform any activities that could create opportunities for your business? Perhaps

you own a sports apparel store and the local barter club runs a community basketball team. This could mean big bucks for your business through sales of uniforms, footwear, equipment, and other sports paraphernalia.

4. *Average age.* Are the residents in Generation X, or are they baby boomers? It is important to define the average age of a community's residents before setting up shop. For example, if your product or service is geared toward 18- to 35-year-olds, but your prospective community is filled with senior citizens, locating there will do little to benefit your business.

5. *Place of residence.* Do the residents rent or own their own homes? Do the renters live in an apartment, a shared co-op, or a high-rise condominium? Where people live can often dictate their spending habits and give insight into their socioeconomic level.

6. *Transportation.* Are residents car-bound or do they ride on public transportation? Do they own mopeds or bicycles? Determine their primary means of transportation. If most are getting around on bicycles, for example, don't locate on a hilltop or in an area that will be difficult for potential customers to reach.

Resident demographics can be obtained from trade associations or the local chamber of commerce. The Bureau of Labor Statistics publishes statistical data on household expenditures ranging from fast food to life insurance. If you decide to plant roots in a particular area, keep a watchful eye for any changes in the community that could impact your success in the future. As people move in and out, the makeup of the community can change. You may have to change with it, to sustain your business (perhaps by redefining your target audience), or move to another location.

Resident Attitude

How does the community feel about its neighborhood? Do residents take pride in its appearance and volunteer or participate in activities to revitalize their area? How a community sees itself will greatly impact your chances for success and survival. Look for a community that is proactive, not passive, and that cares about sustaining a positive way of life, not only for its residents, but also for the businesses that have located there.

Zoning Ordinances

All areas in any city or town are zoned for commercial, industrial, or residential use. Research the zoning for any area that is a possible location for your business. Some communities prohibit certain types of businesses altogether. Others enforce strict limitations (such as the amount of on-street parking that is allowed, or the dimensions of signage) that may make it difficult for you to operate successfully. Visit your local zoning department and inquire about any restrictions that may apply to your type of business.

When you find a community that will permit your business to operate, is bustling with potential customers, has a strong economic foundation, and projects a positive outlook for the future, then begin searching for a facility where you can hang your "Open for Business" sign.

FINDING A "GOOD" FACILITY

If you are setting up your third or fourth business, you will easily recognize a facility that meets your needs because you've developed a keen eye for all the ingredients that make up a "good" facility. If you are a new entrepreneur, you may not know what to look for when choosing a structure.

At the very least, a good facility is one that enhances your business and does not detract from it. The structure that houses your operation is not just an address for deliveries. It is an extension of your company; it makes a statement about you, the type of business you own, and the quality of your product or service. Pay careful attention to even the little things that could mar your business and its reputation. Something as simple as cracked steps leading to your entrance door, or endlessly leaking plumbing in the public bathrooms could cause customers to doubt your ability to deliver a quality product or service.

As a new entrepreneur, you can increase your chances of choosing a good facility if you carefully consider the functions that every structure should perform. An ideal facility will have the traits described here.

Presents a Positive Image for Your Business

Customers will come to your business because they believe you have a product or service that will satisfy their needs. If they have to dodge falling debris or walk up rickety steps to do business with you, they may soon take their dollars elsewhere. Because your business facility makes a bold statement about your company, everything about it, from top to bottom, should present it in the best possible light. Your definition of "best possible light" may depend on the type of business you own. If you sell top-of-the-line products, customers may expect you to have a very posh and spacious facility that supports personalized service, in addition to offering quality goods. If your niche is to provide quality products at prices lower than your competition's, customers may expect your facility to be more modest. In this case, having a luxurious facility could actually hurt your business. Cost-conscious customers may think that your products couldn't possibly be inexpensive if you have lavish accommodations.

If you are having trouble determining how to present your business in a good light, ask yourself what kind of facility would make you want to step inside. At the very least, your building should be clean and well-maintained. Even if customers won't be regularly entering the building to conduct business, don't take the attitude, "No one's going to see the facility, so why bother sprucing it up?" Your employees, suppliers, and banker are going to see your business site, so make it the best that it can be.

Supports Productive Business Operations

What will you need to successfully conduct business? Perhaps you need a facility with a specific interior layout or a state-of-the-art security system; or a structure that is close in proximity to your employees and suppliers. A good facility is one that meets all your requirements for efficiently conducting your business operations. If you are already in business, you should have a clear sense of your facility needs. For example, if you are relocating your company, determining what you will need in your new facility may be only a matter of duplicating those aspects of your old facility that satisfied your needs, and improving or replacing the features that did not measure up to your expectations. But if you are new to the world of entrepreneurship, you may not know where to begin. You can start by evaluating the operating steps of your business: list all the things your operation requires if it is to run like a well-oiled machine.

Encourages Future Growth for the Company

Entrepreneurs often make the mistake of not obtaining enough space to grow their businesses beyond the start-up phase. When choosing a facility, consider whether it will accommodate future growth of your operation. When Clotee McAfee, the founder, president, and designer of Uniformity L.L.C., scoured south central Los Angeles for a facility to house her clothing manufacturing firm, she was looking for a reasonable leasing price. But she was also searching for a facility that would provide enough space to effectively produce her product as her business matured. "I was looking for a building that would accommodate growth and that would allow us to have shipping, a design studio, and a factory," says McAfee, who designs and manufactures school uniforms worn by more than 18,000 middle and high school students in New York, New Jersey, Texas, California, and Washington, DC. McAfee operates her company from an 18,000-square-foot facility equipped with all the elements she required plus two parking lots and easy access to the major highways and transportation facilities. Leasing more space than your immediate needs require carries a high cost. As a new entrepreneur, you must determine whether it makes sense to pay for the extra space now to be ready for easy expansion later. If you reasonably believe that your business will grow in the not-too-distant future (perhaps financial projections in your business plan indicate growth within a three- to five-year period), it may be sensible to assume the added start-up expense. If you're only wishful about future expansion, buying or leasing more space than you need at the moment may place an unnecessary financial burden on your business. Carefully consider your future growth plans before making a final decision.

Fulfills Your Space Needs Economically

Few new entrepreneurs do not use the word "budget." A tight hold on the start-up purse strings is crucial for virtually all new business owners. There's little room for splurging and even less room for waste, so it is imperative to make your facility as cost-effective as possible. If you are not able to buy or lease space at an affordable price, your business is likely to suffer; a high rent will hurt your company's profitability. Overspending for a facility can also damage your operation. Financial lenders may consider your choice of location to be frivolous and irresponsible, which can make it difficult for you to borrow money in the future.

How do you determine when the price is right for a particular piece of property? It's not easy. You must consider two separate price issues: (1) the actual worth of the property and (2) how much you can truly afford. To find a facility that is within your price bracket, it's best to work with a professional real estate agent or broker who can define a property's worth. You must then determine whether you have enough capital to secure the site.

ASSESSING YOUR NEEDS

No two business owners have the same blueprint for mapping out their facility needs. Some owners will require medium-size structures in high-traffic areas; others will need to situate their companies in large plant facilities in remote areas. But whether it is uptown, downtown, or out-of-town, your business needs a place from which to sell its products or services, and you must determine what layout or special features that space will have to have if your operation is to run smoothly.

Vivian Gibson, creator of the famous Vib's Caribbean Heat and president of The MillCreek Company, needed a facility equipped with a kitchen so that she could prepare her hot seasoning sauce. "I couldn't afford to equip a kitchen myself, so I looked for facilities that already had kitchens built-in. I was able to find one that wasn't being used in the upstairs rear of a bowling alley. It had professional sinks, a walk-in cooler, a stove with a hood, and all those things that I couldn't afford to have but needed to meet safety and health requirements, so I used that initially," Gibson explains. "It was a battle because it wasn't ideal for deliveries. For example, I needed vinegar, but the distributor wouldn't deliver it in the 55-gallon drums that I needed because the kitchen I used was on the second floor and there was no loading dock. I had to buy my vinegar in gallon jugs and drag all those gallon jugs up the stairs one at a time, but that was the trade-off. I stayed there until I found out about business incubators and then I moved into one of them."

When selecting a facility, each business owner will have different requirements. Still, there are basic factors that every new entrepreneur should consider. Read the following sections before you close a deal for a facility.

Building Layout, Size, and Appearance

The type of business you operate will determine the general makeup of your facility. Retail and service businesses largely depend on customers to file in and out of their stores, so they must pay special attention to the appearance of the building.

The exterior and the interior should be attractively decorated. Customers should want to step inside. Something as simple as the color of your building can impact a customer's decision to visit your business, so give careful thought to how you will decorate the outside of your facility.

You can construct the interior of your facility in any number of ways. It could be laid out to simply get customers in and get customers out. Hardware and convenience stores are often set up with this purpose in mind. Alternatively, your structure can encourage customers to browse and shop for items besides the one(s) they intended to buy.

Retail and service businesses vary in their size requirements. Businesses that confine customers to a small sales area (e.g., a candy store) and have very little or no inventory storage requirements, can operate in small facilities. However, if your business requires large amounts of space for inventory and customer use (e.g., a beauty spa or car dealership), look for a larger structure.

Wholesale and manufacturing businesses typically require large, open facilities. They place emphasis on buildings that help support efficient handling of their products. For example, an entrepreneur operating a wholesale food distributorship may look for a facility that has large aisles and huge storage racks, the capability to support lift trucks, and large shipping and receiving docks. An owner of this type of firm may seek close proximity to transportation facilities, for the easy movement of inventory and other materials or equipment.

Unlike retail and service businesses, manufacturing firms do not place much emphasis on the facility's interior and exterior appearance. Still, you can't totally ignore how your building looks. At the very least, it should be well maintained and clean. Your facility should motivate you and promote productivity among your employees.

When surveying a prospective facility's size, layout, and appearance, keep in mind that you may be forced to "build out" or renovate your space to meet the specific needs of your business. This could involve replacing doors or updating an existing ventilation system. Renovating your space will create an added expense, so before you picture yourself busy with a hammer, nails, and paintbrushes, consider the following factors:

1. *Cost.* Whether you decide to add a few more light fixtures or knock out a wall to connect two rooms, the cost can be high. Secure estimates of how much the additional work will cost, and compare the bids from the responding contractors before you make a final decision. If doing the build-out on your own will be too costly for your new firm, try to negotiate with your landlord, or the owner of the property, for a package of *rental concessions*— incentives that landlords offer tenants to encourage them to lease a particular space (terms might be a year's free rent or a build-out of the space at the expense of the landlord). If you are leasing a space and the landlord will do some renovation, you may want to negotiate a clause stating that you can terminate the lease agreement if the work is not completed by a specified time or before the deal on your lease transaction is closed.

2. *Length of time for renovations.* Carefully consider exactly how long your build-out will take. There's no standard schedule for completing renovations. Every business is different, and how long your particular modifications will take will depend on the nature of your build-out. If renovations are so extensive that they threaten to extend well into the first few weeks or months of your new business operations, you may want to rethink your plans to build. Attempting to conduct business while construction is ongoing could have a negative impact on your bottom line.

3. *Lease terms concerning build-out.* When renovating your space, it is important that you negotiate contingency provisions—specific terms that could become applicable with the occurrence or nonoccurrence of a particular event. If modifications to your build-out are not made correctly, within budget, or within the promised period of time, you could face financial disaster. Contingency clauses, when outlined correctly, can protect you against tragedies. Contingency provisions must be customized to fit the needs of each business. Check the details with your attorney (preferably, a specialist in commercial real estate).

4. *Zoning regulations.* Wouldn't it be wonderful if you could construct your facility in any fashion that you like? For the most part, you can; however, you must determine whether special permits will be required to perform certain types of work. Ask your local zoning department whether you will need a zoning or building code variance for your planned renovations. A building code variance will allow you to make modifications that would not normally be permitted in a particular area.

Proximity to Customers, Employees, and Suppliers

No matter what type of business you start, three groups of individuals are critical to its success: (1) your customers, (2) your employees, and (3) your suppliers. Without these people, you would not be in business, so carefully consider where they reside before settling on a particular community as a site for your business.

When Byron Stewart launched his architecture firm, Modus Inc. Architects, in 1989, he occupied space in a quiet, residential community on the outskirts of New Orleans. Realizing the need to move closer to his customers, he uprooted his business and headed for the city. "The problem with being remotely located in the suburbs is, if you are a service-oriented business, you have a lot of traveling to do," says Stewart, whose customers include public schools, casinos, and airports. "So I looked for an area where I could be closer to my vendors and clients."[1]

Customers like convenience. They like being able to travel short distances to get the products and services they need. Unless your venture requires acres of land, if potential buyers have to drive or ride a bus for miles before reaching your business, you can expect them to patronize a competitor who offers the same goods or services, but who is closer to their point of departure.

Not every type of business can provide ready and convenient access to customers. For example, manufacturers that sell through wholesalers do not have people filtering in and out of their operations, so their choice of location need not be close to their target market. These businesses are more concerned with proximity to transportation facilities, such as airports or train stations.

Retail or service businesses, like Modus Inc. Architects, depend on a steady stream of customers, so they must locate where their target audience resides if they are to accommodate customer volume and convenience. For this reason, they tend to set up in the midst of heavy car and foot traffic.

If your business depends on a constant flow of walk-in or drive-in customers, you must also consider the side of the street on which you are located. For example, if you operate a hot dog vending cart, choosing the right side of an avenue can make the difference between success and failure. Let's say you roll your cart out to a bustling corner in Philadelphia's center city district. Most of the office buildings are on the east side of the street, but your cart is on the west side. At lunch time, when workers file out of the buildings, they are unlikely to dodge taxicabs and oncoming traffic to buy a frankfurter and some fries. Most of them will go elsewhere, without having to cross a busy main thoroughfare.

If you operate a mail-order business, you are close to your customers practically anywhere in the country. Businesses such as consulting firms and freelance writers enjoy the same advantage.

When recruiting employees for your new business, be aware that your offer will be particularly attractive to applicants who live close to your business. Few employees want to commute for an hour or two at each end of the workday. When you survey a community, investigate whether there is a ready pool of qualified workers who would have to travel no longer than 30 minutes to reach their job. You can contact the closest regional office of the Bureau of Labor Statistics for information regarding employment, unemployment, working conditions, productivity, technology, and other issues that will be useful in your search for a location where qualified workers reside. You can also contact your local chamber of commerce for assistance.

If you will need suppliers (distributors, wholesalers, and manufacturers), start your interviews with those that are nearby, to cut transportation costs and create ease of delivery. If the materials and inventory that you need are produced too distant from your business, and few transportation facilities are available, you will incur enormous shipping costs that could hurt your business financially. Standard practice is to pass along these costs to customers via higher prices, but you then risk losing the customers to competitors who buy their supplies more cheaply and offer their goods at a lower price.

Locating too far from suppliers can also cause potential problems with deliveries, which could cripple your business. Try to locate close to major highways and other means of transportation that will support efficient and quick delivery of shipments.

Closeness of the Competition

When you envision where you will locate your business, give careful thought to the locations of your competitors. Depending on the type of business that you own, you may want to set up shop in the same town, on the same street, or even in an adjacent building. You must determine whether locating near the competition will hurt or help your business in the long run.

Wholesalers generally don't have to worry about competing with next-door neighbors; their customers rarely come to their business premises. For some retail companies, clustering around similar operations can cut operating expenses and create a synergy that allows all of them to prosper. For example, art, jewelry, and clothing stores tend to congregate in the same area, to draw the customers that none of them could attract alone. Most retail and service businesses, however, consider it advantageous to operate away from their competitors.

There is some benefit in locating near anchor or magnet stores, which tend to draw huge crowds. If you set up your retail business on a main road leading to one of these businesses, you could increase the number of potential customers who walk through your doors. For instance, if your business is a small stationery or convenience store, consider leasing space in a facility that customers must drive past to get to Staples or Wal-Mart.

To further increase your chances for inheriting some of the competition's customer base, adjust your store hours so that you open for business before the magnet store and close well after it has shut down for the day. At a minimum, the employees of the magnet store may walk in to pick up odds and ends before heading home for the night.

Another factor that could greatly affect your success is *appearance.* When you're evaluating a potential location, note how the buildings surrounding the facility look. Do they detract from or add appeal to the location and the community? How do they compare to your competitors' facilities? If you do not like how the buildings are decorated or constructed in a particular area, you can simply decide not to locate there and move on to the next community.

When selecting a site, carefully consider what you would like your customers to see as they approach your building. Most new business owners choose to locate in an area where the buildings complement one another. But don't overlook a structure that is architecturally different. Its unique design may help draw attention to your shop or might possibly become your logo.

Nature of the Community

As a first-time homebuyer, you would investigate the local school system, the proximity of police and fire stations, and the nearest hospital. As a new entrepreneur, you should give attention to the same issues when searching for a home for your business.

Why? Because each can impact the survival of your operation. For example, if a prospective community's educational system is top-notch, there may be a ready pool of well-educated high school graduates whom you could hire to work in your business. If a university is nearby, employees might be encouraged to enhance certain skills or gain additional expertise that will improve their job performance.

The makeup or character of a community is vital to the success of your business. Zoning laws and tax rates will give you a sense of whether an area welcomes and is supportive of your type of operation.

When you are surveying a particular community, review its sources for credit and loans, and its utilities rates. Obtaining credit is crucial to the survival of virtually every new and existing business owner. Historically, financial institutions have been more likely to grant loans to businesses within their own communities. If your prospective area does not harbor many financial lenders, you may find it hard to secure needed funding.

Your business cannot operate without power, heat/air conditioning, telephones, and water, so you must locate where these necessities are readily available and affordable. Once you move into a particular facility, you will not have much choice as to which company will supply these utilities. If you are still looking for that perfect spot, consider locating your facility in an area (such as across a county line) where utilities are normally offered at lower rates.

In the event of an emergency (let's say a severe thunderstorm wipes out the power in your company), you may want to keep an emergency generator on hand. This device probably will not be sufficient to sustain your business for a long period of time, but, in a crisis, it could help you avoid losses due to power interruption.

Parking Facilities

How many times have you attempted to visit a particular retail store but could not find a parking space? Probably too many to count, right? If you're like most people, after taking several trips around the lot, you give up and go elsewhere—often to a competitor with a parking lot the size of a football field.

As a new business owner, something as simple as lack of parking can be the downfall of your operation. Carefully evaluate whether enough space is available, not only for customers who visit your business, but also for suppliers and other professionals who impact the success of your operation.

If you are thinking about locating your facility in a neighborhood that supports both residential and commercial uses, check whether the facility's parking lot is used by residents without permission. If so, you may want to regain control of the lot, at least during business hours. Bear in mind that a total prohibition of residents' parking could create ill feelings among potential customers.

If you own a manufacturing or wholesale business, parking space for employees will be your only concern; customers will not be visiting your facility.

Building Dock and Refuse Facilities

Small businesses rarely have enough shipping or receiving to warrant a full-fledged truck dock for loading and unloading goods. Manufacturers, on the other hand, may require large pieces of equipment, oversize inventory items, and raw materials that are too large and heavy to lift off a truck manually or carry through a standard size door. A dock facility, or even separate shipping and receiving docks, may be needed.

Disposable waste varies; small businesses can have small or large amounts, depending on their type of products. For a food business, refuse disposal will be very critical. You may need to use large trash receptacles or compactors. Before you settle on a particular facility, investigate whether you can obtain and legally use certain refuse disposal equipment and, if necessary, private carters.

If your operation handles or generates toxic wastes or other environmentally dangerous materials (such as petroleum products), local, state, or federal disposal laws may govern how you operate your company. You will incur enormous clean-up costs if you improperly dispose of hazardous materials at your facility, so investigate the regulations thoroughly.

Environmental Outlook

If a facility where you've chosen to locate is found to be polluted with hazardous wastes, federal law can force you to pay the clean-up costs, even if you can prove that you did not in any way contribute to spreading the toxins.

If you are a new business owner already strapped for cash, such a clean-up project could bring financial ruin. In your defense, you must prove that you had no knowledge of the presence of the waste and have made extreme efforts to unearth any hazardous conditions.

Before you seal a deal on any facility, consult an attorney about your liability if an apparently "clean" site is later found to harbor hazardous wastes. The lawyer may be able to advise ways that will lessen your liability if the site develops environmental issues. For example, he or she might negotiate, with the seller (or landlord) of the property, some indication in your lease contract as to whether prior uses of the facility made an environmental impact or whether the site was previously cited, by state or federal environmental departments, for violations.

Consult with your attorney about the possibility of having the facility inspected by a professional environmental team. This may or may not be a good move, so before you flip through the Yellow Pages for a "hazardous waste buster," carefully weigh the pros and cons with a professional adviser.

Security

The safety of the area where you locate your business is extremely important to your success. If customers or employees do not feel safe traveling to your facility, they will go elsewhere. Give careful consideration to the crime rate in a prospective community.

If you plan to set up shop in an area that has a high crime rate, you will need to invest in a whole range of security devices. Many business owners will avoid the added expense and locate in a low-crime district. But keep in mind that facilities in high-crime areas tend to offer lower rental fees. You may be able to lease or rent a facility very cheaply (let's say, saving 50 percent of the rental cost), purchase a sound security system, and still come out ahead.

The specific security features that you will need will depend on the type of business that you operate and the potential for criminal threats in your area. The security features used by many businesses are:

- Security alarm systems, window and door alarms, and motion sensors, all of which can be linked to the local police department.

- Security cameras linked to a video recording unit or monitored by security guards stationed on the business premises. The cameras can also be placed to photograph all points of access to the building and all internal areas where theft is most likely to occur (e.g., the sales floor).
- Bulletproof glass. This is generally needed only in areas that pose a very high threat and/or where large amounts of money or valuable items are stored or sold.
- Steel security doors and metal-detecting gates to cover storefront areas. Most business owners prefer not to use the latter because they project a negative image.
- Padlocked cash offices.
- Lighting in all areas that give access into the building, on loading docks, and in parking lots or garages.

You can buttress your security features by using on-site security guards. Either contract with a private security service company, or hire guards as full-time employees. Many businesses station a uniformed guard at their facility around the clock. Other options are: have a guard check the premises periodically after closing time, or arrange for a canine security service to bring in trained guard dogs after business hours.

Before you decide to use an on-site security guard or a watchdog service, check with your insurance agent about potential liability, especially if your armed guard or unattended watchdog mistakes an innocent visitor for a burglar.

Insurance Protection

Your choices of a type of business and a place to hang out your shingle affect your insurance rates. But so does the safety of the area in which your facility is located. If you settle in a high-crime area, you can expect to pay more in premiums than if you set up shop in a lower-crime area. If the surrounding community has a history of fire loss or is susceptible to floods or hurricanes, you will also pay more for your insurance.

To lessen the blow, look for facilities that are structurally sound and well lit, have good fire and security protection features, and offer excellent access to the police and fire departments. If you own an existing business and are looking to relocate, your business's past security record could dictate your insurance rates.

Rental Rates

For most start-up firms, selecting a facility boils down to dollars and cents. How much can you afford? Few new businesses are able to purchase a building, therefore nearly all first-time entrepreneurs start out in leased space. We will discuss leasing later in this chapter.

Prepare a budget that includes *all* expenses associated with occupying a space: your rental rate plus the security deposit; real estate taxes; and various other operating expenses (such as the build-out of your space, if needed). Depending on where your desired facility is located, you could pay rental rates ranging from $10 per square foot to $50 or more per square foot. Keep in mind that central business districts, in any city, generally command higher rental rates than most suburban areas. The trade-off with locating in the suburbs, where rents are cheaper, is the possibility of a longer commute for customers, suppliers, and employees who do not live in the town you've selected.

CHOOSING A FACILITY

When you are searching for a facility to house your business, you have a number of options: an office suite, a freestanding building, a shopping center, a business incubator, and your home. The facility you select must accommodate the type of business you operate.

Many small business owners—unless they operate out of their homes—will occupy space in a business park, a mall, or some other facility. Larger manufacturers or wholesalers, on the other hand, will use freestanding buildings to support their operations. Here are your options as you hunt for the perfect place to locate.

Business Parks

Chances are you have seen one of these business office environments. You may have even worked in one. Business parks generally feature a group of office buildings situated on one tract of land and managed by a professional management company or a land developer. Business parks tend to attract professional businesses: financial organizations, computer technology companies, dental practitioners, and physicians, to name a few.

Office space in a business park is generally leased out; tenants share the maintenance costs of each building. If you locate your business in this type of facility, the major benefit is to your *image*. No matter which type of business you run, you want your potential customers, your suppliers, and your employees to view your enterprise as being competent and professional. The design and layout of most business parks create a very positive image for its tenants.

Shopping Malls

If you own a business that relies primarily on foot traffic, you may want to consider renting space in a shopping mall. These facilities include many small businesses as well as a few magnet stores. Like business parks, shopping malls are generally managed by a professional management company or the developer.

There are many variations of a shopping mall: a community shopping center, factory outlet stores, and minimalls, also referred to as strip malls. Space in any of these facilities is typically leased out to prospective tenants. Retail and service businesses are most likely to lease space in a shopping center or a mall. Malls, which usually command the highest rental rates, charge $4 to $5 per square foot, per month.

Wholesalers and distributors are more likely to locate in factory outlets, where they enjoy immediate access to their target market. Rents for these facilities range from $3 to $5 per square foot, per month.

Business owners find that it is much cheaper to lease space in a strip mall, where rental rates range from $1.50 to $4 per square foot, per month. (The exact price will depend on how close the minimall is to larger malls.) These facilities usually feature open areas and walkways banked by rows of stores, including a number of small shops, one major chain store, and a supermarket.

Business Incubators[2]

Are you looking for a facility that will ease your fears of venturing out on your own and will take the pinch out of those high start-up costs? Then consider launching your business in a business incubator—an assistance program designed to nurture new firms and fledgling businesses. They are owned and operated by a variety of different sponsors: nonprofit organizations, universities, private industry councils, economic development groups, and state and local governments.

According to the National Business Incubation Association (NBIA), located in Athens, Ohio, there are about 1,100 business incubators worldwide, and nearly 600 are operating in North America. New incubators are added at a rate of four to five per month, and their doors are opening in rural areas as well as cities. The incubators' services guide new entrepreneurs through the fledgling years of their business, and they help recently started companies to grow their operations even further. The NBIA lists these as the basic services that incubators provide:

- *Flexible space and leases.* One of the more attractive features of an incubator is its low cost. Incubator fees vary according to the local market (the cost to lease space in an incubator in Peoria, Illinois, will be very different from the cost to lease space in San Francisco, California), but most offer prices that go below the standard market rate. Sponsors and agencies encourage new business development, job creation, and technology transfer. The incubators' flexibility with space is also attractive, because many new business owners are unsure about how quickly their operations will grow.

- *Shared business services.* These include bookkeeping, word processing, telephone answering, and other secretarial duties. Incubators also provide access to fax machines, copiers, computers, and business libraries. These services may be included in your rent, or you can "pay as you go," purchasing each service only when needed.

- *Business and technical assistance.* Using a team of in-house experts and a network of community support, incubators help new business owners in such areas as business planning, engineering and prototype development, marketing, patent protection, legal issues, and marketing. These represent just a few of the services that an incubator can provide. Check with the incubator nearest you for details.

- *Financial assistance.* Whether you need to secure a bank loan or gain access to federal and state research and development funds, venture capital, a revolving loan fund, or "angel" financing, an incubator can give you a helping hand.

- *Network opportunities.* The environment of an incubator allows you to network and bond with other business owners who are facing some of the same issues that your company may encounter. An incubator can also give you an opportunity to create synergies (partnerships) with other businesses housed in the same facility.

Not every incubator will offer the same services, nor will each one accept all types of businesses. Incubators are seldom suitable for retail businesses (e.g., clothing stores), but many accept light manufacturing and service firms or start-ups that develop new products and require research and development. Construction-related firms, sales and marketing agencies, and wholesale and distribution companies are among the businesses incubators are likely to house.

Before you get a nameplate for your door or file a change-of-address card, the NBIA advises that you evaluate a potential business incubator with these factors in mind:

- *Charges for space and services.* How do they compare to the market rates in your area? Do the space, parking, telephone, security, loading docks, and other basic business services meet the needs of your particular operation? What are the lease requirements? Does the incubator allow room for your business to grow?

- *The expertise/experience of the incubator's management team.* Does the staff understand the needs of your business? Can they offer on-site assistance, or, if they are unable to help you, will they let you gain access to valuable contacts and community business services?

- *The incubator's track record.* What is the experience of incubator graduates? How are current tenants faring? During your search, feel free to ask the incubator's management office for references. Call up a few graduates and discuss their experiences in starting and growing their business through this type of facility.

- *Incubator policies and procedures.* Are some services provided free of charge? How long can you remain a tenant? Businesses that start in an incubator stay there for an average of two to three years before graduating to their own space within the community. Does the incubator require that you pay royalties or give up part ownership of your business in exchange for reduced charges? Can you leave easily if your business fails or if you decide that the incubator is just not right for you? Are any free seminars or training programs offered, in addition to the basic business services?

- *Sponsorship.* Who are the sponsors or organizations that support the business incubator? Do they provide ongoing support for the incubator? What are their goals and reasons for supporting the facility? Is the sponsor(s) a member of NBIA or of another professional business organization? Be aware that many private companies set up incubators, but they are only interested in some quick bucks. They may try to force you into a long-term lease or a similar commitment that could jeopardize your business and hinder its flexibility. Their management staff are generally not skilled in offering business-related assistance. Before you choose a private agency, thoroughly check it out and consult your attorney.

You must develop a keen eye when searching for the right incubator to house your business. Before any business is accepted into a business incubator, it must go through a screening process that resembles investigations prior to financing. Here are some things business incubators will look for:

- Your company's likelihood for success.
- The strength and feasibility of your business idea.
- The type of financing you have or are capable of obtaining.
- Your commitment to making your business succeed.
- The likelihood that you will benefit from consulting services.
- Your ability to build a management team.

LEASING VERSUS PURCHASING A FACILITY

After you have determined your facility needs and have chosen the right structure, you must decide whether to lease or buy the property. Most new entrepreneurs do not have bank accounts big enough to purchase a building, so they start out in a leased space. But don't rule out purchasing just because you are a virgin to entrepreneurship and your cash flow is tight. Buying a facility could prove advantageous to your business over the long haul, so examine each choice carefully and weigh it against the needs of your business and your budget.

To Lease or Not to Lease

Should you lease that executive office suite on the 41st floor of the Sears Tower? Or should you plunk down money to mortgage a 50,000-square-foot building on the outskirts of town? Decisions, decisions. As a new entrepreneur, you're destined to make a lot of them, and one of the most important choices will be whether to rent or buy a facility.

The primary advantage of leasing a facility is the low initial cash investment. But if you purchase a structure, you end up paying less in the long run, and you gain an asset that could appreciate in value. Which option should you choose? There is no template answer. Each business owner must decide based on the needs of his or her company. However, there are several factors that can help you make a decision that's right for you and your business.

If you are thinking about leasing a property, consider the following factors:

- *Current cash flow.* In the early years of your business, leasing a space may be more advantageous to your cash flow. When leasing a property, your outlay is generally much lower than if you were to buy a facility. For example, if you lease an office suite, your main expenses will most likely be limited to a security deposit and the first month's rent. If you purchase a freestanding building, you will be required to put down the entire purchase price or a healthy percentage of it. Many new businesses prefer not to tie up money that could be used in other parts of the business (for salaries, purchasing inventory, and office equipment).

- *Mobility.* If you are unsure of the future growth of your business, you may choose to lease simply because when your space needs change, you can easily change your address. Or, let's say your target market migrates to another area, or you find a more suitable property for your company. If you have a short-term lease, you can uproot your business a lot faster and with fewer headaches than if you are locked into a 20-year mortgage.

- *Your company's credit rating.* As a new business owner, you may find it difficult to obtain credit for a mortgage from a financial lender, particularly if your credit history is blemished. Your only alternative will be to lease space. Given the same financial blunders, landlords may still be willing to let you rent space in their buildings.

- *Maintenance of property.* As a new entrepreneur, you will be swamped with the day-to-day tasks of running your business. This may leave little time for such chores as mending the roof, repairing the heating system, or fixing the leaky plumbing. You may even have difficulty finding time to shovel the walkways in winter. As a property owner, you are responsible for these tasks. But if you lease space, these duties are the landlord's, and you are free to meet with suppliers, create ad campaigns, drum up new business, and do anything and everything associated with running your own shop.

- *Declining real estate values.* If you find a facility that meets all your requirements but is located in an area where real estate values have not budged for years, it would make more sense for you to lease than to buy the property. By leasing, you do not incur any potential loss if the property's value drops.
- *Tax savings.* No matter what type of business you start, you will be looking for a tax break. If you lease, you can deduct the money you spend for rent as a business expense. If you buy, the money paid to purchase a facility is not deductible.
- *Unavailability of suitable and purchasable properties.* You may have every intention to buy a facility, but then you find that all the properties that match the needs of your business are offered for lease only. Under these circumstances, you would have no choice but to rent the property.

If buying seems to make more sense for your business, consider these factors:

- *Long-term cost.* Leasing a facility may be more beneficial to your cash flow, but, in the long run, buying a property is generally cheaper. As a landlord, you pay, up front, all the costs associated with purchasing and maintaining the property. Plus, you have the opportunity to establish a profit for yourself.
- *Control of property.* Let's say you want to make extensive renovations to your facility or would like to change your store hours. If you rent a facility, you will need your landlord's permission to make the changes. If you own the property, you can make any modifications you desire, without having to consult a second party (unless your changes could affect the zoning in your area).
- *Permanent location.* For some business owners, especially those offering retail and service businesses, establishing a permanent location is important to their success. If you put down roots in one place, customers will get used to seeing you there and will know how to find you. If you lease a facility with the intention of bouncing around year after year, you could risk losing valuable clients who may not do the legwork needed to reach your new business home. You also run the risk of having to move before you are ready, because

of rent hikes or because the landlord has made other plans for the space. As a property owner, you move when you're ready.

- *Appreciating property values.* If you find a facility in an area where property values are steadily increasing, it would be to your advantage to buy rather than lease. By getting in at the start of land appreciation, you can sell for a hefty profit if you choose to move later. However, if you lease a facility and the land's worth is increasing every year, you stand to make nothing. You could, in fact, end up paying more, if the landlord decides to raise the rent to better match the worth of the property.

- *Tax savings.* You cannot deduct the purchase price of a piece of property on your tax return. However, you can claim yearly depreciation deductions on the building. If you finance your property, you can also claim a deduction for interest paid on your mortgage.

- *Inappropriate spaces to lease.* In your search for a suitable facility to lease, you may find that all the sites that meet your needs are offered for sale only. In this case, you may have to purchase the property.

Look Before You Lease

When many new entrepreneurs begin their search for space, they put on a good pair of walking shoes, grab the Sunday classifieds and a red-ink pen, and head out the door. This is not a bad start for finding a facility, but you should consider adopting a more structured approach. Entrepreneurs who find a space that matches their budget *and* the needs of their business often enlist the help of a commercial real estate agent or broker.

Why? Because these professionals understand the nuances of the real estate industry and can get you a deal that you can afford. As a new business owner, your budget will be a major factor in determining which type of space you lease. The cost of commercial space—which is priced per square foot— varies according to a number of factors, including location and the type of building. However, in most major cities, there are average prices for four classes of space, A through D. This is how these classes are defined:

- *Class A.* Also considered trophy buildings (General Motors or Trump Plaza), these structures are situated in prime locations. They have excellent amenities: indoor restaurants, concierge and messenger services, and secured access to the building 24 hours a day, 7 days a week. These buildings are equipped with the latest technology, including Integrated Services Digital Network (ISDN) lines, which support advanced computer capabilities. The cost to lease a Class A building can range from $30 to $65 per square foot.

- *Class B.* These structures tend to be older and are often located on side streets. They do not have as many upgrades or amenities as Class

A structures, but many business owners still find them to be suitable addresses. Prices can range from $27 to $35 per square foot.

- *Class C.* For new business owners starting on a shoestring budget, these buildings are a viable option. They range in price from $18 to $25 per square foot. However, they may require some build-out on the part of the landlord or the tenant. These structures are at less convenient locations, perhaps a few miles away from the central business district. They have limited access and fewer technological capabilities than Class A and Class B buildings, but, for certain companies, their location could prove advantageous. For example, computer companies tend to lease Class C buildings because they afford the opportunity to create a technology infrastructure customized to the needs of the companies' operations.
- *Class D.* These buildings are generally occupied by manufacturers or wholesale companies. They are at the bottom of the list in terms of extras and price. You can lease space in a Class D building for a minimum of $10 per square foot in some locations.

When working with a broker, it is important that you state: the class of building you would like, the area where you would prefer to locate, how much space you will need, and how much space you can afford. This information will give your agent a clear picture of what you are looking for and will enable him or her to save time by narrowing your search to sites that match your requirements.

Your broker will want to see your financial statements. These documents become particularly important during the lease negotiation process; lessors (a real estate term for landlords) will use them to determine the strength of your company and whether it will be a good candidate for occupancy. Keep in mind that although you may work with a broker, this does not give you carte-blanche access to every space that may pique your interest. Some lessors have restrictions on renting to certain types of businesses. For example, many lessors will not accept personnel agencies, record companies, or city agencies because these businesses sustain a high volume of foot traffic, which places a strain on their buildings' security.

To find a commercial real estate agent, look in the Yellow Pages or ask friendly competitors for a few referrals. When shopping for a broker, look for one who has been in the business for several years and has a good track record of successful placements. Request a list of references, and ask each reference about his or her experiences with the broker. If you run across an agent working for a quick sale, move on to the next. Quick-sale brokers do not have your best interest at heart, and you will waste valuable time by working with them.

When you find a respectable broker, consider signing an exclusivity agreement (perhaps for three to six months) with that broker. Many business owners make the mistake of thinking that if they use two or three different agents, they can speed up the search process and increase their chances of finding a suitable and affordable space. However, split loyalties create chaos and discontent. Brokers will be reluctant to devote valuable time to your search when you are also working with another broker just down the block. Find someone you feel comfortable with, establish rapport with that person, and trust that he or she will find you what you need, when you need it. Searching for a space to lease can be a very time-consuming process, so don't expect to find a building within a matter of days, or even weeks. When you do find that perfect spot, act quickly. In tight markets, space goes fast, and you don't want to be left out in the cold.

Negotiating the Lease Agreement

You've found the perfect facility and made the decision to lease it. Now it's time to negotiate.

In theory, all terms of a lease are negotiable. However, how far you can negotiate depends on economic conditions. For example, in areas where vacancy rates are high, you may get a cheaper deal per square foot than in locations where less space is available. You may also get a price break if you decide to lease space in a newly constructed office building. Most landlords must presell units to obtain financing for construction; in fact, some lenders require that a new building must be 70 percent preleased before the foundation is poured. If you are one of the first to buy, you are likely to get a better rate than if you lease space after construction has been completed.

Here are some points of negotiation to consider as you begin talks with your landlord:

- *Build-out* refers to a renovation of your space. To attract tenants, many landlords will offer a package of rental concessions (or incentives). In soft markets, these benefits can include a year's free rent, and build-out of the space at the expense of the landlord. The average cost is $35 to $40 per square foot. The landlord's willingness to pick up the tab will depend on such factors as the length of the lease, the condition of the building, your type of business, and whether improvements will be useful to a future tenant. If you do the build-out yourself, you may have a bargaining chip to negotiate a lower rental rate. You will need to commission an architect, and it may take longer than the typical three to four months to build-out a space from scratch, but the savings may be well worth the time invested.

- *Rent bumps* is a lease term for increases in rental rates. Landlords will often include in a lease an increase in rent, after a specified period, to stay in line with the Consumer Price Index (CPI). Negotiate a cap on how much the rent can increase (generally, 4 to 5 percent). If there is no cap on a 10-year deal, for example, an escalation in the CPI could cripple your operation.

• *Security deposits* protect landlords against unpaid rent. Generally, your security deposit is tied to your financials, and the amount can differ based on the age of your company. For example, a firm that is 15 or 20 years old may have to put down three months' security deposit and the first month's rent. A newer, unestablished company may have to put down even more. It's up to you, your agent, and your landlord to negotiate the amount of your security deposit.

After all the terms are negotiated, the lease can be drawn. A lease is a written agreement between you (the lessee) and the lessor. On average, it is a 50-to-100-page document that describes in detail all the terms that go along with occupying a space. Each landlord drafts a unique document, but every lease has this standard information:

• The occupant's name.
• The lease premises and its condition upon rental.
• The rental rate.
• Any fees received as a security deposit.
• A breakdown of all operating costs.
• The starting date of the lease.
• The length of the lease.

Most real estate agents advise leasing a space for a period of 3 to 5 years, but some deals are cut for 10 years. It is important that you anticipate your future growth plans when determining the length of your lease. You don't want to lease too little space and be forced to move before your lease expires. This could be very expensive, in terms of moving costs and the expense of renting a bigger place. If you have to break the terms of your lease, you may have to pay a substantial fee to buy your way out. Ask your broker to negotiate your exit if this will be your course of action.

If you would prefer not to break the lease, you can set up a sublease arrangement. Essentially, subleasing is a situation in which an existing tenant leases part or all of a space to another tenant, usually at a discount rate (sometimes $5 to $10 less per square foot than the going rate).

After the leases are prepared, read the fine print. Make sure all costs to the tenant are listed, and all landlord obligations, including maintenance of the building and other services, are spelled out. Most important, have your attorney review the document before you sign it.

Purchasing a Facility

Most small businesses will not have the resources to buy real estate, but some companies do opt for facility ownership. These are generally manufacturing companies, wholesalers, nonprofit organizations, recording studios, and any other enterprises that require the use of large pieces of equipment and inventory.

The process for purchasing a facility is essentially the same as for leasing office space. You will still need a commercial real estate agent, and it's advisable to select one who specializes in investment sales brokerage. When purchasing a building, you will have to solicit a mortgage broker to help with the financing. Depending on the bank that you use, you may need to put down 20 to 25 percent of the purchase price before you can move in.

Setting Up Your Office

There is no template to follow when setting up your office. Each person approaches that task differently. Your space, whether at your home, in an office at the top of a city skyscraper, in a business park, or in a shopping mall, should be productive, efficient, and comfortable.

To set up a productive office, you must ensure that the layout of your space and the organization of your equipment and supplies allow you to get your job done efficiently. For example, if you will use a fax machine, will you have a single line for your phone and fax, or will the fax machine run on a separate line? This may seem trivial, but if you make a large number of phone calls daily (let's say you operate a computer consultant business) and receive a lot of faxes from clients, having a single line for both will slow down your work activity and hinder the productivity of your business.

Something as simple as where you place important reference materials can hurt your company's productivity. If you know that you will need to refer regularly to certain manuals for prices or instructions, you will want to keep those books close at hand.

To create an efficient office, you must lay out your equipment so that you save time and money. Avoid any need to waste valuable minutes running back and forth to consult your references.

These tips may help you as you strive for efficiency:

- Avoid putting equipment and supplies in locations that block other items you may need to perform your work.
- Technology can be both frightening and helpful in running your operation. Organize your computer programs so that the applications you use can be accessed easily from your desktop.
- Use movable furniture. This will allow you to rearrange your office space as the needs of your business change. Avoid built-in desks or similar furniture.
- Organize filing systems that will allow you to easily retrieve papers and documents when needed. Label all files, and neatly place them in a filing cabinet or drawer.

Besides being productive and efficient, your office must also be comfortable if you are to operate successfully. Consider the types of furniture you will use in your work area and in any area where customers may have to spend some time. You need not shell out big bucks for recliners or leather slingback chairs, but your furniture should be attractive and comfortable.

It is very important that you give special attention to the "comfort factor" of working at your computer. Many entrepreneurs have experienced serious health problems (e.g., carpal tunnel syndrome) because of extensive use of their desktops. To help alleviate some of the problems, consider purchasing adjustable computer desks and chairs that will allow you to:

- Position your keyboard so that your wrists remain straight and your elbows maintain a 90-degree angle.
- Place your feet flat on the floor, with your knees at a 90-degree angle and your back against the chair.
- Shift your monitor so that the top of the screen is at eye level or slightly below eye level.

Choosing a location and a facility, and then setting up your office, can be grueling work. Make it also a fun and exciting time as you start your new business. Happy hunting!

CHECKLIST

THINGS TO CONSIDER WHEN CHOOSING A LOCATION

✓ **Facility options.** There are a number of places where you can locate your business. Many business owners who want to save on the costs of rent and avoid the hassles of commuting will set up shop in their home. Other entrepreneurs whose businesses do not lend themselves to a home environment will secure space in an office building, a business incubator, a shopping mall, or a business park. Consider the needs of your business, weigh your options, and select a facility that will serve your business well.

✓ **The community.** Where do you want to set up shop? Would you prefer the suburbs or the city? The type of business you start will help determine where you should locate your firm. For example, retail businesses rely on heavy foot and vehicular traffic, so they must be situated in high-visibility areas where they can be exposed to their potential target markets. Consider an area's population, economic infrastructure, and resident demographics before you hang out your shingle. All of these elements will impact the success of your operation.

✓ **Structure of the facility.** The type of business you operate will determine the general makeup of your facility. Retail and service businesses largely depend on customers' filing in and out of their stores, so they must pay particular attention to the appearance of the building. Manufacturing firms are less concerned with aesthetics because customers don't normally enter their doors. Define the type of business you operate, and your specific needs, when surveying a site's structure. You may need extensive parking, loading dock facilities, and a solid security system to effectively operate your firm. Focus your search on the buildings that match your requirements.

✓ **Cost.** How much you will spend on securing a site will depend on a number of factors, including the location and style of a building. Few new business owners are able to purchase a building outright. Instead, most new entrepreneurs lease office space. Rental rates vary according to the area, but you can expect to pay anywhere from $10 to $50 per square foot.

CHECKLIST *(continued)*

✓ **Proximity to your customers, competition, employees, and/or suppliers.** Depending on the type of business you start, you may need to locate near your customers, competitors, employees, and/or suppliers. Setting up shop near your customers gives them easy access to your company and increases your chances of gaining their business. Locating near the competition can be good or bad, depending on the goals you have set for your business. If you hope to develop a synergy with competing firms, you may want to hang out your shingle in the same area, on the same street, or even next door. Situating your company near employees and suppliers allows easier access to your business. If you need to be in close proximity to any of these groups, review the distance to major highways, airports, bus stations, and other means of transportation.

✓ **Zoning regulations.** Some communities prohibit certain types of business altogether; others impose strict limitations that may make it difficult for you to operate your business effectively. Zoning is a major concern among home-based entrepreneurs. Before you set up shop, investigate the zoning ordinances in your area. Avoid being slapped with a fine by taking the time to find out what is permissible and what is not.

✓ **Leasing a facility.** Because most new business owners do not have enough start-up capital to purchase a building, they lease office space. Leasing a facility requires more than just combing through the classifieds. Work with a commercial real estate agent or broker who can help you find the space that you need, at a price that you can afford.

✓ **Setting up your office.** Wherever you locate your business, you will have to create a productive office environment. Home-based entrepreneurs should choose an isolated part of the house to conduct business. Kitchen tables and family rooms are out. The basement or a spare bedroom is a possibility. If you work in an office apart from your home, the layout of your space should be organized and efficient. Keep all important reference books and materials at arm's length, and pick out comfortable, professional-looking furniture for yourself and the customers who will enter your waiting room.

RESOURCES FOR MORE INFORMATION

ASSOCIATIONS

- *Bureau of Labor Statistics (BLS),* 2 Massachusetts Avenue, NE, Washington, DC, 20212; 202-606-5886; www.bls.gov. The Bureau of Labor Statistics provides economic information concerning employment and unemployment according to region, employment projections, social living conditions, and technology trends in the labor market. You can use this government agency to help you pinpoint the best areas to locate your business and find the most qualified pools of workers.

- *Home Office Association of America (HOAA),* 909 Third Avenue, Suite 990, New York, NY 10022; 800-809-4622; www.hoaa.com. This organization provides a variety of services for the home-based business owner, including a monthly newsletter containing information about trends in the work-at-home environment. It also offers discounts on travel, long-distance phone service, and hotel accommodations, as well as access to group health insurance plans.

- *National Association of Home-Based Businesses (NAHBB),* 10451 Mill Run Circle, Suite 400, Owings Mills, MD 21117; 410-363-3698; www.worldhomebiz.com, www.ameribiz.com. NAHBB is the oldest home-based business group in the country. It services more than 200 classifications of home businesses and offers a home-based business occupational handbook to guide you through the steps of setting up your work-at-home environment.

- *National Association for the Self-Employed (NASE),* P.O. Box 612067, DFW Airport, Dallas, TX 75261-2067; 800-232-NASE (6273); www.nase.org. NASE advises home-based entrepreneurs about how best to operate their businesses, and offers materials detailing the latest news and trends concerning home-based firms. The organization also serves as an advocate for self-employed individuals by defending critical issues in Washington.

- *National Business Incubation Association (NBIA),* 20 East Circle Drive, Suite 190, Athens, Ohio 45701; 740-593-4331; www.nbia .org. NBIA is a nonprofit association that supports the business incubation industry. The organization provides statistical information concerning business incubators worldwide, as well as publications that cater to the needs of entrepreneurs working in these types of facilities.

RESOURCES FOR MORE INFORMATION *(continued)*

- *National Foundation for Women Business Owners (NFWBO)*, 1100 Wayne Avenue, Suite 830, Silver Spring, MD 20910-5603; 301-495-4975; www.nfwbo.org. NFWBO is considered to be a major source of information and statistics for women business owners. The organization assists female entrepreneurs with all aspects of launching their ventures, and provides ongoing support as their operations mature.

- *Small Office Home Office Association International (SOHOA)*, 1767 Business Center Drive, Suite 450, Reston, Virginia 20190; 703-438-3000; www.sohoa.com. This organization extends a variety of benefits to the home-based entrepreneur, including access to insurance programs, leasing services, business consulting, and discounts on office supplies.

- *U.S. Bureau of Census*, 4700 Silver Hill Road, Washington, DC 20233; 301-457-4100; www.census.gov. The Census Bureau is a one-stop shop for social, demographic, and economic data. It is a great tool to use in researching areas in which you would like to locate your business. The government agency provides published reports detailing businesses in several industries—for example, retail, manufacturing, agriculture, and wholesale—and the populations of the areas in which they are located. The bureau operates regional offices throughout the nation.

6

INSURANCE AND LICENSES

From the moment you decide to hang out your shingle, you assume a number of risks that, if not managed properly, can cost you your entire business. Suppose a few of your employees work on inventory after closing time. While counting the stock items, the workers decide to smoke. They crush their cigarette butts too near a stack of papers and cause the entire building to burn down. How would you handle this tragedy? Scream at the workers, then fire them? Throw your hands in the air and decide to scrap the business entirely? Or use your property insurance policy to help you shoulder the loss and begin recovery?

All businesses, large or small, need business insurance to protect against loss. Any uninsured loss can threaten your financial well-being and the livelihood of your operation, so this is one area in which you will not want to cut corners. There are several types of insurance that every business owner has to secure. They may include property, malpractice, liability, and business interruption. The specific coverage you will need will depend on the type of business you operate and where the business is located.

As a new entrepreneur, you may also need to obtain a license and/or permit. Many business owners regard licensing requirements solely as a tax-collecting strategy instituted by city, state, and federal governments, but licensing also protects the general public by showing that a business has complied with local regulations. Many licensing bureaus implement zoning ordinances to control the types of businesses that are permissible in a particular area, so check the zoning laws in your area before setting up shop. Failure to comply with regulations not only puts you at risk, but might expose the general public to potential danger. For instance, if your jurisdiction does not permit home-based businesses that produce food, and you set up a cookie company in the basement of your home, you could be slapped with heavy fines. Your noncompliance could also expose your neighbors to a potential health hazard if, for example, supplies must be stored outdoors and offensive odors are produced.

The first part of this chapter will discuss the types of business insurance that you may need to obtain. The list of insurance types is not meant to be all-inclusive. No two businesses are the same, and some may require additional coverage. To learn about the types of insurance that would apply to your business, check with an insurance agent or an attorney.

This chapter will also discuss the licenses and permits that new entrepreneurs may be required to secure before opening for their first day in business.

INSURING YOUR BUSINESS

Many entrepreneurs view business insurance as a luxury that only large businesses can afford. As a small business owner, you have other start-up expenses to consider, such as paying your employees and suppliers, and creating advertising campaigns for your product or service. Nonetheless, purchasing business insurance should also be at the top of your checklist. Why? Because if you do not have the right type *and* the right amount of insurance to protect you against casualties, legal hazards, and other losses, you could lose your business.

Tuesday Brooks, president of Ajoy Management Enterprises, learned the hard way the importance of having adequate coverage. Brooks launched her company in 1994 as a sole proprietorship. Like many new business owners, she did not have enough capital to acquire all the things she needed to get her public relations/small business services support company off the ground, so she cut corners. Unfortunately, she chose to forgo securing health and disability insurance (coverage that is vital to sole proprietorships), and it cost her plenty. "I became ill and was unable to work for six months," Brooks says. "Not only did I not generate any income for this period (which a disability policy would have helped to cover) but I had to pay all of my medical bills out of my own pocket."

When she decided to obtain the appropriate coverage, in 1996, her insurance company did not want to cooperate. "I went to get a disability policy, but, because I had a preexisting condition, they didn't want to give it to me. They said, 'We'll reevaluate you in a year or two years,' and that's the most that they were willing to offer me. They didn't want to give me insurance at that time, so I had to go back to the agency with all of my paperwork from my doctor and specialist indicating that I was fine and now eligible for coverage. It took nearly two years for me to get everything in order and it turned out fine, but I wish I had put out the money in the beginning to get the insurance that I needed. It would have saved me a lot of time and headaches."

For new business owners, it's often difficult to pull together the money to pay the premiums. But consider the costs if a customer visits your establishment and slips and falls on throw rugs in the lobby. Or if a customer gets food poisoning after eating one of the cakes you've prepared in your small town bakery. Or if a fire damages the area where you keep important computer files and your entire accounts receivable records. Any of these tragedies can turn into your worst nightmare, if you are not properly insured.

Some business owners avoid risks by subcontracting part(s) of the business that may involve potentially dangerous activities. Others prevent risks by instituting safety programs and fire prevention rules for employees. But most business owners share the risks by transferring some of it to an insurance company.

The types of insurance you will need depend on the type and location of your operation. No matter which type of insurance you choose, it will generally fall under one of these three basic types of coverage:

1. *Liability:* General liability, product liability, automobile, workers' compensation, and "umbrella" insurance.
2. *Property:* Vehicle damage, comprehensive damage, fire, crime, and inland marine.
3. *Special coverages:* Surety bonds, plate glass, credit life, and business interruption.

Liability Insurance

As an entrepreneur, you will come in daily contact with customers, suppliers, employees, and delivery personnel, all of whom can file a lawsuit against you if you are negligent. Ignoring such simple tasks as shoveling your entranceway after a heavy snowstorm or installing fire extinguishers and smoke detectors can prove fatal to the life of your business if someone is injured or, even worse, killed.

By purchasing liability insurance, you protect yourself against any devastating claims in the event you are sued. There are five basic types of liability insurance, some of which will apply to your business.

1. *General liability.* This type of policy will protect you from several risks: having to make payments for bodily injury or property damage inflicted by an employee; medical expenses generated as a result of an accidental injury on your premises; legal fees incurred as

a party to a lawsuit, including investigations and settlements; and costs for bonds or judgments required during the appeals process. General liability comes with certain exclusions and limitations; for example, you will not be held liable if an injury is caused by terrorist activities or if someone has entrusted their property to you. The limitations surrounding general liability are determined based on each person and each accident.

2. *Product liability.* An owner's worst nightmare can come true if someone gets sick or injured from using his or her product. In case it happens to you, you will want to be prepared and protected. Product liability insurance protects you by covering the products you manufacture and/or sell. When purchasing product liability insurance, you should provide coverage not only for yourself but for everyone who comes in contact with your product. The amount of coverage you should have will depend on the type of product you offer. For example, your premiums will be high if you manufacture the parachutes for sky diving, and low if you produce the zippers for bodysuits.

3. *Automotive liability.* If you need a vehicle for your business, you should purchase automotive liability insurance simply because if an unrelated business accident occurs, a court could rule in favor of the person filing the lawsuit. When shopping for a policy, make sure that it covers both business-related and non-business-related accidents. Any employee who has a valid driver's license and will be driving the car, van, or truck should be listed on the policy. If workers will use the company vehicle, you may secure "non-owned" coverage, which provides compensation for any injury to individuals, or property damage, caused by your employees.

   A typical automotive liability insurance policy includes liability insurance and property damage insurance. Liability insurance provides compensation to individuals who are capable of suing you for personal injury, damage to their property as a result of an accident, medical expenses, and loss of earnings. Property damage insurance (which generally includes collision and comprehensive coverage) pays you for any damage to your car due to accident, fire, theft, vandalism, earthquake, flood, or riot. Premiums for auto insurance will vary according to the type of vehicle you own. For example, if you use a 1998 four-door Ford Expedition, your premium will be higher than if you have a 1975 Chevy pick-up truck.

4. *Workers' compensation.* This type of insurance is required by law in all states. It protects an employer from liability in the event an employee is injured on the job. Workers' compensation pays for the employee's medical expenses and lost wages. In case of disability or death, the policy will pay a lump sum or annuities to the workers' dependents. You can decrease the cost of this coverage by maintaining a safe work

environment and by implementing and enforcing an employee safety program. Also, consider the types of workers you intend to hire. People who are very accident-prone can quickly raise your insurance rates and create premiums that will eat away at your profits.

5. *Professional malpractice.* Professional malpractice insurance, also known today as "malpractice insurance," "professional insurance," and "errors and omissions protection," is not just for doctors anymore. It is available to a number of different specialists: accountants, attorneys, computer analysts, consultants, dentists, occupational therapists, real estate agents, and data processors. This type of coverage protects you if you make costly mistakes while servicing or advising a customer or client. A physician who misdiagnoses a fatal disease could obviously be sued for malpractice, but so could a real estate agent who sells a house not knowing that it has faulty wiring that could spark a three-alarm fire. A professional policy can cover your client's losses. Consult your insurance agent, local trade association, or business group for information concerning coverage for your particular line of work. Here are a few factors to consider when shopping for your malpractice policy:

- *Coverage will not include intentional wrongdoing.* If you or one of your workers purposely injures a client, most likely your policy will not offer protection.

- *Professional insurance is not your license to be careless.* Remember that there are limits to the amount of expenses your policy will cover. Be careful about making mistakes that could wipe out your maximum coverage and still leave enough expense to substantially hurt your business.

- *The time period of coverage varies.* It may take months or even years before the effects of a bad piece of advice from a financial consultant are felt. Some policies may only pay on claims filed when the coverage is active. Be sure to review the time period covered by the policy before you make your final decision to buy.

Property Insurance

Property insurance can protect you against a loss of business property whether it is a vehicle, inventory, or store fixtures. This type of policy generally covers the building itself and its contents. When securing this coverage, ask about any specific rules that could cause problems for your business.

When Rudy Shepard, president of Soft Stitch, acquired property insurance for his alterations and embroidery shop, he discovered that his business policy would not cover equipment taken off of the business premises. On many days, Shepard loads his company trailer with embroidery machines. He carries the equipment to flea markets, boat and horse shows, and motorcycle rallies, where he performs on-the-spot stitching of hats, T-shirts, and jackets for customers. He needed coverage in case someone hit the trailer and destroyed the equipment inside, or simply stole the vehicle outright, but Shepard's insurance company would not offer the coverage at first.

"My insurance needs overlap because I haul my equipment around to various shows. But when I went to purchase property insurance, the company said it would not cover the equipment I carried inside my trailer even though it was an integral part of my business," says Shepard. "They indicated that my automobile insurance would most likely cover this type of peril, but when I approached my automobile insurance company, they said they would not cover it either because it fell under a different category. I was in a catch-22 situation, so what I did was talk with my property insurance company about creating an overlapping policy and the two agencies worked out coverage that protected me whether my equipment was inside my building or on the road with me. It raised my premiums a little bit, but it was worth it because I use machines worth $30,000 to $40,000, and I can't afford to have somebody run into the back of me and tear them up."

To ensure the broadest and most comprehensive protection for your business, secure "all-risk" forms of property insurance. If you do not, you will have to purchase a separate policy for each item, and this can become very expensive. "All-risk" forms of property insurance cover virtually all mishaps (except for a few exclusions) that may occur during the operation of your business. Here are the types of coverage you should consider buying:

- *Automobile.* If your policy is comprehensive, it will cover expenses for collision damage done to your car, truck, or van, and any physical damage caused by such perils as fire and vandalism.
- *Crime.* This type of insurance can safeguard your business against a number of risks. For example, crime coverage can protect you against losses due to employee theft or the burglarizing of your safe.
- *Fire.* Fire insurance policies are standard in the United States. They cover fire and lightning. When purchasing fire insurance, you should get a comprehensive "all-risks" extended perils policy. This will cover such threats as hail, vandalism, and windstorms, as well as fire. Certain types of policies can be purchased to protect confidential records, important computer files, and accounts receivable records.
- *Inland marine.* This type of coverage protects high-risk mobile items of significant value that are not covered by your regular commercial property policy. However, it can also protect valuable tools, such as those used by jewelry makers, artists, and other skilled tradespeople.

- *Cargo.* A cargo policy covers the cost for any loss involving inventory carried on board a business vehicle.

Special Insurance

A number of additional coverages may be needed to insure your business. These can include boiler and machinery coverage, and rain and water damage. Consult your insurance agent for a complete listing of the types of policies that could benefit your company. Here are just a few that you may want to consider:

- *Business interruption.* If your business has to temporarily shut down because of a fire, flood, earthquake, or other mishap, you may lose sizable profits and the resources to meet operating expenses (employees' salaries, and debts to suppliers). Business interruption insurance will cover the costs of any losses caused by such perils. For small businesses, this type of coverage is crucial because they have limited resources and, more often than not, cannot successfully ride out a time of decreased profits without sustaining significant, if not permanent, damage. According to Sean Mooney, in *Insuring Your Business*,[1] even after your business has resumed normal operations, it may take you a while to regain your customers' trust or to secure new clients who take the place of the old ones. For this reason, you may want to purchase extended business interruption insurance, to cover a specified period of time after your business is back on its feet. You can purchase this coverage in 30-day blocks, to a limit of 360 days.
- *Surety bonds.* Also known as performance bonds, this type of coverage protects against losses that result from others' failure to follow through on a commitment. Construction firms use surety bonds quite heavily. This type of bond guarantees that the promised work will be performed. Some insurance carriers require collateral, and most will ask for extensive documentation to give credence to the contracts you are bonding.
- *Credit life.* If your business will accept credit cards as a form of payment for your products or services, you may want to consider purchasing credit life insurance. This coverage will ensure that you are fully compensated for any outstanding debts of a customer if he or she dies before the payments are made. Typically, large retail firms secure credit life insurance.
- *Plate glass.* The windows of your business are just as important as any other aspect of your operation. This type of insurance covers specified panes of windows, plus signage.

ALTERNATIVES TO SECURING INSURANCE

Not every business owner will be able to afford the types of insurance coverage we have discussed.

If you cannot, don't panic; you can take some inexpensive alternative measures to ensure that your business is safe from harm.

Self-insurance is one alternative to consider if the premiums are just too high for your pocketbook. This type of insurance basically involves setting aside money for any unexpected events that may occur. The amount you choose to set aside is up to you; there is no standard. Many business owners file away the amount they would spend on premiums if they had purchased a commercial policy. Unless you are aggressive and consistent in putting money into a reserve fund, you may be vulnerable to the same risks as someone who has no insurance at all, because what you save may not be enough to cover the costs of major losses.

If you can afford only a little insurance, you may be able to supplement your package by creating and enforcing a solid risk-reduction/management plan. This can include a worker safety program as well as a fire prevention plan. The Insurance Information Institute, in a helpful brochure entitled *Insuring Your Business Against a Catastrophe*, provides the following four-point catastrophe recovery strategy.

1. *Minimize the risk of damage in advance of an emergency.* Fire is always a threat to businesses. To reduce the chances that a blaze could wipe out your operation, teach fire safety to your employees, particularly those responsible for indoor and outdoor maintenance, storage areas, and other sites, throughout the premises, where flammable substances are used or stored. Prohibit smoking, or limit it to certain areas. Update your electrical system and have an appropriate number of fire extinguishers accessible. When choosing your location, look for a site that is fire-resistant, or a building with a fire alarm system connected to the local fire department. To minimize damage from earthquakes, floods, or violent windstorms, make sure the structure of your building is sound and the materials used are top quality.

2. *Develop a disaster recovery plan.* Your disaster recovery plan is underway if you keep duplicate documents. If a natural disaster wipes out important data, such as your accounts receivable records, it is often difficult, if not impossible, to recreate them. To avoid this problem, back up important files and records, and store the copies off-premises, perhaps in a locked safe-deposit box at your local bank or in a secure area in your home. Keep a list of any equipment you own or lease. Note the serial number and model if they are not indicated on your proof of ownership or your lease documents.

Identify your critical business activities and the resources you would need to support them in the event of a disaster. Most businesses, particularly small operations, cannot afford to shut down while disaster recovery is taking place. To keep your operation running as smoothly as possible, decide in advance what you would need to do to sustain your market share. Which activities would need to be carried out? Which employees would you need to perform the work? If you had to lay off some of your workers, could they easily be rehired? What equipment, machines, and tools would you need?

Plan for the worst-case scenario by finding alternative facilities, equipment, and supplies, and by locating qualified contractors. If you need specialized equipment or a special location to operate, consider asking a business counterpart for a reciprocity agreement (a pact that allows one business to share facilities with another in the community). Two businesses often can help each other regain equilibrium by sharing space and equipment, or selling merchandise to each other. To avoid having to fumble around for important papers after a disaster strikes, keep on hand a list of firms that can supply equipment, raw materials, and tools in an emergency. If possible, get an advance commitment from at least one company that, in the event of a disaster, it will respond to your recovery needs.

Next, set up an emergency response plan, and train employees in how to administer it. To avoid panic, make sure that employees know whom to notify and what measures to take to minimize further loss. For example, make sure they know how to call the fire department and to evacuate the building if necessary. Consider the things you would need during an emergency: a back-up source of power, a cell phone, a first-aid kit, and a supply of flashlights, batteries, candles, and matches.

Document each step of the plan, and assign duties to individual employees in clear and simple language. Practice the procedures on a regular basis. Mini-drills will ensure that everyone understands how the plan is to be carried out.

Compile a list of the phone numbers and addresses of your employees, company officials, local and state emergency management agencies, major clients, contractors, suppliers, financial institutions, insurance agents, realtors, and insurance company claim representatives. Keep copies of this list off-premises at a remote area or at home.

Decide on a communications strategy to prevent loss of clients. Whether you decide to set up temporary headquarters or shut down for the duration of the disaster recovery, you will want to notify your customers about your plans to reopen for regular business activity. You can do this by posting notices outside your premises or by contacting your customers via telephone or mail. You can also place a small notice in the local newspaper.

3. *Review your insurance program.* Make sure that your commercial insurance policy covers indirect expenses caused by a disaster, as well as the cost of repair or rebuilding. Review your business's property insurance, business interruption insurance, and extra expense insurance (for outlays beyond your normal operating expenses).

4. *Review on a regular basis all the components of your disaster recovery strategy.* Go over each portion of your disaster recovery strategy, and notify key employees about any changes that have been made.

INSURANCE FOR THE HOME-BASED BUSINESS

According to the Insurance Information Institute, about 12 million Americans are operating businesses from their homes. But when they set up shop at home, many make the mistake of not properly insuring their company. Many business owners assume that their homeowner's policy will cover their business, but home-based firms have insurance needs that are not covered by a homeowner's policy.

A comprehensive homeowner's policy typically covers risks associated with home ownership. Some of the perils covered are:

- Damage to the home and personal property, by fire, storm, or lightning.
- Theft or loss of personal property.
- Damage caused by vandalism or a riot.
- Damage caused by falling objects such as rocks or tree limbs.
- Medical and legal liabilities for individuals who are injured by accident while visiting or staying in your residence.
- For those living in the home, reimbursement for injuries caused by fire, wind, or storm damage.
- Liability for injury or damage caused by pets; however, certain exotic animals are not covered. For example, if you own a baby tiger, most likely your policy will not cover your pet's activities.

The risks generally *not* covered by a homeowner's policy include:

- Liabilities as a result of business activity in the home.
- Damage caused by earthquakes, soil erosion, and other ground movements. (California requires coverage for earthquakes.)
- Flood damage, including water damage caused by a hurricane.

A home-based entrepreneur should obtain several types of insurance. Consult an insurance agent—ideally, one who specializes in home-based businesses—for a complete listing. Here are some of the types of coverage a home-based firm should purchase:

- *Property insurance.* If your home business is burglarized, or a fire wipes out your business equipment and inventory, you will need to purchase property insurance. Most homeowners' policies do not cover such risks. Those that offer coverage for business property have a cap on the amount: up to $2,500 for business property in the home, and up to $250 for damage caused to business property outside of the home.
- *Liability insurance.* Your homeowner's policy will not cover injuries to customers, employees, suppliers, or other professionals visiting your

home business. You will need separate business liability coverage. Home-business professionals will also need to obtain professional liability insurance. If you operate a home business that sells and/or produces food, you should secure product liability insurance to cover the costs of injuries to persons using your product. You may also want to consider an umbrella policy, which would pay for losses in excess of the limits of your existing policy. For example, if you are responsible for a customer's injury that requires $200,000 in medical care, but your liability limit is only $100,000, your umbrella policy will pay the difference of $100,000.

- *Car insurance.* Your home business may require the use of a car or truck. Many personal automobile insurance policies also cover the business use of your vehicle, but, depending on the type of home business you operate and the automobile you have, you may be required to have a separate auto policy. Check with your insurance agent.

- *Business interruption.* If your home is damaged by a fire or other disaster, it may interrupt your normal business activities for a prolonged time. This type of insurance will provide coverage for loss of income, in the event you must temporarily shut down operations.

- *Workers' compensation.* If you plan to have employees, then plan on providing workers' compensation. As previously discussed, this insurance will cover the cost of medical expenses and lost income, in case an employee is injured while on the job.

Obtaining Coverage for Your Home Business

Home-based business owners can purchase insurance for their operations in several ways. Entrepreneurs can purchase an endorsement or "policy rider" for their homeowner's policy. A policy rider is an additional provision, agreed on by you and your agent, that is added to your existing policy at an additional cost. If your home business does not require a constant flow of traffic in and out of the facility, or does not involve storage of hazardous materials or huge amounts of inventory, your agent may be able to offer you a relatively inexpensive rider for your homeowner's policy.

As a policy rider, some insurance companies will offer property and liability insurance for what they consider "incidental" businesses run from the home. Each company may define "incidental" differently; a common description is: those that gross less than $5,000 each year.

If you cannot get additional coverage through a policy rider, you will need to purchase business owner's insurance. A business owner's policy (BOP) covers, for business property, the same kind of risks as the homeowner's policy. For example, if a huge rock from a nearby cliff rolls down, falls through the roof of your house, and wipes out an expensive copy machine used in your home-based public relations firm, your homeowner's policy would cover only the expenses to repair the roof. If you have a business coverage rider to your homeowner's policy or a BOP, your copy machine would be covered as well.

BOPs are usually made available to small businesses, such as retail shops. Restaurants and wholesale manufacturers are generally not eligible for this type of policy because they have specialized insurance needs that a BOP cannot provide. According to Sean Mooney,[2] home business owners are eligible for BOPs based on the following criteria:

1. Size of the premises.
2. Limits of liability required.
3. Type of commercial operation.
4. The extent of off-premises servicing and processing activities.

If you operate a restaurant or manufacturing company and cannot obtain a business owner's policy, you will need to purchase a commercial policy. This type of coverage is generally more expensive than a BOP, but it is more flexible. Commercial policies are also more complex and difficult to understand than a BOP, so consult your insurance agent if this is the type of coverage you will need. These policies protect you against certain basic risks. They may extend to other risks, but only through the purchase of additional coverage based on the needs of your business.

Some insurance companies offer mini-packages designed specifically for home-based entrepreneurs. Most of these policies cover:

- Loss or destruction of business property on or off the business premises.
- Loss of important business information.
- Accounts receivable up to $10,000.
- Money lost on premises (up to $5,000), and off premises (up to $2,000).
- Personal injury and advertising liability.
- Expenses and lost income for up to a year if a risk that is insured suspends business operation for up to one year.

Insurance companies that offer these types of packages often require that your homeowner's and car insurance polices be purchased from them.

Regulations for Your Home Business

If you plan to operate your business from your home, one of your first steps is to research the zoning regulations in your area (see Chapter 5). Not all areas permit home-based businesses; those that do may impose restrictions that make working out of your residence impossible.

Local zoning laws may restrict (1) your right to build a separate structure for business purposes and (2) the number of employees you are allowed to have. If the zoning laws forbid your type of home business, you can try filing a variance or "conditional use" permit (which would allow you to operate your business in an area not zoned for that purpose). Generally speaking, variances are granted only if:

- The existing ordinance would bring financial hardship.
- The type of home business you intend to launch already exists in the area.
- The type of home business you want to start would bring no harm to the community.

To get information about zoning ordinances in your area, contact your local planning department or zoning board; check the Blue Pages of your phone book or contact city hall for the telephone numbers. If you live in an apartment, condominium, or co-op, be sure to check the terms of your lease before setting up shop. If your home-based business violates zoning rules, technically you could be shut down completely, but the laws are generally enforced only when complaints are filed. Before you open for business, talk with your neighbors about what you intend to do. You needn't be specific about the intimate details of your operation. Simply put them on notice that you will be running a business from your home. As long as your business doesn't create extreme noise, offensive odors, tons of traffic, or other residential no-no's, you will probably not run into zoning problems.

When starting a home-based business, the relationships that you establish with residents in your neighborhood are crucial, not only to your business and professional life, but also to your personal life. Your home-based business is not just your place of work, it is also where you live during nonwork hours. If neighbors file enough complaints against your business, you may have to pick up and move altogether.

WEIGHING THE AMOUNT AND COST OF INSURANCE

After you determine the types of coverage you need for your business, whether home-based or not, you must consider how much insurance you will need. Buying too much insurance could drain valuable income from your business, but buying too little protection could leave you vulnerable to losses and liability.

The amount you should devote to insurance hinges on the type of business you operate. The best way to find a figure that is right for you is to discuss your needs with an insurance agent. If you intend to purchase property insurance, you should know:

- *Your property's value.* How much does it actually cost to purchase a piece of property and how much would it cost to replace it if it was damaged? Depending on the type of property that you purchase, you can acquire coverage for the actual or replacement value of the item. If you obtain actual value insurance, the policy will pay for the actual value of the property at the time it was damaged or lost. Replacement value insurance, which can be written for buildings, fixtures, and equipment, pays a specified amount for repairs to damaged property or to replace it with similar property. Insurance for the replacement of property may be more expensive than its actual value, so seriously consider what your company absolutely needs or can do without, before opting to insure a property for replacement value.

- *Your lender's limits.* Most banks specify a certain level of insurance that must be maintained on any piece of property purchased with loan dollars. If you are about to insure some property that you purchased through a loan, determine how much coverage is required under your loan agreement. If you do not meet that level, the bank may have the right to foreclose or to purchase its own insurance on the property.

Determining how much liability insurance is needed is perhaps more difficult for a new business owner. If you intend to obtain liability coverage, you should know:

- *Your people.* Ask yourself a few critical questions about yourself and your staff. Are your employees skilled professionals with years of experience, or high school teenagers? Are you, or your employees, accident prone? You don't want to purchase the minimum amount of liability insurance on your company car, for example, and find out later that several of your workers have numerous violations and outstanding tickets for reckless driving.

- *Your business.* Have you set up a sole proprietorship or a corporation? Each has a different level of liability (see Chapter 4). If you run a corporation and satisfy all the requirements for operating under this legal business form, you may be sufficiently covered if you buy insurance with lower limits. If you are sued, only the assets of the corporation will be tapped to pay any claims. However, if you operate as a sole proprietorship, you are personally responsible for all obligations of the business, and you will need a greater amount of liability coverage.

- *Any legal minimums.* Ask your agent whether there are any minimum insurance levels set by law. Also, find out whether the limits are higher or lower, based on the type of business you operate. For example, if you operate a pizza delivery service, some states will impose higher automobile liability limits.

Buying Your Insurance Package

The general rule of thumb, when buying insurance, is to choose the highest deductible you can afford. Your premiums will then be set at a more manageable level.

Your insurance rates will depend on a number of factors, including the type of insurance you purchase. For example, health insurance rates are typically affected by your age, gender, occupation, and family history, as well as your health. If there is a history of cancer in your immediate family, for example, your insurance company may impose a higher rate on your health insurance.

Life insurance rates are also dictated by your age, gender, occupation, family health history, and personal health. Property insurance rates hinge on where your business is located. For example, if you situate your shop in a high-crime area, your insurance rate may be slightly higher. Auto insurance rates are determined by such factors as the type of vehicle you own, the number of licensed drivers using it, the number of miles traveled to and from work every day, and the installation of anti-theft protection.

You can purchase your insurance policies through an independent agent or broker, or directly from an insurance company (which may then assign an agent to your account), or through a professional or business organization, a bank, or a mortgage/credit company. Insurance providers are listed in the Yellow Pages under "Insurance," but word-of-mouth is perhaps the best way to find a reputable representative. If you know people who operate businesses similar to yours, ask whom they use or would recommend. You can also contact your state insurance department for information about which insurance companies are licensed, and whether any punitive actions have been brought against them.

As a new business owner who must satisfy numerous demands for cash, it is important that you keep your insurance costs as low as possible. Besides opting for high deductibles, you can lower your costs by purchasing your insurance through group plans available from trade associations and other business-related groups and organizations. When shopping for insurance, however, you should never shop for price alone. Look for a package that meets your business budget, but don't sacrifice quality for price.

Here is a list of guidelines for purchasing insurance:

- Choose an insurance company that understands your type of business and exhibits concern about your company. You will want to develop a long-term relationship with the agency you choose, so make sure there is some compatible chemistry.

- Evaluate your relationship with your insurance representative. Are you comfortable sharing your business information? Can you trust that it will be kept strictly confidential?

- Choose a representative who will be willing to help with risk management, in addition to advising which insurance packages to buy.

- Get proposals from two or three brokers and agents. Compare their prices and your general impression of their professional expertise.

- Be forthright with your insurance agent at all times. For example, if you plan to operate your business from your home, say so. It may mean spending a little more for certain coverages, but, in the long run, it will save you money and many headaches.

- Ask about discounts. Many insurance companies offer lower rates to business owners who use smoke detectors or security systems, or who routinely drive a low number of miles each year.

- Keep detailed records of your insurance policies and premium payments. They will be needed at tax time because premiums for fire and burglary insurance of business property are tax-deductible as trade or business expenses.

- Keep in touch with your business's insurance representative. Just as you would notify the agent or representative who handles your homeowner's policy that you will be adding a room onto your house, you should inform your agent about any additional business equipment or inventory that you have acquired and would like to insure. If you do not give that notice and you suffer damage to a piece of new equipment, your existing policy may not provide coverage.

LICENSING YOUR BUSINESS

When Todd Alexander started Vendemmia Inc. (*vendemmia* means harvest in Italian) in 1993, like most new business owners he began the procedure to obtain his license. Because Alexander planned to import fine Italian wines to Atlanta, he had to file for state and federal licenses. Alexander filled out the necessary forms, but, after two months of waiting, he had received no notice or reply.

"I expected it to take about 30 days, so, after two months, I began to wonder about the status of my application," he says. "I contacted the office and they told me that they were working on it and were about to send out an investigator to check out my business. I said okay, but they didn't get around to doing this until 30 days later, and they looked under every rock as if I were doing something illegal. A month after that, I still heard nothing about my license, so I contacted the office again, but this time they told me they lost my application. At this point, I was livid, but how livid can you get with the federal government when you're trying to get your license? So I resubmitted the application. After a few more questions here and another investigation there, they finally issued me a license, but that was nine months later."

Alexander credits the due diligence to the type of business he owns. "They will do a fair amount of research on who they grant a license to because, when you start issuing federal import licenses, it allows you to bring in things from anywhere in the world, which obviously opens up a lot of avenues. But I don't think everybody has to wait as long as I did to get a license."

Securing the appropriate license for your business can be a challenging task; nonetheless, virtually every new entrepreneur must have certification from the outset. Most entrepreneurs will have to secure a local business or "municipal" license, which permits them to operate their company within the confines of their city. Others, like Alexander, may have to obtain a license from the state and federal governments. The certifications you may be required to secure include:

- *County license.* If you want to start your business outside of a municipality, in an unincorporated area, you will be required to apply for a county license.
- *State license.* Also known as an occupational permit or a state occupational license, this is mandatory for doctors, lawyers, general contractors, real estate brokers, insurance agents, and day care providers. Contact your state government for a list of occupations that require this type of certification. Eligible business owners will have to pass a state test before their license is granted.
- *Federal license.* Only a few types of operations are required to secure this type of license. Among them are: radio and television stations, food processors, and businesses involved in alcohol or tobacco products. Contact the Federal Trade Commission to see whether your business qualifies.

The steps to securing a license are fairly straightforward. For an application, you must contact the business licensing division, county registrar's office, recorder's office, city hall, city clerk's office, or whatever agency issues licenses in your jurisdiction. Figure 6.1 is an example of a typical business license application. Licensing requirements vary according to each county, city, or state, so find out exactly what licenses are needed to operate in your area.

Filing fees also differ in various jurisdictions, and may be based on your projected annual gross income, the type of business you own, the number of employees you have, and where your business is located. For example, if you want to operate your business as a domestic corporation in New Jersey, the filing fee for your articles of incorporation is $100. If you set up shop in Tukwila, Washington, and have fewer than five employees, your annual licensing fee is $50. Alexander, whose business is located in Atlanta, Georgia, paid a state fee of $500, a tax liability bond fee of $250, and a registration fee of $125.

Figure 6.1   City of Seattle Application for Business License

FOR OFFICE USE ONLY		
CUSTOMER NR.		
OBLIG. NR.	AMT.	
OBLIG. NR.	AMT.	

CITY OF SEATTLE
Paul Schell, Mayor
APPLICATION FOR BUSINESS LICENSE

PLEASE PRINT OR TYPE

(1) LEGAL NAME _____

(2) TRADE NAME _____

(3) PHONE   (_____)_____

(3a) FAX (_____)_____

(3b) INTERNET ADDRESS _____

(4) BUSINESS ADDRESS _____
_____

(5) MAILING ADDRESS _____
_____

(6) State of Washington UBI # _____

(6a) SIC CODE_____

Federal Employer ID # _____

(7) Type of Business (Check one):

☐ Individual   ☐ Corporation

☐ Partnership   ☐ LLC

☐ Other (describe below)

(8) NATURE OF BUSINESS: ☐ Retail   ☐ Manufacturing   ☐ Printing/Publishing ☐ Wholesale   ☐ Service ☐ Other
  IMPORTANT: *DESCRIBE IN DETAIL PRINCIPAL PRODUCT OR SERVICE RENDERED:*

(9) STARTING DATE OF BUSINESS IN SEATTLE: _____/_____ / 199__

(10) IF YOU PURCHASED THIS BUSINESS, DID YOU TAKE OVER: ENTIRE BUSINESS? ☐   PORTION OF BUSINESS? ☐

FORMER OWNER'S NAME	ADDRESS	CITY, STATE, ZIP	TELEPHONE	CUSTOMER NUMBER

(11) OWNER, PARTNERS, CORPORATE OFFICERS, AND RESIDENT AGENTS: (Attach Separate Sheet, If Needed) List true name(s), residence address, telephone number and date of birth of applicant if a sole owner, or all partners if a partnership. If a corporation, list all officers and directors, giving titles, and all stockholders who directly or indirectly control 25% or more of the company's stock.

NAME AND TITLE	RES. ADDRESS	CITY, STATE ZIP	TELEPHONE DA	TE OF BIRTH

(12) OTHER BUSINESS LOCATIONS IN SEATTLE: (BRANCH LICENSE -- $10.00) Attach separate sheet for additional branches.

TRADE NAME	ADDRESS	CITY	ZIP	TELEPHONE	Separate tax return? ☐ Yes	☐ No
					☐ Yes	☐ No

(13) TAX REPORTING STATUS - CHECK ONE (See separate instructions on BUSINESS LICENSE TAX.)

☐   **QUARTERLY**   ,   Taxable income will exceed $50,000 per year.

☐   **ANNUAL**   Taxable income might (might not) exceed $50,000 per year.

(14) As applicant, I _____ certify or declare under penalty of perjury under the laws of the State of Washington that the foregoing is true and correct.

_____
Print Name

_____
Signature   Date

Office Use Only	Initials	Date
Processed by		
Tax Forms Made		
Reviewed for Reg's by:		
Reg's required?	Yes____	No____
Lic issued:		

(15) **License Fees Due** – MAKE CHECK PAYABLE TO: CITY OF SEATTLE

LICENSE FEE: **$75.00**/calendar year *(exp. 12/31/98)* **$37.50** if line 9 is July 1, 1998 or thereafter *(exp. 12/31/98)*

Additional Locations: _____ X $10.00= _____ , **TOTAL FEE (s) DUE: $**_____

Call or visit the appropriate licensing department in your area, for information on specific fees and necessary forms. If you plan to set up your business at multiple locations, you will have to apply for a license in each jurisdiction.

Your licensing application will be reviewed by the planning and zoning department to determine whether the area's zoning ordinances permit your type of business in that jurisdiction. If not, you could petition for a variance, but, as previously mentioned, these are not regularly granted and can be very expensive to obtain. Check with your lawyer before deciding to apply for a conditional-use permit.

Generally speaking, it can take anywhere from two to eight weeks for you to obtain your license—and it could take longer, depending on the type of business you own and the area where you want to set up shop.

Getting Your Permits

A number of local or state permits may also be required. Permits indicate that you have complied with all local and state laws governing the safety, structure, and appearance of a community. Check with your state government to see which permits may apply to your business. Common permits include:

- *Health permit.* Business owners selling or manufacturing perishable items (food) will be required to secure a health permit from their local or county health department. The fee varies according to the size of your business and the amount of equipment used to produce your product.
- *Fire permit.* If your business will introduce a constant flow of traffic by customers and employees, most fire departments will demand that you have a fire permit. Also, if your business requires the use of flammable and other hazardous materials, you will need this authorization. The types of businesses most likely to require a fire permit include (but are not limited to) restaurants, night clubs, and movie theaters.
- *Seller's permit.* Also referred to as a sales tax permit or number, this is required in states that impose sales tax. If you operate a retail outlet, you will be required to obtain one of these permits. They originate from your State Sales Tax Commission, but each state uses a different agency to issue such permits. Contact the organization that governs your taxes, and ask which agency can supply you with a seller's permit.

CHECKLIST

FACTORS TO CONSIDER WHEN BUYING INSURANCE

✓ **Your business needs.** Every operation needs insurance, but not every company will require the same types of coverage. You must define your business needs and select the coverage that is most appropriate for your firm. For example, if you operate a company that will produce food, you will need to secure product liability insurance.

✓ **Your insurance options.** Generally, the basic types of policy coverage fall into three categories: (1) liability (general liability, product liability, automotive liability, workers' compensation, and professional malpractice), (2) property (automobile, crime, fire, inland marine, and cargo), and (3) special (business interruption, credit life, plate glass, and surety bonds). These apply to home-based businesses as well as operations at a separate site.

✓ **Your alternatives to commercial coverage.** If you can't afford the premiums for certain coverages, you can opt to initiate several alternatives. For example, you can use self-insurance, in which you set aside the amount you would have spent if you had obtained a commercial policy. In addition, you can implement a solid risk reduction/management plan to reduce perils within your operation.

✓ **Insurance needs of a home-based business.** Most homeowners' policies do not cover business-related activities, so you will have to obtain a separate policy for a home-based operation. You may be able to add a "rider" to your homeowner's policy, or to obtain a business owner's policy (BOP).

✓ **Cost of premiums.** The general rule of thumb when purchasing insurance is to choose the highest deductible you can afford. This strategy will drive down your premiums. Insurance rates vary according to a number of factors. Contact your agent for specific rates.

✓ **Business licenses.** Virtually every business owner will have to acquire a county, city, state, and/or federal license. You must contact the appropriate licensing department in your area for an application. The waiting period usually ranges from two to eight weeks, but it can take longer, depending on the type of business you have and where you will locate.

✓ **Business permits.** Some operations will also require a health, fire, or seller's permit. Check with your state government office to see whether this requirement applies to your business.

RESOURCES FOR MORE INFORMATION

ASSOCIATIONS

- *Insurance Information Institute*, 110 William Street, New York, NY 10038; 212-669-9200; www.iii.org. The Insurance Information Institute is recognized by regulatory organizations, universities, governments, and the general public as a major source of information, analysis, and referral concerning insurance. The Institute handles more than 6,000 requests for information each year, including those regarding start-ups and their insurance needs. This organization also produces consumer brochures and studies about the property/casualty industry.

- *Service Corps of Retired Executives (SCORE)*, 409 3rd Street, SW, 4th Floor, Washington, DC 20024; 800-634-0245; www.score.org. Most SCORE offices have a list of the names and addresses of the city, county, state, and federal offices you will have to contact to begin the licensing procedure. SCORE can also provide you with information about permits and registration fees.

- *Society of Risk Management Consultants*, 300 Park Avenue, New York, NY 10022; 212-572-6246 or 800-765-SRMC; www.srmcsociety.org. This organization maintains a body of skilled consultants who examine businesses for potential liabilities and instructs them on how best to protect their operations. It also reviews organizations' insurance and risk management programs and makes recommendations regarding how business owners can improve their coverage.

- *U.S. Small Business Administration (SBA), Small Business Development Centers (SBDCs)*, 409 3rd Street, SW, Washington, DC 20416; 202-606-4000; SBA Answer Desk, 800-827-5722; www.sba.gov. The SBA maintains small business development centers throughout the country. They can provide you with information regarding how to obtain a license for your business, the fees required, and requirements that apply. Call the SBA Answer Desk to find a SBDC near you.

7

CREATING A WINNING BUSINESS PLAN

When Gilda and Amir Salmon decided to open their namesake hair salon (Gilda & Amir's Salon Inc.) in 1994, they visited neighborhood banks in search of seed money. Rarely can new shopkeepers obtain start-up capital from a bank, but the Salmons managed to walk away with a $30,000 small business loan from Bergen Commercial Bank in Paramus, New Jersey, and Paterson Economic Development Corporation, in Paterson, New Jersey.

What was their secret? Luck? A friend of a friend who helped pull some strings to have the loan approved? Neither. The Salmons had a solid business plan that projected the strength and viability of their operation. Throughout the plan, the Salmons indicated a number of crucial elements that helped them to seal the deal. For starters, they included one- to three-year financial projections with estimated earnings of $100,000 (which they exceeded within two years). They also highlighted their combined experience of 15 years in the hair care industry, their average client base of 200 customers per month, and the ability of their small operation to compete in the commercial market of Paterson, where minimalls were becoming a dominant force. In the view of the financial officers at the Economic Development Corporation, the Salmons had offered proof of their mettle as budding entrepreneurs. Today, their shop is still going strong, thanks to their well-crafted business plan.[1]

Whether you are a new business owner in search of start-up capital or an existing entrepreneur planning a new product introduction, you should have a written business plan. A business plan is essentially a blueprint that

149

defines the goals of your company and outlines in specific detail how you will go about achieving those goals. If done correctly, the plan can serve as a road map to guide you through the various life cycles of your operation.

Every business owner should craft this important document before hanging out a shingle, but few do. Instead, many business owners fly by the seat of their pants and manage to successfully sail through the first few years of their operation without a plan. However, when major problems crop up and threaten the life of their company, the owners must scramble to find and apply quick fixes.

Don Sutton, founder and president of Just Chairs, a furniture dealership in San Francisco, California, learned the hard way the value of having a business plan. Several years ago, through private placements, Sutton tried to raise $1 million as expansion capital. Like many business owners, he operated his firm without a business plan. That was his first mistake.

Sutton's second faux pas was hiring a business plan writer and an accountant to create the plan. The business plan writer directed the document's content, and the accountant developed the financial projections. "As a result, the business plan was too long and the numbers didn't pan out," he says.

Because the numbers were off target and the plan was too lengthy, Sutton's pitch to potential investors was flat, and his plans for a private placement stock offering were canceled. Still, Sutton says, creating the plan was a valuable learning experience. It forced him to scrutinize, in detail, his customers and competition. It also helped him to discover a large share of the company's potential market that he had initially overlooked—the discount arena. "We had been sitting on excess inventory that was crying out for an outlet," says Sutton, whose company focuses on corporate customers and the high end of home office businesses.

"Our customers didn't care if a fabric was discontinued. They wanted top quality goods at a good price," he says. To satisfy his expanded market, Sutton soon opened a clearance outlet that sold discontinued products at discounted prices. Just Chairs now competes with office superstores such as Office Depot and Office Max.

By creating a business plan, you can make new discoveries about your operation that could prove profitable, as was the case with Sutton's clearance store. You can also anticipate problems that could negatively impact your operation, and devise workable solutions in advance. But don't think you can craft a winning business plan overnight. Drafting this document is a very time-consuming process. It may take you six months to develop a plan that is solid and attractive to financial lenders, venture capitalists, suppliers, employees, and anyone else you may wish to woo with your venture, but, however long it takes to put your ideas on paper, the time will be well spent.

Having a business plan will impact your ability to secure financing. It will also help you to clearly define a number of other start-up issues, ranging from marketing strategies to operational procedures and equipment purchases.

In this chapter, we will discuss the benefits of crafting a business plan and will outline the main components of this critical document. Step-by-step instructions for developing a business plan will be given, but we advise that you seek assistance from several professionals who can help you pull the whole document together. For example, you may want to work with an accountant and/or a lawyer when crafting the financial plan, which is considered by many business owners to be the most difficult and important part of the business plan writing process. These experts can help you crunch numbers as well as review the financial statements and projections to be included in the plan.

If you are nervous about creating the entire document on your own and you have money to spare, you can enlist the help of a professional business plan writer, but learn from Sutton's mistake: Don't let the business plan writer create the document for you. All of the decisions regarding what information goes into the plan and how it will be structured to best represent *your* ideas, *your* strengths, *your* personality, and *your* goals for the company, rest with *you alone.* You should actively participate in the business planning process from start to finish. No one knows your business better than you.

WHY YOU NEED A BUSINESS PLAN

"If you fail to plan, you plan to fail." How many times have you heard this old adage? How many times have you ignored it or told yourself, "It's just an old cliché that does not apply to my business idea. After all, I've got a sure winner." All too often, entrepreneurs start wonderful businesses, but several years down the road their ventures take a quick nosedive simply because they did not take the time to plan.

You would never set out on a cross-country road trip without a plan outlining the routes you will take, how much money you will need for food and gas, and where and when you will sleep. You should not begin the journey of entrepreneurship without a clear sense of where you want your business to go and how you will get there.

Creating a business plan will force you to think through all of the essential factors that will impact the success of your operation. Virtually every entrepreneur will lay out, in his or her mind, the steps for launching a new business. But the odds are that you will not be able to recall every minute detail unless you put your ideas on paper. Drafting a written plan will help to ensure that you have not omitted any significant factors that could kill your business. With a plan, it will be easier for you to communicate your ideas to potential investors, suppliers, partners, corporate boards of directors, and employees (if you choose to share the document with your staff). It's not practical to have to explain your ideas every time you intend to meet with professionals to discuss your business. With a written plan, you can make copies and distribute them to interested parties for their review.

The structure and content of your business plan will depend on a number of factors: the type of business you operate, your reasons for crafting the plan, and your status as an entrepreneur. For example, if you are a new business owner, you may require extensive planning of all aspects of your venture, from start-up financing to operational procedures. If you are an existing business owner trying to penetrate a new market, you may place more emphasis on the marketing strategies you will use to introduce your product or service into that arena. Whether you are new to ownership or a veteran of the game, a business plan can help increase your chances for success. Essentially, this document can be used for several purposes, as described in the following sections.

A Business Resume

Virtually every job seeker will give potential employers a resume that outlines his or her qualifications and experience. As an entrepreneur, you will need a "resume" to attract the attention of financial lenders, employees, suppliers, and other professionals whose help may be needed to successfully run your operation. Your business plan can serve as that resume. Whether you are starting a new business or growing an existing firm, you may need financing from a bank or other lending institution. To qualify for the necessary funds, you will have to present a business plan. "It's the first thing bankers ask to see," says Amir Salmon. "They want to know how much of your own money is invested in the business, and what you have to offer as collateral."

If you have been in business for several years and you want to obtain a loan—for example, to expand operations into a new market—chances are you have a track record of successes that might persuade lenders to invest in your new idea. Your business plan or resume can illustrate your accomplishments. If you are a new business owner, you do not have a history, financial or otherwise, to which you can refer for support. You must rely on what you *intend* to do with your business. You can outline your business goals, and your strategies for reaching those goals, in your business plan.

Investor "angels," venture capital firms, prospective partners, and even family and friends may also ask to see your business plan before pouring any money into your venture. A business plan can clearly indicate how their money will be used and their potential return on investment.

Suppliers and vendors may also want to review your business resume, particularly when negotiating prices and terms. The points you will be able to negotiate will vary with each vendor, but much of your bargaining power will hinge on how the vendor perceives your business. In short, the vendor will want to know whether your operation is capable of paying for goods supplied, and whether you will become a longtime customer (perhaps eligible for a break on price). Your business plan can illustrate how your cash flow will pay for deliveries, and whether your cash reserve allows you to honor all obligations.

Your business resume can also serve as a handy tool for introducing your business and its goals to potential employees. Not every business owner will want to share the entire document with prospective employees, but presenting portions of the plan to interested applicants (especially senior-level or executive personnel) could be the carrot you need to bring them on board for the long haul.

If you suspect that, to support your business, you will need ongoing funds from any investor, you should document how you have met or exceeded planned goals. The track record you develop could prove useful as your business matures.

A Schedule for Operations

A lot of factors go into running your own business. Everything—from setting the mission of your company to hiring employees, purchasing equipment, and surveying potential locations—must be handled in a timely and orderly fashion. A business plan will help you manage the interaction of all of these activities and create a timetable that will allow your business to stay on track. Essentially, a business plan provides a timeline of the events that will take place in the life of your company. For example, it contains your marketing plan, which outlines how you will define your target audience and how you will position your product or service to reach a selected group of people. It also features your operational procedures, which explain how you will carry out the day-to-day activities of running your own shop. Timing is particularly important. Let's say you have developed an eye-catching 30-second TV spot for a new product, but the product is not yet available. There is no point in running the ad. Your business plan cannot merely state your operational and marketing needs. It must also pinpoint the timeframe in which each activity will be carried out.

A Device for Tracking Business Progress

Every business owner wants to know whether his or her operation is progressing as expected, but many owners find it difficult to implement a simple method that will accurately indicate whether they are forging ahead. A business plan can provide real-time feedback about your firm. For example, if your financial projections indicate that sales will reach $500,000 within the first year, but, by the anniversary of your grand opening, you've barely earned $100,000, you can take the necessary steps to make adjustments.

Perhaps your projections were too ambitious, or you priced your items too high, which sent potential customers to lower-priced competitors. Whatever your problems, your business plan will help you ferret them out and will give you the insight needed to develop reasonable solutions. The only way for you to determine whether your business is progressing is to measure actual performance against expected or predicted performance, as outlined in your business plan.

An Instrument to Adjust Operations

Even if you spend countless hours creating a solid business plan, there is a chance that things may not work out as you had planned. You will then need to revise your document to better reflect your actual business performance. When developing your plan, consider all the factors that can either help or hurt your operation. If things start to go awry, use this information to help pinpoint where your business may have deviated from its predicted performance. For example, perhaps you hired too many employees or overstated your financial potential. Whatever the difficulty, a solid business plan will make troubleshooting within your organization much easier.

A Mechanism for Future Planning

The whole point of creating a business plan is to help you think about and prepare for the future of your operation. It gives you a starting point for considering how your business will fare 10, 20, or 30 years down the road. Developing this critical document forces you to constantly think about how you can improve your business, how you can continue to compete, what types of new products you may be able to offer, the types of new customers you may be able to attract, and a host of other issues. After the initial document is developed, you will need to refine and revise the plan to match the changing needs of your business or of the economy, but taking that first step to put your ideas and the assumptions you have about your business on paper can put you and your operation on the path to a brighter future.

WHEN YOU NEED A BUSINESS PLAN

Who needs a business plan? You do. If you're a longtime entrepreneur, you may consider it a waste of time, particularly if you've been operating successfully without it. But there are many instances in which even you will need to create this invaluable document.

Let's say, for example, that you've been in business for 20 years, and you want to launch a new line of products. To do this, you will need to consider a number of factors, including how much it will cost to launch the products, which customers the products will target, and how the products will be priced and advertised. All of these elements can be clearly defined in a business plan. You may be capable of committing all your plans to memory, but a written plan will help you realize the scope involved in developing your business idea and will red-flag any potential problems. You may find that your idea is not as doable as you had thought, and you will then have saved yourself a lot of wasted time, energy, and money trying to develop a product that is not feasible.

Before you decide to scrap the entire business plan writing process and move on to a "more pressing" task, consider what you're trying to do within your operation. A number of situations will require that you create a business resume. Let's consider each one.

Business Expansion

If your operation experiences growth, it will behoove you to develop a business plan that can explore the opportunities that you may take advantage of as a result of your expansion. For example, if you own a shoe store, and sales far exceed your expectations and projections, you may consider opening a second location. Creating a business plan will help you outline all the costs, advantages, and disadvantages involved in taking on the responsibilities of running a second store.

New Market Penetration

To reach a new market, you will have to address some of the issues you attacked when you first launched your business. Extensive and serious business planning will be needed. You can penetrate a new market in a number of ways: attract new customers, acquire a new distribution channel to reach a different consumer base, or enter a totally different geographic area. Whichever method you choose, you should outline your approach in your business plan.

New Product Introduction

If you are an established entrepreneur and you decide to launch a new product, your business plan can focus on the new item and your goals for promoting, pricing, and positioning it in the marketplace. But if you have not already determined the time and resources it will take to launch your new product, you will need to revisit your existing business plan and integrate these issues into that document. Even if you should decide to modify an existing product or repackage an item, you will need to outline your approach in a business plan.

Acquiring a Business Opportunity

Business opportunities can include the purchase of an existing business or franchise. Whichever you choose, you will need a business plan to help you successfully steer your operation. When they put their company on the market, many sellers use a "selling memorandum," which some experts call a business plan "in reverse." This document is similar to a business plan in that it lists information about the company that is for sale. You can use this document as a starting point for creating your own business plan. If you decide to purchase a franchise, a business plan will help you weigh the benefits of this opportunity against the costs and restrictions that apply to operating such ventures.

WHAT TO DO BEFORE YOU WRITE YOUR PLAN

If you are anxious about introducing your "revolutionary" product or service to the world, you may be tempted to jump feet-first into preparing your business plan. But before you put pen to paper, you must do a certain amount of prebusiness planning if you are to create a document that will successfully guide your operation through and beyond the start-up phase. Here are some issues you should consider before sitting down to write your business plan.

Identify Your Audience

When crafting your business plan, you must consider who will read it. Are you writing the plan for people outside your business (for example, bankers or vendors) or inside it (employees or board members)? By defining your audience, you will get a clear sense of how your plan should be formatted, the content that should be included, and the level of detail that is needed. For example, if you intend to attract commercial bankers with your plan, you will place more emphasis on the financial section of your document, because lenders will be more concerned with the financial stability of your operation than with your facility or salary structure. To help define whom you will target, divide your audience into two categories: internal and external.

Internal Audience
In this audience are key employees, co-owners, a board of directors, partners, and, of course, *you*. When creating a business plan, it may be hard for

you to be entirely realistic about the potential of your idea and its likelihood for success. Every entrepreneur would like to think that his or her idea is a money-making machine, but really good ideas are rare. When you draft your business plan, look at the promise and the pitfalls of your idea. Consider the worst-case scenarios along with the potential reward.

If you will be sharing your business plan with employees and other insiders, you may want to do so after the document is complete, unless you are inviting their input as you are developing the plan. That decision is entirely up to you. Some entrepreneurs offer only certain portions of the plan to employees. For example, a retail store operator may allow workers to view only the operating portion of a business plan, which will indicate, among other things, guidelines for customer service and sales. Providing employees with this type of information will greatly impact their performance because they will have a clear concept of the level of work that is expected of them. Other components of the plan—for example, the financial section—may be too sensitive to be shared with staff members. There is no standard formula for which portions of the plan should or should not be made available to employees. You make the call.

External Audience

This group of people can include bankers, venture capitalists, vendors/suppliers, credit rating firms, family members, and friends. Anyone outside your business who asks to see all or portions of your plan before investing any capital, is a member of your external audience. Financial lenders (bankers) are the external individuals most likely to request a written plan before approving a loan or line of credit. Bankers must be convinced that you have the ability to repay any funds borrowed, so your plan must fully outline your financial standing, both past and present. Most bankers will require you to provide several years' worth of financial projections. Venture capital firms and investor angels will also want to see your financial plan, as well as information regarding your operational and marketing strategies. Because these providers become, in a sense, co-owners of your business, they require details about the vision and goals of your operation. If you plan to borrow money from family or friends, they too may insist on seeing your business plan before plunking down any money. Some relatives will simply seal the deal with a handshake, but, when dealing with close friends or family, it's best to engage in all the formalities that you would endure in conducting business with a banker or other lender. This approach will prevent ill feelings and save you a lot of headaches in the long run.

Specify the Type of Business You Own

Do you provide a product, a service, or a mix of both? It is important that you identify, before writing your business plan, the type of business you own. That description will dictate how your plan will be structured. A product-based business will have a different focus—and perhaps a different audience—than a service-oriented business; in each case, the business plan would reflect the nature of the operation. For example, if you own a product-based business—say, a hairdresser supply store—customers will expect to find products such as shampoos, conditioners, and color treatments that may be cheaper than or different from those offered elsewhere. However, they will not expect you to provide services such as a wash-and-curl or a manicure. If you operate a product-based business, your business plan will need to outline what makes your items different or unique. Perhaps your store is the only outlet that carries a particular hair coloring or scalp moisturizer. Use your business plan to explain any features that set your products apart from the rest. When you outline the elements of your outfit, you need to consider your customers. Will you sell directly to the public or through wholesalers or distributors? Whichever customer base you choose, your business plan must state convincingly that your product is worth carrying (by a wholesaler) and purchasing (by the end users or consumers).

If you operate a service-type business, your customers will expect performance of an activity for them. For example, if you operate a maid service, your customers will look forward to performance of several domestic duties, such as mopping floors, washing dishes, and taking out trash. In preparing your business plan, you must consider all the elements that will impact the success of your firm. Customer service and presentation are just two areas you may need to describe in your plan. Your maid service, for example, might put a fresh red rose on the pillows after making all the beds. Or, you may have your employees dress in traditional maids' uniforms. Remember, when operating a service business, you have to sell customers on what *you* can do, and your business plan is your selling tool.

If your operation offers both products and services, your business plan may be a bit more complex than that of a product- *or* service-oriented company. For instance, if you own a beauty spa, customers will expect to receive great products for their hair and body, but they will also anticipate greetings from a friendly and attentive staff. At beauty spas, personalized service and quality products go hand-in-hand. If your business fails to provide one or the other, you're sunk. The business planning process will give you an opportunity to clearly outline how you intend to handle the relationship between the quality of your product and the delivery of your service.

Gather Available Resources to Help You Write Your Plan

When you craft a business plan, you translate your thoughts about your business onto a written page, but, to bring the entire document together, you have to gather other information that relates to your business. Here are some of the resources you can use to glean important data about your operation.

Marketing Research

When creating your business plan, you will have to include information about the market you intend to target. Whether you are starting from scratch, acquiring a franchise, or progressing through the early years of your operation, you will need specific details about your potential customers, your competition, and your industry before proceeding with your business plan. Conducting market research will reveal this information. Several market research techniques can be used to gather the data you will need (see Chapter 3). Your local chamber of commerce and industry trade associations are good places to start. You may also consult with business owners who run similar companies. Ask them for details about potential markets.

Business Records

Obtaining information from business records is much easier for existing entrepreneurs than for new business owners. If you are already in business, you have accumulated a whole range of documents during the ordinary course of business: payroll records, government documents and tax forms, licenses and permits, personnel files—all of these can be used to create your business plan. Depending on the extent and detail of your recordkeeping system, you may even have spreadsheets and cash-flow projections that you can transfer to the financial section of your business plan. If you are just starting a firm, you do not have a history from which to draw information. But don't panic. Use your knowledge of the type of business you would like to start, and research your industry for specifics. You can visit your local library or surf the Internet for pertinent details about your proposed venture.

Review Your Personal and Financial Blueprint

When starting a business, it is important to be brutally honest about your present situation. A shaky marriage, problems with children, or heavy debt can affect your ability to be successful in business, so carefully analyze your personal situation. Finances are perhaps the most important issue when you are considering entrepreneurship. Kidding yourself about your ability to assume the financial risk that goes with ownership will only hurt you in the long run. Before you create your plan, analyze your assets and liabilities. How much can you personally invest in the business? What collateral would you have if you needed to obtain a loan? If you are presently a business owner, take stock of your financial picture as well as your current operational procedures, other activities, and employees. This overview becomes particularly important if your business plan is focused on how you will expand your business to include activities besides those currently being performed.

Set a Planning Timetable

For business owners, a business plan is an outline of the future of their operations. But how far ahead should the plan project? Should you plan week to week, month to month, or year to year? There is no universal answer; for the most part, you will be predicting how your business will fare, and there are no guarantees of success or longevity. The general practice is to draw up a five-year plan, but this doesn't mean that you can file away the completed document until you're about to enter your sixth year in business. You must continuously update and revise your plan to reflect the changing needs of your operation, or any variations in your competition, market, industry, or technology. The intervals for updating your plan will vary according to your business and your planning needs. However, it's not a bad idea to review your plan every six to twelve months (if not sooner; some businesses plan a quarterly review) and make necessary modifications. We will discuss the business plan as a living document later in this chapter.

Consider Possible Outcomes about Your Business

When creating your business plan, you have no guarantee that the events you are projecting will actually occur. You can't be sure how your operation will actually function, how reliable your equipment will be, whether your employees will be loyal, or whether a fixed interest rate will be applied to your bank loan. You can only assume that several things *will* happen and, in turn, hope that you are absolutely correct or that your assumptions are close enough to actual occurrences to prevent a negative impact on your business.

Two questions remain, and only you, the entrepreneur/owner, can answer them honestly. They involve research and the unexpected, as described here.

Have I Researched All Possible Sources of Information about My Type of Business?

Each entrepreneur has to make predictions about the level of productivity, cash flow, start-up or expansion costs, reliability of employees, "back office" or management duties, and a host of other issues, before creating a business plan. If you are an existing business owner who is introducing a new product, you can use past experience to make your assumptions. For example, based on employees' past performance and their ability to turn projects around, you can make assumptions about their ability to work on your most recent innovations. However, if you are a new entrepreneur, you will have to rely on information from secondary resources—business associations, industry groups, and chambers of commerce—for your estimates. These sources can provide you with information about a variety of general topics as well as details that are specific to your industry and market. Bankers can be approached for analysis of your present and your projected finances. Consider contacting vendors and suppliers, as well as entrepreneurs who may be operating a similar company. As long as you will not be a direct competitor, they may be willing to talk with you and give you the benefit of their experience.

Do I Acknowledge That Some External Factors Are Beyond My Control?

When you think of factors you cannot control, the weather probably comes to mind. How many times have you planned a trip to the beach and had it canceled by a torrential downpour? As a business owner, you will have to make allowances for how external factors, over which you have no control, might affect your business. These factors can range from the weather to bank interest rates, the Consumer Price Index, or the stock market. Let's say you operate a beachfront swimwear boutique and, during one particular summer, the weather is constantly rainy and damp. How will your operation be affected? A good business plan will have a contingency plan for possible occurrences that could affect sales. To create a contingency plan, identify all the environmental factors that could directly impact your business. With a swimwear shop, inclement weather would be the greatest negative factor. Next, quantify how those conditions would impact your operation. For example, if your swimwear shop carries items such as life jackets, goggles, and sailing gear, will those items still be profitable if very few swimsuits (which may be the bread and butter of your operation) are sold that season? At what point would your operation begin to lose money? Is it likely that conditions will change? Lastly, develop several "what if" scenarios. What if it rains off and on during the first full month of the summer and meteorologists are predicting that another El Niño will sweep across the nation? Think through how you would respond to unsettling situations. By anticipating them, you may save your business from financial ruin.

Scheduling Time to Write Your Business Plan

Even when we know they are important, we often put off burdensome tasks. It's hard to make time for activities we really don't want to do, and some of these tasks are ultimately never completed. For many entrepreneurs, writing a business plan is a perennial activity-in-progress. Other start-up activities—securing capital, hiring employees, and finding a good location—are given attention, but business owners will often postpone their completion of a business plan for months, if not years, because they "just don't have the time."

Granted, it may be difficult for you to cram one more "to-do" chore into your busy start-up schedule, but developing a business plan is too important to be perpetually postponed. Reach for a pen, write down a date to get started, and stick to it. Don't worry if weeks or even months have passed since you opened your doors for your first day of business. It's never too late to create a business plan.

If you are a new business owner, you will not have a strategic planning committee to pull the entire document together for you. Nor will you have the funds to hire a professional business plan writer, so the task will ultimately be yours alone. Don't wait until problems surface before you start your business plan. Take the initiative now. Even if you can spare only 15 or 20 minutes each day to think through the goals of your operation, it will be time well spent.

If you think you can sit in your office with the door shut for three days, and hammer out a plan as if it were a high school book report, think again. You will not be able to isolate yourself from your employees, customers, and others with whom you interact on a daily basis, to write the plan. Creating a solid business plan that will prove successful for your enterprise takes time and great effort. You may have to work on it a little bit at a time—perhaps a few hours each evening after dinner, or during a lunch-at-your-desk, or one afternoon on the weekends. Just *get it done.*

To make the process easier, avoid scheduling your planning around the busiest times of the year (the winter holidays), and don't set unrealistic deadlines for yourself. Creating a good business plan can take six months, but, depending on the type of business you own, your reasons for creating the plan, how quickly you can secure the information you need to craft the plan, and a host of other issues, the time needed to complete the plan will vary. A word of advice: Always assume that it will take you longer than expected. In this way, you will not be disappointed if you miss a deadline you have set.

To save time, you can bundle certain business activities with those required to create your business resume. For example, if you are preparing your tax returns, or if your auditors will be arriving around the time you've been thinking about starting a business plan, use the information you gather from these sources as the foundation for the financial and/or management section of your business plan. This tactic can be a great time saver.

Creating a business plan doesn't have to be a difficult process. It can go quite smoothly if you pace yourself, seek assistance where necessary, dig aggressively for all the information you will need to craft the plan, and take the time to think through all of the elements—positive and negative—that will affect your operation.

WRITING THE PLAN—STEP BY STEP

Let's say that you've considered the benefits of developing a business plan, completed your prebusiness planning stage, and scheduled a convenient time to begin the planning process. You can now begin piecing together your road map for success.

No two business plans are exactly alike. The contents of your document will depend on a number of factors, including the type of business you own and your reasons for creating the plan. Your business plan should reflect *your* management style and personality. Ideally, it should be 20 to 30 pages in length (maximum, 50).

Each business plan is unique in content and style, but several major components or sections are common to most plans. These include:

- Cover Page and Table of Contents.
- Executive Summary.
- Business Description.
- Marketing Plan.
- Operating and Management Plan.
- Financial Plan.
- Appendix.

Some business owners, depending on their needs, will also include a Long-Range and Succession Plan in their documents. These are not required elements.

There are no hard-and-fast rules about how you should approach writing your business plan. You can start with your cover page and table of contents and work your way down. Or, you can start with the Executive Summary, jump down to the Financial Plan, and then tackle the Marketing Plan. The sequence for completing sections is entirely up to you. The list given above is how the components *normally* appear in a typical business plan, but if another sequence is more comfortable for you or better matches the needs of your business, use it. Remember, your goal is to give those who will read your plan a clear understanding of your business and what you hope to achieve. If it makes more sense, for your type of business, to list the Marketing Plan after the Operating and Management Plan, feel free to reverse them.

Cover Page and Table of Contents

The cover page, the first component of an average business plan, contains all the information that will help identify your business:

- Address.
- Telephone number(s).
- Fax number/Web address.
- Name of person(s) to contact if those reviewing the plan have questions (most likely, this person will be you).
- The date the plan was completed, and the time period it covers.
- Copy number of the business plan. (Keep a record of each recipient of the document. If you keep the original and one copy, copies

numbered 2, 3, and 4 might be distributed to bankers along with loan applications.)

- Logo or slogan. If you've taken the time to create a unique and eye-catching graphic that will help identify your business and distinguish it from others, display it on the cover sheet.

As with any document, the table of contents should clearly indicate the page on which each section of the business plan begins. Be sure that the page numbers in the table of contents accurately reflect the page numbers listed throughout the document. Any error here is a sign of gross carelessness. When you collate the entire document, triple check the page numbers for an exact match.

Executive Summary

The first major component of the business plan is the executive summary. Also called a "Statement of Purpose," the executive summary is a synopsis or brief "snapshot" of your company's history (if any), objectives, financial status, and management and marketing structures.

This section, which immediately follows the cover sheet, is one of the most important components of any business plan. It must be specific, exciting, and brief (generally no more than one page in length). If you find yourself cranking out a tenth page, you've got some serious cutting to do. Do not fill this section with unnecessary rhetoric or flowery words, in an effort to impress the reader. Simply state what you want. Plain language will prove more advantageous to you in the long run.

If you are a new business owner or an entrepreneur in search of capital, it is especially imperative that you adhere to the rule of brevity. Financial lenders and other investors receive hundreds of business plans each month. Few are actually read from cover to cover. By creating an executive summary that is clear, concise, and eye-catching, you will increase your chances of obtaining assistance. No financial lender is going to spend 30 minutes reading your executive summary. If he or she can't get a handle on the type of business you have, what you hope to achieve, and your capabilities, after a 30-second scan, the lender may discard your plan altogether.

The executive summary typically includes the following items.

A Mission Statement
Outline your company's goals, commitments, and philosophy. For example, if you own an income tax services company, your mission statement could read: "The mission of _____ [give your business name] is to provide quality and accurate income tax services for private individuals and businesses by using a highly skilled staff of consultants."

Objective of the Plan

Every business plan has a purpose. You may want to secure start-up capital or organize a joint venture. Whatever your objective, your executive summary should briefly indicate the purpose of your document and what you hope to accomplish. If you want to obtain a bank loan, for example, indicate the amount required to launch your venture, how much you want to borrow, how the money will be used, the potential return on investment, and the proposed payback period.

Business Description

This portion of your summary should identify the type of business you have. Indicate whether it is a new enterprise or a franchise, or whether you've purchased an existing firm. Define your legal structure (sole proprietorship, partnership, corporation, and so on). Include your company's name, location, hours of operation, and, if you are not a new business owner, how long the company has been in existence. List the principal owners and any other key personnel. You will be providing great detail about your business in the business description section of the plan, so give only the highlights here.

Although the executive summary appears at the beginning of the business plan, it should be prepared last because it summarizes all the details of the document.

Business Description

The business description or "business background" section is a critical aspect of your plan. The information it contains is specific to your operation and should give the reader a clear picture of your resources and your capabilities as an entrepreneur.

If you are a new business owner, preparing this section may be a bit difficult because you cannot supply background information or credentials. State what you *intend* to do. If you are an existing business owner, you can look to past experiences and successes as barometers of your potential for success in the future.

This section of your business plan should include the following elements.

Product or Service Description

State what product you will offer or what service you will provide. If you have a product-based business, explain what your product does, how it works, and any available options. Indicate whether your item is to be sold by itself (for example, candy from a candy store) or in conjunction with other products (such as film from a camera shop). Define how your products will be distributed and to whom you will sell (the issue of target buyers will be reiterated in the marketing plan, which we will discuss next). Explain whether you will sell your items one time only, occasionally, or on a repeat basis. For example, if you open a restaurant, you will be counting on some customers to visit your operation on a regular basis. If you own a computer consulting firm, you will not be servicing the same clients from one month to the next.

If you operate a service-oriented business, use the same approach to explain your services. Define the activities you will perform, and tell how, where, and how often you will perform them. In your description of your products and services, indicate how your business will develop a competitive edge. Perhaps your company will have an advantage because it will stay open 24 hours whereas your competitors operate only from 9:00 to 5:00. Or, your company will provide computer hardware, software, peripherals, printers, and desktop support, but your competitors sell only hardware.

When preparing your business description, include as much detail as possible. Don't assume that the reader will understand the capabilities of your product or service, simply because you do. Remember, the reader does not know your business and will not be able to get a handle on what it entails unless you provide all the particulars.

Business Structure

What type of business do you plan to launch? A retail store? A wholesale manufacturing plant? A service-based business? Your business description should indicate the type of enterprise you intend to start or have already set in motion. Be sure to distinguish whether your company is new or whether you have purchased a franchise or existing business. State your legal form of business, include a list of the principal owners (see Chapter 4), and note your hours of operation.

Facility Structure

Are you operating out of your home or a city skyscraper? Describe your facility and your reasons for choosing a particular site or location. Include such particulars as whether the facility is leased or owned, the square footage of the space, whether there is heavy foot and/or vehicular traffic in the area surrounding the site, and whether ample parking and accommodations for the disabled are available. If your facility is extremely important to the success of your operation, you may choose to devote a separate section to this topic.

Personnel Description

Indicate here all the tasks that will be carried out in your business, and who will be responsible for executing them. Include your intention to use full-time employees and/or temporary help. It may be difficult to pinpoint exactly how many employees you will need (especially if you are a new business owner), but an outline of all the activities that go into running your business will give you a clearer sense of how much assistance you may need. Identify your key employees, and briefly describe their abilities and experience. Include yourself on this list. Present your educational background and prior work experience.

The business background section of your plan need not be long. Its length will depend on the complexity of your plan, but try not to exceed a few pages.

Marketing Plan

Your primary objective in presenting a marketing plan is to persuade current and potential customers that your product or service offers better value than those of your competitors. You might hope to persuade people to buy your goods or services by offering lower prices, personalized attention, or money-back guarantees. Whatever methods you adopt, outline them in the marketing section of your business plan.

This portion of your document helps you analyze your industry. It defines your current customer base, your customers' needs, and how your product or service will satisfy those needs. It also explains your methods for promotion and sales. Your marketing plan should include the following items.

Market Analysis

This is an examination of the business environment in which you will sell your products or services. By conducting a market analysis, you can obtain information about the following issues.

Your Industry. Unless you are planning an enterprise that is common in most business centers—for example, a retail clothing shop or a restaurant—provide some historical information about your field. Explain how your industry has changed over the years, and describe the factors that have contributed to those changes (for example, new technology or reduced economic barriers). Discuss current and future trends that may affect your industry. This information about your industry is available from secondary market research resources such as local chambers of commerce, trade associations, or successful business owners (see Chapter 3).

Target Audience. Do you know who your customers are? When you conduct your market analysis, define your current and potential customers. Are they middle-age women or high school students? Single moms or elderly men and women? Identify their location, how their needs are currently being met, and why these customers will benefit from your product or service.

Competitors. Competition abounds, and you must accurately identify those who will challenge your ability to push your products or services. Define the competition, and describe their strengths and weaknesses, their location, their size (in annual sales), and the percentage of the market they currently hold.

Market Size. Are there enough people in your market to support your product or service? Define your market's size, structure, and growth/profit potential. Be very sure that you are not pursuing a product or service that is not wanted or needed by consumers (see Chapter 2). For example, you may make the most mouth-watering oatmeal raisin cookies in the world—at least, that's what all your friends and family have told you. But with a market fully saturated by brand names such as Nabisco, Keebler, and Famous Amos, there will be little room for your product to succeed. Your market analysis will help you pinpoint your potential market share.

Marketing Strategy and Sales Plans

After you have identified your market, define your customers and competition, and analyze your industry's trends. How will you position your business in the marketplace, and how will you go about reaching the consumer? Your marketing strategy and sales plan will help you answer these questions by outlining the following objectives.

Pricing. Many companies, large or small, lure customers by offering low prices. When you outline your market strategy and sales plans, consider your pricing policy. How much you charge for your product or service will have a significant impact on the success of your operation. If your price is too high or too low, you could drive yourself right out of business. (Chapter 11 describes various pricing methods.) The pricing policies of your competition will give you a sense of how much you may want to charge, but don't simply adopt their pricing structure.

Distribution Channels. Determine how your product or service will be sold. Will you pitch your new products on the Internet, through a mail-order catalog, in a retail outlet, through a broker, via direct sales, or directly from the manufacturer? Survey the competition to gauge which distribution channels you may want to use to transport your product from its place of origin to the end user. But again, don't simply copy what the competition has done. Consider the methods that will most benefit your operation and give you a competitive edge.

Advertising and Promotion. How many times have you seen a television commercial for a hot new car or a kitchen gadget and, soon after, rushed to a store to buy it? Television is a powerful persuader when it comes to convincing potential consumers to open up their pocketbooks. Your marketing strategy and sales plan should include information on the methods of advertising you will use to attract customers. Your options are: TV, radio, newspapers and magazines, flyers, the Internet, and word-of-mouth, which is often the best form of advertisement (see Chapter 9). After deciding which technique to use, determine whether you will outsource your advertising functions to an agency or handle it in-house. Indicate how much of your start-up costs you will budget for advertising expenses, and discuss any public relations activities (such as trade shows or press releases) you will use to further promote your business.

Customer Service. After you recruit your target buyers, you will want to retain them and transform them into loyal clients by offering outstanding customer service. If complaints are filed, will they be handled by phone, in writing, or at a customer service center? Specify who will handle these concerns and how customer satisfaction and customer service performance will be measured (via comment cards or customer surveys).

Operating and Management Plan

This section of your business plan explains how you will operate and manage the day-to-day activities of running your business. Essentially, the operating and management plan helps you think through what it will take to keep your company moving forward. The specific operational issues you will face will depend on the type of business you own. For example, a product-based business, unlike one that is service-oriented, may have to consider how items will be priced, packaged, and delivered to the end user. However, there are certain issues that virtually every company must resolve.

Many large companies hire project managers to prioritize, juggle, and track all their daily business activities. As a small business owner just starting out, you may not be able to afford hiring someone to handle these duties. Instead, you must manage them yourself. As we discussed in Chapter 1, you, as a new entrepreneur, must play many roles, ranging from bill collector to clinical therapist or legal expert. For you to keep your business running like a well-oiled machine, you must outline all the tasks required to operate your business and select those who will be responsible for carrying out each task.

Your operating and management plan should include information about the following topics.

Recruitment/Management of Employees
Choosing the right employees is as important to the success of your business as selecting the right computer equipment. The operating and management plan helps you to define your company's structure and to determine the types of workers you will need to successfully produce and support your

product or service. It can also show potential lenders or investors that you have the right mix of skills, talent, and expertise on board. For start-up firms, the operating and management plan determines what the initial staffing needs are. For the existing business owner, it details both current staff and any additional personnel that may be needed. When creating your plan, discuss your hiring policies. What will potential applicants need to do in order to be considered for employment (physical exam, drug test, background check, aptitude test)? You might also discuss other work-related issues such as union representation, on-the-job training, employee evaluation, promotions, equal employment opportunity, and affirmative action policies. When evaluating your management structure, list your key players and indicate whether they are full-time, part-time, temporary, or consultants. Include information about employee qualifications, such as college or graduate degrees and any professional certifications.

Administrative Tasks

Pushing papers may not sound too exciting when you think about starting a new business, but it will be one of your chores as a new business owner. Someone has to pay the bills, open the mail, maintain the bookkeeping system, and perform collections. These tasks, generally called back-office duties, are not directly linked to providing a product or service. However, they are critical functions that could negatively impact your operation if not handled properly. In your plan, spell out who will handle back-office duties. If you are a one-person operation—for example, a computer consultant—the responsibilities will ultimately fall on your shoulders. If you launch a large toy store, a human resource, sales, or accounting department will handle a number of these tasks. To decrease the amount of time spent on them, you can consider outsourcing, but keep in mind that it can become quite expensive and you will still have to monitor the outsourcer's statements.

Structure of Facility

The makeup of your facility is first discussed in your business description. The purpose of reiterating it in your operating and management plan is to acknowledge that the structure of your facility will have a great impact on the daily activities of your business. Describe your location, including its size and your reasons for choosing that particular site. Include information on any similar businesses in the area; their makeup and appearance could affect the success of your operation. To give the reader relevant details about your facility, you can include floor plans of the work and storage spaces used by employees.

Compensation and Benefits

Explain your compensation procedures (salary, commission, hourly rate) and whether pay will be based on experience level, industry standards, or other factors. Describe any benefits you will offer: medical/dental, vacation, sick leave, and disability. Any other incentives, such as tuition reimbursement, expense accounts, and bonuses, should also be indicated.

Outside Professional Services

Whether you start a sole proprietorship or a corporation, you will probably solicit help from someone outside your organization: an attorney to handle your legal matters, an accountant to help with the books and taxes, a computer consultant to maximize your desktop's functions. These individuals should be listed in your operating and management plan, along with their addresses, specific duties, and method and rate of payment.

Financial Plan

The financial plan is perhaps the most difficult and important section of your business plan. The data in this portion of your document can make or break your firm. And because the goal for virtually any business is to make money, you will want to prepare this section carefully.

Most new business owners create a financial plan to secure a bank loan; lenders often turn to this part of the plan first. But this document serves many other purposes. It can help you create and manage budgets, file your tax returns, and make sound financial decisions regarding hiring additional staff or making major purchases. The financial plan is also critical during audits.

To create your financial plan, you will have to prepare a series of financial statements that lenders, investors, and other recipients of your plan will scrutinize to gauge the profitability of your business. These include a balance sheet, an income statement, and a cash flow analysis (all discussed below). If you are an existing business owner, lenders will judge whether these statements support your projected financial performance. Make sure that you accurately prepare the documents, and present them in a concise and easy-to-follow format. You do not want to force a venture capitalist or other investor to hunt through your business plan and gauge your financial background by piecing together elements from different sections. This will only put your business in an unfavorable light, so take your time and enlist the help of an accountant if you have questions.

If you are preparing a business plan for an existing firm, you can simply glean information from your financial records to prepare your statements. If you have kept records since you first launched your operation, most of your work has already been done. You need only transfer numbers accurately from one sheet to another.

If you are a new entrepreneur, you will not have a business history, so you will have to provide personal financial information as a substitute for historical data. Indicate what personal monies you are able to invest in the business, and provide specific details about personal assets that are available to operate the company. You may be required to present copies of your personal income tax returns, particularly if you are trying to obtain a bank loan. Whether you own an existing or a new business, most lenders will require three- to five-year financial projections.

For the task of preparing the financial statements, it's best to seek assistance from an accountant or a CPA (certified public accountant). By working with a professional, you will ensure that the documents are prepared correctly and fulfill the Generally Accepted Accounting Principles (GAAP). These rules, which were established by the Financial Accounting Standards Board (FASB) and the American Institute of Certified Public Accountants (AICPA), guarantee that the financial information reported is objective, accurate, and consistent for all kinds of businesses. If you work with an accountant, he or she will prepare your financial statements in accordance with the GAAP rules.

Some banks and investors reject financial statements not prepared by a CPA. The accountant's certification gives lenders an added sense of security. If the bank you are looking to tap for funds does not require hiring a CPA, you can prepare the statements yourself. A number of computer software programs provide easy-to-follow formats, but you must understand basic accounting concepts if these programs are to be of any use to you.

Most lenders require three financial statements as part of your business plan: (1) balance sheet, (2) income statement, and (3) cash flow analysis.

Balance Sheet

This statement indicates the financial condition of your business at a specific point in time. Referred to as a "snapshot," it provides a picture of what your business owns and owes at a particular date (see Figure 7.1 for an example of a balance sheet[2]). The balance sheet does not indicate how your business arrived at its current financial standing or make projections for the future, so this statement must be viewed along with other financial documents to show a total picture of the financial well-being of your firm. The balance sheet consists of the following categories.

Assets. Anything of monetary value that your business owns is an asset. Assets are subdivided into current assets and fixed or long-term assets. Current assets—assets that will be changed to cash within one year—include such items as accounts receivable and inventory. Fixed assets—assets that will not be converted to cash within one year—include land, buildings, and equipment.

Liabilities. Any debts that your business owes to creditors or other lenders are either current liabilities or long-term liabilities. Current liabilities are those that are payable within one operating cycle—for example, accounts payable, taxes payable, or payroll. Long-term liabilities represent an outstanding balance minus a current amount that is due. Business loans, car notes, and mortgages would be considered long-term liabilities.

Figure 7.1   Balance Sheet

Jon's Jazzy Designs

Balance Sheet

November 30, 1998

Assets	
Current assets	
Cash	$ 33,621
Accounts receivable	45,000
Inventory	50,000
Prepaid expenses	500
Total current assets	129,121
Property, Plant and Equipment net of accumulated depreciation of	
$35,500	186,000
Total assets	**$315,121**
Liabilities and Stockholders' Equity	
Current:	
Accounts payable	81,000
Accrued expenses	20,000
Total current liabilities	101,000
Stockholders' Equity	
Common stock, $10 par value-share authorized 1,800; issued and	
outstanding 1,800 shares	18,000
Retained earnings	196,121
Total stockholders' equity	214,121
	$315,121

Net Worth. Also referred to as owners' equity or stockholders' equity, net worth represents claims the business owner(s) makes on the company assets. Net worth will vary according to a company's legal structure. For example, a corporation would figure its net worth by taking the sum of financial contributions by its stockholders or owners and adding the earnings retained after dividends are paid.

To determine your company's financial health, use the following mathematical formula:

$$\text{Assets} - \text{Liabilities} = \text{Net worth}$$

If your business has more assets than liabilities, the net worth will be positive. Conversely, if your company harbors more liabilities than assets, your net worth will be negative.

Balance sheets allow you to identify and analyze trends that impact the financial status of your operation. They should be prepared at the close of an accounting period and should follow a generally accepted accounting format.

Income Statement

Unlike a balance sheet, which gives you a snapshot of your company's financial standing at a particular time, an income statement indicates your business's financial activity over an extended period—generally, your tax year. An income statement—also referred to as a "profit and loss statement," "report of earnings," or "statement of incomes and losses"—should also be compiled at the close of each business month (see Figure 7.2 for an example of an income statement[3]). The income statement is prepared by using actual business transactions listed in your income and expense accounts. After the close of each month, the accounts in the general ledger are balanced, and the balances from both the income and expense accounts are transferred to

Figure 7.2   Income Statement

Jon's Jazzy Designs

Statement of Income and Retained Earnings

November 30, 1998

Fee income	
Design	$122,300
Photo	23,000
Printing	2,300
Total fee income	147,600
Operating expenses	
Printing and reproduction	13,300
Supplies	850
Payroll	38,000
Repairs & Maintenance	1,100
Training and seminars	650
Professional fees	940
Interest expense	1,350
Insurance	800
Utilities	300
Travel and entertainment	900
Contributions	1,000
Dues and subscriptions	150
Bank service charge	150
Total operating expenses	59,490
Income before taxes	88,110
Tax provision	3,000
Net income after taxes	$ 85,110
Retained earnings, December 1, 1997	111,011
Retained earnings, November 30, 1997	196,121

the profit and loss statement. If your records are set up properly, the transfer of data should be relatively easy, provided you have a working knowledge of what information is needed and the records from which you should draw figures. If you need help, consult an accountant. There are also easy-to-use computer software packages that can set up income statements for you. A typical profit and loss statement lists the following data.

Income. Revenue, cost of goods sold, and gross profit all affect income. Revenue equals gross sales minus allowances and returns. Cost of goods sold (COG) represents the cost of purchasing or producing products to be sold during a particular period. This includes beginning inventory (product available at the beginning of an accounting period); purchases (labor or material purchased during an accounting period); and ending inventory (product available at the close of an accounting period). To calculate COG, use the following formula:

COG = Beginning inventory + Purchases – Ending inventory

Gross profit is net sales less cost of goods sold.

Expenses. This category consists of variable expenses and fixed expenses. *Variable* expenses are those that are directly linked to the sale of a product or service. Vehicles, travel, depreciation of production equipment, advertising/marketing, and sales salaries would be considered variable expenses. Variable expenses vary according to the extent of business activity. *Fixed* expenses are your overhead costs: rent, utilities, insurance, and office supplies. Fixed expenses generally remain the same, regardless of business activity.

Net Income from Operations. To calculate this, use the following formula:

Net income = Gross profit – Variable expenses – Fixed expenses

The income statement is a very effective tool for assessing your company's financial health. Because it indicates the origin of your money and where in the business it has been spent over a period of time, you can use this document to spot weaknesses in your operation and make plans for necessary modifications.

Cash Flow Analysis

A cash flow statement documents the movement of cash in and out of a company (Cash flow = Cash in – Cash out). It indicates how much money you will need to meet certain obligations, when you will need the funds, and where you will obtain them. A cash flow statement also alerts you to when credit or cash will be needed to pay particular expenses (see Figure 7.3). This document is particularly important to financial lenders; they will want

Figure 7.3   Monthly Cash Flow Projection

MONTHLY CASH FLOW PROJECTION

NAME OF BUSINESS		ADDRESS						OWNER		DATE		
	Pre-Start-up Position		1		2		3		4		TOTAL	
YEAR MONTH											Columns 1—4	
	Estimate	Actual	Estimate	Actual	Estimate	Actual	Estimate	Actual	Estimate	Actual	Estimate	Actual
1. CASH ON HAND (Beginning of month)												1.
2. CASH RECEIPTS												2.
(a) Cash Sales												(a)
(b) Collections from Credit Accounts												(b)
(c) Loan or Other Cash injection (Specify)												(c)
3. TOTAL CASH RECEIPTS (2a + 2b + 2c = 3)												3.
4. TOTAL CASH AVAILABLE (Before cash out) (1 + 3)												4.
5. CASH PAID OUT												5.
(a) Purchases (Merchandise)												(a)
(b) Gross Wages (Excludes withdrawals)												(b)
(c) Payroll Expenses (Taxes, etc.)												(c)
(d) Outside Services												(d)
(e) Supplies (Office and operating)												(e)
(f) Repairs and Maintenance												(f)
(g) Advertising												(g)
(h) Car, Delivery, and Travel												(h)
(i) Accounting and Legal												(i)
(j) Rent												(j)
(k) Telephone												(k)
(l) Utilities												(l)
(m) Insurance												(m)
(n) Taxes (Real estate, etc.)												(n)
(o) Interest												(o)
(p) Other Expenses (Specify each)												(p)
(q) Miscellaneous (Unspecified)												(q)
(r) Subtotal												(r)
(s) Loan Principal Payment												(s)
(t) Capital Purchases (Specify)												(t)
(u) Other Start-up Costs												(u)
(v) Reserve and/or Escrow (Specify)												(v)
(w) Owner's Withdrawal												(w)
6. TOTAL CASH PAID OUT (Total 5a thru 5w)												6.
7. CASH POSITION (End of month) (4 minus 6)												7.
ESSENTIAL OPERATING DATA (Non-cash flow information) A. Sales Volume (Dollars)												A.
B. Accounts Receivable (End of month)												B.
C. Bad Debt (End of month)												C.
D. Inventory on Hand (End of month)												D.
E. Accounts Payable (End of month)												E.
F. Depreciation												F.

evidence of your ability to repay them and to pay your vendors, suppliers, and other creditors. If you are an existing business owner, you can use historical information to prepare your cash flow statement. If you are a new entrepreneur, you will have to use the income and expenses listed in your projected profit and loss statement to estimate your cash flow analysis. The items listed in a typical cash flow statement include:

1. Cash sales.
2. Credit sales.
3. Loans.
4. Accounts receivable.
5. Material and other merchandise.
6. Overhead expenses (utilities, rent, phone, office supplies).
7. Advertising/marketing.
8. Taxes.
9. Administrative fees and salaries.
10. Research and development.
11. Labor costs.
12. Cash flow.
13. Cumulative cash flow.

Your cash flow analysis should be prepared on a monthly basis, at least during the first year of operation. During the second and third years of business, you can prepare this document quarterly and annually, respectively.

Appendix

The appendix consists of items that are not a part of the business plan itself, but serve as useful aids to those who will read the document. For example, an appendix might include ancillary materials that support assumptions you may have made in your business plan, or notes that will help the reader better understand the accounting principles and other terms that are used. You can also include marketing materials such as copies of newspaper or magazine advertisements. If you decide to include employee biographies and resumes within your business plan, place these items in the appendix.

ADDITIONAL BUSINESS PLAN COMPONENTS

Virtually every business owner will include the basic components of a business plan, as discussed above, but there are two additional sections that you may want to incorporate: (1) a long-range plan and (2) a succession plan. These sections are not generally required by financial lenders and other investors, but their presence in your business plan can further increase your chances of obtaining a bank loan or line of credit, and will establish more credibility for your firm.

Long-Range Plan

Statistics indicate that nearly half of all businesses fail within their first four years of operation. Some falter because of mismanagement of finances; many others are driven out by their competition. A long-range plan can help you avoid these pitfalls and position your business for the long haul. A long-range plan, also known as a strategic plan, can help you establish new goals and objectives or revise existing ones.

Before you create a long-range plan, assess the present state of your business. Are you operating in the black or the red? Determine what impact external factors (such as shifts in industry trends, or inflation) will have on your bottom line. If you are an existing business owner, you can project the future growth of your operation by reviewing several of your earlier financial statements (for example, the profit and loss statements). If you are a new owner, you will have to use financial and historical data gleaned from a series of secondary resources (the Internet, local chambers of commerce, business publications, and trade associations).

After gathering your information, prepare a written analysis of your findings. A good way to clarify and unify your goals is to solicit input from key employees operating in various functions throughout your business. For example, consult your marketing and sales representatives, and your customer service and human resource personnel. What is their take on the future progression of the business? If you don't have a ready pool of workers from whom you can draw ideas, consult trusted colleagues in your field.

A very effective way to dialogue with your employees about the future is to hold brainstorming sessions or retreats. To get the most out of these meetings, hold them in a distraction-free environment, perhaps off-site at a hotel or resort. If your shoestring budget will not allow an off-premises meeting, gather in your conference room and start talking. Prepare an agenda for the meeting, appoint a facilitator to oversee the discussions, and have an employee record the minutes. Matters that you should discuss and agree on in these sessions include: the strengths and weaknesses of your company, and how each will impact such things as revenues, keeping pace with the competition, productivity, and customer service.

A crucial part of a long-range plan is your mission statement. Although mentioned in your Executive Summary, you should restate the purpose of your organization in your long-range plan, along with a list of your goals. Your long-range plan should be updated yearly. When compiling your information, be sure to prioritize your objectives and assign certain tasks to individual employees. Most importantly, set realistic dates for implementation. Setting dates that are overly ambitious will render your plan useless.

Succession Plan

A succession plan is a multipart process in which a company's founder plans for the cross-generational transfer of the ownership, management, and wealth of the business. Family-owned firms frequently use this document.

Lenders don't normally require this level of detail in your business plan, but it can make a positive impression on creditors. Here are some of the issues you must consider when creating a succession plan.[4]

Short- and Long-Term Goals

What are your plans for the business and how do family members' views of their participation match your goals? Some family members may be interested in running the business for generations to come; others may only want a quick payout. Determine what each party involved hopes to gain from the business, and outline short- and long-term goals within your succession plan.

Transfer of Ownership/Management

A transfer begins with choosing a successor. This is not always easy—in fact, it is often a challenging and emotional task, particularly for family-owned firms in which multiple siblings are interested in running the business. In your succession plan, you must outline who will take over in the event of the death, disability, retirement, or withdrawal of the founder or key executives. You should also describe the successor's or cosuccessors' level of experience and vision for the company.

Transitional Stage

When you are no longer able to run your business, into whose hands would you like to place it? A longtime partner? A particular family member? Or would you prefer that the business be liquidated or sold? With each option comes a series of legal and financial ramifications that can be handled through your attorney and accountant, respectively. Your attorney can assist you with drawing up legal documents (such as a buy–sell or partnership agreement) that can protect your shares in the business in the event of your death or retirement. Your accountant can help with financial projections and tax planning and can also provide information regarding state, gift, and estate taxes, all of which, if not handled properly, could force the sale of your business.

PRESENTATION OF YOUR BUSINESS PLAN

After spending countless weeks, if not months, preparing your business plan, the last thing you want to do is slap a huge paper clip on it or throw it into a manilla folder. You want your presentation to look professional; the aesthetics of your business plan are just as important as its content. Consider the following tips for showcasing your business plan.

- Use a typeface and font size that are easy to read. Italic type may tickle your fancy, but it is impractical for a business plan since it is somewhat difficult to read at first glance. Choose a conservative typeface and a font size that is large enough to be read easily. (You may have to spread your financial statements over several pages.)
- Put your plan in a three-ring binder, or have it professionally bound. Using a binder allows you to easily add, update, and replace pages. Avoid a presentation that looks cheap or sloppy. Your local stationery store should have a wide selection of presentable covers you can use. Do not staple the document or use binder clips to fasten it together.
- Spell-check your document three or four times after it is finished. Misspellings and grammatical errors do not make a good impression.
- Create standard margins or borders.
- Make more than one copy of your business plan, and be sure you have a binder for each copy. Each lender you intend to approach should be given a copy, in a binder.
- If acronyms are used every day in your business, you can use them in the document as long as you define them at first mention. Terms with which a person outside your field may not be familiar can be listed and defined in the appendix.
- Use plain, high-quality paper, and print on one side only.

USING BUSINESS PLAN SOFTWARE

You don't have to be a rocket scientist to prepare a business plan, but you must understand the generally accepted format if you hope to attract lenders and other investors. If you would like some assistance but cannot afford to hire an accountant or CPA, research some of the easy-to-use computer software packages. But beware of the "canned, fill-in-the-blanks" programs. These are quick and easy ways to prepare a business plan, but the standard approach they use could actually hurt your business. Your business plan should reflect *your* personality and management style. If you use a boilerplate program, it will be difficult for readers/investors to get a sense of what makes your operation unique.

Bankers and other lenders can quickly spot a business plan that has been prepared using a fill-in-the-blanks program. This could be an immediate turnoff because lenders will conclude that you have spent minimal time preparing your business plan and know very little about your operation's chances for success. As a result, they may consider your business a poor risk and decline your request for a loan or line of credit.

Effective software programs allow you to research and create your own statements about how you will approach your particular business idea.

With these types of programs, you have an opportunity to make your business stand out from the rest and to show that you have spent a reasonable amount of time thinking through all the elements required to successfully operate your firm.

When preparing the financial portion of your business plan, you can use automated financial statements or spreadsheets. These will save you time because you need only insert the amounts; the program will do the math for you. These spreadsheets will also allow you to make changes and create "what if" scenarios to see how things could pan out, given a particular financial situation.

Visit your local office supply store or a computer shop and review the business plan writing software. Prices vary according to each application. One of the more notable programs is Business Resource Software Inc.'s Plan Write Expert Edition 5.0. With this software, even a novice can prepare a professional business plan. Unlike many other applications, Plan Write not only helps you write the plan, it also analyzes your document and provides suggestions for how to improve your business. Plan Write is only available through mail order. To order a copy, contact Business Resource Software Inc. at 512-251-7541, or visit their Web site at www.BRS-Inc.com.[5]

PUTTING YOUR PLAN INTO ACTION

How many times have things gone exactly as you had planned? You can probably count the number of instances on one hand. When you begin operating your business according to the objectives and assumptions outlined in your business plan, you may find that your company is not performing as you had expected.

You will then have to assess the problem and decide how best to resolve it. Your first step should be to review your contingency plans. When you first outlined your business plan, you considered all the factors, negative and positive, that could impact your operation. Review this information to identify the factors that may be causing your business to deviate from your business plan.

Review your contingency plan to determine whether the problems you are experiencing are caused by internal or external factors, or a combination of both. Internal factors that could impact your business can include poor employee performance or antiquated office equipment. External factors that could cause your firm to deviate can consist of a dip in the economy or the use of an unreliable vendor or supplier. Seldom will you find a single cause of your business problems, so always consider *all* the reasons that may be hindering your operation.

After you identify the problems, determine which solutions you will use. Some resolutions may come quickly. For example, if a particular supplier is late with orders every other day, you can simply use another vendor.

However, if you operate a kiosk in a neighborhood mall, and several of the anchor stores—which have helped to feed your small operation via residual walk-in traffic—close, you may not be able to just pick up your business and leave. You will have to rethink your business strategies and rework your business plan to coincide with the current situation. Just make sure that you get all the necessary information regarding the situation before making a move. For example, if the magnet stores close, there may be plans for new ones to open in the next several months. Consult your financial plan to determine whether you can ride out the period of decreased revenue or will be forced to relocate to save your business.

MAKING YOUR BUSINESS PLAN A LIVING DOCUMENT

Many business owners create a business plan only to secure financing. When the requested loan comes through, they file their business plan away in a drawer or on the top shelf of a bookcase. A business plan is a living document that should be updated and revised as your business grows. Remember, your business plan can serve a number of functions besides wooing creditors and other financial lenders to invest in your venture. But if your plan is not updated to reflect changes in your industry and other external factors, the plan will ultimately become useless.

Here are some of the occurrences that may cause you to revise your business plan:

- *When your business changes.* Are you going to hire additional staff, create a new position, take on a partner or two, or add a new line of products? Whatever changes you make in your business should be documented in the business plan.

- *When your customer base changes.* Customers' needs change all the time. When you started your business, the products you offered may have attracted a certain clientele. Now, these same customers may request a different type of item. If you want to maintain their business, you must make modifications to satisfy their needs. For example, retail clothing that you stocked just two years ago may be unsalable today because of new styles and customers' preferences.

- *When technology changes.* Are you visiting Web sites or creeping along with 1980s technology? Advances in communication require you to change the way you do business and the way you write your business plan. You may have to revise your document to reflect changes in computer technology, such as new software packages, Internet resources, and desktop environments.

Plan a midyear or quarterly review of your business plan to ensure that your operation is meeting your own expectations. Enlist the help of employees to track specific changes in their areas of expertise. For example, have your marketing representatives monitor changes in the advertising and promotions industry. You can then analyze the information and decide how to implement these changes in your business plan.

A business plan can be a lifesaver for your business. If prepared properly and updated accordingly, it can become a useful management and operational tool throughout the life of your operation. Don't let it wither on the vine!

CHECKLIST

FACTORS TO CONSIDER WHEN PREPARING YOUR BUSINESS PLAN

✓ **Your audience.** Who will read your business plan? A bank officer? Suppliers? Employees? Partners? Family members? By defining your audience, you will get a clear idea of how your plan should be structured and the level of content that should be included.

✓ **The type of company you own.** The business plan of a product-oriented business will have a different focus than that of a service firm. Take into account whether you are peddling goods, performing a service, or providing a mix of both.

✓ **Your customers.** How will you reach them? Will you sell directly to shoppers from your storefront, or offer your products through mail order, wholesalers, or distributors? Your business plan should indicate how you will attract customers and why they should buy from you instead of from your competitors.

✓ **Access to resources.** Creating a business plan requires that you gather a lot of information about your business and your industry. Everything from personal resumes to financial statements will need to be included. Determine what types of information you will require, and consider where you will obtain the data needed to pull the entire document together.

✓ **Your timetable.** Business plans are all about strategizing for the future of your operation. But how far out should you plan? A general rule of thumb is to create a five-year plan and schedule frequent updates and revisions.

✓ **Time to plan.** There's little chance you will be able to call a "time out" from the daily grind to pen your business plan. But that doesn't mean you should scrap the idea altogether. Spend several minutes a day working on some aspect of your business plan. Set a schedule for writing it, and stick to that schedule.

✓ **Length.** No two business plans will look alike. However, the average length that is recommended is 20 to 30 pages (50 maximum).

CHECKLIST *(continued)*

✓ **Professional consultation.** You should never totally surrender the responsibility of preparing your business plan to someone else, but it doesn't hurt to solicit some expert advice, particularly when preparing the financial section of your document.

✓ **Business plan software.** If you can't afford to hire a professional business plan writer, but you'd rather not tackle the task alone, try using business plan writing software. There are a number of computer programs that can assist you with all sections of your document. Just beware of the "fill-in-the-blanks" programs. They can hurt you rather than help you.

✓ **Presentation.** How your business plan looks on the outside is just as important as the information contained on the inside. Secure your document in a three-ring binder or have it professionally bound. Use plain, high-quality paper and easy-to-read typefaces. Spell-check it at least three times.

✓ **Revisions.** Business plans are living documents. Don't spend countless hours compiling your plan and then file it away in a draw to collect dust. Update your plan to keep pace with changes in your business, the economy, your industry, and business technology.

RESOURCES FOR MORE INFORMATION

ASSOCIATIONS

- *Minority Business Development Agency (MBDA),* 14th & Constitution Avenue, NW, Washington, DC 20230; 202-482-5061; www.mbda.gov. Through its nationwide Minority Business Development Centers, the MBDA offers start-up and existing business owners financial, technical, and managerial assistance. Among other services, counselors in the MBDAs help start-up firms prepare business plans and loan packages.

- *National Black Chamber of Commerce (NBCC),* 2000 L Street, NW, Washington, DC, 20036; 202-416-1622; www.nbcc-e-train.org. The NBCC is an umbrella for 170 black chamber of commerce affiliates in some 43 states. These chapters offer a number of services to new business owners, including conventions, black business directories, and a variety of workshops and seminars. The topics covered during these meetings include securing capital, hiring and training employees, and writing business plans.

- *Service Corps of Retired Executives (SCORE),* 409 3rd Street, SW, 4th Floor, Washington, DC 20024; 800-634-0245; www.score.org. SCORE is a nonprofit association comprised of 12,400 volunteer business counselors who provide entrepreneurs with a variety of managerial and technical support. SCORE counselors also offer advice to business owners on a number of topics, including how to write a business plan, improve cash flow, and integrate technology into their concerns. There are 389 SCORE chapters located throughout the United States.

- *U.S. Small Business Administration (SBA),* 409 3rd Street, SW, Washington, DC 20416; 202-606-4000; www.sba.gov. The SBA administers the Small Business Development Center Program, which provides management, financial, and technical assistance to new and existing business owners. There are about 56 SBDCs throughout the country. They deliver a myriad of services to entrepreneurs, including business plan writing. To find a list of SBDCs by state, visit the SBA Web site.

8

FINANCING YOUR START-UP

No matter what type of business you start, you are going to need money. Your good looks and charm won't be nearly enough to successfully sell your products or services, so you will have to secure the cash needed to get your company off the ground and running smoothly.

As a new business owner, you will need start-up capital—"seed" money—to finance every aspect of your venture, from securing a location to selecting letterhead stationery. If you're an existing entrepreneur, you may have to obtain funds to open a new branch, introduce a new product line, update your equipment, or simply meet your payroll obligations. If you do not have enough money to accomplish these objectives, you may have to borrow funds to keep your business afloat.

How much money will you need, to fund your venture? If you've been in business for five years, determining how much cash will pay for certain day-to-day tasks is relatively easy. But if you are a new business owner, you will have to estimate your expenditures.

The costs associated with starting a new business vary according to several factors: the type of business you operate, where you locate, the type of equipment you use, the number of employees you hire, the types of professionals you consult, and a host of other factors. If you research the market you intend to enter, and write a solid business plan, you will be able to (1) identify all the elements required to run your operation and (2) make accurate cost estimates for equipment, personnel, transportation, and other start-up necessities. You can then begin your search for capital.

The first place many entrepreneurs look, when deciding how to finance their operations, is their savings account. Using personal assets is the most ideal way to start a new business because you will avoid or minimize outstanding debt. But if you are unable to make a personal investment, you will have to look to outside resources. Funds can be obtained through a number of channels: commercial and community banks, trade credit, family and friends, venture capital, investor "angels," small business investment companies (SBICs), bartering, Susus (explained later), factoring or government-assisted loan programs. The type of company you own, where you are within the life cycle of your operation, and your legal form of business can all impact the type of funding you will be able to obtain. For example, if you are just starting out as a sole proprietorship, you may find it difficult to secure venture capital. Venture capital firms typically invest in large established businesses (often, corporations) with a proven track record and credit history. A start-up firm may find a warmer reception at a bank, although new business owners are often given the cold shoulder there as well.

Traditionally, commercial banks have been less than friendly toward new small businesses. They consider small ventures bad risks, and many new entrepreneurs have found it difficult to obtain seed money. Minority business owners have found it especially challenging to obtain fair access to capital because of racism and discriminatory loan practices.

Fortunately, times are changing. Start-up firms are increasingly finding greater access to capital from neighborhood banks and other lending institutions. Augmented loan programs initiated through government organizations such as the Small Business Administration (SBA) and Minority Business Development Agency (MBDA), both located in Washington, DC, are making financing easier for black-owned businesses. Also, regional and national banks are increasingly competing for small business dollars. Many have set up small business departments and charged them with the task of soliciting local businesses. Others have sponsored local business events and established small business seminars and programs to assist owners in readying their operations to obtain financing.

None of the capital access improvements allows you to walk into a bank and request a stack of bills just because you're a neighborhood shopkeeper with a grand idea. You must do the planning needed to make your firm an attractive investment opportunity.

Begin by creating a business plan. As we discussed in Chapter 7, writing a business plan will help you think through all the essential factors that will impact the success of your operation. Developing this document will also help you pinpoint your start-up costs, which will be of great interest to potential lenders. Whether you borrow money from a bank, a venture capitalist, or your Uncle Joe, the lender will want to know how much you will need and how the money will be used. If you don't take the time to thoroughly plan your business idea, estimate your start-up costs, and identify where you will use the funds, you will lessen your chances for acquiring financial assistance.

In this chapter, we will discuss a number of financing issues. We will examine some of the major start-up expenses for most new business owners, and help you to project your cash outlays. We will also discuss the more common methods of financing for new *and* existing entrepreneurs: commercial bank loans, investor "angels," factoring, credit cards, and venture capital. As a new business owner, you may not be able to secure venture capital right now, but, as your operation grows, you may want to call on this type of investor for support. Therefore, we also provide the nuts and bolts of financing options that you may find beneficial as your business matures.

The Small Business Administration is a great source of financing for new businesses, particularly minority-owned firms. To wrap up the chapter, we will discuss some of the SBA's loan programs and how you can qualify for federal financial assistance.

DETERMINING YOUR CASH NEEDS

Before you go hunting for start-up capital, you must determine your cash needs. How much money will you require to operate your business? Don't omit the funds you will need to support your company beyond its first day of operation. At the very least, plan on cash outlays for the first 90 days.

Obtaining start-up capital is crucial to the success of your business, but acquiring "working capital" is just as important. Working capital is the amount of money needed to sustain the day-to-day activities of your operation, such as paying bills or compensating employees. By projecting costs for the first three months of your operation, you will safeguard your business against any unplanned occurrences. For example, let's say sales are slower than you had anticipated, or unexpected expenses surface. If you've obtained only enough money to finance your first day, you could end up killing your business before it even gets off the ground. Every new business owner would like to think that sales during the grand opening will immediately push the company into the profit zone, but, realistically, this will not happen. Project several months' worth of costs, to keep your venture from taking a quick nosedive.

There are several ways in which you can determine your start-up costs. You can project your sales for the first 90 days of your business, craft a budget based on some basic start-up expenses, and review the financial statements and projections included in your business plan (see Chapter 7). You may also want to refer to any personal documents or statements you have prepared that list your assets and liabilities. These statements will not provide specific information regarding your initial start-up costs, but they will help you determine whether you can actually afford to open your own shop, and what personal assets, if any, you may be able to invest in your business. Remember, starting a new business requires serious financial risk. If you have extensive personal debt that could be exacerbated by taking on the additional costs of operating a new business, you may want to rethink your plans for entrepreneurship.

Projecting Business Sales

Although you may not be able to predict the *exact* amount of money you may need to borrow, you at least want to generate a figure that is within the ball-park of your actual costs. One method is to project how much revenue your business is likely to produce during the first three months of operation.

Estimating future revenues may be your most difficult prediction regarding your new business. However, it is important because your potential sales will affect your chances of securing financing. To pinpoint sales figures, you must consider a number of factors, including your competition, geographic location, and marketing strategies.

Depending on the type of business that you start, a number of forecasting methods can be used to generate the figures you will need to convey to lenders. The methods most used originate from the Bureau of the Census, suppliers, or trade associations and publications.

Bureau of the Census

This government agency tracks information on the sales volume of several types of businesses within designated geographic areas. It provides such demographic information as: the number and size of households in a particular region, and the average income levels and classes of people (according to age, gender, ethnicity, occupation, and so on), in a certain geographic location. These data can help you pinpoint your projected sales, which translate into your start-up costs. For instance, if you plan to open an upscale clothing boutique, but the sales of similar businesses in the area where you plan to set up shop are meager, you can use this information to gain insight into how you might fare. Other factors may be affecting the success of surrounding shops; perhaps the businesses in the area are poorly staffed or have cash-only policies. Whatever sales figures you derive, use them as a reflection of how you *may* do, not how you *will* do. You may also want to consult such publications as the *Census of Selected Services, Census of Manufacturers,* and *Census of Retail Trade,* for more specifics about your industry and related costs. (See Chapter 3.) To find these and other publications, check the reference section of your local library.

Suppliers

Product vendors are excellent sources for gaining insight into potential sales, particularly if you operate a business that is inventory-intensive. Let's say you want to open a neighborhood minimarket at your favorite corner. If you purchase inventory from a major food-and-snack distributor, that supplier could provide useful sales information. Generally, larger suppliers keep a record of sales generated by any store to which they distribute goods. This information could form the foundation for your own calculations. You will have to adjust your figures based on such factors as your marketing efforts and competition, but, for the most part, using these data will give you a good start. A word of caution, however. If you are going to speak with suppliers about your potential sales, always get a second or third source to confirm what a supplier has told you. Some distributors may tell you what you want to hear—instead of the truth—simply to gain your business.

Trade Associations and Publications

These very popular secondary market research resources are used by many new business owners for industry-specific information. For instance, if you decide to open a Mexican restaurant, you may want to consult representatives at the National Restaurant Association in Washington, DC. This organization provides useful data concerning potential sales of restaurants, according to their location, food type, category (fast food versus four-star dining), and marketing area. It also supplies statistical information, such as operational costs and gross profit margins. Trade associations typically offer access to information to their members only, and many produce their own publications. However, if you are not a member of a particular organization, you can view a variety of industry-specific materials in your local library. Like trade associations, trade publications generally provide sales data for individual enterprises, and most break out sales according to geographic location and business type.

Creating a Basic Business Budget

The costs associated with starting a new business will vary from one entrepreneur to the next, but there are several basic expenses that virtually every shopkeeper will share. For example, whether you start a four-star restaurant in the heart of a major city or a tiny flower shop in the bowels of suburbia, you will be required to pay rent. How much you will have to pay depends on a number of factors, including the amount of space you lease and where your facility is located. Nevertheless, as a business owner, you will have to fork over money at the beginning of each month.

Here are some of the expenses you should consider when tabulating your start-up costs:

- Lease payments.
- Phone and utilities.
- Advertising.
- Inventory.
- Equipment.
- Transportation.
- Business licenses/permits.
- Office supplies.
- Business insurance.

- Office furniture.
- Legal/Consultant fees.
- Employee salaries.

You may incur more, or perhaps fewer, costs; the exact number depends on a variety of factors regarding your business. In the sections below, we will discuss two major expenses that you may face.

Using Vehicles for Your Business

Depending on the type of venture you start, you may require the use of a car, truck, van, or other vehicle to successfully operate your business. For instance, if you open a pizza delivery shop, landscaping firm, plumbing business, dog catching service, furniture store, or limousine service, you will have to obtain a set of wheels if your business is to stay afloat.

Before you plunk down the cash for a new car or truck, consider whether a vehicle that you already own can be used for your business activities. If you have two vehicles, can one of them be converted into a business-mobile? If so, you will be able to use the money you would have spent on car payments for other expenses of your company.

If you are unable to use a personal vehicle for business, leasing a vehicle is a low-cost option that offers many advantages. For example, if you decide to lease a car, you may not be required to place a down payment on the vehicle. You've seen the tantalizing commercials: "Toyota Camry, Mitsubishi Galant, no money down, with monthly payments of x dollars." This is music to the ears of cash-strapped entrepreneurs who need wheels to deliver their products or to perform a service.

Leasing also gives you the opportunity to deduct your lease payments as a rental expense on your income taxes. Just keep in mind that if the business use of your leased car, truck, or van is less than 100 percent, the rental deductions you can claim must be proportionate to actual business use. In other words, if you use your 1995 Chevy pickup 50 percent of the time for business, you can deduct only 50 percent of your lease payments. You may also deduct vehicle operating expenses on your tax return if the costs you incur are business-related (see Chapter 13).

Virtually every new business owner would like to show off a brand-new car to clients and potential customers, but few are able to afford one. To save costs, you may want to consider buying a used vehicle. New cars are not good investments. As soon as you turn the corner to leave the car lot, a new car decreases in value, becoming worth much less than the amount you paid for it. Buying a used car lets you hold on to some money you would have doled out for a new car, and you can spend it on other start-up necessities. But be careful in your search. Many used car dealers will knowingly sell you a lemon just to make a sale. Here are some tips for buying a business-mobile:

1. Before closing the deal, have a trusted mechanic thoroughly inspect the car, truck, or van you intend to buy.

2. Secure any warranty information in writing. This should not be a problem. Most dealerships are required, under federal and state laws, to provide these data to customers.

3. When you find a car you are interested in buying, research its value in the *Blue Book,* a reference that lists the "book value" or actual worth of cars according to their make, model, and year. If a car salesperson is asking a price that goes well beyond the book value of the car, be wary. He could be trying to take you for a ride. You should be able to find the *Blue Book* in a local bookstore.

4. If the car has minor defects that you can live with, use them to drive down the asking price.

Whether you lease or buy a used car, you will have to obtain automobile insurance. The two types of car coverage you should obtain are liability and property damage insurance. Liability insurance provides compensation to individuals who are capable of suing you for personal injury, damage to their property as a result of an accident, medical expenses, and loss of earnings. Property damage insurance (which typically includes collision and comprehensive coverage) pays you for any damage to your car due to an accident or other incident such as a fire, theft, vandalism, or flood. Most states require that motorists secure a certain amount of liability coverage. If your car will be financed through a bank or other commercial financial institution, you will have to obtain both collision and comprehensive coverage. Even if you will not finance your automobile, you may want to carry both types of coverage, especially if you will use a new or valuable antique car.

When purchasing automobile insurance, make sure that your policy will cover business-related as well as non-business-related accidents and business travel. If not, you can still get the coverage by adding a "rider" to your policy (see Chapter 6).

Your premiums for automobile insurance will vary according to your location and the type of vehicle you own, but you can take the following steps to cut the costs:

1. *Request a higher deductible.* A deductible is the amount of loss paid by the policyholder. By choosing a higher deductible, you can lower your premium costs significantly.

2. *Shop around.* It is not unusual for the same type of coverage to vary in price by hundreds of dollars from one company to another, so do some comparison shopping before settling on a policy. Get referrals from family, friends, and existing business owners. Check the Yellow Pages under "Insurance" for a list of insurance agents or companies, or consult your state insurance department for prices and

financial ratings. While searching for the right coverage, remember never to shop for price alone. You want to get the right package at the right price, but you also want to ensure that you are getting quality service.

3. *Purchase an inexpensive vehicle.* To lower your insurance costs, buy an automobile that will cost less to repair and is less of a target for thieves. If you purchase a Mercedes sport utility vehicle to support deliveries from your flower shop, you are likely to spend more on insurance coverage (not to mention excise taxes, which we will discuss in Chapter 13) than if you buy a Dodge Caravan. The greater the cost of your vehicle, the greater the risk and the higher your premiums. Consider using a low-profile automobile to lessen your insurance burden.

4. *Make use of discounts.* Several discounts are available to help defer some of the costs of your insurance. Some companies provide allowances to motorists who travel a certain number of miles each year or who have no accidents within a specified time period. Other insurers offer discounts on cars that have air bags, automatic seat belts, and/or antilock brakes or antitheft devices. Ask your insurance agent about available discounts.

Equipping Your Company

Computers. Office furniture. Light fixtures. Filing cabinets. Telephones. Fax machine. Photocopier. These are only some of the items you will need as a new business owner, to make your company fully operational. But how will you acquire the necessities, and how much will they cost?

The type of business you operate will determine what types of equipment you will need. Let's say you want to open a bakery. Some of the items you will have to obtain include heavy-duty ovens; a cash register; cookie sheets, spatulas, measuring cups, rolling pins, and various other baking supplies. To estimate the costs of these materials, you can use a number of resources. For starters, you can visit vendors for price quotes. Be sure to comparison shop before settling on one place to plunk down your dollars. Talk with other bakers about how much they spent on outfitting their shops. Also, check catalogs issued by general merchandise stores and supercenters.

After you figure out the costs, you must determine how you will finance your purchase. Ideally, you would want to purchase brand-new equipment: it looks good, it's less likely to give you immediate problems, and it gives you a hard asset for your business. But if you are strapped for cash or unable to obtain the financing to "buy new," you will have to find more cost-effective ways to get the materials you need.

You can save significant costs by leasing or purchasing used equipment. Depending on the piece you need to obtain, buying used equipment could allow you to save up to half the cost if the same item were purchased new. Don't buy an item just because it's cheap. Look for a high-quality product, but at a reasonable price, and be careful where you make your purchases. You can find used equipment in a number of places, including the following:

- *Yellow Pages.* Check for a listing of consignment shops, thrift stores, and other secondhand outlets.
- *Local newspaper.* The classified section of most newspapers generally has columns listing "Equipment for Sale."
- *Yard and garage sales.* These can be great places to find used equipment. Often, the items for sale are in top condition. If you have the time and patience to pore over a yard or garage sale, you could find a bargain or two. You should be able to find upcoming yard and garage sales listed in your community newspaper, or you can simply watch for signs in and around your neighborhood.

You may find that the used equipment you purchase is still covered by a warranty. If so, make sure you read the fine print to ensure that the benefits described in the original service agreement are transferable to you. If not, you may have to obtain coverage to protect your investment.

Insuring your equipment should be only one part of your overall plan to protect your business. When shopping for equipment insurance, look for an "all risks" policy. This type of policy provides protection against virtually all mishaps or perils. It also prevents gaps in or duplication of your coverage (see Chapter 6).

Leasing equipment is another cost-saving option. You can lease virtually any type of equipment from computer systems to office chairs to security devices. According to the U.S. Department of Commerce, about 80 percent of all U.S. businesses lease all or some of their equipment. A report by the Equipment Leasing Association, based in Arlington, Virginia, states that small business owners, as a group, are the biggest users of leased equipment.

Deborah Sawyer, president and CEO of Environmental Design International Inc., leases just about everything she uses to run her full-service environmental consulting firm. "We're a little company, so we don't have a lot of cash to throw around buying stuff. Therefore, we lease pretty much everything, including our copiers, furniture, cubicle system, and telephone system," says Sawyer, whose company offers professional engineering, industrial hygiene, and environmental services.

"We particularly try to lease things that have short-term value, like computers. The kinds of computers we have to use are expensive. Some of them are just for word processing, but many of them have to be capable of running our desktop publishing system, so they cost a pretty penny. We've found that it is much cheaper for us to lease them because you don't have to put out thousands of dollars up front for a system, and when they become outdated or you need to upgrade, you simply turn them back in with no hard feelings. You only pay for the time that you use," she says.

Leasing equipment is not unlike leasing an apartment or office space. The materials you lease are either purchased or owned by a second party; in the case of equipment, the owner may be a manufacturer, broker, financial institution, or dealer. When you lease the materials, you make monthly payments to the leasing company for a specified period of time. You may have to make first and last payments when signing a lease. The lease terms vary, but can range from six months to six years. The average rental time is three years. After the lease term expires, you have an option to return the equipment, buy it, or extend the terms of your agreement.

There are several ways in which you can lease equipment. You can lease it through a vendor or dealer that has its own subsidiary leasing company; obtain it from a lessor, who buys the equipment from a manufacturer and then leases it directly to you; or order the equipment and then seek financing through a lessor. If you are going to lease equipment through a leasing company, bear in mind that you will be charged a monthly "lease factor" rate not unlike the interest payments on a bank loan. The difference, however, is that lease rates are often low. The exact amount depends on the cost of the equipment, the type of lease you select, and the lease term.

Several types of equipment leases are available. They include the following:

- *Operating lease.* If you do not plan to buy the equipment at the end of the lease term, or if you will use it for only a short period of time, consider obtaining an operating lease. The terms of this lease are shorter than the useful and expected life of the equipment. You will be gaining expensive equipment for much less than its overall cost.
- *$1 Buyout lease.* If you are nearly certain that you will buy the equipment when your lease term expires, a $1 Buyout lease may be best for your business. By simply paying $1 at the signing of the lease, you become the owner of the equipment. Still, monthly payments are required, and they are generally higher than those associated with other lease forms.
- *Finance lease.* Unlike an operating lease, a finance lease requires a longer term and costs less. Under the terms of this agreement, the lessee (you) is responsible for insurance, taxes, and maintenance of the equipment. However, once leased, the equipment becomes a depreciable asset that you can identify as a liability on your balance sheet.
- *Master lease.* This option allows you to lease equipment under the same terms and conditions used to negotiate the original contract. In other words, if you obtain certain materials at the beginning of your

initial lease agreement, but find later that you need other assets to support your business, you can obtain the additional materials without having to negotiate a new agreement.

These are not the only lease agreements that are available. To attract potential lessees, many leasing companies concoct their own variations of the general lease types. When deciding which type of agreement is best for your business, consult your accountant.

There are several advantages and disadvantages to leasing equipment. The advantages are:

- *Minimal start-up cash expenditure.* The main advantage that leasing provides is the immediate use of a hard asset without the cash outlay that would be required to purchase it. Like vehicle leases, equipment leases rarely require initial down payments, and they offer 100 percent financing for all the materials you may need to operate your business.
- *Flexible credit terms.* Most likely you will be able to secure a lease for equipment much quicker and more easily than a line of credit from a bank, and with minimal paperwork. Lessors are more flexible than, say, commercial bankers, when it comes to financing equipment because, in most cases, the ownership stays with the lessor. If the lessee fails to make payments, the lessor can simply retrieve the equipment. A lease arrangement also offers an opportunity to negotiate a longer lease term or a more flexible payment schedule. The terms of a bank loan are often more rigid than those of a lease.
- *Convenience.* Many business owners opt to lease rather than buy equipment because of the convenience that leasing provides. As a new business owner, you will need equipment immediately. Banks may take weeks to approve a loan; leases can be approved overnight. It is not uncommon for some lease companies to approve terms via fax communication.
- *Maintenance.* Some lessors will assume the responsibility of maintaining and repairing the leased equipment. The cost will most likely be factored into your monthly rental payments. The added bonus is that you don't have to scout an experienced repair person to service your equipment when needed.
- *Tax benefits.* If you use leased equipment in your business, you can claim a full deduction for monthly rental payments on your federal income tax return.
- *Fewer financial restrictions.* Unlike the terms of some bank loans, which may prohibit you from using borrowed funds to purchase additional equipment without the lender's permission, a lease arrangement can offer you the flexibility to obtain materials for future operations.

- *Reduced risk of equipment obsolescence.* Leasing is a smart option for new business owners who will need equipment that is subject to periodic improvements and advances. For example, computers and communications devices are technological tools that often become obsolete within a matter of a few years. If you buy the materials outright, you will soon have an asset that is worthless. Moreover, you may not have additional funds to invest in the new equipment because the initial purchase depleted your funds. But if you obtain equipment under a short-term lease or one that provides equipment substitutions, it will be easier and less costly for you to update your tools.
- *Ability to be flexible in needs.* There may be a time in which you are uncertain whether you actually need an item for your business. If this time comes, leasing provides a smart option for obtaining equipment. You can rent it for a short period to gauge whether it is something you will need for the long term. You can also use leasing as a low-cost way to compare different pieces of equipment.

The disadvantages of leasing include:

- *Lack of ownership.* You will make monthly payments under a lease agreement, but you have no ownership in the property. In other words, when the lease expires, you will not have a tangible asset that you can credit to your business. However, you can obtain equity by securing a $1 Buyout lease, as stated above.
- *Total cost.* Lease arrangements typically require no down payment, but the costs of leasing equipment over the life of the item will be higher than if you had purchased the equipment. To estimate the cost differential between purchasing and leasing equipment, conduct a thorough cash analysis of your business.
- *Obligation to fulfill lease terms.* Once you sign on the dotted line, you are committed to making all payments for the full lease term, even if you no longer need the equipment. For example, if you negotiate a two-year lease for the use of computer equipment, but you end up using it for only one year, you would be charged for the second year as well. Some leasing companies will not allow you to break the contract. Others will offer an exit, but charge you a hefty fee to terminate the agreement.
- *Loss of tax benefits.* With ownership come many tax advantages, one of which is the depreciation deductions allowed for a tangible asset. If you lease your equipment, you can deduct your rental payments, but you will lose the tax benefit of depreciation.

You can find leasing companies by checking the Yellow Pages under "Leasing Service" or searching the Internet. You may also want to contact the Equipment

Leasing Association of America, based in Arlington, Virginia, for referrals of reputable lessors in your area. Before you contact a leasing agent, make sure that you have mapped out exactly what you need and how much you are willing to spend. It's not a bad idea to provide a written explanation of your equipment needs to potential lessors. Cost may be the most important factor as you shop around for the "perfect" contract, but pay close attention to the leasing company's reputation with other lessees. You will be bound by a contract for at least a few years, so make sure that you feel comfortable working with the company, that you are treated fairly, and that the lessor is responsive to your needs. Whenever possible, retrieve references from current or former lessees of the company. Your local Better Business Bureau can tell you whether any claims have been brought against the organization.

When you find a lease that looks attractive, make your move but *do not sign* until you are certain that you understand all of the terms. To be on the safe side, have your attorney review the contract before you sign it.

GETTING FINANCING FOR YOUR FIRM

Every aspect of starting a new business is important, but perhaps the most critical factor is financing. Without cash or a sensible line of credit, your company is sunk.

Many new business owners will use personal or "owner" financing (money in savings accounts or retirement funds) to launch their ventures. For some entrepreneurs, this is the only way they can hang out a shingle. Many lenders are unwilling to lend capital to a new company unless the owner (or owners) has a vested interest. It is highly unlikely that any investor will assume 100 percent of the financial risk. In fact, some lenders will expect you to put up at least 25 to 30 percent of the start-up costs before they commit any additional funds. If you were thinking that your neighborhood bank would foot the entire bill for your venture, think again.

Even if you are able to find an investor willing to fork over the total start-up costs for your business, you must ask yourself: At what price? What will you have to give up in exchange for total financial support? Will it be a half-ownership interest in your company, or high interest rates on a loan? Carefully consider the trade-off before you say yes to any lender.

If you volunteer your own money, you will reduce your chances of having to surrender control of your business to an investor. You will also make your enterprise more attractive to commercial lenders, who will view your investment as a strong sign of your commitment to the venture.

If you do not have personal funds that can be poured into your operation, don't panic. Your dreams of becoming an entrepreneur can still come true. The ways in which you can finance your company range from credit cards to venture capital. Realize, however, that the life cycle or state of your business development may impact the type of financing you will be able to obtain.

As a new entrepreneur, your best bet may be to acquire debt financing (a loan; typically, from a bank). Remember, however, that this will not be easy. A lack of performance record and credit history may affect your attempts to obtain the funds you need. The cost of borrowing money (interest payments) may also affect your chances of securing a loan. Although the rates vary from one lending institution to the next, they are typically high for new entrepreneurs. You can reduce the cost by investing your own funds in the business or using collateral to secure the loan. It always helps to have a solid business plan at hand to prove the value of your idea.

If your bank says no, consider sharing ownership in your business by soliciting an equity investor. You will surrender total autonomy over your firm, but it may be a small price to pay to see your dream come true.

If you decide to purchase an existing business, you may have an easier time obtaining funds than if you were starting one from scratch. Financing is more readily available to you because the business you intend to buy already has assets, a credit history, and a proven track record. Your task of finding money is also easier because you may take advantage of seller financing. Seller financing is a process in which the owner of the property participates in the financing of the sale of his or her business. By using seller financing, you may get more reasonable interest rates than if you were to secure a conventional loan on your own. Other advantages include a less stringent credit review and the use of existing assets as collateral to secure the loan. Seller-financed loans generally do not require a pledge of personal or additional assets to secure financing.

Entrepreneurs who want to grow their operations experience fewer headaches when they seek money for their firms. Compared to a start-up firm, an existing business owner is more attractive and creditworthy (to a lender) because it has an established credit history, firm assets, an efficient operational structure, a loyal customer following, a sophisticated marketing and advertising plan, committed suppliers and vendors, and a positive cash flow.

Debt versus Equity Financing

You can use two types of financing to jump-start your operation: (1) debt financing and (2) equity financing. With debt financing, you borrow funds from a bank or other lending institution and repay them in a specified period of time, typically with accumulated interest. Debt financing can be either short-term or long-term. To obtain the funds they need, smaller businesses seeking debt financing may have to supply collateral or personal guarantees. The collateral—property (such as equipment or inventory) used to secure a loan or other debt—can be seized if the debtor fails to pay back monies owed. A personal guarantee is a pledge, made by a person other than the borrower of the funds, to repay the loan if the debtor becomes delinquent or any other deficiencies on the loan become apparent.

Debt financing requires that you repay a loan, but, for what may be an extended period of time, it is an attractive financing vehicle for new business owners. Why? For starters, by using debt financing, you do not have to sacrifice equity (ownership in your business) to an investor. Your only obligation is to repay the loan. The interest on the loan is deductible, and the financing cost is generally a fixed expense.

You can secure several types of debt financing for your new or existing business. They include the following:

- *Commercial/community bank loans.* New or existing entrepreneurs can obtain a number of different bank loans: short-term and long-term commercial loans, working capital lines of credit, equipment leasing, letters of credit, or credit cards.
- *Asset-based financing.* Typically, existing business owners use this to satisfy specific short-term cash needs or to generate working capital. Short-term assets such as accounts receivables or inventory can be used as collateral to secure a commercial bank loan.
- *Family and friends.* A sister or brother-in-law may be your ticket to entrepreneurship. Many business owners tap family members or close friends for needed funds because this lending practice is likely to be informal and unsecured (no collateral will be required). If you intend to borrow money from a realtive or friend, seal the deal with more than a handshake. Engage in some written formality to prevent future conflicts or damage to the realtionship.
- *Trade credit.* Under this type of financing, suppliers extend the terms under which payment of goods is due, or they allow the business owner to pay for products in installments. This system is very common for both start-up firms and growing companies.
- *Leasing.* As discussed earlier, leasing equipment or a vehicle can reduce your cash outlays and channel more money toward other critical start-up expenditures. Some lessors require no money down for equipment leases and provide 100 percent financing.

Unlike debt financing, equity financing requires that you give up equity (an ownership interest in your business) to a lender in exchange for capital. However, the benefit to acquiring this type of financing is that you incur no debt; repayment of a loan is not required. Still, the trade-off is loss of total autonomy in your business and possibly of control and management of the company, because investors may want to actively participate in running the business.

Equity financing can come from family, friends, or interested strangers. Business owners who consider this method of raising capital for their companies often wrestle with how much of an ownership interest they should surrender to potential investors. The amount of equity you sell will depend on the value you place on ownership. If you are not interested in maintaining the business indefinitely and merely want to make a short-term investment to gain a sizable profit a few years down the road, you may want to sell off a sizable portion of your business to acquire, up front, as many dollars as you can.

As a new business owner, you may have to relinquish at least 50 percent of your venture to an investor; in fact, a 50–50 split of equity is not uncommon for start-up firms. However, a 51–49 split is also popular because equity investors are increasingly willing to invest capital in new ventures for a lesser share in the business.

We will discuss some common types of equity financing later in this chapter. They include venture capital, investor "angels," and small business investment corporations. The type of equity financing you will be able to obtain may hinge on your legal form of business. Remember, there are a number of issues to consider when choosing a legal entity: your financial goals, the tax consequences, and the amount of liability you are willing to shoulder. However, your ability to obtain financing is another concern when you are selecting your business's legal structure.

Sole proprietorships are the easiest businesses to form but the most difficult to finance. Equity financing for a sole proprietor is often limited to the amount of personal funds the owner invests, unless the owner is willing to sell an ownership interest to an investor. Debt financing is also limited to the amount of personal assets the owner pledges to secure a loan.

General partnerships are similar to sole proprietorships in their ability to obtain financing. If you operate your business as a general partnership, your individual creditworthiness will define the value of your operation. For example, if you are bombarded with personal debt, potential investors will consider you a bad risk.

If you form a general partnership, your equity financing is likely to come from the capital contributions of your general partners in exchange for a larger share of the business, or from the increased funds generated by adding new partners. Debt financing may be easier to obtain for a general partnership (versus a sole proprietorship) because there is more than one owner. Remember, however, that your business reputation and credit are only as good as those of each individual partner. If one partner's credit is severely blemished, it could kill your operation's chances of securing funding.

Investors are attracted to limited partnerships because of the "limited liability" status they can acquire. As discussed in Chapter 4, a limited partner contributes capital to a company, but has no hand in running the operation. In fact, limited partners are prohibited from participating in the day-to-day activities of the business. If they participate, they forfeit their limited liability status. Limited partners are also not responsible for any obligations to the business. The losses they suffer are limited to how much they have contributed to the partnership.

Limited liability companies find little difficulty in soliciting investors because, like a limited partnership and a corporation, they offer a limited liability status. However, unlike a limited partnership, members of a limited liability company are permitted to engage in the day-to-day activities of running the business without sacrificing their limited liability status.

Perhaps the easiest way for you to raise equity capital for your business is by forming a corporation. It may be easier for you to convince 10 people to each invest $10,000 in your new venture than to convince one person (a banker) to fork over a lump sum of $100,000. Forming a corporation can provide you with the widespread ownership you may need to get your business off the ground.

Whether you file as a C corporation, closed corporation, or Subchapter S corporation, you will obtain money for your business by selling shares of stock to interested parties. As a budding entrepreneur, you may be reluctant to dole out several portions of your business to complete strangers. However, you can maintain a certain level of ownership control for yourself by limiting the number of stock shares sold and the rights that accompany each class of stock. For example, if a family member is not interested in an active role in the business but would like to contribute, you may issue nonvoting shares of stock in exchange for his or her capital investment. Keep in mind that not all potential shareholders will settle for a small stake in your business. Investor angels and venture capitalists may demand a more active role.

Securing capital for your business is not an easy task. However, it is not impossible. With the proper planning and persistence, you can get the funds you need to set your operation on the road to success.

THE BANK LOAN

For start-up or working capital, many business owners will turn to their neighborhood bank. Although it is convenient for obtaining cash, this method of financing is not easy to secure, especially for a new business owner. In fact, many new entrepreneurs find themselves faced with an all-too-familiar catch-22 when trying to tap banks for money: "Without credit and a proven track record you can't get a loan, and without a loan you can't establish credit and a proven track record." This scenario drives many new business owners to alternative resources for funding, such as family and friends, investor angels, and SBA-guaranteed loans (all discussed later in this chapter).

If, as a new shopkeeper, you initially visit a bank in search of funding, there are several types of bank loans that you can acquire. However, before you stroll through the revolving doors of any financial lending institution, consider the needs of your business. Whether you are starting a business from scratch or expanding an existing firm, you must accurately estimate how much money you will need. A lender will want to know the amount of capital that you require, how the funds will be used, and how the money will be repaid or will generate a profit for the business. These figures should be outlined in your business plan and confirmed in your financial projections. You may be tempted to forgo this exercise in favor of another start-up task, but it is important to map out *all* your costs as proof of the viability of your idea and of your own understanding of your business and the marketplace.

Numbers are important to lenders, but they are not the only variables by which your company's creditworthiness will be measured. Bankers will also take a subjective approach to evaluating you and your business. For example, if you are an existing business owner in search of a loan to purchase inventory, a lender may use your prior success in raising capital to determine whether monies should be granted. If you are a new business owner, a lender may pore over your personal resume, as well as reference letters from community professionals and other business counterparts, to gauge your reliability and reputation. And, to spread the risk of loaning money as widely as possible, a financier will also look more favorably on new business owners who have secured financial commitments from other investors and who have made a substantial contribution of their own.

After you determine your cash needs, you can select a bank or other lending institution to approach about financing your operation. Federal and state laws govern bank operations, credit unions, and other investment entities, but not all financial institutions are the same. Each lender will establish its own policies regarding:

- Interest rates.
- Criteria for loan qualification.
- Types of products and services offered.
- Fees for account services.
- Minimum required account balances.

One bank may specialize in commercial loans for small businesses; another may focus on home loans, consumer loans, or auto loans. It's important to determine the needs of your business before visiting a banker.

When shopping for a bank, you will want to go with the one that offers you the funds you need. However, be sure you are doing business with a financier who will provide ongoing support and business expertise for your operation.

Choosing a Lender

Puzzled by which type of lender to approach for money? A number of financial institutions can be tapped for cash or a line of credit, but not every financier will be right for you or your business. Consider carefully what each has to offer, match that offer against the needs of your operation, and choose one that has your best interests at heart.

Lorraine Carter, president of Caption Reporters Inc., based in Alexandria, Virginia, distinctly remembers making a bad choice when selecting a lender. Carter, whose company provides closed-captioning services for newscasts and other programming, started her business from her home, in 1993, with a $30,000 advance from an account she landed with WUSA/Channel 9 in Washington, DC. She approached a neighborhood bank about acquiring additional monies to fuel her new venture. "They said they would give me $50,000 if I put up my $30,000 as collateral, plus my house, plus my equipment. So I was being triple-collateralized and paying interest on my own money, but I followed through because it was the first bank that ever said yes to me, and I thought it was a good way to develop a rapport with my bank. Also, I figured that if I made my payments on time, which I did, I could go back a year later and borrow some more money," explains Carter.

"But I was wrong because when I lost my contract with Channel 9 after three and half years, I went back to them about refinancing my house to free up some money, but they said they would not help me. I asked them if they could take their name off of my house just so I could refinance and then they could put it back on. I didn't think that was asking a lot because I only owed them about $28,000, and I had $15,000 sitting in a C.D. [certificate of deposit] that they wouldn't let me touch. But they said no without hesitation. It didn't seem to matter that I had good credit and made all my payments on time; they told me they were not going to give me any more money. As you could imagine, I was devastated because I couldn't do anything for my business without getting the house refinanced. So I wouldn't take no for an answer. I sat in the bank for the whole entire day, from the time it opened until it closed, waiting for somebody to talk to me about options. Around three o'clock, someone came out and told me that if I didn't leave they were going to call the police. Still I sat there, fuming, but I didn't show it. I just sat there in my suit and read the paper. They let me sit there the entire day and at closing time they turned out the lights so I had no choice but to leave. But the next morning I got up and went back. They were so surprised that I had returned. I brought all my stuff with me—my laptop, my cell phone—and set up office right there in their lobby. I said to them, 'Whenever you get a minute just let me know; I'll be over here.' Well, after that, they hurried up and called me into an office and did what I had initially asked them to do. I was so mad because they made me go through all of that when what I was asking for was so simple. So the moral of the story is that you have to find a bank that has your best interests at heart and is willing to work with you because you can have good credit and you can make your payments on time. If a bank does not understand the needs of your business and is not willing to work with you, it won't."

Obtaining a loan from a financial institution can be a challenge. Here are some types of lending institutions that you may want to consider in your search for capital:

- *Conventional bank.* This is typically the first source new business owners think of when looking for a loan. Conventional banks may be large commercial banks or small community banks. Historically, large commercial banks have not been a viable source of funding for start-up firms. These institutions look more favorably on operations with a sizable amount of collateral to secure a loan and a proven track record. Some large banks are increasingly improving their small business lending record, but their major focus is still on big businesses. As a small business owner, your best bet may be your local or community bank.

- *Credit union.* A credit union is owned by the employees of a company or members of another group. Because the regulations that govern credit unions differ from those of a conventional bank, they can provide interest rates and other loan terms that may be more favorable than those of a commercial lender. Typically, you may not be able to borrow huge sums of money from a credit union, but the amount that you are able to obtain can put your business on the path toward profitability.

- *Consumer finance company.* This type of institution generally makes small (usually, several thousands of dollars) secured personal loans. The interest rates and processing fees are typically higher than those offered by a bank or credit union. For this reason, most new small businesses do not use this type of lender for access to capital. However, a consumer finance company is less conservative than a bank when issuing loans. In special circumstances, it may offer a high-interest loan to someone who has a poor credit history but a viable idea and an attainable goal.

- *Commercial finance company.* If you have a sizable amount of collateral to secure a business loan, you may want to approach a commercial finance company for capital. This lending institution offers business loans to enterprises that can secure the debt with readily accessible and marketable commercial assets such as accounts receivable, inventory, or equipment. This type of lender typically deals with existing entrepreneurs rather than start-up firms because of the high collateral requirement. High interest rates also deter most new small business owners. However, some entrepreneurs are still drawn to these lenders because they are willing to make riskier loans, offer flexible lending terms, and provide both short-term and long-term loan options.

In your search for a bank or other lending institution, start with where you conduct personal business. Perhaps the institution where you've opened a savings and/or checking account also maintains a good record of small business or minority lending. Meet with the bank manager or other officer of your local branch, and inquire about debt financing. Get referrals from your accountant, lawyer, or local chamber of commerce. Bankers are often involved in the activities of chambers of commerce and other business-related organizations. By attending a few of their meetings, you might be able to network and acquire general information about their lending practices. When you find a potential lender, you will be better prepared to discuss the type of loan your business will require.

Types of Bank Loans

Several types of bank loans are available to start-up and emerging new businesses. *Before signing any documentation,* make sure that you understand the major characteristics of your loan and all of its direct and indirect costs.

Bank loans will vary according to their terms and the security or collateral required. A loan *term* is the amount of time you will have to repay the debt. Short-term loans (which are paid back within 6 to 18 months) are generally used to raise capital for such things as accounts payable, working capital, or inventory. Long-term loans (which are repaid in less than 5 years) are typically used to purchase, improve, or expand fixed assets such as your business facility or major pieces of equipment. The interest rates on long-term borrowing tend to be higher than those on short-term loans, and more collateral is required to secure a loan.

Bank loans can be either secured or unsecured. With a secured loan, the borrower offers the creditor collateral (a fixed asset) to support the loan. If the debtor does not repay the debt according to the terms of the loan, the creditor can seize the collateral and liquidate it as payment for the debt. Most lending institutions will require that start-up firms in search of short- or long-term financing provide collateral to secure loans. By doing so, the financiers reduce the risk of default.

Lenders will also minimize their risk by granting a loan that is only a percentage of the value of the collateral. This is defined as the loan-to-value ratio (the maximum loan amount versus the value of the collateral). For example, a lender may agree to grant 65 percent of the appraised value of a piece of equipment. If the item is valued at $200,000, the creditor may approve a loan for $130,000.

With an unsecured loan, the debtor promises to repay the amount borrowed but does not provide collateral to support the loan. When issuing an unsecured loan, a creditor relies on a company's trustworthiness and reputation for repaying its debts. If the debtor defaults on the loan, the creditor has no property that can be seized as a form of repayment. However, the lender can file a claim, in court, against the borrower for monies due. Unsecured loans are generally offered to businesses with an established credit history. New small businesses are not likely to obtain this type of debt financing.

New and existing business owners must also consider the financial costs of a loan, which can be either direct or indirect.

The direct financial costs typically include:

- *Interest rates.* Typically, the longer the term of the loan, the higher the interest rate. On most loans, you can expect to pay one or two points above the bank's prime lending rate, but this percentage may be negotiable with your financier. Your interest rates will be either variable or fixed. Variable interest rates, also known as floating interest rates, change over the term of the loan. If you are a new small business owner who is strapped for cash, this type of loan could hurt your operation: the rates might increase far beyond the prime lending rate. Try to negotiate a maximum cap on any variable rate you are considering. Floating-rate loans may also implement a minimum or "floor" rate below which the rate cannot drop. A fixed-rate loan offers a fixed interest rate that is slightly higher than the current floating rate. Whether you are considering a variable or a fixed-rate loan, shop around. Small community banks and even larger commercial lenders sometimes announce reduced interest rates as a way to attract new borrowers.

- *Account balance requirements.* Some financiers may require that you establish and maintain a minimal balance in an account at their institution as a condition of a loan. This is called a compensating balance and is often kept in a low-interest-bearing account. Many banks implement this policy as a way to make outstanding loans more profitable. You may be able to negotiate this policy with your banker. Some financiers only request that you establish and maintain a general depositor relationship with the creditor through a traditional savings account or credit card. In this case, no set balances are required.

- *Prepayment penalty.* Just about any business owner would like to repay his or her debt early. Even if you can do so, this may not be a good idea. Some lending institutions charge borrowers for prepaying *any* of the loan principal. If you make payments ahead of schedule, your creditor does not get the expected interest. To discourage such aggressive tactics, many lenders charge a fee for prepayment of certain loans (generally, long-term loans).

- *Bank charges and fees.* There are a number of up-front bank charges that you can assess when securing a loan. Points or one-time charges can be tacked on for such things as credit checks and the review and preparation of bank documents. These charges are typically a percentage of the total loan amount. If you obtain a line of credit, the lender may charge a "commitment" fee for keeping the credit open to you.

The indirect financial costs or other loan conditions to which you may be subject include:

- *Personal guarantee.* This is a pledge made by a person, other than the borrower, to repay monies owed if the debtor defaults on the loan. Most personal guarantees encompass "joint and several liability." This means that each person who signs the guarantee form can be held responsible for the entire debt. Even if you own a mere 5 percent of a particular business, you can be held 100 percent liable for the amount of a loan that is guaranteed. The guarantors can be sued collectively or individually. Some lending institutions will assume a "take-it-or-leave-it" attitude and require that all the individuals they want to sign a guarantee do so, or the loan will not be granted. However, there is room for negotiation, especially if your business has good credit and a sizable amount of collateral to offer. You can also negotiate substituting higher interest rates or a higher compensating balance for a personal guarantee. If, like most new small businesses, you are unable to avoid this requirement, try to negotiate the terms of the agreement itself. As your business grows and establishes a credit history, the need for personal guarantees should subside. Also, if you take on partners throughout different stages of your business, try to get them to commit to a personal guarantee for preexisting loans. This will allow you to spread out the risk as wide as possible. There may be tax consequences by initiating such a move, so consult your tax attorney for guidance.

- *Financial restrictions.* Large commercial lenders may institute a series of agreements in accordance with your loan. For example, certain financiers may place restrictions on how you may spend your loan dollars, the number of mergers and acquisitions that can occur, or the amount of dividends payable to shareholders (if a corporation). They may also require that you track and maintain several financial ratios such as debt-to-equity and current ratios, and perform the proper maintenance on your business location. Small community banks are less likely to enforce such policies because they do not have the time or resources to support such a policing function. Small lenders generally enforce restrictions on using collateral to secure other loans and on establishing and maintaining informal depositor relationships.

- *Status reports.* You may be required to present a periodic report card indicating the financial status of your operation. The requirements of how you should report will vary according to the financier. Small community banks are likely to request quarterly or annual financial reports (your income statement and balance sheet), yearly personal financial statements, and personal income tax returns. Some banks may require that your documents be prepared by a CPA.

Now that you understand some of the basic loan practices, you can proceed with choosing the type of debt financing that is right for you and your business. Here are some of the more common types of loans issued by banks:

- *Short-term commercial loan.* This type of loan is obtained by new or existing business owners and is used for a specific purpose such as an equipment purchase or payment of a debt. The term of the loan can range anywhere from 90 to 120 days, although it is not uncommon for this type of loan to extend from one to three years. Because the duration of the loan term is brief, the lender may offer you a fixed interest rate, payable on the total amount of the debt. Short-term commercial loans generally require collateral as security, although lenders will also consider other factors such as your cash flow and sales history. For start-up firms, this is the most common type of bank loan.

- *Long-term commercial loan.* Unlike a short-term commercial loan, a long-term commercial loan is difficult for new small businesses to obtain. Essentially, the longer the loan term, the greater the risk. Most lenders, unwilling to gamble on an assumption that a start-up will still be solvent 10 or 15 years down the road, choose not to offer this type of financing to new businesses. For new entrepreneurs, the term of a commercial loan, if granted at all, is generally limited to five to seven years. Business owners seek long-term commercial loans for a number of reasons, including the purchase of a business facility or of large pieces of equipment, and expansion costs. These loans are usually secured by a fixed asset, and financial restrictions or agreements are often applied.

- *Working capital line of credit.* A line of credit represents the funds (up to a certain amount) made available by a creditor for a borrower to draw on at any given time. It is generally used by an existing business owner for purposes of working capital, hence the term *working capital line of credit.* A loan may be offered for a period ranging from 90 days to several years. The maximum amount that can be offered varies according to the lending institution. Interest rates typically change over the term of the loan, and interest is paid only on the outstanding balance. Business owners obtain this type of financing to fuel the day-to-day activities of their operations (e.g., purchase of inventory). Collateral (often in the form of accounts receivable or inventory) is needed to secure this line of credit, and a commitment fee is usually applied by the bank. Bankers will carefully consider your cash flow before granting a working capital line of credit.

- *Credit card.* If you are unable to obtain a working capital line of credit, consider using a revolving credit/charge card to finance your business. With a revolving line of credit, the amount of money being used changes continually at any given time, and interest is assessed only on the amount that you actually borrow. Revolving charge cards can be used to acquire working capital. They represent a quick and relatively easy way to access needed funds. Unfortunately, the downside of their convenience is the cost. The interest rates on a revolving credit card are close to the rates applied to consumer cards. In short, they're sky-high and many have lending limits that barely reach beyond $15,000. However, to compensate for the cost, many lending institutions will offer incentives to attract borrowers to use the cards. For example, bankers may package the cards with different types of insurance or with discounts on car rentals and hotels. A number of organizations, including American Express and VISA, have small business credit card programs. If you apply for a card, you will have to provide a business and personal credit history.

- *Equipment leasing.* Fixed assets that are normally leased by new and existing business owners include vehicles, facilities, equipment, and real estate. As discussed earlier, you can lease the materials you need (1) through a vendor or dealer, who may own a leasing company; (2) from a lessor, who would buy the equipment from a manufacturer and then lease it directly to you; or (3) by purchasing the equipment and then seeking financing through a lessor.

Securing a Bank Loan

If you want a lender to supply your business with the capital it needs to grow, you will have to provide more than just a winning smile and a great business idea. You will need a solid business plan, and, as Deborah Sawyer will tell you, a healthy dose of persistence and patience.

Sawyer, who holds a master's degree in petroleum microbiology from Eastern New Mexico University, worked for the Ohio Environmental Protection Agency before launching her company, Environmental Design International Inc., in 1991. Like most start-ups, she did not have an adequate amount of capital to effectively finance her firm.

"We were so dramatically undercapitalized. I should have had $300,000 and I had nothing close to that. I had $20,000 to start with," says Sawyer.

After operating her firm for three months on a shoestring budget, Sawyer carried her receivables to a bank to try and secure financing. But she was rejected by 23 banks that refused to even glance at her business plan.

"I had done two start-ups for companies in the past, using other people's money, so I had all kinds of charts and graphs and was able to show what I had done elsewhere, but I wasn't even asked to sit down. The bankers said they didn't provide loans for small businesses or they didn't fund service-based businesses. Eight years ago, small businesses were not what they are today. Women-owned businesses were not what they are today, and banks really did not have a facility, an instrument, for dealing with small companies, especially service-based businesses. If you didn't have widgets or something tangible to use as collateral, they really weren't interested in talking to you, and they didn't talk to me," she explains.

But Sawyer did not become discouraged. "You stop counting the rejections after 15 because you feel like people are saying *no* all day, every day; but I've always been one to persevere, so I hung in there. I have worked in the environmental field for the last 15 or 20 years. It's the thing I know best, and it's the thing that I knew I wanted to do. And since I'm usually at my best when people are telling me *no*, the rejections only made me want to try harder."

And she did. Sawyer approached bank number 24, but before walking through the doors she did a little homework. "With the 24th bank, I called the lender and developed a phone rapport before I went inside. You see, every time you meet with a lender, they generally give you five minutes in the front hall of the bank, and each time I went inside, there was a new excuse as to why they could not grant me a loan, so I made a list of the excuses and spent quite a bit of time on the phone with the lender asking her to explain certain things. Looking back to the 23 rejections I experienced, I think part of it was my fault because I didn't spend time learning how to talk to bankers. They have a vocabulary and a mindset that are truly all their own, but I didn't know how to talk to them and they didn't know how to talk to me at first. But when I visited the 24th bank, I was better prepared and was able to secure a line of credit for $50,000. It wasn't half of what I needed, but it helped."

Sawyer's advice to new business owners in search of start-up capital: "If you are thinking about starting a business, get very familiar with your bank and their procedures. Find out if the bank where you have your savings account or checking account deals in small business lending. Do all of this before you need a loan because the worst time to ask for money is when you desperately need it."

Each financier will follow a number of basic lending principles in determining whether to grant a loan. The five criteria (known in the banking industry as the five "Cs" of credit) that a potential banker will examine when reviewing your request for cash are:

1. *Cash flow.* The flow of money in and out of your business is a major concern for lenders. Financiers will want to make sure that your company's sales and collections supply a sufficient and regular amount of cash for repaying the loan. For new small businesses, this is a sore spot; maintaining a positive cash flow is often difficult. As a new entrepreneur, you will be required to provide a lender with projected cash flow statements as well as historic financial reports.

2. *Capital.* Do you plan to invest any personal funds in your new business? A financier will want to know how much of your money, if any, you plan to use to help finance your venture. Banks usually require that borrowers make an equity or cash investment ranging from 25 to 30 percent (if not more) of the total projected start-up costs.

3. *Collateral.* The property used to secure a loan can be seized by the lender if the borrower fails to repay the debt. Lenders require that many borrowers (especially new business owners) provide collateral as a way to reduce the risks of offering credit. To make sure that the collateral being offered provides enough security, the lender will

often demand an item that matches the term of the loan. In other words, the useful life of the collateral will have to match or exceed the loan term in order for a lender to accept it as security. Some lenders will also require that the collateral being offered must have no prior liens that could take precedence over the lender's. This is called *first secured interest collateral*, and it ensures that the lender will receive its share of any foreclosure monies before any other person who may be entitled to the proceeds. Among the personal assets that you can use as collateral are: accounts receivable, equipment, inventory, life insurance policies, an employee retirement plan, and stocks and bonds. The most common collateral is real estate. New business owners will often use their home as an asset to obtain a first or second mortgage, to acquire a home equity loan or line of credit, or to refinance their current mortgage. Putting up your home may increase your chances of securing a loan, but you should weigh this option carefully. Remember, you risk forfeiture of your residence if the loan is not repaid.

4. *Credit.* If you are operating an existing firm, a lender will want to review the credit history of your business as well as a personal credit profile. Before you apply for a loan, you should request a business and consumer credit report so that if any problems or inaccuracies appear, you can correct them before submitting a loan application. If possible, try to find out which credit reporting company a potential lender will use, and request a copy of your report from that agency. If you have been in business for several years, you can obtain a copy of your business credit report, free of charge, from Dun & Bradstreet (1-800-234-3867). If D & B does not have your company listed, you will have an opportunity to provide information about it. The most common consumer credit reporting agencies that you can contact regarding your personal credit history are: Equifax (1-800-685-1111), TransUnion (1-800-916-8800), and Experian (1-800-682-7654). Keep in mind that most conventional lenders will want to see that you have at least four or five years of credit experience before considering your application for a commercial loan. If you have been operating your firm without credit or by using personal assets, you may want to make some trade credit purchases before seeking a loan.

5. *Character.* How a lender will judge the character of a potential borrower will vary from one financial institution to the next. Here are some of the more basic characteristics that most financiers will consider when reviewing loan applications:

   - Your success rate.
   - References from professionals—attorneys, business advisers, and accountants.
   - Past or present lender relationships (e.g., a traditional savings account).

- Community participation.
- Personal financial investment.

In addition to the five Cs of credit, financiers will ask for a series of bank loan documents that borrowers must provide when applying for a loan. The documents will vary according to the type of loan you are trying to secure and whether you are already in operation or are starting a business from scratch.

The documentation usually required of start-up firms includes:

- A business plan that outlines how you will use the money and how the debt will be repaid. You can include a personal resume of your past business experience, and reference letters from respected professionals.
- Projected start-up costs.
- A projected income statement and balance sheet for at least the first two years. (Include it in your business plan.)
- A projected cash flow statement for the first 12 months, at least. (Include it in your business plan.)
- A personal financial statement, and copies of your federal income tax returns for the past three years.

Existing business owners can expect to be asked for the following documents:

- Projected balance sheets and income statements for two years.
- Projected cash flow statements for one year.
- Balance sheets and income statements for the past three years.
- A business plan. (You may not have to provide this document if you have a good credit history.)
- Business and personal income tax returns for the past three years.

Some financiers will also request a break-even analysis. This document, which can be presented as a financial statement or a graph, indicates how long it will take your company to turn profitable. Essentially, you break even when your revenues match your total costs.

Obtaining a bank loan may be one of the most challenging tasks you encounter as a new business owner. A good rule of thumb for making the process easier is to establish a rapport with your banker before you actually need to borrow money. For starters, you can develop a lending relationship by opening a traditional savings or checking account. If you are an existing entrepreneur, you can also establish a small line of credit with a bank, even if you don't need the money right away. During periods in which you have a positive cash flow, borrow several thousand dollars from your bank every 90 days, place the money in an interest-bearing account, and then repay the loan about a month before its due date. This strategy will enhance your borrowing power in the future.

You may also want to invite your banker to your facility and introduce him or her to key personnel. A personal tour will make the lender more comfortable with the type of business you operate and with your managerial practices. Remember, the more comfortable a financier feels with you, the greater your chances of obtaining a loan.

If your loan application is rejected, find out why and how you can improve your chances for accessing capital in the future. If, after several attempts, you are still finding it difficult to secure a bank loan, don't give up. Persistence is the key. Try a second, a third, or even a 15th time, if you have to.

OTHER SOURCES OF DEBT FINANCING

Trade Credit

If your vendors and suppliers offer trade credit, they can be reliable sources of financing for your new business. Trade credit is a process whereby a seller of goods (a supplier) finances a purchase by delaying the date on which a buyer must make payment. For new business owners who are tight on cash but need the supplies to put their operation in motion, trade credit represents a viable option. Suppliers have a vested interest in your business. If you're successful and happy with their products and supplies, you will most likely continue to purchase from them.

In addition to delayed payments, suppliers may extend credit by offering equipment loans and sales on consignment. Equipment loans come in the form of a lease agreement in which you rent tools and other supplies from a company for a specified period of time. With sales on consignment, the supplier allows the buyer to pay for the goods only if and when they are sold. The supplier retains ownership of the property until the goods are sold, at which time you keep a portion of the sale and return the remaining balance to the supplier. Sales on consignment are an attractive option for new and existing businesses. They require no up-front costs, and any goods that are not sold are simply returned to the supplier.

Trade credit is a good financing method for new business owners, but it has a few drawbacks. When purchasing goods on credit, you are subject to a higher purchase price than if you were to buy your supplies with cash. To help secure the loan, you may have to personally guarantee a portion of the purchase price. And, as a condition of credit, the supplier may ask that you do no business with any other company. For a start-up firm, this may not be a bitter pill to swallow. Many new entrepreneurs rely on one supplier to meet their needs anyway.

Before you begin to shop around for potential suppliers, draft a proposal outlining the amount of inventory your business will require to get started, and how much you would like to purchase from the company of your choice. Suppliers are interested in your cash flow, so you may want to present your business plan as well. Discuss an option for renegotiation if prices change during the course of your agreement. And sign on the dotted line only after all terms are explained and understood. Some suppliers may want to do business with a handshake. Put every agreement in writing, and have an attorney review the language.

Family and Friends

If you're like most new business owners, you've probably thought about hitting up an uncle or aunt for a loan to get your business off the ground. Asking family members to pitch in a few dollars requires fewer formalities than trying to secure a conventional bank loan, and less hassle than preparing a slide presentation to give to a roomful of potential investors. But although family financing may seem like the easiest way to get the money you need to fulfill your lifelong dream of entrepreneurship, it could turn into your worst nightmare if not approached correctly.

Too often, entrepreneurs borrow money from family and friends without drafting so much as a promissory note—a written agreement stating that the borrower will repay the monies loaned, with interest. "A simple handshake will do," contends your brother-in-law. "I trust you." But if the business goes belly up, the same brother-in-law who congratulated you at your grand opening will be screaming about his lost investment and demanding an explanation.

Borrowing from family and friends is a viable financing option, especially for start-up firms, but you should engage in the same formalities that you would endure if you were dealing with an outside lending institution. If you don't, you could destroy family relationships and suffer dire tax consequences.

If a relative or friend is going to contribute capital to your business, state in a written document whether you are receiving a loan or a gift. If the money is a gift, it may be subject to taxes. The Internal Revenue Service allows an individual to give a gift of $10,000 a year tax-free. Any larger amount would count against the gift giver's taxes and may require filing of a gift tax return.

If the money is a loan, a promissory note should be drafted stating the terms of the loan, the date the loan was issued, the date the debt will be repaid, the schedule for payments to be made, and the interest that will be applied. The lender should charge an interest rate that falls in line with the fair market value. If below-market rates or no interest rates are applied, the money could be subject to a federal gift tax.

After preparing the document, have it witnessed by a notary public (not a family member), and get ready to hang out your "Open for Business" sign.

SOURCES OF EQUITY FINANCING

Venture Capital

Venture capital firms, a source of equity financing, pool money from private resources and invest in certain companies. They expect a high annual return (20 to 40 percent) on their investment and a chance to exit on their timetable. Most venture capitalists invest in companies for a period ranging from three to seven years. Before you plan to meet with a roomful of these financiers, carefully consider whether this method of financing is a viable option for your business.

Not every company will be able to secure funds from venture capitalists. These professionals typically invest in large companies (the average venture capital recipient has revenues in excess of $2 million) that have a high growth potential and require huge sums of money. If you are starting a small business and need about $50,000 to get it off the ground, this may not be your best method of capital access. However, if you're operating a $10 million company, with the potential of making, let's say, $30 million in the next five years, you will find it easier to attract a venture capitalist. Still, as a new business owner you should keep this financing method in mind. As your business grows, you may find yourself calling on a venture capital firm to help finance changes you would like to make in your operation.

Among the businesses that venture capitalists target are technology-driven firms such as computer and electronic companies. Health-related companies are also a favorite among these investors.

For existing business owners, venture capital firms can provide large amounts of money as well as expert business advice. However, the cost of using this type of financing is high. It is not uncommon for a venture capitalist to demand an equity interest of 30 to 50 percent in a company (usually in the form of a common stock purchase or straight business loan). And although most investors will not want to participate in the daily operations of your firm, they may want to sit on the board of directors and participate in all major decision-making activities. If you are reluctant to sell off large portions of your business for fear of losing control, seek an alternative method of financing your firm.

When a venture capitalist decides to exit your business (or you decide that you no longer require his or her services), you can offer an initial public offering of your company's stock ("go public"), partner with another venture capital firm, or repurchase the original investor's stock. All exit options should be discussed before partnering with a venture capital firm.

To find a venture capitalist, ask your attorney, your banker, or other business owners for referrals. Word-of-mouth can serve as a convenient way to find these investors, but make sure that the persons you approach for contacts know the venture capitalist well. You will want to know what to expect. Venture capital firms have a reputation for being tough, so you will have to be on your toes. When a meeting is set, come equipped with a solid business plan, wear your best power suit, and project healthy doses of confidence, drive, and commitment.

You can also find these investors by contacting the National Association of Venture Capital in Arlington, Virginia. For a nominal fee, this organization provides a directory of venture capitalists scattered throughout the country.

African American business owners in search of equity financing may want to contact the Black Enterprise/Greenwich Street Fund, a $60 million private investment initiative, located in New York. The fund, launched by Earl G. Graves Ltd., publisher of *Black Enterprise* magazine, and the Travelers Group, a financial services company with over $150 billion in assets, targets established (not start-up) black businesses with $10 million to $100 million in revenues.

A word of caution: when shopping your ideas around to several potential investors, exercise caution in sharing any proprietary information. Although your ideas may be protected via a trademark or patent, you could still find yourself defending your rights in court. Try to limit the details you provide during meetings with a venture capitalist, and/or obtain a confidentiality agreement with the investor as an extra measure of protection.

Investor "Angels"

Whoever says angels cannot perform financial miracles has not spoken with Johnny Johnson, CEO of Community Pride Plus Food, in Richmond, Virginia. Johnson started his career in the food business as a grocery bagger for a Farm Fresh supermarket in Virginia. However, he quickly rose through the ranks, became the store manager, and was given the opportunity of a lifetime when an "angel," in the form of a supermarket executive, paid him a visit. "It turns out this businessman was literally watching over me while I rose through the ranks [at Farm Fresh]," says Johnson. "He knew I was a good manager and he was willing to take a chance on me."

And that he did. The angel loaned Johnson $700,000. Raising another $300,000 by acquiring a second mortgage on his home and cashing in profit-sharing stocks from his current employer, Johnson combined the funds and used them as collateral to secure a $3 million loan. With that money, he opened four grocery stores in 1992. Today, Community Pride Plus Food is one of the nation's largest black-owned businesses, with a chain of stores and $46.7 million in sales.

Looking back on his path toward entrepreneurship, Johnson says, "I would not have been able to do it without this investor. Richmond is a close-knit town and blacks typically don't get loans."[1]

If you find that commercial banks are giving you the cold shoulder, or that you are an unlikely candidate for venture capital, you may want to call on some angels in your area. Investor angels are usually wealthy individuals, or groups of businesspeople or professionals, who provide capital to new companies—often, companies that can improve the community.

Compared to venture capitalists, investor angels are less demanding in their financing terms. However, they are not pushovers. Angels tend to be less interested in helping manage the business, but they want an advisory position within your company. Some investor angels will offer loans with low interest rates. Others will require a specific return on their equity investment. For example, some angels may require, within a five-year period, a return on investment (ROI) of three to five times their initial offering. Still, for some businesses, this is a better alternative than a venture capitalist, who may demand a return that is five to ten times the initial investment. Investor angels may also request guaranteed exit provisions in the form of an initial public offering of company stock or a mandatory buyout of ownership interest.

You can locate an investor angel in a number of ways. A good place to start is in your local community. Ask for referrals from business and trade organizations, civic groups, chambers of commerce, your neighborhood banker, lawyer, accountant, and fellow business owners.

To increase your chances of finding an angel to watch over your firm, try tapping an angel network—a matchmaking database that pairs interested investor angels with entrepreneurs nationwide. Here's how it works: angel network firms request background information from business owners and potential investors who subscribe to their matchmaking service. If you want to list your company in the database, you will have to supply a business profile outlining many specifics about your operation, including its age, type, and location. You will also be required to indicate how much money you will need. Investor angels are asked to supply a profile that details the kinds of businesses they are interested in supporting, and the amount of investment they are willing to make. After all of the information is gathered, the angel network firm sends a list of potential candidates (business owners) to compatible investor angels. The angel network firm then steps out of the picture and allows the potential investor and business owner to make a decision to partner.

Here are some angel network firms you can contact:

- *Angel Capital Electronic Network (ACE-Net)*. This angel network is sponsored by the Small Business Administration's Office of Advocacy. It is an electronic network that allows interested investors to view the securities offerings of small businesses. Companies listed are generally looking for equity financing in the range of $250,000 to $5 million. If you are interested in listing your securities information in ACE-Net, you must file an application and pay an annual fee of $450. For more information about this resource, you can visit the ACE-Net Web site at http://ace-net.sr.unh.edu, or call the SBA Office of Advocacy at 202-205-6532.[2]

- *The Capital Network.* This nonprofit economic development organization is the nation's largest matchmaking service for investors and business owners. The network, which is associated with the University of Texas in Austin, typically invests in emerging businesses that have quick growth potential. If you would like your firm to be paired with an interested investor, you must file an application, complete a questionnaire, and submit a business plan to the network. For $450, the network will match your business with interested investors. Investors who want to be listed in the database must pay $950. For more information about this resource, call 512-305-0826 or visit its Web site at www.thecapitalnetwork.com.

- *Technology Capital Network (TCN) at the Massachusetts Institute of Technology.* The nation's longest established venture capital network, TCN introduces start-up firms and high-growth companies to potential investors via a computerized matching system called TECNET. TCN maintains a confidential database of business and investor profiles. To use the services, business owners must complete an application and include a two-page summary of their business plan (not the entire plan) and a one-page summary of their projected financial information. Investors who want to be listed in the database must also complete an application stating their investment criteria or preferences, and show proof that they are qualified investors. When all of the necessary information is gathered, TCN enters it into TECNET, which searches the database for matches between an investor's requirements and a business owner's capital needs. When a match is found, initial introductions are made between the potential investor and the prospective business owner. To be listed in the database, entrepreneurs must pay an annual membership fee of $300. Investors are required to pay $350. For more information and an application, call TCN at 617-253-7163 or visit its Web site at www.tcnmit.org.

Some angel network firms include both venture capital firms and private investors. When searching for an investor angel, try to locate one who will be able to offer business support beyond financing. In addition to money, many angels can provide contacts for suppliers, new customers, and other lending resources (if additional capital is needed in the future).

Small Business Investment Companies

Small Business Investment Companies (SBICs) are government-operated investment firms that provide venture capital to small businesses. SBICs pool monies from private investors and the federal government to fund fast-growing, existing concerns. Like venture capital firms, these organizations do not typically fund start-ups. They offer loans ranging from $200,000 to $4 million to prospective borrowers, and are more likely to finance general business types rather than high-tech or biotech firms.

SBICs are licensed by the SBA, but they are privately managed companies that enforce their own policies and guidelines regarding investment decisions. They provide long-term loans (with maturity up to 20 years), equity capital, and management and technical assistance to eligible entrepreneurs. Since their inception, SBICs have disbursed more than $13 billion to over 78,000 small businesses.

To qualify for financial assistance through an SBIC, you must have a net worth of less than $18 million, and your average after-tax earnings for the past two years must be no more than $6 million. Each SBIC has its own lending criteria. To apply for a loan, you must submit an application to an individual company, and provide an extensive business plan that includes your company's name, location, and legal form of structure. The document should also give details about your product, competition, finances, marketing strategies, management, and facility.

In addition to SBICs, the SBA licenses Specialized Small Business Investment Companies (SSBICs). Created in 1971, these firms generally operate as SBICs, but they invest solely in socially or economically disadvantaged businesses.

To locate an SBIC or SSBIC, you can order a copy of the *NASBIC Membership Directory* from the National Association of Small Business Investment Companies, in Washington, DC. The directory lists, by state, the addresses and phone numbers of over 200 SBICs and SSBICs. It also includes details about a member's preferred limit for investments and loans. Cost to nonmembers is $25.

If you are short on cash, request the *Directory of Operating SBICS*, a free publication, from the SBA Office of Investments (202-205-6510). There are some 270 licensed SBICs nationwide.

Not all SBICs are the same. When deciding which SBIC to approach, consider the following:

- *Amount of money you require.* Before approaching an SBIC for money, determine how much it is willing to offer. SBICs vary in size, and the amount of money loaned to businesses differs from one SBIC to the next.

- *Policies regarding investments.* SBICs make equity investments and straight business loans. However, they vary with regard to their investment policies, so make sure you match your needs with the type of investment an SBIC is willing to make.

- *Geographic location.* Typically, SBICs prefer to grant loans to and invest in businesses that are in close proximity to their offices. Contact the SBICs in your area about possible assistance before branching out regionally or nationally.

- *Industry.* Not every industry will be served by an SBIC. These investment companies have a wide array of experienced personnel and will often specialize in making loans and investments in particular industries.

For more information about small business investment companies, visit the NASBIC Web site at www.nasbic.org.

OTHER METHODS OF FINANCING

Bartering for Business

According to the International Reciprocal Trade Association (IRTA), a non-profit corporation that supports the barter industry, over $7.5 billion in sales is transacted annually by the commercial barter industry.[3] In short, swapping goods and services has become big business. For new and existing entrepreneurs, it is a way to finance their operations and avoid cash outlays.

For example, if you own a manufacturing concern, you may be able to get a better price on certain pieces of equipment if you promise to display the maker's trademark or logo on the finished product. Trade-offs like this can help you stay afloat when cash crunches occur.

Bartering provides a number of advantages. It allows business owners to generate new sales, unload slow-moving inventory, increase the volume of their business, reduce unit costs, and retain cash for other operational expenses. However, the drawbacks include a limited number of available products or services, and tax consequences. Because the IRS categorizes bartering as a cash transaction, you are required to report bartered goods and services on your income tax return. Another disadvantage to bartering is that you may not always get goods and services when you want and need them.[4]

There are about 600 barter companies in the United States and abroad. These companies are generally designated as either barter exchanges or corporate trade companies. Barter exchanges serve as clearinghouses for the exchange of goods and services among members. Let's say you are a member of a particular barter exchange organization. If you want a swap, you must list the products and services you want to trade. In exchange for the products and services, you may receive trade credit based on their value. You can then use the credit to purchase products or services offered by other members of the exchange.

The barter exchange company charges an individual who wants a swap a 10 to 15 percent commission on each transaction, and it institutes a yearly fee ranging from $100 to $600. About 500 barter exchanges are currently active.

Corporate trade companies exchange goods and services on behalf of their clients. The companies negotiate favorable prices for media time and other products and services, and exchange these for excess assets or their clients' cash surplus. There are about 100 corporate trade companies.

To establish a barter relationship, you must first contact an individual or individuals willing to exchange goods and services. Try approaching other business owners about the possibility of swapping products and services, or join a barter club or exchange. There are several of these organizations throughout the country. For a list of barter exchanges, contact IRTA in Chicago, Illinois, at 312-461-0236.

Susus

If you are looking for seed money for your new business, chances are that you have *not* considered a Susu. In fact, you may have never heard of a Susu. A Susu is a rotating credit association used primarily in parts of the Caribbean (and, increasingly, in minority communities throughout the United States) for raising capital for home mortgages, cash flow management, and start-up financing.

Susu is derived from the Yoruba word *esusu*, which roughly translates into "pooling the funds and rotating the pot." In a Susu, a group of individuals, usually five to ten family members or friends, each contribute money to a pot over a specified period of time. The amount of contributions varies but can range from $500 to $5,000. Each week, a member of the Susu receives a "hand," or the entire amount of the pool collected for that week. Payouts depend on the size of the Susu, but can range from $5,000 to $15,000. After every participant receives a hand, the Susu is dissolved.

Creating a Susu is a great way for new or existing business owners to raise capital without the headaches and paperwork of trying to secure a traditional bank loan. However, operating a successful Susu is not easy.

Here are some tips on how to keep the pot full and the participants happy:

1. Select as the Susu banker a person who is well known and trusted by all Susu participants. He or she should collect and document all contributions made.
2. Deposit contributions into an account at an accredited financial institution. This will assure members that the money is safe and not finding its way into someone's pocket.

3. Conduct background checks on all participants, even if they are family members. Consider their salaries, employment history, and credit ratings. Remember: Your Susu is only as good as the people in it.

4. Keep the length of the Susu short. Susus generally operate between two and four months.

5. Make weekly contributions realistic. Not every participant will be able to contribute the same amount. Set reasonable amounts for contributions, and never give more than you can afford.

6. Limit the number of members. With too many participants, it will be hard to run your Susu smoothly. Keep the number low.

For more information about Susus, contact the Caribbean American Chamber of Commerce and Industry (718-834-4544; www.internationalcacci.com).

Factoring

Every business owner wants his or her customers to pay for goods and services on time. But entrepreneurship is not utopia. Business owners often struggle with customers who are either late or delinquent with payments. W.C. Miles, owner of Miles-Chicago Transportation Company, in Chicago, Illinois, was feeling a pinch when many of his clients were coming up short, so he decided to factor some of his accounts to get the money he needed to keep his limousines and sedans on the road.

"The banks wouldn't touch me, and I had a logjam of receivables and no systematic way of getting the money in a timely fashion," says Miles. "While money slowly rolled in, I had cars to service and drivers to pay."

Miles needed quick cash, so he sold $9,000 in accounts receivable to the Camaron Group, a Maryland-based factoring company. He got immediate results. "Only a few days after faxing the invoices to the company, I received a check. It gave me the cash I needed to pay my employees and keep things running," says Miles, who factored accounts for two and a half years until he was able to get his customers to pay up more quickly.[5]

If you are an existing business owner and you need money fast, you may want to consider *factoring*, a method of asset-based financing that allows business owners to sell their accounts receivable to a third party in exchange for cash.

Commercial finance companies and even some banks will factor accounts. Here's how it works. When the factor company purchases your receivables, it takes over ownership of the invoices and collects payment from the customers directly. In exchange, the business owner pays a finance charge or "discount" on the total amount of the receivables. The percentage of the finance charge depends on the size of the receivable; it can range any-where from 2.5 percent to 15 percent.

In addition to assuming title to the invoice, the factor company takes responsibility for all the costs associated with tracking down the debtor, and endures the hassle of trying to get payment.

Factor companies are generally used by businesses that have annual sales ranging from $125,000 to $10 million and are experiencing temporary cash flow problems. Factoring is not a financing method for a start-up firm. Still, it is a capital access option to keep in mind as you start and grow your new business.

Here are the advantages to factoring accounts:

- *Fast money.* Factoring provides relief for business owners who find themselves in a cash crunch. Ordinarily, it may take you 30, 60, or 90 days to collect payment from a customer. However, by factoring your accounts receivable, you can receive a check in just a few days, or even sooner. If you are using a factor for the first time, you may have to wait one to two weeks. The factor company will want to check the credit history of the customers whose accounts are being factored.

- *No hassle with collection.* By factoring accounts, you have the ability to eliminate the need for collections, depending on the type of factor company you contact. There are two types of factors: nonrecourse and recourse factors. Most factor companies are nonrecourse factors that purchase all rights to the accounts receivable and assume com-plete responsibility for collections. Recourse factors are obligated to perform collections, but they are not totally liable for any accounts that go unpaid. In other words, when selling receivables to a re-course factor, you are ultimately held responsible for repayment of any portion of an account that is not collected.

- *Debt-free.* If you are wary about taking on debt, factoring may be just right for you. Factoring involves the sale of an asset (your receiv-ables), so no loans are needed and you remain debt-free.

The disadvantages to factoring are:

- *High cost.* Factoring is a relatively easy way to get quick cash, but the price of convenience is high. The discount charges applied to your accounts receivable can be as much as 15 percent. Also, the longer the invoice period, the higher the rate. In other words, if you would like to sell receivables that are 90 days old, you are more likely to pay a higher discount price than if your accounts were only 30 days old. Typically, factors will not take invoices with an allowable payment period of more than 90 days.

- *Fractured customer relations.* Factors are less interested in preserving your relationships with customers than they are with collecting monies due. Therefore, the approach they take to collecting payments may be too aggressive and somewhat offensive to a long-time customer. Ultimately, factoring could destroy your business relationship with loyal clients.

Before you decide to hand over a stack of receivables to a factor, consider the credit history of your customers. Conduct your own credit check if you have to. Factor companies are less concerned about your credit rating than they are about that of the customers you're sending their way. If the customers' credit rating is poor, it could impact your costs, so do your homework.

"Factors" is a topical heading in the Yellow Pages; you can also contact your local bank officer for referrals. The Commercial Finance Association, in New York (212-594-3490; www.cfa.com), can supply more information.

SMALL BUSINESS ADMINISTRATION LOAN PROGRAMS

Established in 1953 by the U.S. Department of Commerce, the Small Business Administration (SBA) has long been a ready source of financing for new and existing business owners. Entrepreneurs who are repeatedly turned down for commercial bank loans, or rejected by some other financial lender, often turn to the federal government for a helping hand. That's exactly what Jill Patton did when she purchased Essentially Chocolate, a gift-basket business, in 1995.

"I initially went to NationsBank for a loan, but they basically said that the amount I was asking for was too small and that they really weren't interested. I realized then that it was probably not a good environment for me to be with such a huge corporation because my business would probably get lost in the shuffle, so I went to a very small bank, with only two branches in the entire state, to try and get the money I needed," says Patton.

"I started a new relationship with the bank and they handled everything regarding my SBA loan. I just went in, completed the forms, and submitted a business plan about what I would do once I had acquired Essentially Chocolate. The whole process just took four weeks, and that's from start to finish. The bank turned it around quickly, submitted it to the SBA, the SBA granted approval, and the funds were transferred over. It was very quick and easy." Patton obtained an SBA-guaranteed loan of $50,000 to purchase her business, which she later merged with the Basket Gallery, which she had bought in 1992.

If large commercial banks turn you down for financing, you may want to consider applying for an SBA loan. The SBA rarely uses government money to make direct loans to start-up firms and existing businesses.

However, it does guarantee a certain percentage (typically, up to 90 percent) of loans made by private lenders.

Small business owners like SBA-guaranteed loans because they give them access to capital that might not otherwise be available to them on reasonable terms. New entrepreneurs also favor this method of financing because they are able to acquire long-term loans. An SBA guarantee can cover loans up to 10 years, and some real estate credits stretch to 25 years. This far exceeds the typical three- to five-year maximum doled out by most private lenders.

Lenders prefer an SBA guarantee because it reduces their risk. If a debtor fails to repay a loan, the lender can recoup the guaranteed portion of the loan (generally, up to 80 percent of the outstanding principal) from the SBA.

Currently, the SBA guarantees business loans up to $750,000 or 75 percent of the loan amount. The SBA will also guarantee 80 percent of loans under $100,000. Keep in mind, however, that the SBA may require that you provide an equity investment of at least 25 percent of the total start-up cost. Also, because the SBA does not make the loan itself, it does not set the interest rates on the loan guarantee. The rates that a lender charges are based on the prime rate. However, the SBA can govern how much interest a lender can charge an SBA borrower. For example, if the term of a loan exceeds seven years, the lender cannot charge more than 2.75 percent above the prime rate. If the loan term is for less than seven years, the charges cannot exceed 2.25 percent of the prime rate.

Several types of SBA-guaranteed loan programs are available. Before you fill out an application, determine whether your operation is eligible for assistance. Here are the criteria that potential borrowers must meet in order to qualify:

- *Fit the SBA's definition of a small business.* Generally, the SBA considers a business small enough to receive assistance if it has fewer than 500 employees. However, the agency follows several industry-by-industry standards in making its decisions. For example, in the retailing industry, a business can qualify for an SBA guarantee as long as annual receipts do not exceed $13.5 million. A manufacturing firm that has between 500 and 1,500 employees can still receive a SBA loan.

- *Be for-profit.* For the most part, nonprofit organizations are not eligible for assistance unless they operate in the interest of the disabled. A for-profit company that owns a nonprofit organization still qualifies.

- *Be rejected by a conventional lender.* If more than one private lender rejects your loan application, revisit your business plan to find out what factors may be causing trouble.

- *Be independently owned and operated.*

- *Be ordinary, not dominant, in its industry.*

Some types of businesses are not eligible for an SBA guarantee. Your particular business may not be on this list, but that doesn't automatically mean that you can apply for and receive an SBA loan. To ensure that you qualify, contact your local SBA office. To find the one nearest you, call the Small Business Administration's Answer Desk at 1-800-8ASK-SBA (1-800-827-5722).

Businesses that are ineligible for SBA assistance include:

- *Gambling enterprises.* However, small businesses that generate one-third of their income from the sale of lottery tickets under a state license, or from gambling that is licensed and supervised by states in which gambling is legal, are eligible.
- *Academic schools.* Vocational, trade, and technical schools qualify, as do preschools and nurseries, as long as their curriculum is less than 50 percent academic.
- *Lending or investment concerns.* Pawn shops are eligible because they typically generate most of their income through merchandise sales rather than interest payments.
- *Businesses that produce and distribute illegal products.* Loan applicants who are incarcerated, or on parole or probation, are also ineligible.
- *Media-related concerns, such as cable television systems.*
- *Amusement parks and facilities.*

SBA Loan Guarantee Programs

When starting a new business or expanding an existing one, you often have no guarantees of success. To increase your chances, the SBA offers several financial assistance programs to put you on the path toward profitability. Perhaps most accessible to new business owners is the SBA microloan program.

Entrepreneurs who need a small amount of financing and technical assistance can obtain as little as $25,000 through microloans. These short-term loans, maturing in six years, are approved by the SBA and administered through reputable nonprofit organizations such as state finance entities and local economic development groups. The SBA lends money to the nonprofits. They pool the SBA funds with others drawn from the community, and grant loans directly to prospective business owners.

The proceeds from these loans can be used for several purposes: working capital, or the purchase of equipment, inventory, supplies, or furniture. However, the loans cannot be used to repay existing debts.

If you are unable to obtain a microloan, consider these other forms of federal financial assistance.

7(a) Guaranteed Loan Program

If you need a loan in excess of $100,000, consider applying for this program. It provides SBA loan guarantees up to $750,000 or 75 percent of the loan amount, whichever is less. Small business owners can use the monies to start a new business, acquire an existing business, or expand an established firm. Many entrepreneurs who are already in operation use proceeds from a 7(a) loan as working capital (e.g., to purchase inventory and equipment or to finance the construction or remodeling of a facility). Through this program, the SBA will finance up to 90 percent for construction and real estate loans, and up to 100 percent for working capital and equipment purchases. The interest rates, which can be fixed or may fluctuate over the life of the loan, are based on the prevailing prime rates. As discussed earlier, if the loan term is less than seven years, the maximum interest rate allowed is the lowest prime rate plus 2.25 percent. If the loan term is longer than seven years, the maximum interest rate permitted is 2.75 percent. An SBA 7(a) guaranteed loan is a popular financing tool for new small businesses; however, the loan application is more complicated than those used for other loan guarantee programs, and you would be wise to seek professional assistance. Many local or state economic development agencies would be willing to offer you assistance at little or no cost. A good place to start is with the Minority Business Development Centers (MBDCs). Established by the Minority Business Development Agency (MBDA), these centers help minority entrepreneurs with a number of operational activities, including the preparation of loan packages. MBDCs are scattered throughout the nation. To locate the one nearest you, call the Minority Business Development Agency (202-482-5061). For assistance, you can also consult the Yellow Pages for a listing of professional loan packaging services. Realize, however, that you may have to spend from $1,200 to $5,000 for these services. The paperwork involved in applying for a 7(a) loan is enormous. It can take a minimum of 25 hours to prepare a successful loan package, so be patient when filling out the forms and waiting for a response. Turnaround time ranges from a few weeks to several months.

LowDoc Loan Program

Established in 1993, this program provides guarantees on commercial loans under $100,000. Unlike the 7(a) Guaranteed Loan Program, LowDoc requires less paperwork, and the processing time is generally less than one week. The interest charged on a LowDoc loan varies according to the loan amount. For loans of less than $25,000, the maximum rate is 4.75 percent above the prevailing prime rate. For loans between $25,000 and $50,000, lenders can charge no more than 3.75 above the prime rate. But if the loan amount is $50,000, the cap is determined by the loan's maturity. If the loan is for less than seven years, the cap on interest is set at 2.25 percent. For loans beyond seven years, the maximum rate is 2.75 percent. As with any loan, LowDoc requires that applicants meet certain criteria before financing is made available. Essentially, any business that qualifies for a 7(a) loan is eligible to apply under the LowDoc program. However, this is not the only requirement that must be fulfilled. Your staff can be no more than 100 persons (including the owner, partners, or principals), and your average sales over the past three fiscal years must be less than $5 million. LowDoc requires less paperwork than 7(a), but there are certain documents that the SBA will still want to see. If you are seeking a guarantee on a loan of $50,000, you will have to provide:

1. A LowDoc application. This is a one-page, two-sided form. On one side is the prospective borrower's SBA loan application. On the flip side is the lender's request for the loan guarantee.
2. A personal financial statement.
3. Evidence that you were denied a loan from a conventional lender.
4. A personal guarantee from any individual who owns 20 percent or more of your company.

If the guarantee is for a loan that ranges between $50,000 and $100,000, you will have to supply all of the above documents plus:

1. Personal financial statements from all owners of the business and any other guarantors.
2. Your income tax returns for the past three years.
3. Year-end statements, if you are already in business.
4. Cash flow projections.

Since its inception, the LowDoc program has made financing available to nearly 90 percent of its applicants.

Section 504 Loan Program

Essentially, this program provides long-term and fixed-rate financing for firms that want to invest in fixed assets such as land, vehicles, equipment, construction, buildings, renovations, and intangible property such as patents and trademarks. These funds cannot be used for consolidating or repaying debt, working capital, or inventory. Section 504 loans are typically used by existing business owners who want to expand their operations. However, start-up firms can also make good use of the loan guarantee, particularly if the business will involve property ownership. For example, manufacturing companies may apply for 504 loans because the majority of these enterprises tend to purchase rather than rent or lease real estate for their operations. Section 504 loans are also targeted to businesses that will aid local economies by increasing job opportunities. The loans are administered through SBA-approved companies called Certified Development Companies (CDCs). A CDC is a private nonprofit entity established to help improve the economic development of a community or region. Participants in a CDC in-clude professional organizations, private investors, banks, and utilities. The average cost of projects financed through CDCs is $1 million. A Section 504 loan may be attractive, but not every business owner will qualify for funds. To become eligible for the loan guarantee, you must:

1. Own a for-profit sole proprietorship, partnership, or corporation.
2. Indicate that your after-tax profits for the previous two years aver-aged less than $2 million.
3. Sustain a net worth of less than $6 million.

If you are going to apply for a Section 504 loan, know that the CDC will require that you make some contribution. Start-up firms are generally re-quired to commit an equity investment of 20 to 30 percent and to meet the following criteria (in addition to the general requirements set by the SBA):

- Create or retain one job for every $37,500 of the total costs.
- Pay any legal fees assessed by the CDC.
- Pay a one-time processing fee (generally, 1.5 percent of the total loan amount).
- Prove that your cash flow is stable enough to allow repayment of the debt.
- Supply collateral to secure the loan.

Other contributions required before the CDC will approve funding in-clude the following:

- Existing firms must contribute 10 percent.
- Banks and other private lenders must commit 50 percent. The bor-rower has to provide collateral (such as a mortgage or personal guar-antee) to secure the loan.
- The SBA will have to dole out 40 percent. The business owner also must provide collateral in the form of a mortgage and personal guarantee.

Minority Business Development Agency

Black business owners have long been the victims of discriminatory loan practices when dealing with conventional lenders. To overcome this chal-lenge, many have participated in financial assistance programs such as the 7(a) Guaranteed Loan Program. Still, many African American entrepre-neurs are finding it difficult to gain access to capital. But because of federal organizations such as the Minority Business Development Agency, black-owned companies are increasingly obtaining the funds they need to start and grow their operations.

The MBDA was formed in 1969 as a unit within the U.S. Department of Commerce. It is the only federal agency designed specifically for the creation, maintenance, and growth of minority-owned firms. Groups that can receive assistance include: black Americans, Native Americans, Asian Pacific Americans, Asian Indians, Spanish-speaking Americans, Puerto Ricans, Hasidic Jews, and Eskimos/Aleuts.

The MBDA provides support to minority-owned firms in the form of technical, managerial, and financial assistance. The agency helps new business owners with a number of issues that impact start-up financing. For example, through its minority business development centers, the MBDA helps needy entrepreneurs prepare loan packages, write business plans, and fine-tune financial statements for review and consideration by potential lenders. The MBDA does not make grants, loans, or loan guarantees to business owners, but it identifies sources of funding and helps prospective borrowers qualify for 7(a) loans and other lending programs. In fact, most of the financial support provided through the centers is in the form of helping minority business owners acquire debt financing from banks and other lending institutions.

MBDCs are spread throughout the country. There are regional offices in Atlanta, Chicago, Dallas, New York, and San Francisco, and district offices in Boston, Miami, Philadelphia, and Los Angeles. For a location nearest you, call 202-482-5061. Keep in mind that the MBDCs charge a nominal fee for some of their services.

Whether you are a new business owner or an existing entrepreneur, finding capital for your business is not easy. It can be one of the great frustrations of starting or expanding your business. Don't quit after just a few attempts at meeting with a banker, an investor angel, or another financial lender. Hold fast to your dream of entrepreneurship. Prepare your business to access the capital you need, and wait patiently. The money *will* roll in.

CHECKLIST

THINGS TO CONSIDER WHEN SEARCHING
FOR SEED MONEY

✓ **Your cash needs.** Before you approach any bank or other lending institution, you must determine how much money you will need. No two businesses require the same amount of capital, but virtually all start-ups have expenses for rent, equipment, inventory, insurance, and advertising. Determine your start-up costs by creating a business budget and forecasting your business sales.

✓ **Equipment required.** The type of business that you operate will dictate the equipment that you will need. If you will require computers, fax machines, or xerox copiers, you have the option of purchasing or leasing. Many new business owners lease equipment because it allows them to set up quickly without making a huge cash outlay. Consider how equipment-intensive your firm is, and choose a financing option that best matches your needs.

✓ **Vehicle use.** Not every business owner will require the use of a car, truck, or van to operate the business. If you do, you can either lease or purchase your vehicle. Most new business owners finance their vehicles through a lending institution. Before you close any deals, consider whether a vehicle that you already own can be used for business activities. If so, you can save a lot of money.

✓ **Debt financing versus equity financing.** No matter what type of financing you secure, it will fall under either debt financing or equity financing. Debt financing is essentially borrowing funds from a bank or other lending institution and repaying them in a specified period of time. With equity financing, you give up an ownership interest in your business to a lender, in exchange for capital.

✓ **Financing options.** There are many ways to secure money for a new business. The neighborhood bank is the natural choice for most small business owners. Other sources of cash are: investor angels, venture capital firms, small business investment companies, factors, suppliers, the SBA, and family and friends.

RESOURCES FOR MORE INFORMATION

ASSOCIATIONS

- *The Capital Network (TCN),* 3925 West Braker Lane, Suite 406, Austin, Texas 78759; 512-305-0826; www.tcnmit.org. The Capital Network, the nation's largest and most successful venture capital network, provides a matchmaker service that pairs business owners with potential investors. TCN also offers educational programs, venture capital conferences, software, seminars, and literature useful to new entrepreneurs.

- *Caribbean American Chamber of Commerce & Industry (CACCI),* Brooklyn Navy Yard, Building 5, Mezzanine A, Brooklyn, New York 11205; 718-834-4544; www.internationalcacci.com. Founded in 1985, CACCI promotes economic development among Caribbean American, African American, and other minority-owned businesses. This organization provides technical assistance, referrals, business development seminars, and training programs such as "How To Start, Operate and Manage a Business." CACCI also provides information on how you can start and maintain a successful susu.

- *Commercial Finance Association (CFA),* 225 West 34th Street, Suite 1815, New York, NY 10122; 212-594-3490; www.cfa.com. This organization provides a number of financing services for business owners, including equipment financing, factoring, equipment leasing, and inventory financing. CFA also publishes *The Secured Lender,* the only publication devoted exclusively to the asset-based financial services industry.

- *Equipment Leasing Association of America (ELA),* 4301 North Fairfax Drive, Suite 550, Arlington, Virginia 22203-1627; 703-527-8655; www.elaonline.com. This association promotes and represents the interests of the finance and equipment leasing industry. ELA provides information regarding how business owners can finance their equipment, and offers referrals to entrepreneurs in search of a lessor.

- *International Reciprocal Trade Association (IRTA),* 175 West Jackson Boulevard, Suite 625, Chicago, IL 60604; 312-461-0236 www.irta.net. IRTA is a nonprofit corporation that supports the commercial barter industry worldwide. Through its barter exchanges and corporate barter companies, IRTA allows business owners to swap their goods and services. IRTA also serves as a watchdog for the entire barter industry, and it represents the interests of its members before public bodies.

RESOURCES FOR MORE INFORMATION *(continued)*

- *Minority Business Development Agency (MBDA)*, 14th & Constitution Avenue NW, Washington, DC 20230; 202-482-5061; www.mbda.gov. Through its minority business development centers, the MBDA assists start-up and existing business owners in obtaining financing for their firms. It also helps entrepreneurs prepare loan packages, write business plans, and create financial statements for review and consideration by potential lenders. Although the organization does not issue grants, loans, or loan guarantees to business owners, it does identify sources of funding for start-ups and helps borrowers qualify for lending programs.

- *National Association of Small Business Investment Companies (NASBIC)*, 666 11th Street NW, Suite 750, Washington, DC 20001; 202-628-5055; www.nasbic.org. NASBIC provides legislative representation for business owners, and information regarding venture capital available to small entrepreneurs. Its publications list small business investment companies throughout the United States.

- *National Association of Trade Exchanges (NATE)*, 27801 Euclid Avenue, Suite 610, Cleveland, Ohio 44132; 216-732-7171; www.nate.org. NATE is considered to be the premier organization for trade exchange owners throughout the world. The organization's newsletter highlights trends and news in the barter exchange industry. Annual conventions are held for members of the trade industry.

- *National Venture Capital Association (NVCA)*, 1655 N. Fort Meyer Drive, Arlington, Virginia, Suite 850, 22209; 703-524-2549; www.nvca.org. This association was formed in 1973 to represent the interests of the private equity and venture capital industries. NVCA sponsors a management liability insurance program, regional venture capital/entrepreneurial networking luncheons, and provides research and publications that highlight issues germane to the venture capital industry.

- *U.S. Small Business Administration (SBA)*, 409 Third Street SW, Washington, DC 20416; 202-606-4000; www.sba.gov. The SBA is one of the greatest financial resources for new and existing entrepreneurs. Through its guaranteed loan programs, it offers business owners access to capital that they might not otherwise be able to obtain. Among the loan programs the organization maintains are: the microloan program, the 7(a) Guaranteed Loan Program, and the LowDoc loan program.

9

ADVERTISING YOUR BUSINESS

"Yo Quiero Taco Bell." Who can forget these words uttered (digitally, of course) by the doe-eyed Chihuahua as it beckoned hungry mouths. What began as a single 30-second television commercial mushroomed into perhaps one of the most memorable fast-food advertising campaigns of 1998. Taco Bell released nearly a dozen TV spots featuring the pint-size pooch. As a result, fans erected Web sites in honor of the cute canine, Chihuahua sales went through the roof, and the billion-dollar franchise raked in yet more *dinero*. That's the power of advertising. And, like customers, it's something that no new business owner can do without.

Advertising is one of the most important aspects of building a new business. To succeed, your firm must generate sales. But you can't make sales unless you attract potential buyers, and you can't attract potential buyers unless you spread the word about what you have to offer. Having a good idea is not enough to create a successful business. You have to let consumers know that you exist, describe the products or services you provide, and communicate how those products or services will benefit them. As a new shopkeeper, you may not have the financial resources to employ a lovable dog to push your products or services during prime time. However, in many inexpensive and creative ways, you can market your operation.

When husband-and-wife team Rudy and Sharon Shepard launched their alterations and embroidery shop in 1992, they used several "bootstrapper" techniques to build their customer base. They issued flyers advertising their services to their customers. But they also hauled their embroidery machines (via their customized trailer) to boat shows, motorcycle rallies, and other gatherings throughout North Carolina, their home state. "A lot of times when we go to the shows, they are very slow, so we get a chance to meet a lot of people and talk about our business and the service that we provide. We pick up a lot of business that way," says Rudy Shepard. "At one time, I thought about providing giveaways at the shows, but I decided that the only thing I would give away is my business cards."

Although a large portion of their business is generated by visiting area shows, Shepard says he has acquired a number of new customers by simply putting his company name on throwaway placemats in major restaurants throughout the area. "We were listed on placemats used in restaurants in Charlotte, Greensboro, and Raleigh, and that brought in quite a bit of business. By having our name on the mats, we actually reached an audience 90 miles from our shop. But the first time I really noticed how far our name was going was when a customer from Charlotte came into the store. I asked him how he heard about us and he said he was eating dinner at a restaurant in Charlotte one evening and noticed our name on one of the placemats, so he tore it off. He planned to make his way through Greensboro and said that he would stop and he did. It ended up being a sale for me because he bought some jackets and several other items."

Shepard says the cost to have his name on the placemats was about $200; the listing ran for about six months.

As you plan your marketing push, keep in mind that advertising is just one part of the process. Successful marketing also includes market research (see Chapter 3), pricing (see Chapter 11), promotions, public relations, and sales and distribution. In this chapter, we will discuss some common advertising, promotions, and public relations techniques. It's important to carve out an advertising campaign that will knock the socks off potential customers and put you ahead of the competition, but you must not forget one key factor in the midst of all the brochures and billboards: YOU. How you market yourself is just as important as how you market your business. You might think that slightly scuffed shoes and a bright orange suit are sufficient for behind-the-desk duties. But your appearance can greatly impact the image your company portrays and the amount of sales you generate. Even your telephone etiquette and how you enter a room can say a lot about you and your abilities as an entrepreneur.

This chapter will offer some tips on how you can market yourself. You never get a second chance to make a first impression, so you should put your best foot forward from day one.

THE MARKETING MIX

When you think of marketing, what comes to mind?

_____ (a) Glitzy ad campaigns.
_____ (b) Aggressive selling techniques.

_____ (c) Competitive pricing.

_____ (d) All of the above.

If you checked (d), you were right. According to the American Marketing Association, marketing is "the process of planning and executing the conception, pricing, promotion, and distribution of ideas, goods, and services to create exchanges that satisfy individual and organizational goals." In other words, marketing involves identifying what product or service you will sell, the people you will sell it to (your target audience), how you will price it, how you will make potential buyers aware of it (advertising, promotions, or public relations), and how you will make it available to the consumer (sales and distribution channels).

By now you should have identified what goods or services you will sell, what audience you will target, and how much you will charge for your product or service. The next step is to determine how you will reach your potential customers. Will you use flyers or word-of-mouth? Trade shows or direct mail? Billboards or the Internet? Press releases or product demonstrations? There are a variety of techniques that you can adopt. Whichever method you choose, it should produce more exposure for your business and ultimately increase your sales.

GETTING YOUR MESSAGE ACROSS

Advertising your products or services can be an exciting part of starting your new business. It's a chance for you to unleash the creative side of your personality and go for broke (figuratively speaking, of course). Unlike other marketing techniques, such as public relations, when advertising your business, you have total control over the message that you will convey, where the ad will be placed, and how often it will run. Choosing the right medium to spread the word about your products or services is not always easy. Not every technique will suit the needs of your operation. For example, you may want to use a billboard to advertise your products, but if you operate a gift basket company, this may not be the most effective or most affordable way for you to reach your target audience. Before you plunk down money for a splashy ad campaign, consider the following factors.

Your Objective

What are you trying to achieve by advertising your product or service? Do you want to create greater awareness about your company, or increase sales in five years? Before you select an advertising tool, clearly establish your specific goals. For example, don't simply say you want to increase sales or build your staff. Instead, you may want to indicate that you will "boost sales by $15,000 during our first year in business," or "grow our staff by eight new employees within three months." By pinpointing exactly what you want to achieve, you will be able to choose an advertising medium that will be most effective in helping you accomplish your goals. Write down your objectives, to force yourself to be specific. When setting your goals, realize that not all of them may be directly related to sales. Perhaps you want to improve your company's image. If so, your ad campaign will focus on changing your customers' perception of your business rather than on making a buck.

Your Budget

When deciding what medium to use, always consider your budget. You may want to use radio spots to advertise your business, and it may make perfect sense to do so, but can you afford it? As a rule of thumb, you should earmark between 2 and 5 percent of your projected gross sales for your advertising budget. As a new business owner, you may not be able to devote this much cash to your marketing push. If you cannot, don't panic. There are many "bootstrapper" or "shoestring" techniques (discussed later in this chapter) that you can use to advertise your operation. When making a selection, choose a medium that you can afford to use more than once. One of the keys to a successful advertising campaign is frequency. To persuade prospective customers to buy from you and not from your competitors, you must hit them with your message again, and again, and again, and again. Some marketing experts say that potential consumers must be exposed to an ad seven times before they consider making a purchase. Don't blow your entire budget on a flashy 30-second television commercial that your target audience will see only once. Instead, put your message in a less expensive medium (such as a newspaper or magazine) that you can afford to use week after week or month after month. Cost should not be the only factor you weigh. Take into account the frequency of each medium, the types of people it attracts (they may or may not be within your target audience), and how effective each medium will be in conveying the message you want to get across.

Your Audience

Who are the people you want to reach with your advertising? Where are they located? You must answer these two very important questions when deciding which media to use. Some media have a strong appeal with particular groups of people. To determine the best way to spend your ad dollars, you must match your potential customers with the kinds of media that they see and hear. For example, if you operate a young adult nightclub and an area radio station targets the 18- to 35-year-old crowd, you may choose to saturate the airwaves with a message about your new venture during early evening. If you decide to launch a fishing supply shop, you may opt to take out a half-page ad in a magazine that's geared toward fishing enthusiasts. Determining which media will reach your target audience can be challenging, but assistance is not far away. If you can't identify your audience's media preferences, call the sales department of the particular outlet and ask for demographic information. Newspapers, magazines, and radio and television stations maintain reports indicating specific details about their subscribers or audiences, including age, income, product brand preferences, and other key attributes (see Chapter 3). Never try to sell to just anyone who has a few dollars to spend. Your ad campaign could be costly and yield little or no return on your investment. Focus on your target audience. You will make smarter and more cost-effective advertising choices.

Your Message

Determine what you will say to your audience and how often you will say it. No matter which method you choose, you should convey how your product or service will benefit your customers. Explain the features of your product or service, but focus even more attention on what your business can do for the end users. Customers buy benefits, and they want to know why they should buy them from you. Will your product or service save customers time or money? Will it improve their appearance or stamina? Whatever the benefit, clearly indicate the advantages customers will enjoy by purchasing your products or using your services. Be careful about the length of your message. If you have lots of information to disseminate, don't use a 30-second radio spot for advertising. If you can convey your message better by giving a product demonstration, don't place a print ad in the local newspaper. Carefully consider the content of your message, and then choose a medium that can effectively accommodate your needs. Lastly, determine how often you will need to post your ad. The timing needed will help you choose the right medium. If you plan to advertise a weekend white sale, your best bet would be to use radio. You will have the opportunity to run your ad several times a day, for the entire week leading up to the sale.

Your Positioning

Positioning is a process whereby you add brand value or personality to your business by communicating the differences between your company and the competition. By positioning your product or service, you are communicating the features and benefits that make your business unique. This is a very important aspect in creating effective advertising because how you position your product or service dictates the content of your message. When developing your positioning strategy, the key is to determine how important product differences are to your potential buyers. If they are not important enough to influence a customer's buying decisions, they really don't matter. You can set yourself apart from the competition in several ways. For example, you can offer special packaging, discount prices, or personalized service. In some instances, the differences between your business and your competition will be difficult to see and even harder to communicate. Take McDonald's and Burger King as an example. Both are fast-food restaurants that offer burgers and fries. But each has developed a loyal following because of unique differences that have been communicated to customers. You must create a difference for your business even if it is similar to others. To determine how potential buyers value your business differences, you can conduct qualitative market research (interviews or focus groups) or quantitative market research (consumer surveys; see Chapter 3). When devising your strategy, be careful not to "overposition" your company by promising features and benefits that your product or service cannot deliver, or to "underposition" it by failing to indicate all the features and benefits that your goods or services are capable of providing. Clearly state which aspects are features (packaging, price, color, and style) and which are benefits (time-saving and cost-saving advantages, pain relief, greater strength, and faster service).

To help with your positioning strategy, consider creating a unique selling proposition (USP)—a single, concise statement that describes the unique qualities of your business versus the competition. Savvy business owners often create a USP in the form of a slogan or catchy phrase, and carry it throughout their advertising and promotional activities. Some well-known commercial slogans include Sprite's "Obey Your Thirst" and Nike's "Just Do It."

A memorable USP is perhaps the best way to succinctly describe what sets your business apart from the rest. To help you craft your statement, ask yourself the following questions:

- What is unique about the product or service versus the competition?
- Which differences are most important to target buyers?
- Which factors can be easily communicated and understood by potential consumers?
- Which differences are not easily duplicated by competitors?
- Is it possible to develop a USP based on the differences that have been identified?
- How can the USP be conveyed to the target audience?

Advertising can help you build a successful business. But, for advertising to be effective, it must be credible, interruptive, unique, memorable, and consistent. Good advertising makes customers stop eating, talking, flipping through the comics, or drinking a cup of coffee, to take a peek. If you don't agree, think back to some of the Nissan car dealership advertisements in which playful pups were used to sell the four-wheel-drive line. Or how about the "Khaki Swing" commercials from The Gap. Honestly, didn't they make you stop for at least 30 seconds to catch a glimpse?

Here are eight tips to help you create a memorable ad that sells your product or business:

1. *Convey a simple, single message.* Remember the KISS principle: Keep It Simple, Stupid. No matter which advertising medium you use, you have only a few seconds to grab a potential customer's attention and persuade him or her to make a purchase. Don't overload your ads with unnecessary jargon or too many features. Cut to the chase. Tell potential buyers what they can gain by buying from you. Some key words you may want to include in your broadcast or print ad are: "free," "guarantee," "money," "easy," "fun," "fast," and "now." For example, if you operate a tax services company and you want to run a print advertisement several weeks before April 15, your headline could read: "Need Your Taxes Done in a **Flash?** Come Down to Bob's Tax Planning Services **Now.**"

2. *Portray credibility.* If your ad will say "Service in 20 minutes or it's free," make sure that you can deliver. If customers find out that you can't, your advertising efforts could damage your business. Also, don't use your ads to browbeat the competition. Focus on what *you* can do. As long as you can do it better, perhaps cheaper, and with a smile, customers will eventually come your way.

3. *Stick with one style.* Perhaps the worst thing you can do—even worse than imitating a competitor's ad—is to develop five wonderful and memorable ads, each with a different style. Advertisements take on a personality and style of their own. Changing ads too quickly will only confuse potential buyers and ruin your chances of gaining memorability. Find one style that you like and stick with it.

4. *Go for the sale.* Ultimately, you want a potential buyer to open his or her wallet and make a purchase, so give consumers the opportunity to do just that. In your advertising, invite buyers to come into your store or to call you for more information. State clearly your location, telephone number, fax number, and Web site address (if you have one). Mention your store hours and the methods of payment you accept. If your ad says "We accept personal checks," you may be guaranteeing more sales.

5. *Be competitive.* Whatever type of business you start, you will face some competition. Create an ad that will stand apart from the rest. Research the advertisements of your competitors in the media that you want to use. Match them against yours for uniqueness, credibility, and recall. To gauge how your ad might fare in the marketplace, conduct a focus group or survey with members of your target

audience. Depending on their responses, you have an opportunity to make changes or additions before investing any money in a final advertising choice.

6. *Create a professional look.* Appearance is key in creating ads that sell. No one will want to buy from you if your ad is poorly written or designed. Unless you are a professional writer or artist, commission an advertising professional or an agency to lend a hand. You will be buying superior writing and artistic skills and computer savvy that can create eye-catching, vibrant ads. It is particularly important that you seek outside help if you plan to advertise on commercial or cable television. Don't even think about using your home video camera to shoot a commercial. Outside professionals' fees are not cheap, but they may save you money and time in the long run. To cut costs, consider hiring college journalism and/or advertising students. They may be willing to do the job in exchange for the experience. Contact the administration or marketing departments of your local colleges and universities for more information.

7. *Be honest.* Honesty is the best policy in *anything* you do, but it becomes extremely important in advertising. Potential buyers want to know that they can trust your products or services to deliver certain benefits, and, more importantly, that they can trust you. Whichever advertising technique you adopt, ensure that it will convey your message in a truthful manner. Communicating deceptive practices and false advertising could cause you to be heavily fined or could land you in jail.

8. *Create ads that reflect your positioning.* Make sure your ads coincide with your positioning strategy. If your position statement conveys particular features and benefits, duplicate them throughout all of your advertising efforts. This will add *consistency* to your ad campaign and create *memorability*—two critical aspects of any ad campaign.

Advertising Myths

The purpose of advertising is to make potential customers *aware* of your products or services. However, many business owners assume that just because they advertise, they will automatically generate sales. According to the SBA's Office of Women's Business Ownership (OWBO), this is one of several advertising myths. The Online Women's Business Center, an Internet resource created by the OWBO, lists these three myths surrounding advertising:[1]

- *Myth 1: If a product isn't selling well, advertise it.* You can spend thousands of dollars to create a colorful, eye-catching ad to unload last year's inventory, but unless customers truly want or need a product, they will not make a purchase. You may be able to get a potential buyer to come into your store, look at the items up close, and ask additional questions (possibly about a discount for discontinued merchandise), but the bottom line is: If the item is not wanted or needed, no amount of advertising will help you generate the sale. Your best bet is to spend your ad dollars on promoting new and existing products.

- *Myth 2: Advertising can create sales.* Many people think that advertising and sales are one and the same. They are not. Advertising is one part of the marketing process, which involves product, price, place, and promotion. These entities have to work together if your cash register is to be ringing. No part of the process can function by itself to get potential customers to buy your products or services. Your advertising makes customers aware of your offers, communicates how they will benefit by buying from you, and distinguishes your products or services from the competition. But unless consumers are comfortable with other marketing variables, such as the price of the item or the place in which it can be purchased, they will not spend their money.

- *Myth 3: Advertising can manipulate people to buy.* Every consumer chooses whether to buy a product or service. No advertising can force an individual to make a purchase that he or she does not want or need. Advertising appeals to emotions, so if your print ad, television commercial, or radio spot can persuade customers that your product or service can fill a need, you have a good chance of gaining a sale.

Low-Cost and No-Cost Advertising Methods

The amount of money you will need to spend on your advertising campaign will depend on the industry that you serve, your competition, and your personal preference. For some entrepreneurs, money is no object when they are advertising their operations. But most new business owners will have to curb the amount they spend on pushing their products or services. That's not to say that you must sacrifice quality for cost. You can advertise your business in many appealing low-cost and no-cost ways. Perhaps the most effective—and definitely the cheapest—way for you to spread the word about your products or services is through word-of-mouth.

Many experts consider word-of-mouth to be the most effective form of advertising. By using this technique, you can pass on information about your products or services free-of-charge. And what better way to attract new clients than by having satisfied customers tell their friends, who tell their friends, who tell their friends, about the benefits of purchasing from you?

Not every new business owner will want to rely on word-of-mouth to build a business. You can use the following bootstrapper techniques if you are operating on a shoestring budget.

Business Cards

It's virtually impossible to conduct business today without having a colleague, customer, banker, supplier, or other interested party ask for your business card. Using a business card is one of the least expensive and most effective ways for you to advertise your business. (You should be able to have a couple hundred printed for less than $100 at any stationery store.) However, many business cards do not generate a lot of business because they are not created properly. A business card is more than just a reminder of your company's name, address, and contact numbers. It is an important marketing tool that reflects the image of your business. Everything from the paper stock to the size of the lettering and the graphic design (if any) can affect whether someone will be willing to do business with you. Pay as much attention to creating your business card as you would to any other part of your advertising campaign. For starters, consider the size. The average business card is 3.5 by 2 inches. Avoid creating a bigger card. (It won't fit nicely into a prospective customer's wallet.) If the card is not wallet size (or can comfortably fit into a rolodex), it may end up in the trash or beneath a stack of papers on top of someone's desk. Use at least 80-pound card stock. Anything else will be too light and will appear cheap. Like a handshake, a business card should be firm and solid. Lightweight cards may create an impression that you too are lightweight in your business dealings and lack credibility. Remember, it's important that your advertising efforts are credible. On the card, indicate your company's name, logo, and address, your telephone number and extension, your fax number, a Web site address/e-mail if you have one, and your title. You may also want to consider listing some of the features your product or service will provide. Don't list prices or fees. If you run out of space on the front of the card, put lesser details on the back. Don't use a typeface smaller than 10 point. If a potential customer has to squint to read your card, you are likely to lose a sale. Pass your cards out. Don't order them and then let them collect dust. Make it a point to pass out at least ten cards each day.

Flyers

Anyone who drives can recall a time when they've come out of a shopping mall and noticed a flyer advertising a new restaurant opening in town. Flyers are a cheap way for you to spread the word about your new business. You can create them on your own personal computer or contact a neighborhood print shop to give you a hand. Using colored paper and a few creative designs, you can create mini billboards for your business that can be distributed all over town. You can post them on free bulletin boards in laundromats, grocery stores, or beauty parlors and barber shops. You can also place stacks in the lobbies of office buildings, tuck them beneath car windshield wipers, hand them out to shoppers in a bustling shopping center, or go door-to-door throughout your community. You can also insert them with bills to your suppliers and other outgoing mail.

Brochures

Brochures afford you the opportunity to provide detailed information about your business and the products or services that you offer. Most business owners will use triple-fold brochure stock and computer software to create professional, sleek-looking brochures at little cost. You should be able to find user-friendly desktop publishing software in a local computer supply store. Quick-print places such as Staples and Kinko's may be able to assist you in your creative endeavors. When developing your brochure, consider the graphics or art you will display. If you have a company logo or slogan, give it a prominent spot. If you already have a few loyal customers on board, ask their permission to include their testimonials. Most satisfied customers will be more than happy to comment on how your business has benefited them. By incorporating these blurbs, you will encourage customer loyalty and increase your chances of making future sales.

Yellow Pages

When you are looking for an inexpensive way to advertise your business, remember to "Let your fingers do the walking." Listing your company in the Yellow Pages is a great way to promote your business. People use the Yellow Pages to locate restaurants, law firms, florists, hotels, shoe repair shops, clothing boutiques, cleaning companies—you name it. The cost of a listing varies, depending on the size and complexity of the ad. Call the sales office of your local Baby Bell for specific rates and for the deadline date of the next annual printing. To list your company in the Yellow Pages, you must have a business telephone line. To set your ad apart from your competitors, use solid black borders (if possible) and boldface type, even if you will need only a single-line entry. Also use a bit of color where you can. (Red is generally permitted.) When buying into the Yellow Pages, be careful about the number of categories under which you list your company. What starts as an economical way to advertise your business can quickly turn into an expensive tool.

Per Inquiry

This bootstrapper advertising technique is generally associated with radio and is widely used among product-oriented businesses. Somewhat like bartering, it is a process in which you pay only for the responses that are generated as a result of your advertising message. In other words, you pay the station a percentage of your product's price (generally, 50 percent) for each sale that is generated from the radio spot. The station does not get involved with handling or filling the orders. It simply plays your commercial. When the orders start pouring in, the station counts them and forwards them to you to be filled. If this is the method you want to use, you will have to identify the stations that are popular among your target audience. A listing of radio outlets nationwide is printed in the *Broadcast Yearbook,* a resource usually available in the reference section of libraries. Make a list of the stations you want to contact. Call the station managers, explain that you have a product that you feel will sell extremely well in the station's market, and ask whether the station would be interested in a Per Inquiry advertising arrangement. If so, ship a packet of information off to the stations immediately. This packet should include a written or taped copy of the commercial you intend to use (most likely, you will need two 30-second and two 60-second commercials), a brief description of your product, a proposal outlining how you will handle orders as well as complaints, and when and how you will pay the station its percentage of the sales. Also, be sure to include a self-addressed, stamped, reply postcard and ask the station manager to inform you about when the commercials will air, during which periods of the day, and how often. A few weeks before your ads are scheduled to air, call the station manager to make sure everything is on track and there are no last-minute questions.

Company Logo

If you've created an eye-catching logo or slogan for your business, you should place it on all printed collateral, including your business cards, flyers, and brochures. You may even want to create a pin in the shape of your company logo. It will make a great conversation piece and will give you the opportunity to talk about your business in just about any setting where you will wear the pin.

Doorhangers

And you thought they were just for "Do Not Disturb" signs. Doorhangers make great economical tools for advertising your business. They are widely used among fast-food restaurants and other service-type businesses. If you decide to create a doorhanger for your operation, don't cut corners on the stock. It should be heavy enough so that it will not blow off the doorknob. You should be able to have doorhangers made at any stationery store.

Printed Bags

If you have a company logo or slogan, you may want to print it on the bags that you will give to customers when they purchase a product from your store. Print the bags on both sides. They can serve as walking billboards when departing customers make their way back to their cars or go in and out of other businesses in the area. If someone in another store sees a bag that carries your company name, that person may make a stop at your doorway.

Company Baubles

A number of inexpensive trinkets can be imprinted with your company name, logo, and/or slogan, and given away to customers. Some popular baubles include: pens, pencils, coffee mugs, keychains, bumper stickers, buttons, and calendars. If you buy these items in bulk, wholesalers may offer you a discount.

Gift Certificates

Selling gift certificates is a great way for you to recruit your existing customers as sales representatives. They will purchase them for family or friends, so they are introducing your business to more potential buyers.

Holiday Cards

Christmas, Kwanza, Chanukah, and other holiday cards establish courteous contacts with your customers, clients, suppliers, and banker. They also give you an opportunity to advertise your business inexpensively. Like your business cards, holiday cards can show off your company logo and/or slogan.

As you can see, there are many ways in which you can advertise your business at little or no cost. If you have enough cash in your coffers, you can hire a professional advertising agency to work on your campaign. Check the Yellow Pages for a list of firms, or ask other business owners for referrals. Outline your advertising objectives clearly. Keep in mind that not all ad agencies are the same. Some will put together entire marketing campaigns. Others will work only on advertising. What services will you need to spread the word about your firm? How much are you willing to spend? Select an agency that has the skills needed to help you meet your advertising goals.

Whether you decide to go with a professional ad agency or adopt a shoestring technique, always deal with each ad message separately. A print publication may convey one message well, but that doesn't mean that it will make sense to use print media for all future advertising efforts. When calculating your costs, always spend wisely. Get the biggest bang for your buck, but make sure you are using the medium that will be most effective in reaching your target audience.

Putting Your Business in Print

The "classifieds" aren't just pages where the jobless look for employment. Interested buyers look there for deals on cars, clothing, furniture, real estate, appliances—you name it. When looking for a place to house your ad, try your local newspaper. Taking out a classified or small display ad in a daily or weekly paper, and running it constantly under the right category, can generate a huge response for your business. But before you call an ad department to reserve your space, request a media kit from each publication in which you would like your ad to appear. These kits provide rate information as well as demographics concerning the audience the publication serves. The cost to place an ad in the classifieds varies according to the size and structure of the ad.

There are several advantages and disadvantages to using newspapers for advertising. The advantages are:

- *Popularity.* With so many advertising tools from which to choose, newspapers are still the number-one advertising medium in terms of where U.S. ad dollars are spent. In fact, 25 percent of the average U.S. ad dollar goes toward newspapers.
- *Diverse audience.* Daily newspapers are capable of reaching a broad audience that encompasses all races, ethnic backgrounds, and social and economic classes.
- *Timely delivery.* Because newspapers have a regular publishing schedule (daily, weekly, or monthly) ad messages can be tailored to current events.
- *Immediacy.* Newspapers are an immediate form of communication that readers pick up within a certain time frame. In other words, if it's Sunday, readers will read the Sunday paper. More than likely, they will not read Saturday's paper on Sunday afternoon. Because newspapers are immediate, you will have a clear sense of when a potential consumer will see your advertisement.
- *Unlimited space.* As long as you have the money, advertising space in a newspaper is unlimited. You can have a one-column, a half-page, or a full-page ad. The choice is yours. Realize, however, that the bigger the ad, the more money you will be charged.

Some disadvantages of newspaper ads are:

- *Poor reproduction of photos.* Technology has allowed some improvements, but the quality of photographs in newspapers is not top-notch. To cut costs, newspapers typically use a lower grade of paper that reduces the clarity of pictures. If you must have photos to convey your message, inquire about space inside a four-color magazine or trade publication.
- *Limited readership among particular age groups.* Most 14-year-olds do not read a newspaper, so if your target audience is preteens, you are not likely to reach them by advertising your products or services in a newspaper. Baby boomers and seniors tend to be newspaper readers.
- *Difficulty in reaching target audience.* You may want to hone in on skiers, chefs, or musicians, but you will be paying to target a much broader audience because newspapers reach a diverse group of people.

Another print alternative is magazines, including regional, national, or industry trade publications. Securing space in one of these periodicals will give you a chance to reach a wider audience, but the cost may be significantly more than a newspaper ad. However, the response you may get from a four-color quarter-page or half-page ad may be well worth the money you spend.

The advantages to magazine advertising include:

- *Targeted audience.* There are hundreds of specialty magazines geared toward certain groups of people. You can easily select a target audience by simply securing ad space in a magazine geared toward the people most likely to purchase your products or services. For example, if you operate a golf shop, you may want to advertise in *Golf Digest.*
- *Flexible layouts.* Like newspapers, magazines are very flexible with space. You can use a couple of lines, a quarter-page, or a whole page. You can also create ads with color, fragrances, and pop-out or foldout pictures. Magazines offer a great opportunity to create eye-catching ads.
- *Quality photos.* Many magazines are four-color and are printed on glossy, high-grade paper. This approach allows for quality photographs and clearer ads.
- *Long shelf life.* People generally save their magazines for a time when they can sit down and enjoy reading them. The longer shelf life works to your advantage because when the potential customer is in the mood to buy (perhaps when on vacation or during a weekend) and picks up the magazine to begin leafing through, your ad will still be there.

Some disadvantages to magazine advertising are:

- *Cost.* Because most magazines use high-grade, glossy stock, the cost to print is expensive. This translates into higher costs for your ad.
- *Advanced deadlines.* Most magazines schedule their publications three or four months in advance. To obtain space, you will have to ready your ads well ahead of time. If you are bogged down in the day-to-day activities of running your business, you may not have the time to prepare ad projects well in advance.
- *Timing of ad exposure.* There's no way to pinpoint when a potential customer will see your ad. Magazines generally include a slew of feature articles that readers tend to pore through before anything else, so days or even weeks may pass before your ad is actually read. Your ad could possibly become outdated by the time someone notices it.

If neither newspapers nor magazines pique your interest, consider creating a company newsletter. By using this publication, you will be able to (1) advertise your products or services in greater detail than in a classified ad and (2) stay in touch with your customers on a regular basis by offering news about the business. It's also another way for you to display your company logo and/or slogan.

Internet Marketing

Chances are you know someone who has purchased at least one item on the Internet. Perhaps you've even traveled throughout cyberspace to go on a shopping spree of your own. Increasingly, customers are browsing and buying online. Statisticians predict that, by 2002, consumers will conduct more than $300 billion in online transactions. What does this mean for a new business owner? A chance to make big bucks, provided he or she advertises on the Internet.

Internet marketing, also known as "cybermarketing," allows entrepreneurs to advertise and sell their products or services online. Cybermarketing is becoming very popular among small business owners who relish the opportunity to reach millions of potential customers around the world, at minimal cost.

Using his interactive Web site, Tony Haywood has lured customers from Canada, Chile, Turkey, Mexico, and Japan to his turbo shop, A-1 Turbo Industry Inc., in Santa Monica, California. "I decided to set up a Web site because I realized how accessible it would make us to international customers. I didn't have to spend hundreds or thousands of dollars placing ads in international newspapers. I could just build a Web site and still reach the same audience," says Haywood, whose company builds and rebuilds turbochargers and superchargers for cars, trucks, and buses.

Haywood braved the world of HTML coding and created the site himself. He contacted the World Business Exchange (WBE), an online service provider for small business owners (see Chapter 10), to host the site, and spent only $700 in initial costs to get it up and running. He pays $25 per month to have WBE maintain and update the site. Customers who type in www.a1turbo.com can view turbo models and prices for such cars as Audi, Saab, Toyota, Chevrolet, Chrysler, Porsche, Pontiac, and Dodge.

Like Haywood, you can advertise your business by setting up a company Web site. You don't have to have deep pockets to create dazzling and professional Web pages, nor do you have to have a graduate degree in computer technology. With just a few lessons in HTML coding, you can create a site yourself, but most business owners enlist the help of a professional Web designer to build a site, and a local or national Internet Service Provider (ISP) to host the site. (See Chapter 10 for specifics on how to develop a Web site, and typical costs.)

To support your e-commerce needs, you should invest in some "shopping cart" software. These programs provide a convenient and easy way for customers to make a transaction and receive their items in a timely fashion.

For example, shipping software allows customers to choose their preferred method of delivery, and cross-selling software gives customers an option to purchase companion products at the time of their initial purchase. For instance, if a customer orders a pair of shoes, the cross-selling software program would automatically suggest other related items such as trouser socks or hosiery.

Other features you may want to add to your virtual storefront include e-mail updates and virtual customer software. By using e-mail updates, you give customers the option of receiving information on new product releases. Once a customer visits the site, he or she can register for the service, input information about the types of products he or she likes, and instantly receive bulletins when the products become available. Virtual customer software allows buyers to provide feedback to the business owner and communicate with other customers via a customer comments page or chat room.

Just because you build a Web site, you are not guaranteed that consumers will come, especially if they don't know that the site exists. Publicize your site. Register it with the major search engines such as AltaVista (www.altavista.digital.com), Infoseek (www.infoseek.com), and Lycos (www.lycos.com). Enroll in a program such as LinkExchange (www.linkexchange.com), and print your URL on all of your print collateral, including your business cards and stationery.

You may also want to join an Internet mall or "cybermall," a collection of companies listed on a single Web site (see Chapter 10). Cybermarketing is the new frontier for entrepreneurs. However, it does not go unchallenged. Some consumers are increasingly comfortable with doing business electronically, but many others are still wary of giving credit card information over the Internet. Therefore, business owners must ensure potential buyers that their transactions will be secure.

To ease these fears, credit card companies have developed Secure Electronic Transactions (SET), a program that encrypts credit card information after a consumer makes an online purchase. Another program that provides security over the Internet is Secure Links. This device protects the link between the business and the customer, and keeps information from being intercepted during the transaction process.

Direct Mail

Remember the old saying, "One man's junk is another man's treasure?" This could very well be the mantra for business owners who use direct mail to advertise and sell their products or services. Often viewed by the consumer as endless junk mail, direct mail is one of the most effective and fastest growing marketing tools in use today. The primary purpose of direct mail is to make a sale, but this medium can also be used to increase awareness about your product or service. This section will explain the nuts and bolts of the entire process.

Also known as direct marketing or direct response marketing, direct mail is a technique in which an advertiser (the business owner) sends messages directly to potential buyers through the mail. Unlike newspaper or television advertising, direct mail allows you to have total control over how your message is presented. You do not use another medium to convey your ad message. You create the message and then place it directly into the hands of your target audience. Moreover, direct mail allows you to present your product or service, make an immediate offer, and go for a quick sale—all at the same time. Some types of direct mail include sales letters, brochures, catalogs, and other product literature that gives consumers an opportunity to place an order.

What makes direct mail such an effective medium is that it enables you to target very specific groups. For example, using a mailing list, you can mail to potential customers living within a particular zip code area, to senior-level managers in a certain industry, or to potential buyers of a specific type of product. However, a main challenge is market saturation. By initiating a direct mail campaign, you will be in competition with thousands of other companies vying for the same consumer dollars. Therefore, you must make your direct mail stand apart from the rest. This is no easy task, so before you affix stamps to a stack of envelopes, consider the following factors:

- *Target audience.* Consider the people to whom you will sell. The more you know about your potential customers, the easier it will be to tailor your mailing to them. Determine whether the customers will purchase your products through the mail. There would probably be little point in preparing a direct mailing for a used car dealership, because people do not purchase cars through the mail.

- *Your objectives.* Determine what you hope to accomplish by using direct mail. Are you looking to net immediate sales or to simply give more exposure to your company? Perhaps you just want to spread the word about your product or service and give potential buyers a chance to mull over your offer before making a purchase at a later date. When developing your direct mail campaign, you must remember that this marketing technique requires a long-term commitment. You can't expect to send out a single mailing and generate a quick return. Response takes time, so be patient.

- *Budget.* How much are you willing to spend to bring a customer on board? Not every product or service will make money the first time around. In fact, some goods and services may generate sales only when companion or ancillary products are offered. Determine how much cash outlay you can comfortably part with to acquire potential buyers.

- *Buyer motivation.* As with any form of advertising, when developing your direct mail campaign, you must give considerable thought to what motivates potential buyers. Are they moved by fear, love, need, or greed? Determine why customers would be willing to purchase your products or services. Often, a key to mail order success is offering products that no one else provides.

- *Geographic location of buyers.* Where do your prospective buyers live? Is there a mailing list available that includes your target market? Not every product or service sells the same in all locations, so you must find out where your potential customers reside. For example, if you operate a pool cleaning service, you will want to target higher-income neighborhoods as opposed to lower-income communities.

- *Market size.* Determine whether your market is large enough to support your business. If your market consists of only 15,000 people and you plan to sell your product at $5 a pop, it's highly unlikely that you will be able to keep your business afloat, especially when most direct mail campaigns garner only a 3 percent response rate.

It's important that you consider these factors, but the real key to a successful direct mail campaign is your mailing list. You can have the most colorful, well-written, inviting sales letter or brochure, but if it's sent to the wrong individuals, you have defeated the purpose of direct mail. Direct mail experts indicate that 50 percent of direct mail's success hinges on the mailing list used; 40 percent, on the product offer; and 10 percent, on other variables. A mailing list is simply a list of names. A list can be created in a number of ways. Some lists are generated from publication subscriptions. Others are compiled based on customers of particular companies or people of a certain age group who have purchased specific products or services.

To obtain a mailing list, you can contact a list broker or list house. List brokers are companies that represent the owners of mailing lists and arrange to rent them to individuals interested in direct mail. After you pay the fee, the list becomes yours to handle in whatever way you choose. The broker receives a commission from the owner of the list for each rental made.

There are many ways to find a list broker. For starters, look in the Yellow Pages under "Mailing Lists," or surf the Internet using one of the major search engines. Publisher's Yellow Pages, at www.morganprice.com/pyp /000002nq.htm, is one site that offers a list of brokers. You can also ask for referrals from other business owners who've used direct mail. The costs for mailing lists vary according to the type of list. Compiled lists—those generated using sources such as industry directories or telephone books—are usually the least expensive. They typically rent for a charge of $20 to $80 per 1,000 names, but be aware that they usually garner the lowest response rates. Lists created from subscriptions to publications generally rent for $75 to $150 per 1,000 names, and more specialized lists cost hundreds of dollars per 1,000 names. You can fine-tune your lists by renting "selects"—list subsets that are broken down by criteria such as gender, age, location, the size of customers' purchases, or a position as a top-level executive. Selects generally cost from $5 to $20 per 1,000 names. The standard rules of the direct mail business state that individuals must rent at least 5,000 names at any given time. For the more popular lists, a rental of at least 10,000 names is required.

Finding the right list for your business is not always easy. Your list broker should be able to identify lists that match the needs of your operation and predict how a list might perform. The best lists are usually those that have worked well for a product or service that is similar to yours. Your broker should also be knowledgeable about how well a list is maintained. Beware of slick, fast-talking brokers. When meeting with a broker, ask the following questions to make sure that you are getting names that you can use:

- *What is the source of the list?* Each list gives a profile of prospective customers: their educational status, gender, age, and other attributes. It is important to determine where the names originated. You can then ascertain whether the people on the list have been so inundated with direct mail that they may not be open to receiving information about your product or service.

- *How often is the list updated?* Fifty percent of the names on a mailing list are useless after one year. Determine when the list was updated or you may be paying for names that you cannot use. For example, if you wish to target new car buyers, make sure the list you obtain is current. A list of last year's buyers will not suffice. Brokers are responsible for removing duplicate names and outdated addresses from the lists.

- *When are the lists of names compiled?* Mailing list houses gather their names at different times. Some compile lists once a year; others generate names more frequently. Determine when the lists are created and whether they are sufficiently up-to-date.

- *What is the pricing structure?* Prices for mailing lists differ because of a number of factors, including the methods used to compile the names. Ask your broker what your list will cost.

- *What is the broker's professional experience?* Just as you would with any professional, ask the list broker about his or her work experience. Some brokers are more knowledgeable than others. Try to find a broker who works with other clients whose needs are similar to yours.

Before purchasing a particular list, ask the broker for the names and telephone numbers of businesses that have used the list in the past six months. Call a few of those operations and ask what their response rate was and how many returns they received because addresses were incorrect or outdated.

Give careful thought to the materials you will use for your direct mail campaign. Your direct mail message can affect your response rate. Here are some tips for creating a winning direct mail piece:

- *Focus on customer benefits.* Your direct mail piece should clearly indicate how your product or service will benefit the recipient. Use the lead paragraph or the first few sentences of your sales letter or brochure to talk about benefits. Don't put your company's history, or information about the features of your product, at the beginning. Prospective buyers might discard your mailing before getting to what the product or service can do for them. Remember, customers buy benefits.

- *Use the KISS principle.* Keep your message simple, easy to understand, and persuasive. Don't use unnecessary jargon to try and impress the customers. Just give them what they need.

- *Ask for the sale.* The beauty of direct mail is that you can increase awareness about your products or services while also going straight for the sale. Make it easy for potential buyers to place an order. List your toll-free number (if you have one), fax number, street address, and e-mail address. Include order forms, and designate the methods of payment you will accept. Use phrases such as "Call today," or "Order now," to encourage customers to act.

- *Use a personalized writing style.* You want the customer to feel and know that you have his or her best interests at heart. Use a personal and friendly writing style to convey a sense of one-on-one communication.

- *Include a self-addressed reply card.* Even if you don't generate a sale as a result of your direct mail piece, you would at least like some customer feedback. Include a response card and invite customers to submit their opinions about your products or services. You can use this information to tailor your next direct mail campaign and other advertising efforts.

- *Create multiple direct mail pieces.* Even if you are offering the same product or service, it may have different benefits for various age groups. For example, your product may serve seniors differently than young married housewives. Create a different direct mail piece of the same offer for each known audience.

- *Make the offer for a limited time.* If potential customers see that they have only a few days to make a buying decision, they may be more apt to act quickly. Set limits to your offers, to encourage potential buyers to pick up the phone and place an order.

When orders begin to roll in, you must be prepared to handle them. As a small business owner, you may not have the in-house resources to handle all the calls, shuffle and process the order forms, deliver the goods, and handle customer complaints (should they occur). To relieve the burden, consider outsourcing your direct mail responses to a fulfillment house, which, for a fee, will field your calls, handle the transactions, and deliver the product to buyers. This is an expensive service to use, but it may be a wise choice until you build a staff capable of handling your complete responsibilities to customers.

Signs and Displays

Signs and billboards are great advertising tools. You can use bright colors, neon lighting, and fancy designs to attract potential customers. Many business owners use reader boards—signs that use individual lettering to provide information about a company. To be effective, a reader board must be positioned in a well lit and carefully maintained area. Avoid misspellings, and update the board frequently. If you decide to use a reader board, keep in mind that zoning ordinances limit their use. Check your local laws before positioning your board.

There are several advantages and disadvantages to using billboards or signs. The advantages are:

- *High visibility.* Most billboards and signs are hung high, where passersby can see them easily. Your message is bound to attract some attention.
- *Diverse audience.* People walk and/or drive by billboards and signs every day. Many of these people could be potential customers. A big splashy ad could make them decide to head straight for your store.
- *Maximum impact.* You can use a number of features on your signs, to gain maximum impact. Billboards that talk, move, or twinkle are great attention getters and show that you are a creative business owner.

The disadvantages to using signs and billboards are:

- *Cost.* The price for renting billboard space varies according to the location and the size of the ad, but be prepared for a major outlay of funds, particularly if you choose to use the more advanced features described above.
- *Inability to target a specific audience.* You may be able to target a specific neighborhood, but it will be virtually impossible to be any more specific than that. Billboards may be viewed daily by millions

of travelers, but many are just passing through. It will be difficult to identify your target market.

- *Exposure to wear and tear.* Signs are subject to inclement weather and vandalism. Graffiti can turn a beautiful and expensive ad into an eyesore that is an irritant to the surrounding neighborhood.

A sign or display need not be stationary. Create traveling billboards by tacking rubberized magnetic signs to your car or van. They can be easily removed when the vehicle is used for nonbusiness activities.

Point-of-purchase displays—signs, posters, custom display racks, or video monitors—are other alternatives. Consider using register tape with coupons printed on the flip side, to encourage customers to return at a later date.

YOUR PUBLIC RELATIONS PUSH

Public relations is another marketing technique that can increase awareness of your products or services. Public relations gains free publicity for your company through appearances on radio or local television shows, press releases for your local newspaper, participation in community activities, or a hosting role for special events. To execute a public relations campaign, you must use the same procedures you use to create an advertising campaign: define your objective, identify your target audience, set a budget, determine your message, and review your positioning statement. Initiating a strong public relations push is not difficult, but only careful planning will make it effective.

Some people think that public relations and advertising are the same activity. They are not. When you advertise your business, you control the message, its placement, and how often it runs. If you write a press release, hoping that a local editor will then write a story about your company, you have very little control over the outcome. The newspaper may discard the incoming press release. If it is judged newsworthy, you will have no control over the content that is used, or the date, page location, or accuracy of its publication. Nonetheless, using public relations is a great way to push your products or services into public view, and the rising costs of some forms of advertising make free publicity an attractive option.

Preparing a Press Release

A little "good press" about your company can go a long way. Perhaps no one knows that better than Vivian Gibson, president of The MillCreek Company in St. Louis, Missouri. By issuing press releases about her Vib's Caribbean Heat, a hot seasoning sauce, she has appeared on numerous television and radio shows and has been featured in articles in the *St. Louis Post-Dispatch*, *Black Enterprise* magazine, and *St. Louis Magazine*. Now she writes a monthly cooking column for the *St. Louis American Newspaper*.

"I write an article on food and recipes, and half of the recipes have my sauce in them. The arrangement is very nice because I get to talk about food, the newspaper gets a food section that they never had before, and I get free publicity," says Gibson, who also sets up tastings of her hot sauce in stores throughout her area, and teaches cooking classes at a local school.

Potential customers who read an article about your company in a well-known and popular print publication will look favorably on your operation and may be persuaded to visit your store.

Gaining free publicity for your company can begin with a single press release. A press release, also known as a news release, is a one- to two-page announcement about your company and the products or services that you offer. Press releases are sent to local newspapers, magazines, trade publications, and television and radio stations. They are also included in press kits, which we will discuss later in this chapter.

Many of the stories you see on the evening news or read in the Sunday morning paper are generated from press releases. The next feature you see could be yours, if you plan properly. The key to getting a newspaper editor or station manager to notice your press release is to make it newsworthy. You must convince the recipient that your company has something valuable to offer readers, listeners, or viewers. If you tie your story into current events, you will increase your chances of getting coverage. Here are some topics typically included in press releases:

- New product releases, services, or innovative ideas.
- Survey or research findings.
- New staff appointments or promotions.
- Upcoming activities or special events such as grand openings or anniversary celebrations.
- Reactions to decisions made by competitors and other businesses.
- Scholarships and other award presentations.
- Sponsorship of community programs.

Journalists receive hundreds of press releases every day, so competition is stiff. Rarely do reporters or editors have the time to read every release from beginning to end. If they can't decipher, in the first few sentences, who you are and what you have to offer, your release may be sailed into a wastepaper basket. When creating a press release, use the inverted pyramid model: structure your article so that all the important information is summarized in the beginning. The five "Ws" (who, what, where, when, and why) of your story should be indicated in the first few sentences. Follow these statements with a few important details, and leave the less important, less interesting data for the end of the article. When articles are too long, journalists cut them from the bottom. By listing all the important information at the top, you will not have to worry about losing any critical details that could impact a potential customer's decision to make a purchase from you.

The information included in a press release will vary from one business to the next. However, there is a basic format that every business owner should follow when creating this document. Here are the general guidelines:

- *Length.* Press releases are usually one page. If your information must spill over onto a second sheet, try to end the first page with a complete sentence or paragraph, and center the word "more" at the bottom of the page to alert the reader that there is additional information. On the second page, place a brief heading at the top (flush left or flush right; not centered). Include your company name, the page number, the date, and the topic of the release. At the end of the press release, center the word "end" or the symbol "###" at the bottom of the page.

- *Message.* Always use the KISS principle (Keep It Simple, Stupid). Your release need not be complex or "deep." Simply state who you are and how a story about your company will benefit the audience. Use the active voice when you write, and keep your sentences short and punchy. You may want to include quotes from key personnel in your company or experts within your industry, to add credibility to your story. Avoid using too many acronyms. At its first appearance, indicate what each one stands for. Tell readers how to contact you for more information. Double-check the correctness of all names used. An editor may decide to use your press release exactly "as is." Lastly, spell check the entire document. One misspelling can ruin an otherwise perfect press release.

- *Format.* Print the release on your company letterhead. If you don't have business stationery, use an 8½" × 11" sheet of white paper and list your company name, address, telephone number, fax number, and Web site and/or e-mail address (if you have one). Provide a contact name (most likely, this will be you) and telephone number that readers can call for additional information. Use one side only, and double space the text. Set your margins at one inch on both sides, and indent all paragraph openings. At the top of the page, type the words "News Release" or "Press Release" so that the editor or reporter can quickly identify it. Indicate whether the information is for "Immediate Release" or can be used at a later date. For example, you could type "For Release on September 11, 1999" or "For Release on or after September 11, 1999." Begin your opening paragraph with a dateline (the date and location of the news event). Your dateline might look like this:

PHILADELPHIA, Pennsylvania (September 11, 1999)—Bob's
Bagel Barn is introducing a new. . . .

Provide a short headline that describes the content of the story. The reader should be able to grasp what the article is about by simply glancing at the headline. Try to include your company name in its wording.

- *Photos.* You do not have to include photos with your press release, but they make a nice addition, especially if your press release will discuss a staff appointment or promotion, or a new product. Newspapers generally use 5″ × 7″ or 8″ × 10″ black-and-white photos, but always confirm the preferred size before sending any photos. Magazines generally use color prints, so you may need to send a quality color slide for reproduction. Make sure you include a caption, keyed correctly to each print. Use the active voice when writing the descriptions, include the five "Ws," and identify all photo subjects from left to right. Do not write on the back of the photographs. Type each caption on a separate sheet of paper and attach it with a paper clip (not a staple) to the correct photo.
- *Timing.* Each publication's or station's schedule varies, so you should call the appropriate person at each facility to find out the best time to send your press releases. Generally, releases to daily newspapers should be sent at least one week in advance. Most major magazines are published monthly and operate on a three- to four-month advance schedule, so you will have to send your releases well in advance if you are targeting a particular publication date.

Along with the press release, you may want to create a fact sheet—a list of additional features of your product or service that do not appear on your press release. Your fact sheet should be one page and should give only facts (no quotes) about your product or service. List the features in an outline format or as bulleted points.

When your press release is complete, choose a medium that is most likely to run a story about your type of business. Before mailing your release, review several publications to gauge their style and format, and the types of articles they include.

To locate newspapers, try the *Editor and Publisher Yearbook* or *Hudson's News Media Contacts Directory.* For radio and television, search the *Broadcasting/Cable Yearbook.* And for magazines, flip through *Writer's Digest.* You should be able to find these resources in the reference section of your local library.

If you are sending your release to newspapers or magazines, address it to the managing editor. You can follow-up a few days later to see if the editor would like to discuss your release. The best times to call are during the morning or evening hours. This is typically "down time" for reporters.

When you call, don't jump right into what you want to say. Ask the editor if he or she is working toward a deadline and whether it's a good time to talk. If so, be ready to make your pitch in a couple of minutes. Never demand to know whether your story will run. This will only anger the editor and could ruin your chances of dealing with the publication in the future. If one editor does not use your press release, don't give up. Review your story. Perhaps write it from a different angle and forward it to another publication. If an editor does decide to use your story, make yourself available for additional questions. After the story is printed, send a thank-you card.

If you choose to send your release to radio or television outlets, address it to the news director or program director. If you are invited to appear in person, get additional information about the station and the specific program involved. Is the format talk, news, or lifestyles? Is it a live call-in show, or will you appear before a studio audience? Meet with the interviewer a few days before the show, to go over what you will discuss. Find out how long the interview will last, and where it will take place.

Radio and tv are media that require quick and clear delivery, so you must give short, but natural, answers or sound bites. To help guide you through the interview, draft an outline listing specific points of discussion or objectives. Also prepare opening and closing statements. To ease your fears, conduct a mock interview with a friend or family member, and time your answers. Avoid being long-winded.

If you are invited to be on a radio program, your attire is of less concern than if you were to appear on television. For either medium, wear business attire. Women should not change their daily make-up (a television station may have a make-up artist who can assist you) and their hairstyle should accentuate their face rather than hiding it.

On the day of the interview, arrive 30 minutes early. Relax and be natural. After the interview, send a personal thank-you note to the interviewer/reporter and the station manager.

Creating a Press Kit

To achieve the greatest impact with your public relations campaign, you may want to consider creating a press kit or media kit—a collection of materials designed to convey a detailed message about your product or service. Press kits give reporters and editors an in-depth look at your business and what you have to offer. Send your media kit to newspapers, magazines, radio, cable, and television stations when you are making a major announcement, or you wish to highlight a discussion during a meeting with various media representatives.

Press kits are usually presented in a standard two-pocket folder, although you can choose to create a fancier container. Media representatives get hundreds of press kits each year, so you may want to develop a unique design that will entice an editor to open your kit and take a closer look.

Here are some typical items found in a standard press kit:

- *Press release.* As discussed earlier, a press release is a one- to two-page story about your company and its products or services.
- *Business card.* Include your business card or that of the appropriate contact person. Virtually all press kits have a slot on the front inside pocket where you can display a business card.
- *Photographs.* You can insert a black-and-white or a full-color glossy photograph. Photos are particularly important if you plan to introduce a new product or make a staff announcement. The photo size will depend on the preference of the publication or station.
- *Biographies.* Include profiles of your key employees and yourself. Indicate educational and professional work experience as well as community service and other activities that may interest the reader.
- *Testimonials.* Success stories from satisfied customers can enhance your press kit immensely and add credibility to your company. If others have positive things to say about you, an editor may be more inclined to run a story about your business.
- *Company backgrounder/fact sheet.* A company backgrounder is a one- or two-page summary that provides background (history) about your business and your goals. A fact sheet gives information about your product or service, and highlights its features and benefits.
- *Charts/graphs.* Statistical charts and graphs can add credibility to your product or service. Savvy business owners include charts that compare their products or services with those of their competitors.
- *News clippings.* Next to testimonials, article reprints are the next best thing to present when you are trying to persuade an editor to run a story about your business. If other media have interviewed you, the editor may be more inclined to offer coverage. Include copies of any past press coverage you have received.
- *Newsletters, brochures, or catalogs.* If you have created a small brochure or newsletter, include it in your press kit.
- *Question and answer sheet.* This list suggests the questions an interviewer may want to ask if he or she decides to do a story. This approach may appear to be aggressive, but it can actually work in your favor. Editors may be impressed with your attention to detail and, if they do conduct an interview, you will have saved them time by preparing the unit yourself.

Before sending off your press kit, draft a pitch letter—a one-page piece that serves as the motivator to get an editor to open up the kit. A pitch letter quickly and clearly explains why your company would be of interest to the media's audience. Within the letter, you should also suggest possible approaches or "angles" to the story.

Performing Community Service

You can cast your marketing net even wider by participating in community-related activities. Besides earning you free publicity, your involvement will help you build good will among potential customers and others in your community.

Some of the activities you may want to consider participating in include community sporting events. Perhaps you can sponsor the neighborhood softball or basketball league, and your team could wear your company logo on the back of their uniforms.

Consider donating your time and products or services to local civic organizations, schools, and churches. For example, if you operate a bake shop, you could donate refreshments for the monthly chamber of commerce meetings. Look for opportunities to meet other entrepreneurs and build name recognition for your company.

Hosting special events is another public relations option. Anniversary celebrations, grand openings, fashion shows, and other fundraisers are always great attention getters. Search your local newspaper or church bulletins for information about upcoming events. Volunteer to host the events, and invite your potential buyers to attend.

PROMOTING YOUR BUSINESS

Everyone can recall looking under a bottle cap or inside a candy wrapper to see whether it revealed a $2 million prize. Many large commercial companies use this promotional technique to initiate sales and promote their products or services. As a new business owner, it's highly unlikely that you will be able to give away millions of dollars, but you can still award prizes to your target audience in an effort to generate sizable sales for your firm.

Like advertising and public relations, promotion is a marketing technique that builds buyer awareness of a product or service and also initiates immediate purchases. Some promotional activities are prohibitively expensive, but there are other inexpensive ways to promote your business. Some typical promotional activities include product demonstrations, contests and games, gift giveaways, and offering coupons. Whichever promotional method you choose, make sure it conveys the right message about your business.

Product/Service Demonstrations

Perhaps the best way for you to persuade potential customers to buy your products or services is to show them what they can do. Holding product or service demonstrations ("demos") at your store is a clever and cost-effective way for you to promote your business. Statistics indicate that, because of product demonstrations, 51 percent of shoppers experiment with products that they normally would not try. Just think about how many purchases a supermarket or grocery store realizes, because of in-house demonstrations. Some grocers maintain a movable feast inside their walls to persuade customers to try new brands.

A demo is often accompanied by a free product sample or free trial service, but not every business will be able to provide free samples. For example, if you operate a jewelry store, this technique will not bode well for your company's bottom line. However, many enterprises (ice cream parlors, coffee houses, or snack shops) can use it for a short time to generate appeal among potential buyers.

You can use all sorts of demos to promote your products or services—everything from open house days (to introduce customers to your new facility) to taste tests or test drives (for car dealerships). Service-oriented businesses (tax or financial planning services, or antique dealers) can use free seminars as a way to display their expertise. One of the most popular demos is the trade show.

According to *The Power of Exhibitions II,* a study conducted by Deloitte & Touche and published by the Center for Exhibition Industry Research, trade shows have a greater effect on sales than direct marketing and telemarketing. Business owners spend about $16.5 billion a year on exhibits. Lusetha Rolle, owner of Cadtech Group, spends about $3,000 each year on trade shows.

"I go to very specific shows where I know the attendees are looking for drafting services or engineering support, rather than general membership shows," says Rolle, whose company creates drawings of mechanical parts for government aircraft and architectural floor plans.[2]

Trade shows are usually grouped according to industry, product, and market. They vary in size and cost and can be general shows or more specialized events. For example, some trade shows will bring together small business owners and corporate buyers; others will allow business owners to sell directly to potential customers and other operations. There are a number of trade shows that you may want to attend. For starters, consider reserving space at the Business-to-Business Expo held annually during the Black Enterprise/NationsBank Entrepreneurs Conference in Orlando, Florida. The conference brings together scores of business owners to network and discuss entrepreneurship. Ron Riley, marketing manager of Kemi Laboratories, reserved a booth at the 1998 Business-to-Business Expo, hoping to net some valuable contacts for distribution of the company's line of skin and hair care products. And he did. "We signed up seven or eight new distributors on the spot," Riley says.

Many major organizations, including the National Association for the Advancement of Colored People (NAACP) and the National Urban League, sponsor trade shows during their annual conferences to give African American business owners a chance to promote their products and services to conference attendees.

Trade shows can be an excellent way for you to make valuable contacts and attract new customers for your business, but they are not cheap. Costs vary according to the type of show and its size, but you can expect to incur these average expenses:

- *Exhibit space.* A space measuring 10′ × 10′ is standard for each exhibit. To reserve this amount of space, you may have to spend from $500 to $1,200.

- *Display units.* The cost for an area to display your products can run about $3,000.

- *Lights, graphics, and other features.* To make your booth stand out from the rest, you may want to use bright bold lights and colorful graphics. These can cost you up to $15,000.

- *Carpet rental.* Carpet adds a warm touch to your booth and creates a more professional look than the hardwood floor. Expect to pay around $85 for carpet rental.

- *Electrical lines.* You will need to install lines for your lights, computers, and any audiovisual aids you may use. The cost: about $80 to $100.

- *Draped table.* This item for your booth is priced at about $50. The more tables you have, the more expense you will have. A word of advice: Place your table at the back of your booth and set chairs up front. It creates a more inviting look to passersby.

- *Chairs.* Visitors to your booth may want to sit and discuss your products or services in great detail, so have a few chairs handy. They may cost you about $40. A word of advice: Don't sit longer than you have to. Unless you are talking with customers, remain standing. If you sit, you will look tired and disinterested.

- *Telephone line.* You have to have a phone. You may need to keep in touch with your office, so plan to spend around $150 for the line and about $50 to rent the phone itself. You can also bring a cell phone along.

- *Freight services.* You can use your own dolly to transport your materials from your car to your booth, but you probably will not have to. Most trade shows offer freight services and will carry your materials from the loading docks to your booth and back, for between $30 and $50 per 100 pounds.

Cost is a critical factor in any decision to attend a trade show, so choose carefully the shows you will attend. You want to get the most for your money, and if you attend the wrong show, you could end up losing dollars. Don't assume that bigger shows will land you more sales. You could actually make out better by setting up a booth at a smaller show where attendees will have a greater opportunity to visit all of the booths, including yours. At a large show, potential customers may not make it around to your exhibit, particularly if it's set far away from the exhibit hall entrance or other prime locations. To locate a trade show that will serve your business well, visit the Trade Shows News Network Web site, at www.tsnn.com, or the Trade Show Central Web site, at www.tscentral.com.

Realize that although you may promote your business through a trade show, you may not net immediate sales. Many attendees simply browse while they make their decisions about whether to purchase your products or services. To reel in customers you meet during a trade show, you must follow up after the event is over. Send a note to the people you meet; thank them for stopping by your booth. If you don't make contacts right away, don't feel discouraged. Just keep trying. Rolle spent two years following up on a lead she obtained at the Virginia Regional Minority Supplier Development Council trade show. Rolle was bent on securing a contract with Alliant Techsystems, managers of a Virginia military base, so whenever she came into contact with the firm's buyer she would sell herself. "Every time I saw her at a show, I'd talk to her. I sat next to her at banquets and chatted her up at receptions. When the show would end, I'd send faxes and newsletters keeping her informed about our company." The hard-sell paid off. Rolle was asked to bid for a job.[3]

Contests and Games

Many small business owners will create games and contests to lure potential customers to their shops. For example, restaurants may have customers fill out a card before leaving, and drop it into a fish bowl. Several weeks later, the owner of the eatery will hold a drawing and award a free meal or other prize to the winner.

Holding drawing contests and other games is a great way to build loyal customers and attract new ones. You can hold something as simple as a "Guess How Many Jelly Beans Are in the Jar" contest and award the winner with a gift certificate to use in your store, a T-shirt, a hat, or a similar item. Your prize need not be extravagant to attract attention. Virtually everybody enjoys a good contest, so you should have little difficulty getting people to play along.

Whatever games you decide to play, make sure they are fair—and free—to all customers. Indicate how many winners will be selected, and the prize that will be awarded. If relevant, note that any taxes due will be the responsibility of the winner. It's not a bad idea to check with your attorney about local laws before holding any contests.

Gift Giveaways

"Free" is the magic word when you want to attract customers. Who would turn down a chance to get an item without spending any money?

To promote your business, you can provide gift giveaways of T-shirts, pens, coffee mugs, keychains, and other specialty items that have your company name and logo printed on them. But before you indulge in this promotional activity, make sure that the cost of the gifts will be recovered through increased sales. One way to determine whether your giveaways are netting more sales is to ask customers how they heard about your business. If the majority of them reply that they spotted your company in the classifieds or saw your flyer tacked to a church bulletin board, giving away free items may not be worth the money you're spending.

Coupons for Your Customers

Virtually everyone has used coupons at least once in their life. Many people have entered a store just to redeem a coupon they clipped from the Sunday paper. That's the whole point of coupons—to get customers into your store, where they can get their discount and see all the other products you have to offer.

Most coupons offer customers a price reduction. However, many reward loyal customers for their patronage. For example, some card shops offer their customers a card that is punched every time an item is purchased. When the card is fully punched, the customer can receive a free item or a sizable discount on a future purchase.

Coupons are a good way to promote your business, but the redemption rates are low. Only a small percentage of coupons are actually used. (Newspaper coupon redemption rates hover between 1 percent and 5 percent.) If you already have some customers, you may have more success if you attach your coupons to products. This approach generally earns redemption rates of 20 percent to 50 percent.

If you decide to use coupons, make sure you offer at least a 10 percent discount off the retail price, and don't forget to announce an expiration date.

SELLING YOURSELF

When you're spending countless hours preparing your advertising, public relations, or promotional campaigns, it's easy to lose sight of *you*. However, it is important to spend some time working on how you will market yourself. Something as simple as wearing scuffed shoes or a loud tie is sure to send the fashion police your way; more importantly, your attire can send the wrong message to customers about how you do business and may raise serious questions about your professionalism.

In this section, we offer some tips on how you can look your best, some advice on phone etiquette, and some suggestions about nonverbal communication. Each plays a significant role in your ability to sell your products or services.

Avoiding Fashion Faux Pas

Your wardrobe is an important part of your life, socially and professionally. What you wear speaks volumes about your personality, style, and competence. When dealing with potential customers, suppliers, and other business colleagues, you want to look your best. Carelessness here could mean forfeiting a potential partnership or sale.

Consider the following factors when you dress for success:

- *Fit.* Even the most expensive Armani suit looks bad if it's two sizes too big. Make sure all of your clothing fits. If you find an article of clothing that you like but it's not your size, have it altered. Consider your body type when picking out clothes. Be honest about how you look. If a healthy midsection will not allow you to wear double-breasted suit jackets comfortably, go for single-button jackets instead. It will give you a more attractive look.
- *Style.* The style of clothing you wear should complement your body type and lifestyle, and the industry you serve. For example, if you work in the banking industry, you will want to dress conservatively. Tailored suits in rich colors would be a smart choice. If you work in a less conservative environment, you may adopt a "business casual" dress code: khakis, sport jackets, and loafers. Just don't go *too* casual. Remember, you're still conducting business, so leave the tennis shoes in the closet.
- *Colors.* Colors can convey authority, power, and personality. As a new business owner, you want to appear confident and in-charge. When picking out your wardrobe, choose solid colors such as blacks, blues, and browns.
- *Fabrics.* The textures you choose should be attractive as well as comfortable. Natural fibers such as silk or wool are the best. They look professional and are long-lasting.

Shoes are an important part of your attire. Try all-leather shoes. They are comfortable, attractive, and durable. Women should select shoes with one- to three-inch heels. The choice of colors is up to you. Navy blue, brown, and black are the most practical colors for pumps. They're sure to complement virtually any outfit you have. Gentlemen should choose a black or brown laced shoe.

Minding Your Telephone Manners

Often, it's not what you say that turns customers away, but how you say it. As a new business owner, you will have to talk with customers, clients, suppliers, bankers, and other professionals. Many of these conversations will take place on the telephone, so you must develop a pleasant phone manner. If things start out badly on the first call, there may not be a second.

Use the following tips to improve your telephone skills:

- Smile while talking on the phone. Believe it or not, customers can tell that you are smiling.
- Never talk on the phone with food (or chewing gum) in your mouth.
- Never do paperwork, open mail, read a magazine, or perform some other task while talking on the phone. It's rude and very distracting to the other party.
- Return telephone calls promptly—within 48 hours, if not sooner. If more time passes, you could end up losing a potential customer.
- Answer the phone with a pleasant greeting. For example, "Good morning, this is Alice Walker. How may I help you?"

Nonverbal Communication

You can say a lot by not saying anything at all. Sound impossible? Not when you use such things as facial expressions, handshakes, and hand gestures. Each of these can create an impression about you as a businessperson, so you must be careful that your nonverbal communication does not send the wrong message.

A handshake is perhaps the most powerful form of nonverbal communication in the business world. A firm handshake exudes strength, power, and authority. A flimsy handshake says you are weak and perhaps shy. When meeting with a customer, always begin with a firm handshake and make eye contact with the other person.

Pay attention to how you enter a room. You need not flip on Hollywood-style floodlights to make your entrance, but enter with confidence and a purpose. Don't peek around corners; it could be a sign that you are timid. Maintain a strong stride and firm posture as you enter the door. Then extend your hand and begin your meeting. During the conversation, be aware of your body language. Whether you are talking one-on-one or in front of a room filled with people, always maintain eye contact, and keep friendly, relaxed facial expressions. Oh yes—don't forget to smile.

CHECKLIST

FACTORS TO CONSIDER WHEN
ADVERTISING YOUR FIRM

✓ **Your objective.** Determine what you want to achieve with your advertising campaign. Do you want to build buyer awareness about your products or services, or do you want to increase sales? Be sure to quantify your goals. If your goal in advertising is to increase sales, indicate by how much and within what time frame.

✓ **Your target audience.** Identify your target buyers and their geographic location. You must match the media members of your target audience to the type of medium that will best convey your advertising message.

✓ **Your Budget.** Money is perhaps the most important factor when determining how you will advertise. Review your budget to determine the amount you can afford. It may make perfect sense for you to advertise your products on television, but you may not have the financial resources to use this medium. You need not have deep pockets to launch a successful ad campaign. Several bootstrapper techniques can be used to advertise your products or services.

✓ **Your message.** Define what you want to say to your target audience, and decide how frequently you will need to say it. Your ad message should focus on how your product or service will benefit the customer. Remember, customers buy benefits, and although you will want to explain some of the features of your product or service, you should clearly state what customers stand to gain by buying from you. Be careful about the length of your message. This awareness will help you make a smarter choice when deciding which medium to use to deliver your message.

✓ **Your positioning.** Determine what makes your product or service unique. Ask yourself what distinguishes your business from the competition. After you identify these differences, determine how important they are to potential customers. Are the differences great enough to persuade consumers to buy your products or services? How you position your product or service will dictate the content of your advertising message.

(continued)

CHECKLIST *(continued)*

✓ **Your marketing tool.** Remember, advertising (via billboards, flyers, or word-of-mouth) is only one aspect of marketing communications. You can also increase awareness of your product or service by using public relations (press releases) and promotions (contests and games). Choose a marketing tool that suits *your* business. Cost may affect your selection, but you must also consider the media that your target audience is more likely to use.

RESOURCES FOR MORE INFORMATION

ASSOCIATIONS

- *American Marketing Association (AMA),* 250 South Wacker Drive, Suite 200, Chicago, IL 60606; 312-648-0536; www.ama.org. AMA is the world's largest and most comprehensive professional society of marketers. Through its 500 professional and collegiate chapters, AMA serves its members by organizing workshops, meetings, and seminars to discuss a number of topics, including marketing research, consumer marketing, and business marketing.

- *Association for Interactive Media (AIM),* 1301 Connecticut Avenue NW, 5th Floor, Washington, DC 20036; 202-408-0008; www .interactivehq.org. AIM is a nonprofit trade organization that supports companies that conduct business on the Internet. This association promotes consumer confidence in companies that do business online, defends the rights of Internet users in Washington, and provides business-to-business networking opportunities for cyberpreneurs. AIM also provides timely news about Internet developments via its newsletter and research on the Internet market.

- *The Center for Exhibition Industry Research (CEIR),* 2301 S. Lake Shore Drive, Suite E 1002, Chicago, IL 60616; 312-808-2347; www.ceir .org. CEIR maintains the world's largest database on the exhibition industry. It publishes reports and other studies highlighting exhibit industry trends. The organization has also produced "The Power of Exhibitions: Maximize the Role of Exhibitions in Your Marketing Mix," a brochure that discusses the benefits of exhibiting.

- *Public Relations Society of America (PRA),* 33 Irving Place, New York, NY 10003-2376; 212-995-2230; www.prsa.org. PRA is the world's largest organization dedicated to public relations professionals. It offers its more than 18,000 members professional enhancement through seminars, publications, national conferences, videos, and other materials. PRA also maintains the Professional Practice Center, an information center that provides low-cost access to hundreds of public relations campaign profiles and industry research findings. The Center also assists individuals in finding public relations service organizations.

10

CYBERPRENEUR

Think back to the last time someone handed you a business card. Chances are it contained more than just the person's name, address, and telephone number. More than likely, it also listed an e-mail and/or a Web site address. A few years ago, this would have been a rare find. Today, it is virtually impossible to locate anyone, especially an entrepreneur, who has not established a presence on the Web.

Business owners are increasingly using information technology, particularly the Internet, to start, maintain, and grow their firms. For many entrepreneurs, using the Internet to conduct business activities has become as natural as picking up the telephone. At the very least, owners use it to gather information about their industry and to exchange electronic messages (e-mail) with their counterparts and customers. Many shopkeepers also use the Internet to recruit employees, secure suppliers, advertise their products or services, and seal deals with colleagues who are oceans away. Just the potential to reach millions of customers throughout the world has many entrepreneurs cruising through cyberspace. Still, droves of others continue to creep along in the shoulder lane because of their unfounded fears about computers.

Despite the emergence of the Black Digerati, a group of African American professionals working in the information technology (IT) field, many black business owners still fall behind in their efforts to fully embrace technology.[1] According to a study conducted by the National Foundation for Women Business Owners, "Embracing the Information Age: A Comparison of Women and Men Business Owners," entrepreneurs are

274

integrating sophisticated computer systems into their companies. But although the report indicates that one-third of minority business owners use technology on a regular basis, it also states that another one-third never even log on to the Internet.[2]

As a new business owner, you will have to tackle a number of tasks to get your venture off the ground. Among other things, you will have to obtain financing, secure a location, purchase insurance, and hire employees, so surfing the Net may not be at the top of your "things-to-do" list. However, if you are to maintain a competitive edge in the Information Age, it is important that you use the Internet. This doesn't mean that you have to create a colorful, interactive Web site. You may not need one to successfully operate your company. However, you should have at least a basic understanding of the technology that is driving today's business environment.

The computer sits at the core of this technology, so, if nothing else, you should at least acquire a decent piece of hardware and some managerial programs to assist you in the back-office duties of running your shop. Computers are time-savers. They are able to do in seconds what used to take hours to complete. For example, by using a computer, you can create electronic spreadsheets to record and track inventory. Or you can prepare your payroll and print and issue checks. If you have a computer, you are basically just one click of the mouse away from the Internet, so we advise you to take the plunge.

Using the Internet will afford you a number of advantages. For starters, it will give you immediate access to information that could assist you in running your operation. It will keep you up to speed with what your competition is or is not doing. And it will level the playing field by giving you an opportunity to compete with the big boys of business. There's no guarantee that use of the Internet will bring riches your way, nor is it a panacea for any problems that you may have in building your business. However, if you embrace the technology and carefully plan your approach, it can help you improve your chances for profitability.

This chapter discusses some of the benefits and challenges of going online, and how you can establish a presence on the Web. To help you decide to create a Web site for your firm, we provide a crash course in Web site development. We also review fifteen business-related sites that you will want to bookmark, and provide a glossary of tech terms to familiarize you with all of the lingo.

THE BIRTH OF A NET-TION

You've heard the term *Internet* a million times. You've used it to research information for your child's book report and to unearth directives about how to finance your new catering business. But do you really understand what the Internet is, all that it has to offer, or even how it came into existence? If someone were to ask you to define this technology, what would you say?

The Internet is the term used to describe the vast, complex network of computers that gives businesses, government agencies, schools, nonprofits, trade and civic organizations, and the general public the ability to exchange information on a variety of topics ranging from cooking to sports to politics. In essence, the Internet (often referred to as "the Net," "cyberspace," "the Information Superhighway," and "the World Wide Web") is a worldwide communications medium that allows users to perform a number of tasks including (but not limited to) downloading files, sending and receiving e-mail, conducting live chats with fellow Net users, and conducting business transactions (electronic commerce). With all of its bells and whistles, it's hard to believe that only a few years ago the Internet, as we know it today, did not exist.

The Internet was born in 1969 as an outgrowth of a project created by the U.S. Department of Defense Advanced Research Projects Agency (ARPA). Then called ARPANET, it was initially designed and used to connect military installations and key educational institutions. From this project, a standard networking protocol (a communications etiquette, or "Netiquette," for exchanging information between computers on a network) was created. Once these customs were put into place, much of the software and services that make up today's Internet were developed. For example, such basic services as remote connectivity, e-mail, and file transfer appeared. However, not until the 1980s and early 1990s did the more advanced features, such as Usenet (discussed later in this chapter) and the World Wide Web (WWW), come into existence. The World Wide Web, the multimedia branch of the Internet, can be accessed by using "browsers" or software programs such as Netscape Navigator or Mosaic.

According to Roosevelt Roby, president of World Business Exchange, a Santa Monica, California-based company that allows small business owners to post Web pages to sell their products worldwide, the World Wide Web was not the place for commercial use until 1994. In prior years, the Internet's text-based design and complex user interface made it a difficult medium for conducting commercial enterprise. However, when Mosaic was created, it opened up the flood gates for the multimedia capabilities of the WWW. With Mosaic, users could experience sound, see colorful graphics, view videos, and fill out forms on the Internet. This software program also made it possible for users to begin creating Web sites—electronic pages filled with graphics, text, and/or sound.[3]

The Internet has become a household word and a tool used regularly by housewives, CEOs, bankers, teachers, students, consultants, engineers, entrepreneurs—the list goes on and on. It is estimated that there are over 24 million Internet users worldwide, and that number is growing every day. Dr. Vinton Cerf, one of the inventors of the networking protocols, predicts that over the next 10 years, the number of Net users will climb to over 100 million worldwide.

Besides being extremely popular in the United States, the Internet has a significant presence in other parts of the world. In the Pacific Rim, Japan,

Singapore, Hong Kong, Indonesia, Taiwan, Malaysia, and Korea have Internet access. Australia and New Zealand are plugged in, and even parts of Antarctica have connectivity. Africa is the least connected continent, but the Net does have a presence in Egypt, South Africa, and Zaire.

Suiting Up for Cyberspace

Before you begin your journey through cyberspace, decide how you will use the Internet. Will it be a tool for retrieving information for your business, or for providing details about your products or services to potential customers, clients, suppliers, and others whom you hope to attract? By defining your Internet needs, you will be able to determine what hardware and software you will need in order to achieve your objectives.

Whatever your purpose for going online, you will first have to gather these basic items:

1. *A computer.* You may think that the old PC you have tucked away in your basement will support your Internet needs, but it may not. To achieve effective use of the Internet, you will have to have hardware that is capable of handling the speed of the connection between your computer and the server computer. You can enjoy cyberspace with a good entry-level PC or Macintosh, but to get the most out of the Web, you should obtain premium hardware. You will need at least a 286 PC to access the text interface of the Internet. Surfing the Web requires at least a 486PC.

2. *A modem.* A modem is an electronic device that transforms data from digital signals to analog signals and vice versa, giving computers the ability to communicate over telephone lines. Modems come in varying speeds, such as 28.8K bps or 56K bps, and can be either internal or external. Many computers come with a built-in modem, but you can purchase an external one to support your Internet connection.

3. *Internet Service Providers (ISPs).* These are local and national organizations that provide connections to their servers, usually over phone lines, giving you access to the Internet. Examples of ISPs include America Online, Worldnet, MCI, Earthlink, and AT&T. To gain entry to the Net, you must subscribe with an ISP. Fees vary but typically cost as little as $20 per month. Some ISPs charge according to the amount of time you spend online. (We will discuss how to choose an ISP later in this chapter.)

4. *Basic communications software.* Just obtaining the hardware is not enough to get online. You must also acquire the software that will manage the communications to the server computer. Many ISPs provide software programs such as Netscape Navigator or Microsoft Internet Explorer, when you purchase a package from them. But not

all ISPs do, so you may have to purchase and install the software on your computer yourself.

5. *Additional hardware.* Depending on your business needs, you may have to purchase additional equipment. For example, if you plan to create documents with color photographs and other graphics, you will need a scanner and/or digital camera. If having multimedia capabilities is paramount, you will have to purchase a CD-ROM drive (although many now come built into computers), a sound card, and speakers. If you plan to have several employees working on individual terminals, you may want to invest in a local area network (LAN). Your LAN will connect multiple PCs and other pieces of hardware such as fax machines and printers, allowing more efficient use of your resources.

The Internet in Action

With just the click of your computer mouse, you can find just about anything on the Internet, from weather reports to wildlife preserve organizations. Essentially, having access to the Net is like having the contents of the world's largest library right at your fingertips. But the Internet is more than just a place to dig for information. It is also a place where you can sell your products or services via a Web site (which we will discuss later in this chapter) or just network with your fellow "Net-izens."

Anita Brown, a resident of Washington, DC, founded Black Geeks Online (www.blackgeeks.net) in 1996 to promote computer literacy, give fellow techies a virtual place to meet, and encourage other African Americans to log on. Like many other black business owners, Brown was initially fearful of the Internet. "I thought it was a Big Brother and not to be trusted," she says. But after taking her first trip through cyberspace in 1994, she was hooked. Shortly thereafter, she developed a virtual community for techies and nontechies to congregate, share their thoughts, and educate others about the power and potential of the IT industry.

Through its newsletter *bLINKS,* and Heads-UP bulletins, Black Geeks Online provides job listings, company announcements, new media developments, and information about software and hardware. Its members are scattered throughout England, Japan, South Africa, Hawaii, Alaska, Australia, and the Ivory Coast. Don't picture the members as bespectacled kids who wear pen-pocket protectors and checkered bow ties. They are educators, entrepreneurs, government officials, students, parents, technical professionals, and community leaders.

In addition to its virtual meeting of the minds, the organization takes its educational forum offline by setting up workshops and seminars throughout the United States. To become a member of Black Geeks Online, visit the Web site to fill out an application, or send an e-mail to Anita Brown at MissDC@BlackGeeks.net.[4]

Engaging in group forums like Black Geeks Online is just one of the many things that you can do when traveling through cyberspace. The number of services that the Internet offers are too varied to list in one chapter (and perhaps even in one book), so we encourage you to surf the Net and find something that interests you. In the meantime, here are a few of the basic services that you can expect to find on the Internet.

Electronic Mail

You may have used electronic mail (e-mail) on your job. Essentially, e-mail is an electronic messaging service that allows you to send and receive communications from other e-mail users on the Internet. To use e-mail, you must first subscribe with an Internet Service Provider (ISP). Once you sign up, you will be issued an e-mail address (for example, wendybeech@aol.com) and space on the ISP's server to store your messages until you are ready to read them on your computer. You will also be assigned a password, which will give you access to your mailbox. No one else is able to read your mail. When you use e-mail, you can issue group mailings so that when a message is sent to one particular address it is also distributed to several other simultaneously. You may also send attachments (reports, memos, and other documents) along with a single e-mail message.

The World Wide Web

The World Wide Web (WWW) is a hypertext-based information service that provides access to a wealth of information on the Internet. The WWW, the multimedia branch of the Internet, can be accessed through browsers or software programs. To access the Web, you must first sign up with an Internet Service Provider (ISP) to obtain an access account and password. You then need only to dial your ISP, wait for the connection, enter your password, and start surfing. With a worldwide library of information accessible in cyberspace, finding specific documents and materials can be a frustrating and time-consuming chore. To cut down your search time and relieve any anxiety about getting lost among the links, you should use an Internet directory or search engine to unearth the data that you need. Internet directories—databases that list sites according to topics—are good tools if you are looking for general, subject-oriented information. Yahoo (www.yahoo.com) is one of the more common Internet directories.

To focus your search, you can enlist a search engine, which will allow you to enter key words that will prompt the engine to scan its databases for links to any sites that are relevant to your topic. (Internet directories only take you to the sites that are listed in their databases.) Some popular search engines are: Lycos (www.lycos.com), InfoSeek (www.infoseek.com), AltaVista (www.altavista.digital.com), and Excite (www.excite.com). If you need to find a particular company but don't know its Web site address, use LocalEyes (www.localeyes.com), which functions like the Yellow Pages but provides the immediacy of the World Wide Web. If you key in a geographic location and a topic or name, this search engine/directory will find all related businesses in a particular area, whether they have a Universal Resource Locator (URL) or not.[5]

Usenet Newsgroups

If you're looking for a virtual buddy who will exchange thoughts about politics, education, or some other topic, you may want to join a Usenet newsgroup. These "groups" are actually electronic bulletin board systems that allow users with similar interests to interact with people throughout the world. As a participant in a newsgroup, you can post a message about a particular topic on the bulletin board. Other group participants can respond on the board or send e-mail directly to you. Discussions revolve around a variety of topics: religion, social and cultural issues, computer problems, and just about anything else you can imagine. Subscribers to newsgroups receive the posted messages of all other group participants. This service is a great research tool for your new business, but can be used for social purposes as well. To find a newsgroup, query a search engine for a listing and for the topics to be discussed, or visit www.dejanews.com. Before you jump into the ongoing dialogue, read the frequently asked questions (FAQ) section linked to the newsgroup you intend to join. This file will give you a clear understanding of the topic that will be discussed and the rules that govern the group. If you can't find the file, observe the group discussion for a short time before joining in. When you finally do begin to participate, post only messages that are relevant to the discussion. Stay clear of providing any advertisements for your business. Although not illegal, posting ads in a newsgroup (unless it is a commercial newsgroup) is not tolerated. Participants may respond in anger—or not at all. If you persist, you could lose your privilege of subscribing to the newsgroup, so save your advertisements for another place.

Entrepreneurship and the Internet

Now that you know some of the things that the Internet can do, you may be wondering how it can help you start your business.

There are several advantages to accessing the Internet. Here are just a few of the business benefits that you can achieve by logging on:

- *Immediate access to information.* Need to find information about venture capital, business plan writing, advertising, and insurance, without spending a lot of time? By using the Internet, you can access information concerning these start-up issues, and a whole lot more, in a matter of seconds. The Internet is a quick and easy medium for retrieving all the data you need.

- *Increased customer base.* According to Nielsen statistics, Internet users average 5 hours and 28 minutes per week surfing the Net. These users are from all walks of life and could be potential customers for your business. If you properly position your company on the Internet (set up a Web site), you have the potential of building your client base a lot faster than if you were to take out an ad in the local newspaper or rely on word-of-mouth.

- *Advertising of products or services.* Many business owners use the Internet as an electronic bulletin board to advertise their products or services. This method may be more expensive than using the typical brochure or Yellow Pages advertisement, but it can pack a bigger punch and give you the opportunity to reach customers beyond your geographic location (see Chapter 9).

- *Recruitment of employees.* As a new business owner, you may need to hire a few employees to get your company off the ground. The Internet contains resume databases, list servers, and local bulletin boards filled with qualified applicants in search of employment. By traveling through cyberspace, you can quickly scout the talent that might help to put your venture on the path to profitability.

- *Low-cost transfer of documents.* Sending a single document via fax or standard carriers can cost you much more than transmitting materials via the Internet, and you save time as well. If you ship important documents through regular mail or even overnight, you run the risk of late delivery, loss, and damage, all of which translate into greater costs for your operation. However, if a document fails to transmit over the Internet, you can simply send it again with little hassle and no additional cost beyond the original dispatch.

- *Rapid communications.* How many times per day do you play telephone tag? Probably too many to count. The Internet's e-mail capability offers a solution to this problem and provides a quick way for you to touch base with anyone you may need to reach (as long as he or she also has connectivity). As a new business owner, it is important that you maintain consistent contact with your customers, suppliers, bankers, consultants, and others who could impact the success of your operation. If they can receive your Internet messages, your communication link is quick and firm.

- *Access to new business opportunities.* When you first decide to brave the world of entrepreneurship, the Internet may be the first place to look for business ideas. By querying one of the search engines, you can unfold a wealth of information regarding a wide range of industries, plus the skills required to work in each field, start-up costs, and profit potential.

- *Market research assistance.* One of the most taxing projects you will encounter in starting your new business is market research. This is a critical part of launching your new venture because how a customer feels about your product or service will ultimately determine your level of success. By using the Internet, you can distribute surveys to a large number of potential consumers and gauge the feasibility of your business idea before investing a lot of time and money.

- *Professional advice and consultation.* The Internet is filled with experts, in a variety of fields and industries, who can give you advice on starting a new business. Many will offer their services free-of-charge and, if they are unable to assist you in a particular area, will provide additional referrals and resources to meet your business needs.

- *Electronic commerce capability.* According to the U.S. Department of Commerce, electronic commerce ("e-commerce") is expected to exceed $300 billion by 2002. Increasingly, companies are conducting business over the Internet. If you hope to throw your hat into the ring, you have to begin by obtaining connectivity. Companies that want to do business with the federal government need Internet access and have to become familiar with Electronic Data Interchange (EDI), a facility that the transportation industry has been using for well over 20 years. For business transactions, including purchasing, pricing, shipping, receiving, invoices, payment, order status, and other day-to-day contacts initiated between business partners, EDI exchanges the data, via a computer, in a standard format called ANSI X-12, and consequently reduces operating costs, delivery delays, and administrative errors, and speeds the payment process. The technology may sound complicated, but EDI is pretty straightforward. To get started, you need a computer, a fast modem, and EDI software. An Internet consultant or your local Procurement Technical Assistance Center (PTAC) can help you with the process. PTACs are designed to help small operations do business with the government. To locate a list of these centers, visit www.softshare.com:80/ptac.

ESTABLISHING A WEB PRESENCE

Although the Internet began as a tool used among the military, nearly two-thirds of today's entire Internet population are using the Internet for commercial enterprise. For many entrepreneurs, general access to the Internet and an e-mail address are not enough to sustain a competitive place within their markets. Many are developing a Web presence beyond their general fact-finding missions. In short, entrepreneurs are developing Web sites to attract customers and boost their bottom line. A Web site is basically a series of Web pages or computer files stored on a computer and connected to the Internet for the dissemination of information about a business or the sale of products or services.

Richard Waller Jr., owner of Waller & Company Jewelers, in Richmond, Virginia, launched his company's Web site in March 1998, at the suggestion of his sister, Jewel Waller Davis. "It was my feeling that we really needed to go after a national client base, and since we have a small business located in Richmond, the most effective way to expand without spending a lot of money was to go on the Web because it would give us the opportunity to reach a wide constituency," says Davis.

Davis worked with MelaNet's African Marketplace (www.melanet .com/market), a cybermall in Norfolk, Virginia, to pull the Web site together. "I handled the planning but the technical expertise was handled by MelaNet. They gave me some advice on the kinds of things that they felt we would want to consider putting on the site. It took about three months to plan and about $4,000 to create," she says.

By visiting the Web site, (www.wallerjewelry.com) customers can view the style and prices of Waller & Company's fine jewelry and place their orders online. The Web site includes a variety of tools, such as a page that details the history of Waller & Company Jewelers. A newsletter, *The Waller Review*, provides information on new merchandise and jewelry trends, tips on purchasing jewelry, and access to The Waller Club. "When people join the club, they are eligible to receive discounts on purchases made over $250, free catalogs, and special gifts," says Waller. "By joining the club, visitors can also have their name added to our mailing list. Offering the club is just a way for us to keep our communications with our customers intact," Waller says.

Waller and Davis say the site's number of hits is steadily increasing, and they expect it to become popular among customers. To publicize the Web presence, Waller places the Web site address on his business cards, in an advertisement he runs in a weekly newspaper, and on the sales slips he issues to customers.

Like Waller, many entrepreneurs create a Web site to expand their customer base. Here are eight more reasons why you may want to consider putting your business on the Web:

1. *Twenty-four-hour access.* At first, this may not sound like an advantage, but it is actually a big plus for your operation. By creating a Web site, you allow potential customers to find out about your products or services 24 hours a day, 7 days a week. This provides convenience for customers who may not be able to inquire about your company during your normal office hours, and it saves you the headache of having to answer a call at 6:00 A.M. from a client who lives in a time zone that is three or more hours ahead of yours.

2. *An enhanced company image.* When starting a new business, you want to make a good impression on your competitors, your banker, your suppliers, and, most importantly, your customers. If done properly, a Web site will let potential clients know that your company is professional and credible. It will also let the public know that you mean business and are fully capable of meeting their needs. If you are a home-based entrepreneur, a Web site can increase the perception that you are fully prepared to serve customers' needs, and may open up business opportunities with individuals who otherwise may have passed you by.

3. *Quick updates or changes in product/service information.* If you develop print brochures, catalogs, and other sales collateral, it will be

difficult and costly to update them or make changes at a moment's notice. However, with a Web site, you can initiate changes in seconds, with just a click of the mouse and a minimal charge.

4. *Immediate promotion of specials.* If you're launching a new line of products for your company, you want your customers to know as soon as possible. Sending out faxes, making sales calls, or printing up flyers or brochures promoting the new items takes time and is costly. With a Web site, you can simply post the information on your home page or send an e-mail to your best customers, informing them about the new products.

5. *Response to frequently asked questions.* As a new business owner, much of your time is spent answering customers' basic questions about your business. You can use your Web page to post these facts, and free up some time to focus on more pressing issues.

6. *Customer feedback.* If you send out a company brochure or catalog outlining details about your product or service, and attach a reply card to gauge customers' likes and dislikes, you will probably get few responses. Customers tend to lose the card, or forget to return it, or simply trash it because of their lack of interest in, or dissatisfaction with, what you have to offer. You'll never know whether price, style, color, or some other factor kept them from responding. By creating a Web site, you give customers an opportunity to provide immediate feedback about your products or services. If your Web pages have an instant e-mail response feature, potential clients can reply while ideas are fresh in their minds.

7. *Penetration of international markets.* Internet users from around the world may be interested in purchasing your product or service. Creating a Web site gives you the opportunity to reach a global marketplace and open a dialogue with potential customers and/or partners in foreign countries. And the contact can all be done with minimal cost as compared to advertising in the *Tokyo Daily* or the *London Times*, for example.

8. *Communication with customers who speak other languages.* Although English is the universal language for conducting business, having a Web site affords you the opportunity to translate your messages into foreign languages. When users come to your home page, they can choose to view your site in English or another language. Offering this type of service can do wonders for your image and provide convenience to partners or customers who, like you, are more comfortable communicating in their native tongue. You also gain the opportunity to learn the rudiments of a second or third language—a handy facility if you visit your market countries sometime in the future.

Before you begin searching for a professional Web designer or take a beginner's course in HTML (the hypertext markup language used to create

Web pages), clearly define your reasons for wanting to develop a Web site, and determine whether you can afford it. You will not need deep pockets, but you will be required to fork over dollars for set-up costs, hosting fees, maintenance costs, and site publicity. Depending on the type of site you want to create, and the host, you can spend anywhere from $500 to $250,000 (or more) to launch your Web site. Does your marketing budget allow such an expenditure?

Developing a Web Site

If you build it, will they come? The answer depends on what your Web site offers and how well you publicize it. Building a Web site is not as difficult as it may seem, but careful planning is required if it is to be a success.

After you've justified your reasons for building a site and carved out monies from your budget to fund the project, you must determine how complex you want the site to be. There are any number of ways to structure a Web site. Surf the Net to see what's out there. Study and bookmark sites that have earned success, and refer to them when you begin designing your Web pages. Look at what your competitors are doing. What ideas might work for your business?

If you plan to sell products via your Web site, you will face the issue of security. Customers are wary about giving out their credit card numbers over the Internet. You must provide them with a secure and convenient way of doing business online.

Here are three types of Web sites to consider when drafting your blueprint:

1. *Online brochure.* This static and low-cost type of site typically includes one to four pages. It generally lists the company's name, information about the products or services, an e-mail link to the operation, and a few photos (perhaps of key personnel or the facility itself). Use this type of Web site if you intend to offer only general information about your business to prospective customers. It requires no multimedia elements or frequent updates, but its potential is limited. If you hope to create a storefront with your Web site and offer products for sale, this is not the type of site you should create.

2. *Interactive site.* An interactive Web site offers customers extensive information plus a reply form or an online ordering capability. Interactive sites are updated frequently. They incorporate new information about products or services to attract new customers and keep the current ones coming back for more. How much you spend to build this type of site will depend on the design.

3. *A "strictly business" site.* This type of site requires a significant investment in time and money, but the results can be spectacular.

When creating this type of Web site, some business owners use a full range of Web tools, such as "shopping cart" software to conduct full-fledged business activities on the Web. Others incorporate sophisticated methods to gather marketing research and gauge what potential customers want and need.

It is important to think through what you want your Web site to do and what types of content you will provide. Will you post photos and graphics as well as text? Will you incorporate sound? Will you provide an e-mail link so that visitors can send questions and comments instantaneously? Will you ask visitors to sign a guestbook? If you are going to sell products on the Web, will you provide a downloadable catalog for customers to view? These are just some of the design questions you should ask yourself before getting started. If you decide to incorporate graphics and other art elements into your site, there are a number of places where you can get low-cost, if not free, materials. FrontPage and HomePage come with a collection of free art such as arrows, page backgrounds, and other visual elements that will help visitors navigate your site.

After determining the structure and content of your site, decide whether you will build it yourself or hire an outside professional. A widespread perception is that Web site development is for the technically inclined, but you can build a site with little knowledge of computer technology. However, you will have to learn HTML (hypertext markup languages) coding. Don't panic. User-friendly books and software packages are available to guide you through the process. Microsoft's FrontPage (www.microsoft.com/FrontPage) is a great tool for site management and HTML authoring. It cost under $200 *at the time of publication.* You may also want to try FileMaker's Home Page, formerly Claris's Home Page, (www.claris.com). FrontPage, which can build Web sites of any size, provides blueprints that allow you to create a customized Web site. Home Page ($100 *at the time of publication*) provides polished pages as templates for you to use in constructing your site. When using this software, you simply follow the instructions and type in your information over the boilerplate models.

If you want to forgo the task of developing the site yourself, you can outsource the entire function to a professional Web site developer. The fees of Web designers vary, but you can expect to pay a minimum of $500. When choosing a site developer, follow the same criteria you use when selecting any other professional for your business. Study the designer's online work and check his or her references. Shop around for the best price, but don't sacrifice quality. The site will represent your business worldwide.

When the site is complete, you will have to find a host (a place to store your site). You can launch a Web site by (1) setting up your own Web server, (2) placing it on an existing server for a monthly rental fee, or (3) joining an Internet mall or cybermall. For most new business owners, setting up a site on an existing server is the most cost-efficient means of establishing a presence on the Web. Building a Web server is a complex task and requires significant expenditures (as much as $250,000, in some cases). Most ISPs will host a Web site for a monthly fee ranging from $25 to $100. Some will even store a site free-of-charge. America Online and Earthlink are two online service providers that offer their members free space, so check with your current Internet account before shelling out money for hosting fees. One of the drawbacks of using free space offered by a service provider is that the provider will often require that you advertise its services on your Web pages.

By using an ISP to launch your site, you essentially become a content provider rather than a host of your own site. One of the benefits of being a content provider is that your setup costs are less. You will not have to have the knowledge or hardware needed to get your site up and running. You simply hand over the content and, for a monthly fee, the ISP will post it and maintain it. Maintenance costs depend on how often you update your site (daily, weekly, or monthly). They can range anywhere from $30 to $500.

A drawback of using an ISP is that if something goes wrong with your site, you have to wait until the online service provider gets around to fixing it. Herein lies the beauty of establishing a Web server. As a Web site host, you can control the material, make changes faster, and troubleshoot problems as soon as they appear. Also, when hosting your own site, you get to keep all revenues that are generated, without having to pay a hosting fee. Only you can decide which approach is best for your business. Most new business owners choose to launch their sites through an ISP.

Here are some issues to consider when choosing an ISP:

- *Access to the World Wide Web.* Make sure that the online service providers you are surveying support the multimedia capabilities of the World Wide Web as well as just plain text. ISPs that have high-quality connectivity to the Internet are those that offer a T1 line.
- *Software.* Many ISPs offer, free of charge, the software you need to access the Internet. Others charge a minimal fee. Ask what software will be provided and what programs you will have to acquire yourself. You can cut costs by downloading shareware software or freeware from the Internet. These packages allow you to do just about anything on the Net.
- *Pricing.* Review all available packages, and ask which fees will apply. You may find some low monthly fees, but the trade-off may be a set number of hours. Higher fees generally afford you unlimited access. If you find an ISP that will offer a flat fee, do some investigation on your own. Dial the number at different times during the day to see when it is busy. Midday and prime time are generally the busiest periods of the day, so if the ISP you dial won't give you

access at midnight, try another service provider. Also ask about any surcharges that apply.

- *Connection capability.* Ask an ISP these three questions about its connection capability:
  1. What is the speed of your connection?
  2. Where is the bottleneck of your network?
  3. Do you have more than one connection to the World Wide Web?
- *Worldwide e-mail capability.* Ensure that your ISP allows you to send and receive e-mail, with text and other documents, to and from anyplace in the world. Also inquire about any limits to the number of e-mail messages you can send, receive, or store.
- *Technical staff.* You may experience problems with your site from time to time, so make sure that the ISP you choose is capable of handling any faux pas. Ask how many technical people are on staff and how long they've been working with the company. Also check their professional background in the field.
- *Reliability.* The last thing you want to do is choose a lazy ISP. Ask about the process of monitoring Internet activity and the peak times. The service provider should be able to show you statistics regarding server traffic. If you come across something you don't understand, ask for an explanation. A provider that wants your business will take the time to discuss any complexities involved.

When shopping for an ISP, consider local as well as national providers. National providers offer more POPs (points of presence) or local dial-in numbers that you can use when traveling on business throughout the United States. However, local providers generally offer more services for the price, such as free space to host your Web site. To find an ISP, visit the Netscape Partner Directory Web site at http://dev1.netscape.com/directory/index .html. Click on the icon labeled "Internet Service Providers" and begin your search among Netscape's premier lineup of ISPs. This directory allows you to select an ISP according to the type of connection you would prefer (e.g., ISDN or T1). You can also find an ISP by searching *The List, The Definitive ISP Buyer's Guide.* Visit the Web site at http://thelist .internet.com.

After you sign up with an ISP, the provider will usually register a domain name or Web site address (e.g., www.blackenterprise.com) for your business through the Network Information Center (InterNIC). InterNIC (www.internic.net) is a division of AT&T and the governing entity of Internet addresses that end in .com, .org, .net, and .gov. Registration ($100) is for two years. The registration process should take no longer than three weeks. However, the turnaround time often depends on the backlog at InterNIC, so you may have to wait a bit longer.

After your site is completely finished, test it and work out any kinks before introducing it to the world. Here are some general tips to help you create a winning Web site:

- *Update your site regularly.* More than 10,000 Web sites take their place in cyberspace every day. To keep your customers interested, you will have to give them something fresh and new to see, while still providing access to older or basic information. Not all visitors to your site will want only the most up-to-date data about your products or services.

- *Create an e-mail link on every page of your Web site.* This link gives customers an opportunity to respond immediately to something they see. On your part, make sure you respond within a reasonable amount of time. Most Internet users expect a response within 24 hours. Letting too much time elapse before you answer a customer's question, or not answering at all, will negatively impact the image of your company. Delegate this task to one of your employees if you are too busy to handle it yourself.

- *Use navigational tools.* Scatter some indexes, search windows, frames, icons, and sidebars throughout your Web pages so that customers can easily find their way around your site.

- *Load your site quickly.* You have about 10 seconds to catch a visitor's attention and keep it. If your Web site loads too slowly, the customer may go elsewhere for the information he or she needs. To make sure your site loads fast, keep backgrounds simple and graphics files small. Use height and width tags with every graphic. These tags allow the text to load first, giving customers something to read while they wait for the graphics. Also, use ALT tags (graphic identifiers) to indicate to the customer where graphics will appear on the page. These are inserted during the HTML coding process.

- *Provide different points of contact.* Don't set up an e-mail link and leave it at that. Offer several ways in which your customers can reach you. For example, offer a phone number (an 800 number, if you have one), fax number, and mailing address. A customer who does not have online access could be using a friend's terminal to make contact.

- *Provide directions to your business.* Include a street map and/or written directions so that customers can find you after viewing your wonderful Web site. If you have multiple locations, let customers know which facility is in or closest to their area.

- *Display a company logo on the homepage.* What entices many Web users to take a closer look? Often, it's the design of the homepage. Consider displaying your company logo or some other colorful graphic at the top, to invite visitors into your Web site.

- *Maintain consistency.* Your Web pages should have similar backgrounds and the same number of links or navigational tools.
- *Use clearly defined links.* Be sure to use self-explanatory words or icons to describe your links, so that customers know what to expect when clicking their mouse. Also, carefully consider the outside sites to which you will link. Unless they truly benefit your business, stay clear of sending customers to them. You may never get those customers back.

Setting Up Shop in a Cybermall

If your objective for your Web site is to sell, sell, sell, consider setting up shop in an Internet mall. Also referred to as a virtual mall or cybermall, an Internet mall is a collection of different businesses arranged in a single Web site.

According to *IMALL Tipster*, a newsletter that assists business owners in finding the right cybermall to set up a shop, or in contacting other owners who might join in forming a new mall, virtual malls are a growing industry that generates nearly $40 million per year. When Anthony N. Jones decided to expand his wedding invitation business, Nicholas J. Video Company, he created both a Web site and an Internet mall. Using $9,000 in personal savings and loans from a few friends, Jones launched the African American Community Mall (www.aacmall.com) in 1996. The mall now hosts about 100 stores. Each store owner pays $570 in start-up costs and $75 in yearly fees.[6]

Kim T. Folsom, president and CEO of The Business Source Technology Solutions Inc. (TBSTS), an Internet commerce provider, offers secure encrypted Web stores to small business owners through her Internet mall, the Online Marketeer (www.onlinemarketeer.com). For small business owners interested in establishing a Web presence, the Online Marketeer provides a variety of services: the store's design, hardware and software, and maintenance; and catalog and order form conversions into online marketing materials. Prices range from $1,000 to $7,000 per year, depending on the complexity of the storefront. The setup cost is $750, and there's a monthly fee of $50 for up to 100 products, plus $.50 per processed order.[7]

You can choose from hundreds of cybermalls. You may want to check out MelaNet's African Marketplace (www.melanet.com/market/), MarketPlaza (www.marketplaza.com), and Majon's Cybermall (www.majon.com). When poring over your choices, consider the following factors:

- *Connectivity.* The mall you choose should have high-quality connectivity to the Internet (a T1 line). You don't want potential customers to visit the mall's site and then have to wait light-years to view your products or services. Make sure the mall's connection is fast.

- *Web site address.* No customer will remember a domain name that is 80 characters long. Create a Web site address that is easy to remember and to type.
- *User interface.* Sloppiness will turn potential customers away. Ensure that your mall owner sustains an attractive and easy user interface. How many bells and whistles does the mall use? Some customers want simplicity: get in, get the information, and get out. Your business will be targeting these customers. Keep them in mind as you shop around for a virtual mall.
- *Publicity.* The company that operates the mall should have some knowledge of how to promote and publicize the site. If it doesn't, move on to another mall. Don't post your Web site in a place that will do nothing to highlight what you have to offer.

For their services, online malls will generally charge storeowners a flat fee ranging from $200 to $1,000. An alternate charge is 15 percent of a store's gross annual sales. Shop around for the mall that will best serve your business needs.

Publicizing Your Web Site

Even if you spend thousands of dollars and countless hours laboring over your Web site, there's no guarantee that visitors will come. To bring traffic your way, there are several publicity methods that you should adopt. For starters, list your Web site address with the major search engines such as AltaVista, InfoSeek, Lycos(www.lycos.com), and HotBot (www.hotbot.com), as well as Internet directories such as Yahoo (www.yahoo.com). Each search engine and directory will explain the procedure for registering your site. Basically, all you need to do is type in your Universal Resource Locator (URL) and provide a brief description of your site.

To increase your exposure, enroll in a link exchange program. These programs, offered free, will display your company banner on other sites, provided that you display the other banners on your site. An Internet banner is an icon that allows surfers to link to your Web site when they click on the banner. Two link exchange programs to check out are: LinkExchange (www.linkexchange.com) and Smart Clicks (www.smartclicks.com). To register with these programs, you simply have to fill out an enrollment form. The program will provide you with a hypertext code, which you then paste onto your Web pages.

Include your Web site address on all your print collateral: business cards, office stationery, company brochures, press materials, fax cover sheets, and so on. This is a low-cost way to spread the word about your site. Also list your URL in any advertisements (e.g., Yellow Pages ads) that you use to promote your business.

Creating a successful Web site is no small task, but, with the proper amount of planning, it can become a profit center for your new business. Remember that, like your new venture, a Web site is a work in progress. Update it as your operation matures and as the needs of your customers change. By doing so, you will make your Internet experience a successful journey through cyberspace.

POINT-AND-CLICK YOUR WAY TO SUCCESS

A wealth of information is waiting for you on the World Wide Web. In this section, we review fifteen business-related Web sites that can help put your business on the path toward profitability. Ready your browser to bookmark these sites (and remember that all Internet Web site addresses begin with http://).

American Express Small Business Exchange: www.americanexpress.com/smallbusiness

As a new business owner, you're bound to use at least one credit card to make equipment purchases or buy office furniture. Why not use American Express—or this site, at least—to arm yourself with the information you need to get your venture off the ground and running smoothly. This site features a bundle of resources ranging from buying and selling a business to hiring and firing staff and the basics of law and insurance. Using the Business-to-Business Directory, you can locate potential partners, suppliers, or customers and even add your name to the list. You can also post free advertisements for your firm, ask questions of a small business expert, and apply online for the platinum small business corporate card, if you decide that plastic is the way to go.

Black Enterprise Online: www.blackenterprise.com

The authority on business news, strategies, information, and resources for African American entrepreneurs, corporate executives, managers, and professionals, Black Enterprise Online provides everything entrepreneurs need to make their mark in the business world. Visitors to the site can view the contents of the latest issue of *Black Enterprise* magazine, including features and department stories highlighting critical business issues; interact with other visitors; ask questions or exchange views on current topics; and share information via the *B.E.* Bulletin Board. For new entrepreneurs, there is a business resources links page that connects business owners to sites maintained by the Small Business Administration, the U.S. Chamber of Commerce, the International Franchise Association, and similar organizations.

The site also offers links to venture capital firms and job search Web sites. Entrepreneurs and other business professionals can gather details about the annual Black Enterprise/NationsBank Entrepreneur's Conference and the Black Enterprise/Pepsi Golf & Tennis Challenge.

Bureau of Labor Statistics: www.bls.gov

You could spend at least a week at this site, but it would be well worth your time. The Bureau of Labor Statistics provides mounds of economic information concerning employment and unemployment according to region, technology trends in the labor market, employment projections, and social living conditions. You can download a number of publications and research papers, so get your disks ready.

Internal Revenue Service (IRS): www.irs.ustreas.gov

As much as you might like to zip past this site, stop and take a look. As the official site of the Internal Revenue Service, it provides answers to some of the most commonly asked tax questions. You can download current and past tax forms plus a variety of tax publications. If you have questions about how to transfer the files, don't worry. The site provides easy-to-follow downloading directions so that you can get all of the documents you need. If you like, you can view 86 IRS publications online. They include *Employer's Supplemental Tax Guide, Tax Guide for Small Business, Partnerships, Corporations,* and *Business Use of Your Home.* The amount of information available on this site is well worth a trip through cyberspace and will put you in fine form for April 15th.

Minority Business Development Agency (MBDA): www.mbda.gov

The MBDA, a unit of the U.S. Department of Commerce, is the only federal agency designed specifically to support the creation, growth, and expansion of minority-owned businesses in the nation. Visitors to this site can register their company with the MBDA "Opportunities Database," a matchmaking service that pairs eligible entrepreneurs with contract opportunities. When navigating this site, you will find a list of MBDA centers across the country. Through these centers, minority entrepreneurs can receive assistance with business functions such as business plan writing, loan packaging, and access to capital (from conventional lending institutions, and through the SBA loan guarantee programs). A number of useful links to government agencies, minority business sites, and procurement resources are provided. There are also handy fact sheets concerning the African American, Hispanic, Asian, Native American, Alaskan Native, and Hasidic business communities.

National Association of Home Based Businesses (NAHBB): www.usahomebusiness.com

Millions of Americans set up shop in their home. Some choose a home-based business because of the low cost and convenience. This site offers information on how to start and manage a home office. Among other useful tools, the site provides information about marketing services (how you can share the expense of advertising and promoting your products or services) and offers an Internet Homesite System (home-based entrepreneurs learn how to design their own Web pages and/or create links to other sites on the Internet). The U.S.A. Home Based Business Information Superhighway is part of a Worldwide Internet Access System for home-based businesses. Type in the URL: (www.worldhomebiz.com) and you can access the home-based business sites in Europe, the Caribbean, the Middle East, Africa, South America, Asia, and the Pacific region.

National Minority Supplier Development Council (NMSDC): www.trainingforum.com/ASN/NMSDC /index.html

The NMSDC was established in 1972. Its purpose is to provide procurement opportunities for minority businesses of all sizes. This organization works as a matchmaking service partnering minority enterprises with corporations that are interested in purchasing particular goods and services. On this site, you can search the Associations Database, an interactive search engine, to locate business organizations nationwide. You can also view the Events Calendar, which lists upcoming activities such as the NMSDC annual convention, and trade fairs across the map. The NMSDC's Information Center provides extensive information concerning minority business development and trends. Among the resources you will find at the Center are: access to online databases; a vast collection of magazine, newspaper, and journal articles about minority business development; statistical data from the U.S. Census Bureau; reference books containing corporate facts and figures; and current information on legislation affecting minority business development. You cannot view the contents of the Center from this site; however, a contact number is listed if you want more information.

Netnoir Online: www.netnoir.com

All work and no play is not good for anyone, even new entrepreneurs, so we've added this site to give you a place to go and just have some fun. Netnoir is a popular interactive online community that provides articles on a variety of lifestyle topics, plus interviews with prominent African American citizens and celebrities. On this site, you can shop, browse a bookstore, check your horoscope, or just get up-to-date with the news in the African American community. For people who insist on working, there is information on marketing, taxes, and information technology. Netnoir's Biz Page provides quick links to other business-related resources, including *Black Enterprise* magazine, the Minority Business Development Agency, and the Small Business Administration.

Online Women's Business Center: www.onlinewbc.org

This site is the brainchild of the SBA's Office of Women's Business Ownership. A very comprehensive find that loads quickly, the site includes sections on marketing, finance, management, technology, and procurement. You can take a quick tour of the Center or navigate yourself through a candyland of start-up, expansion, and management information. The site also provides success stories, upcoming events, Internet sites specific to the female business owner, and global links en Español. *Muy Bien!*

Service Corps of Retired Executives (SCORE): www.score.org

Known as the counselors to America's small businesses, SCORE provides an array of services to new entrepreneurs: counseling, workshops, and seminars on such topics as product promotion, business plan development, and securing start-up capital. The Web site guides visitors through a number of business resources, including *The Networking Buyer's Guide* (an overview of how to set up your computer network) and the Business Resource Index (an alphabetical listing of business-related sites on the Web). Visitors to this site can receive, via e-mail, free and confidential counseling with a SCORE expert. One of the more interesting and motivating parts of the site is the client success stories icon. Click here and you can read about how SCORE mentoring helped small business owners build their ventures. A partner with the SBA, SCORE is a national nonprofit association of 12,400 volunteer members scattered through 389 chapters nationwide.

Small Business Administration (SBA): www.sba.gov

The SBA has a wealth of information for new and existing business owners. It provides information about critical start-up issues such as writing a business plan, securing trademarks and patents, and conducting market research. Utilizing sidebars throughout the site, the SBA easily points entrepreneurs to documents about international trade, government contracting, finance, and franchising. The site examines the SBA loan guarantee program and any legislation affecting small businesses, and it lists the nationwide Small Business Development Centers. This site also offers links to other government Web sites such as the Office of Minority Enterprise Development (MED); ProNet, a service that pairs businesses with procurement officers; and the Service Corps of Retired Executives, plus a slew of outside resources ranging from nonprofits and home businesses to trade shows and travel.

Smart Business Supersite: www.smartbiz.com

Nicknamed "The How-To Resource for Business," the Smart Business Supersite is a valuable tool for new and existing entrepreneurs. It contains hot tips of the day, information on thousands of trade shows, hundreds of feature articles pertaining to entrepreneurship, and a user-friendly reminder service. With all that you will have to do as a new business owner, you'll want to take advantage of this service. Visitors can browse through 60 categories of business-related information, including cash flow management, franchising, home-based ventures, employment procedures, intellectual property rights, advertising, and research. A message center lets you communicate with other business owners and with monthly advice columns written by experts in fields such as technology, law, and marketing.

U.S. Business Advisor: www.business.gov

If you're looking for how-to information on just about any topic, you will not want to skip over this site. The U.S. Business Advisor's homepage features a clean design that easily guides you through its Web pages. Click on the "Common Questions" icon and you will find answers to popular questions surrounding taxes, export trade, social security, and safety. Click on the "How To . . ." icon and you will find tools, guides, and forms to help you solve problems involved in doing business with the government. This site also provides links to agencies with business-related news, such as the Federal Communications Commission (FCC), the Department of Labor's Occupational Safety and Health Administration (OSHA), and the White House.

U.S. Census Bureau: www.census.gov

This site is a great tool to use in market research efforts. It is a one-stop shop for social, demographic, and economic data. The Census Bureau provides statistical information about businesses in several industries (e.g., retail, manufacturing, agriculture, and wholesale) and lists statistical agencies worldwide. The site lists a number of surveys about housing, population, finance, education, and minority- and women-owned businesses. It also examines the Bureau's State Data Center Program, which provides training and technical assistance in gathering Census data for research, administration, and planning by the government, the business community, university researchers, and other census data users. Visitors can link to the Web sites of individual State Data Centers.

U.S. Department of Commerce: www.doc.gov

Just point and click your mouse and you can search all Commerce Department Web sites for information that you need. You can conduct a more focused search by limiting your queries to information specific to one Bureau, such as the International Trade Administration, National Institute of Standards and Technology, or U.S. Patent and Trademark Office. This site's news and events page will point you to the hot topics of the day, as well as press releases and speeches given by the Secretary of Commerce and Deputy Secretary of Commerce. Die-hard fact finders may also want to pore over congressional testimonies documented by the Office of General Counsel. They include dialogue concerning such topics as electronic commerce, trade relations, domain names, and the Year 2000 problem.

GLOSSARY OF TECHNOLOGY TERMS

Treading the often rugged terrain of the information technology field is not easy. We've defined these terms to make your trips through cyberspace a little easier.

Backbone. A major communication link on the Internet. Backbones are typically high-speed, long-distance networks that connect other networks to the Internet.

Bandwidth. The transmission capacity of a computer channel or communications line (e.g., a telephone line). Bandwidth is measured in cycles per second.

Bookmarks. A list of Web site addresses maintained by a browser to assist users in navigating the World Wide Web. Bookmarks prevent users from having to retype long Universal Resource Locators (URLs).

Browser. A software program that reads hypertext markup language (HTML) and allows Web users to find and view information anywhere on the Internet. Examples of the more popular browsers are Microsoft's Internet Explorer and Netscape Navigator.

CPU. Central processing unit. Also known as the microprocessor, it is the heart of any PC.

Cybermall. Also known as an Internet mall or electronic mall. A collection of virtual storefronts listed on one Web site. African American Community Mall is an example of a cybermall.

Cyberspace. A term used to refer to the Internet.

Domain name. The word address of a Web server. The domain name usually ends with a three-character extension such as .com, .net, .org, or .gov.

Download. The act of transferring files from one computer to another or to a peripheral device.

E-mail. The abbreviation for electronic mail, a messaging service that allows users to send and receive communications on the Internet.

E-mail address. A unique information sequence that indicates a location for sending and receiving electronic messages. It is composed of the user's name and the domain name (for example, wendybeech@aol.com).

Encryption. The process of encoding information so that unauthorized users are not afforded access.

FAQ. Frequently asked questions; generally, a list of commonly asked questions and their answers. Usenet newsgroups and most mailing lists provide FAQ files on a regular basis.

Hardware. The physical pieces of equipment that are components of a computer system: a computer, a modem, and other associated materials.

Homepage. A page or a series of pages stored on a Web site.

HTML. Hypertext markup language. The computer language used to code information on the World Wide Web.

HTTP. A signal to a computer to read a file through *hypertext transfer protocol.* All Web site addresses begin with http://.

Hypertext. A form of multimedia document that includes graphics, sound, text, special programs, links to other documents, and other features. Essentially, hypertext is a generic term that describes any media format and is not limited to the Internet.

Information Superhighway. An early term used to describe the global communications and information network that (in theory) links users worldwide through fiber optics.

ISDN. Integrated Services Digital Network. ISDN lines transmit voice and data in a digital format. This type of line is much quicker than normal telephone lines, and it carries huge amounts of information. ISDN lines cost more than regular phone lines and require special equipment for their use.

LAN. Local area network. Offers speedy communication and efficient use of resources by connecting multiple PCs to other peripheral devices such as printers, fax machines, and modems.

Link. A connection made between two Web sites or two informational objects.

Modem. A device that connects a computer to a data transmission line, usually a telephone line, and allows computers to communicate.

Netiquette. The unwritten "rules of the road" for the Information Super-highway. For example, when participating in a Usenet newsgroup, you are discouraged from posting advertisements for your business.

Post. To publish or place a file or message on a Web site or Usenet newsgroup.

RAM. Random access memory. A way of describing the amount of working space that is currently available on your computer. Each software program that you load onto a computer requires a certain amount of RAM in order for it to operate properly. Most of today's computers come equipped with 16 or 24 megabytes of RAM.

Search engine. A database of Web site addresses and page contents to which you can refer for information on a particular topic.

Server. A computer that shares its resources with other computers on the same network.

Service provider. A commercial vendor that sells connections to the Internet. America Online is an example of an Internet Service Provider (ISP).

Software. The program, programming languages, and data that a computer runs. Software controls the functioning of the hardware and directs its operations.

Spam. Cyberspeak term for unsolicited and unwanted postings of advertisements or messages on the Web or a Usenet newsgroup.

T1. Designation for a digital carrier facility used to transmit a DS-1 formatted digital signal at 1.544 megabits per second. Any ISP you are considering to host your Web site should have a T1 line.

Usenet. The Internet news and online bulletin board system.

URL. Universal Resource Locator. The specific Web site address or identifier of a Web page or file on the Internet. For example, the URL for the Service Corps of Retired Executives is http://www.score.org.

WAN. Wide area network. A linkage of computer systems over long distances, usually using leased lines or radio and microwave transmissions.

Web page. A page or a series of pages stored on a Web site.

Web site. An address on the World Wide Web, indicating where proprietary information is stored.

World Wide Web. The multimedia portion of the Internet that can be accessed using browsers. Information on the WWW is coded into HTML, allowing users to view color, animation, graphics, audio, and video.

CHECKLIST

THINGS TO DO WHEN PUTTING ON
YOUR HIGH-TECH HAT

✓ **Define your Internet needs.** As a new business owner, will you play the role of information provider or information seeker? Decide how using the Internet will benefit your operation.

✓ **Gather necessary equipment.** Whether you decide to use the Internet to retrieve general information or to push your products or services, you will need basic equipment to get started: a PC that can handle the speed of the connection between your computer and the server computer, a fast modem, and the right software to manage the communications to the server computer.

✓ **Draft a blueprint for your Web site.** Will you offer an online brochure or an interactive Web site? Decide how complex your site will be, and what you will include (an e-mail link, photographs and other graphic elements, downloadable files, or links to related sites).

✓ **Choose a host.** You can host your own Web site by building a Web server, or you can rent space on the server of a local or national Internet Service Provider (ISP). Many business owners also join Internet malls. Weigh your options, and choose a host that will bode well for your business.

✓ **Publicize your site.** After investing a significant amount of time and money into creating your Web site, lure people to your URL by promoting what you have to offer. Register your site with the major search engines, Internet directories, and free link exchange programs. Print your Web site address on all print media that you use: stationery, business cards, press releases, and fax cover sheets.

✓ **Update your Web pages frequently.** Your Web site is one of millions floating throughout cyberspace. To keep the hits coming, update your Web pages regularly.

RESOURCES FOR MORE INFORMATION

ASSOCIATIONS

- *Black Data Processing Associates (BDPA)—Information Technology Thought Leaders,* 8401 Corporate Drive, Suite 405, Landover, MD 20785; 301-429-2702; www.bdpa.org. Through its 40 chapters across the country, BDPA educates the African American community about information technology. The BDPA centers offer career counseling, technical assistance, workshops, networking opportunities, and computer competitions for those eager to join the Information Age as IT professionals. BDPA also holds an annual conference at which workshops and seminars covering entrepreneurship, leadership, and technology trends are held.

- *The Internet Society (ISOC),* 12020 Sunrise Valley Drive, Suite 210, Reston, Virginia 20191-3429; 703-648-9888; www.isoc.org. Established in 1992, this professional membership organization serves as a global clearinghouse for information concerning the Internet. ISOC addresses the issues confronting the future of the Internet. Through its worldwide chapter organizations, members are able to network with fellow Internet enthusiasts to discuss how the technology affects their communities. ISOC chapters are located in Brazil, Canada, Japan, Sweden, and Peru.

- *Small Business Administration's Office of Women's Business Ownership,* 409 Third Street, Suite 4400, Washington, DC 20416; 202-205-6673; www.sba.gov/womeninbusiness. The SBA's Office of Women's Business Ownership (OWBO) provides expert advice, training, and network services to female entrepreneurs to help them start, maintain, and grow their businesses. OWBO helps women business owners prepare loan packages, secure federal procurement dollars, and penetrate the international marketplace. The organization also offers loan guaranty programs for female entrepreneurs who have found difficulty securing capital through conventional lending channels. OWBO maintains nearly 70 women's business centers in 40 states.

11

PRICING YOUR PRODUCT
OR SERVICE

When Clotee McAfee first priced her products, like many new business owners, she exercised caution. "I didn't want to price too low, but I didn't want to price too high, either," says McAfee, president, founder, and designer of Uniformity L.L.C. Located in south-central Los Angeles, Uniformity manufactures school uniforms consisting of walking shorts, French-cuff blouses, wrap culottes, overalls, reversible bomber jackets, and cropped denim vests.

"I worked in better garments for years and have always sold upper-end clothing. When I sold my couture line, my jackets cost $300 to $400 apiece, so I had always worked with the better markets," says McAfee. "So when I started designing and manufacturing school uniforms, I had to make a decision whether I wanted to stay in the better market or offer low-end merchandise. My experience and my resources had been in the better garment industry, so I decided to maintain that level."

After deciding how she wanted to position her product, McAfee looked at the demographics of her customer base and then researched her competitors to see how they were pricing similar items. "I pretty much worked my costing backward. After I did the research and I knew what price points I needed to fall into, then I found fabrics and styles. I design my own styles, so I knew what labor costs were involved, and that's basically how I built my pricing structure. I have used a different method of pricing in the past where I have costed-out the whole garment and then I sold it for what it cost to make. But with my 15 to 20 years' experience in the garment industry, I realized that for the product I wanted to do, I needed to see what the consumer was doing first, and then build my price structure from that."

The prices McAfee has set for her school uniforms range from $36 to $110. Thanks to thorough research, she now sells a competitively priced product that has earned her nearly a half-million dollars.

Pricing is one of the most important aspects of starting a new business. How much you charge for your product or service will have a direct impact on the success of your operation, so this is one start-up task that you will not want to take lightly. Many business owners think that if they merely pattern their prices after the competition's, their bottom line will increase. Others reason that if they determine the cost of making a product or providing a service, and multiply that figure by an arbitrary number, they will net a sizable profit. It's important that you look at your costs and the competition when setting your prices, but there are other factors to consider as well. For example, you should weigh such things as overhead expenses, customer perception, desired profit margin, distribution channels, and price elasticity. If you ignore any of these elements, you could end up pricing yourself right out of business.

Pricing is not easy. To choose a dollar amount that will bode well for you and your customers, you must be familiar with pricing structures. In this chapter, we provide some basic guidelines for pricing products and services, and we identify five methods of pricing.

As much as you might like to leave the number crunching to your accountant, you should know how to calculate your gross profit margin, markup, and break-even point, all of which are essential to setting your prices correctly. When you find a price that works for your business, you can't chisel it in stone. Circumstances may arise that force you to reprice a product or service. We will discuss some common situations that may cause you to rethink your pricing strategy.

THE BASIC RULES OF PRICING

How much should you charge for your product or service? Should you set your prices high, low, or somewhere in between? Choosing the right price for your product or service can be challenging. You have to establish a price that maximizes your sales and profits but also provides enough margin to support your expenses. This is no small task, especially for a new business owner who may be unfamiliar with the concepts of pricing. Here are the universal rules that you can follow to find a figure that's right for you:

- Prices must cover all the costs of doing business: fixed and variable costs, and costs of goods sold. (These are discussed later in this chapter.)

- Prices must be consistent with the market. If you decide to develop a non-revenue-generating department within your company and you raise your prices to offset the costs, unless the competition raises its prices as well, you could price yourself out of the market.
- You must adjust your prices frequently to reflect changes in: the marketplace, costs, the competition, and customer demand.
- You must price to sell. Do not set a price only to butt heads with the competition. Select a figure that will attract paying customers to your business.
- If you want to slash your prices, the best thing to do is to lower your costs.

Most business owners will abide by these rules when setting their prices, but not every enterprise will adopt the same method of pricing. There are numerous approaches to establishing prices; some are scientific and some are not. When selecting your approach, you must keep in mind that pricing is subjective. What works for one company may not necessarily work for another, so don't simply copycat a competitor. Choose a pricing tool that will best serve the needs of your business and your bottom line.

Five Methods of Pricing

When starting a new business, time is of the essence. You will have a hundred things to do, and you may sometimes feel that you have to take care of all of them at once. If you're tempted to skimp on areas that you feel are less important, pricing is *not* one of them. Cutting corners on your pricing methods could mean undercutting your profits, so spend some serious time calculating what you will charge your customers.

Here are five methods you can use to establish your pricing strategy.

1. *Competitive pricing.* Having trouble determining what you should charge for your product or service? Try using competitive pricing. This method is generally used in markets where the differences in products or services are minimal and the price for a particular product or service has already been set. For example, if you want to open an antique clock store and all of your competitors are charging $2,000 for their grandfather clocks, you should charge $2,000 as well. To effectively use this method, you must find out the amount each of your competitors is charging, determine the price you want to set, and then match your price against the market as a whole. If you decide that you want to charge more than the market value, you will have to defend your price to customers. In other words, you will have to indicate why your product or service deserves a higher price. Is it because of the materials that you use, or the personalized, in-home service that you provide?

Unless customers perceive that your product is worthy of a price tag higher than the competition, they will not be willing to pay for it. Before selecting a final price, make sure that your target audience is aware of how your particular product or service is normally priced. They could be less inclined to purchase from you simply because they are uneducated about how much your product or service usually earns. McAfee found that she had to justify her prices by educating some of her clients about the kinds of fabrics used to make her garments. "Because we're selling to public schools and because that customer has not been educated about a uniform fabric and the performance of a uniform fabric, we've been faced with questions about the price points," says McAfee. "So we actually made a decision to add an educational piece on our hang tags, teaching them about the fabrics, why we use a uniform fabric, and what a uniform fabric is. My customers at private schools understand the cost and pricing structure because they use the same fabric that we use to make our garments. But the public schools, who have not been exposed to these types of garments, don't understand and we have to educate them about that. When we began getting questions about our pricing, we basically had to make the decision of whether we wanted to lower our price points, with the possibility of jeopardizing our durability and performance, or did we want to educate the customers and bring them up to our level. We decided that we needed to do both."

2. *Demand pricing.* This procedure is generally used among product-oriented businesses such as retailers, wholesalers, or direct mail companies. To properly calculate your prices through demand pricing, you must consider the ratio of sales volume to profit. To illustrate, let's say you operate a wholesale food company and your competitor runs a retail food store. As a wholesaler, you are more likely to purchase products in larger quantities than the retailer. As a result, you are able to purchase goods at a lower unit price, sell them at a lower price to the consumer, and generate a profit based on a greater volume of sales (demand). However, the retailer, who purchases and sells a smaller quantity of products, must pay a higher unit price. Therefore, the price the retailer sets for consumers must be higher than that of the wholesaler in order to achieve a profit. Also, keep in mind that the higher the demand for a product or service, the higher you may be able to set your prices. Just think back to the 1997 and 1998 Christmas seasons. What was the hot toy in each of these years? Tickle Me Elmo and Furbie. The public went wild over the dolls and with their popularity, retailers could (and did) justify driving up the price. Demand pricing is not an easy method to use. For it to be effective, you must calculate what price will give you the best profit-to-volume ratio. If in doubt, enlist the help of an outside professional who is familiar with this concept of pricing.

3. *Cost-based pricing.* This method of pricing is used widely among business owners. Whether you sell a product or perform a service, if cost-based pricing is to be effective, you must weigh all of your overhead expenses (such as office equipment, rent, salaries, and advertising) and add on

the percentage of profit you want to realize. If you adopt this method, make sure you factor in *all* of your costs. If you don't, the cost you omit could cause a substantial reduction in your profit.

4. *Markup pricing.* When you think of the kind of business that would use markup pricing, the first industry that comes to mind is retail clothing, but markup pricing is used by manufacturers and wholesalers as well. To calculate markup, you add a certain amount to the cost of your product to gain your desired profit. That figure then becomes the selling price to the consumer. For example, if your price tag says $300 and the cost of your product is $250, your markup is $50. The percentage of your markup would be 20 percent (the markup in dollars [$50] divided by the cost of the product [$250] = 20 percent). We will explain markup in greater detail later in this chapter.

5. *Value-based pricing.* How much are potential customers willing to pay for your product or service? You must ask yourself this important question when you are setting your prices. If a customer doesn't think that your product or service is worth the asking price, he or she is not likely to buy it. Value-based pricing (also described as pricing that reflects what the market will bear) requires (1) considering how customers perceive the value or benefit of your product or service and (2) defining the maximum amount they are willing to pay. Perceived value is created by a number of factors: your company's image, how customers compare you with the competition, your marketing messages, the sales environment, and the packaging. You can initiate value-based pricing strategies in a couple of ways. You can set your prices low compared to the competition, to secure a large number of customers in your market, or you can position your product or service as a high-end entity. By establishing low prices, you can attract interested buyers and achieve nonfinancial objectives. For example, you may simply want to create product awareness. By pricing your product several dollars below the competition's price, you can draw attention from buyers and educate them about the features and benefits of your product. If you position your product as a high-end item and your target audience consists of wealthy individuals, you could charge a higher price. The BMW automobile is an example of high-end pricing. Along with the inflated price tag come the status and the prestige of wealth. The autos don't cost that much more to make, nor do they last any longer than lower-priced automobiles. However, the way in which the manufacturer has positioned the vehicle allows it to command a higher price that consumers in that target market are willing to pay. In short, they place a high value on this particular vehicle.

To effectively use the value-based method, ask yourself these questions before setting your prices:

- *Do customers save money or time using my product or service?* Customers buy benefits. If they can save time or money, or become more attractive, slimmer, or younger looking by using your product or service, they are more likely to buy from you than from a competitor whose products may not offer any real value.

- *Are my customers placed at a competitive advantage by purchasing my product or using my service?* Perhaps your product will allow customers to complete a task faster or more efficiently, compared to someone who does not use your product or service.

- *Does my product or service offer convenience?* Even if your product or service is priced slightly higher than the competition's, customers may be willing to pay a few extra dollars for its convenience. A good example is a neighborhood minimart. The price you pay there for items such as bread, milk, or cold cuts may be astronomical, but these stores can inflate the cost because many customers will pay the extra money rather than drive several miles to the nearest supermarket.

- *What choices do my potential customers have?* Are you the only game in town, or are there other stores that offer the same products or services? If you offer a product that is unique and customers cannot get it anywhere else (at least, not easily), you can pretty much control the price that the market will bear. However, if you want to charge more than your competitors but your product is very similar to others offered in neighboring stores, you will find it difficult to attract customers unless you offer a unique incentive—for example, a money-back guarantee or an in-house demonstration.

When setting your pricing structure, think about offering discounts to customers who provide benefits for your business. One strategy is to offer discounts on seasonal items to customers who make their purchases off-season. For example, if you operate a clothing retail store, you can mark down unsold summer pieces during the fall and winter months, to reward off-season buyers.

You can also offer discounts to customers who pay their bills in cash and at the point of purchase. This rewards customers who help you to maintain a positive cash flow and to lower the costs for credit collection. Providing reduced rates to customers who buy in large quantities is also a possibility. Remember, keeping the customer happy is paramount. Otherwise, you're out of business.

PRICING YOUR PRODUCT

As you can see, several methods can be used to help generate a price for your product or service. But no matter which pricing procedure you adopt, before settling on a final figure for your product, you must first determine your costs. As previously mentioned, your product price must cover all your costs of doing business. To help you to identify your expenditures accurately, divide them into the following two categories:

1. *Fixed costs.* These expenses, often referred to as "overhead," do not vary according to your level of sales. They stay the same whether you sell 1, 10, or 1,000 products at any given time. A perfect example of a fixed cost is rent. Regardless of your profits, on the first day of every month, you must pay a specified amount of money in order to occupy your facility. If your flat rental fee is $800 per month, you must pay $800 per month, every month. Other fixed costs include: office equipment (such as telephones, fax machines, and computers), employee salaries, utilities, legal costs, depreciation on vehicles, insurance, and business license fees.

2. *Variable costs.* Unlike fixed costs, variable costs fluctuate from one month to the next in relation to your sales volume, your seasonal shifts, price changes among your vendors, and your advertising and promotional campaigns. Examples of variable costs include: shipping and delivery, office supplies, equipment replacement, marketing communications (such as advertising, public relations, promotions), printing, packaging, and wages for independent contractors and for part-time and temporary workers.

Cost of goods sold (also known as cost of sales) is another expense you must consider when setting your prices. Cost of goods sold represents the cost of purchasing your products for resale or the cost of producing or manufacturing the product yourself. This expense, expressed as a percentage of your total sales, varies from one business to the next.

Computing Gross Margin, Markup, and Break-Even

To accurately set your prices, you must be familiar with certain pricing structures, so get ready to put on your mathematical hat here. Three of the more important equations that you must figure when determining what to charge your customers are: margin, markup, and break-even.

Margin, also referred to as gross margin, is the difference between your total sales and the cost of your sales. Gross profit margin can be expressed as a percentage or a dollar amount. When your gross profit margin is expressed as a percentage, it is always communicated as a percentage of net sales.

First, let's look at how you can calculate your margin—the difference between your total sales and the cost of your sales. If your total sales are $5,000 and your cost of sales is $3,000, your margin is $2,000 ($5,000 − $3,000 = $2,000). To express your gross profit margin as a percentage, you would use the following equation:

Total sales − Cost of sales ÷ Net sales = Gross profit margin

$$\frac{\$5,000 - \$3,000}{\$5,000} = \frac{\$2,000}{\$5,000} = 40 \text{ percent}$$

To determine your net profit (before taxes), you would have to subtract all of your expenses, both fixed and variable, from your gross profit margin. If your gross profit margin is low, you will have little or no profit.

You may think that obtaining a high gross margin is the only way to make a profit, but not every shopkeeper will have to do so. Every business is different. If, for example, your operating expenses are relatively low, you could very well generate a nice profit even if your gross profit margin is low.

Margin is expressed as a percentage of the seller's *price*. Markup represents a percentage of the seller's *costs*. Using the figures from the example above, the equation would be:

Total sales − Cost of sales ÷ Cost of sales = Markup

$$\frac{\$5,000 - \$3,000}{\$3,000} = \frac{\$2,000}{\$3,000} = 66 \text{ percent}$$

This equation means that if you purchase your products for $3,000 and you want to sell them for $5,000, your markup would have to be $2,000. Expressed as a percentage, your markup would be 66 percent. To show the relationship between margin and markup, if you require a 40 percent margin to net a profit for your business, the markup on your products will have to be 66 percent.

It is imperative that you recognize and understand the correlations and differences between margin and markup. They may be the same dollar amount, but as a percentage they differ. To avoid undercutting your profit, don't assume that just because the markup on your products is a certain percentage, your margin will also take on the same proportion. It could kill your business.

Lastly, let's take a look at how to conduct your break-even analysis. A break-even analysis is a method that indicates when revenues equal total costs. In other words, your break-even point represents the point at which you neither make nor lose money in producing your product or providing your service. As a simple example, if you spend $50 to make a widget and you sell that widget for $50, you break even. To calculate the revenue you must generate in order to break even, you must first tabulate your fixed and variable costs. The trick is to set the price of a unit of product or service at a level where it will cover all of these costs.

According to the Online Women's Business Center, a unit of the SBA's Office of Women's Business Ownership, you can use the following equation to calculate the dollars you will need to stay afloat:[1]

$$\frac{\text{Fixed costs}}{\left(\dfrac{1 - \text{Variable costs per unit}}{\text{Selling price per unit}}\right)} = \text{Break even revenue}$$

Let's say you are trying to calculate how much you should charge for your residential cleaning service. If your fixed costs total $50,000, your variable cost (e.g., hourly pay to a full-time worker) is $20, and your unit selling price is $40, you will need to generate $100,000 in annual revenue in order to break even. If you earn more than $100,000, you're in good standing and will take home a profit. But if you earn less, you will have to rethink your pricing strategy.

PRICING YOUR SERVICE

When pricing your service, you will have to consider some of the same factors as when pricing a product. The procedure you use in setting your price will vary according to the type of service business that you operate. However, whether you start a cleaning service or a computer consulting firm, you will have to apply these elements within your pricing structure:

- *Costs for labor and materials.* Labor costs encompass the monies paid—usually, in the form of an hourly wage—to your employees, independent contractors, or others who work within your service business. To calculate your labor costs, you must determine how long it will take you to complete a particular job, and multiply the number of hours by the hourly rate you require.

- *Overhead expenses.* Recall that overhead represents all of the expenses required to operate your business: equipment depreciation, advertising, salaries, business forms, and office supplies. Overhead expenses will vary from one business to the next. To calculate your overhead rate, add up all of your expenses for an entire year, except for the costs of labor and materials, and divide that figure by your costs for labor and materials.

- *Profit.* Profit is every business owner's goal. It represents the money earned after all costs for providing a service have been paid. To calculate your profit for providing a service, you would use the same method as when figuring your markup on the cost of a product.

- *Image.* When pricing a service, you must consider how the customer values it. When Lorraine Carter, president of Caption Reporters Inc., first priced her closed captioning for newscasts and other programs, she used an hourly rate based on the amount other businesses were charging for the same service, or so she thought. "Some of my competitors were charging $1,000 per broadcast hour, so when customers would call up and ask about my prices and I told them my hourly rate, they would say, 'Oh, is that all.' So there was a point when I realized that I was pricing my service too low, so I had to bump up my rates and I did, about $100 per hour. In good conscience, I couldn't charge exactly what some of my competitors were charging because I thought it was outrageous, but I did go up on my rates to fall in line with how my services were priced in the marketplace." Carter charges $350 for one hour of broadcast, and a flat day rate of $1,300 for real-time captioning. If you are unsure about how customers regard your service, collect pricing information from your competitors (if possible), your business allies, and the customers themselves. It worked for Carter and it can work for you.

TESTING YOUR PRICE

After a price for your product or service is established, it is important that you test it. If you don't, you're running on guesswork. Examine every technique, strategy, and concept that you use to arrive at your final price. When testing your pricing, you should especially observe these elements:

- *Parity with competitors.* Are you getting as much in price for your product or service as your competitors?
- *Competitive advantage.* Does your product or service provide better value than your competitors'?
- *Reflection of brand positioning.* Positioning refers to the brand value or personality that you add to a product by communicating the differences between your company and the competition (see Chapter 9). If you position your product as a high-end item, the price should be higher than the cost of similar products positioned in the marketplace.

To try out your prices, you may want to perform consumer testing. You can hold a focus group with members of your target audience or perform a field test. A field test is a relatively cost-effective method of experimental, primary research that uses "real-world" tests in a controlled group of stores to gauge the effects of particular variables (see Chapter 3).

Repricing Products and Services

Many business owners make a common mistake: they set their prices and then leave them exactly the same. This would be an ideal practice, particularly if customers continued to purchase from you forever, but it is not realistic. You cannot set your prices in stone. You must constantly check them to make sure that they are in line with the market and that your customers are getting the best price that is available.

Among the situations in which you may have to reprice your product or service are the following:

- The competition changes its prices.
- You release a new product or series of products.
- You penetrate a new market.
- Inflation or recession occurs.
- You restrategize your sales plans.
- Your testing reveals your price is too high or too low.

Other Pricing Considerations

Computing your costs, whether for overhead or labor, is perhaps the most critical step when you must set the price for your product or service, but some other important factors bear mentioning as well. They include:

- *Market size.* If you are going to successfully sell your product or service, you will have to take a piece of your competitor's market share. But is the market large enough to support your products or services and hundreds of others? When deciding what prices to set, consider the potential sales volume in the market you intend to serve. By conducting secondary market research, you should be able to determine what share of the market you can obtain (see Chapter 3). Pay close attention to your competitors' strengths and weaknesses. By capitalizing on their shortcomings, you could carve a niche in a market that is nearly saturated. By leveraging that niche, you could become the market leader and dictate a price that all others would have to follow.
- *Distribution channels.* The methods you use to make your product available to the consumer have great price implications. Select a distribution channel that will yield revenues, not detract from your profits. There are many ways to distribute your product to your target audience: wholesale, retail, direct mail, the Internet, and telemarketing.
- *Price elasticity.* A product is considered to be elastic if the demand for it changes dramatically as the price changes slightly. If the volume of a product does not fluctuate with a change in price, then it is not considered to be elastic. The general rule of thumb is: The greater the elasticity of your product, the closer you should price it to match the amount your competitors are charging for similar goods. With respect to elasticity, if you're thinking about pricing

well above your competition, think again. Your product may be unique, but customers will not pay a premium price for a similar product that is available at a lower cost from your competitor.

As you can see, pricing is not easy. It can be confusing if you are not familiar with pricing concepts. However, you can survive this start-up task. Just remember, with any business that you start, the key to pricing is to find the price (1) that customers are willing to pay, (2) that is competitive in the marketplace, and (3) that will produce a profit for your business. If you don't, you may find yourself here today and gone tomorrow. And that surely is not a price you will want to pay.

CHECKLIST

FACTORS TO CONSIDER WHEN PRICING
YOUR PRODUCT OR SERVICE

✓ **Your costs.** As a general rule of thumb, when pricing your product or service, you must cover all the costs of doing business, including fixed and variable expenses.

✓ **Methods of pricing.** You can use several procedures to price your product or service, including cost-based, competitive, demand, markup, and value-based pricing.

✓ **Margin, markup, and break-even point.** To effectively set a price for your product, you must calculate your margin (a percentage of the seller's price), your markup (a percentage of the seller's cost), and your break-even point (the point at which revenues equal total costs).

✓ **Labor costs, overhead, and profit.** These factors apply to setting prices for a service-oriented business. To determine your labor costs, you must estimate the amount of time it takes for you to complete a job. Your overhead represents your costs, such as salaries, rent, and equipment depreciation. Your profit is the income earned after all costs for providing a service have been paid.

✓ **Market size.** To sell your product, your must cut into your competitors' market share. Make sure there are enough customers in your industry to support your business *and* those that have already positioned themselves in the marketplace.

✓ **Distribution channels.** How you choose to make your product available to your target audience will greatly impact your pricing decisions. Select a distribution channel that will allow pricing levels to generate a reasonable profit margin.

✓ **Price elasticity.** If the demand for your product or service shifts dramatically with a change in price, your product or service is considered to be elastic. As a rule of thumb, the greater the elasticity of your product or service, the closer it should be priced to the competition.

CHECKLIST *(continued)*

✓ **Price testing.** Without testing your prices, you're merely guessing at what might work. Organize a focus group or perform a field test to gauge what price the market will bear.

✓ **Repricing.** You cannot set your prices in stone. You must constantly monitor them to make sure they are in line with the marketplace. If changes in the economy occur, or the competition raises its prices, or you penetrate a new market, you must revisit your pricing strategy.

RESOURCES FOR MORE INFORMATION

ASSOCIATIONS

- *American Management Association International (AMA),* 1601 Broadway, New York, NY 10019-7420; 212-586-8100; www.amanet .org. This organization provides educational forums at which its members can learn practical business skills. It operates management centers throughout the nation and, through its library, provides over 10,000 management books covering a variety of business-related topics.

- *The Educational Society for Resource Management,* 500 West Annandale Road, Falls Church, VA 22046-4274; 800-444-2742 or 703-237-8344; www.apics.org. Formerly known as the American Production and Inventory Control Society (APICS), founded in 1957. This nonprofit international educational organization is recognized as a global source for information and expertise in the manufacturing and service industries. It is also a clearinghouse for hundreds of business management publications and other materials that should assist you in pricing your product or service.

12

BOOKKEEPING FOR YOUR BUSINESS

As a new business owner, the thought of having to maintain your financial record books is probably alongside your reaction to a visit to a dentist for root canal work. What person (other than a CPA) wants to spend hours, each day, pushing papers and balancing debits and credits? If you're like most entrepreneurs, you probably feel that your time would be better spent selling your product or service, not filling out accounts receivable ledgers and general journals. However, if you want to operate a successful firm, you will have to perform bookkeeping for your business.

Bookkeeping involves the daily recording of a company's financial transactions. By maintaining a record-keeping system, you will be able to determine the financial health of your business (whether you are making or losing money), identify and resolve potential cash flow problems, define your tax liabilities, craft your tax-planning strategies, prepare your financial statements, and complete your income tax returns.

Unless you are adept in accounting or bookkeeping, you should enlist an accountant or CPA to *assist* you with your record keeping. This doesn't mean that you can just dump a box of canceled checks, bank deposit slips, invoices, and bank statements into your accountant's lap and call it a day. You must develop an understanding of basic bookkeeping procedures that will enable you to track your day-to-day transactions. You should only have to call on your accountant for the less routine tasks of record keeping, such as preparing monthly, quarterly, or yearly financial statements, and adjusting and closing book entries. If you plan to use your accountant to prepare your daily financial records, be aware that this solution can be very costly. Depending on the size of the accounting firm you hire, you will spend anywhere from $10 to $100 per hour for those services. Carefully match your bookkeeping needs against your budget before you schedule frequent visits from your accountant. Consider what you can and cannot do on your own. A variety of inexpensive accounting software programs are available to help you prepare your books and possibly cut the number of your accountant's visits in half.

Before you set up your system, you must first understand the basic principles of accounting. In this chapter, we will discuss the basic records you should keep and how you should maintain them. Most business owners will work with an accountant or will purchase accounting software to support their record-keeping efforts. We will examine how you can choose an accountant who is right for your business, and will review a few software packages that are available if you decide to automate your bookkeeping system.

WHY YOU MUST MAINTAIN FINANCIAL RECORDS

If someone were to ask you how much money you have deposited in your business bank account, would you be able to respond accurately? Many business owners are unaware of their company's financial status. They know that the business is generating sales and that their cash flow is active, but they have little knowledge about how much money is moving in and out of their operations, or where that money is going. As a business owner, you should know, at all times, the financial condition of your venture. You should know exactly how much money you have in the bank on any given day, and how and where that money is being spent. The only way you can stay on top of these issues is by creating and maintaining complete, accurate, and timely financial records.

Monitoring the financial status of your operation is only one reason for maintaining a solid record-keeping system. Here are some other reasons why you should keep good financial records.

To Prepare Your Business Budget

No matter what type of business you start, you will have to prepare a budget to help you forecast your cash needs and track your expenses. It can also aid you in securing financing for your firm, because bankers and other lenders may ask for this documentation as evidence that you have the resources to repay a loan. To prepare a budget, you must have sound financial information.

You can easily glean the data that you need from your bookkeeping system, as long as your records are complete, accurate, and up-to-date.

To Secure a Bank Loan or Other Financing

If you want to obtain a bank loan, you will have to present a series of financial statements, including a balance sheet, an income statement, and a cash flow statement. You can use the information stored in your record-keeping system to prepare these documents. A prospective lender may even ask to see some of your bookkeeping procedures, to determine whether you have a solid and professional operation. If you hope to convince a partner or two to join your venture, you will have to share your financial records with them. Potential partners will want to become familiar with the financial status of your operation *before* wedding their resources with yours. One of the best ways for you to give them a bird's-eye view of where your company stands financially is by opening up your books.

To Make Sound Business Decisions

No matter what decisions you make regarding your business, they are likely to be grounded in your financials. In other words, if you decide to hire additional workers, purchase a new piece of equipment, lease a company car, or introduce a new product line, your decision to do so will hinge on whether you can afford it. By keeping accurate financial records, you will be able to pinpoint the financial impact of the decisions you make.

To Meet State and Federal Tax Obligations

As a new business owner, you will have to pay a number of taxes. For example, if you have employees, you must pay payroll taxes, which entail a number of regulations and strict deadlines which, if not followed to the letter, could prove damaging to your operation. For instance, as an employer, you must file a payroll tax return every quarter, and issue, at the end of every year, a W-2 form to all of your employees and to the Social Security Administration. If you keep clean and accurate records, complying with payroll taxes becomes very easy. You can simply use the information in your records to determine how much payroll tax you need to pay, and when. But if your bookkeeping system is incomplete and sloppy, this one task could become a nightmare and might cost you thousands of dollars in late penalties. In addition to payroll taxes, you may be responsible for collecting and paying sales tax. Your records can help you pinpoint how much sales tax is due and prepare the necessary forms for issuing payment. We will discuss taxes in greater detail in Chapter 13.

To Prepare Your Income Tax Returns

Every business owner has to pay income taxes. It's probably the only constant of entrepreneurship, but it need not be a "taxing" task. Sound financial records will ease the stress of preparing your annual returns. They will also make the job easier for the accountant or tax preparer who fills out your tax forms. If you are careless in your record-keeping activities, you could end up paying too little or too much in taxes, or filing after the extension deadline, which could result in a nasty penalty. Incomplete records could also result in higher accounting fees because your accountant will need additional time to sort out the disheveled mess you compiled.

To Distribute Business Profits

If you decide to operate your business as a partnership or corporation, keeping solid financial records will help you determine the amount of profit or dividends that should be paid out to each partner or shareholder.

Bookkeeping is one of the most important tools for conducting a financial analysis of your business. Set aside time every day to perform routine bookkeeping chores. If you let the paperwork pile up, you will be less inclined to do it. Procrastinating also increases the potential for errors, so don't stall. Remember, if done correctly, bookkeeping can help you manage your company's activities and foster business success. If handled haphazardly, it could cost you a lot of wasted time and money. If in doubt about how to set up and maintain an effective bookkeeping system for your operation, don't go forward alone. Consult an accountant for details.

Working with an Accountant

Setting up and maintaining a reliable and solid bookkeeping system is not easy. In fact, it requires knowledge of some basic accounting principles. For this reason, many business owners will hire an accountant to set up their books.

Your first step should be to determine how often you will need the services of an accountant. Weigh the possibilities of hiring a full-time bookkeeper, using an outside accounting firm on an as-needed basis, or scheduling year-end meetings with a CPA to close your books, prepare your financial statements, and fill out your tax returns. How often you will need to meet with an accountant will depend on the needs of your business and the type of company that you operate. At the very least, you should meet with your accountant at year-end to close your books and file your income tax returns. If you need to prepare monthly or quarterly financial statements to keep a more accurate account of your business dealings, you should meet with your accountant more often. For example, retail stores, which are required to collect and pay state sales tax every month, may require their accountant to close their books every 30 or 31 days.

After you decide how often you will need an accountant's services, you can begin your search. Where should you look for a reputable accountant? Ask other business owners for referrals, or inquire about the accountants they use. You may also be able to get a few recommendations from your banker or attorney. Contact some candidates to schedule interviews. Most CPA firms will provide interviews at no cost.

Accountants have many professional designations: Accounting Practitioner (AP), Registered Public Accountant (RPA), or Certified General Accountant (CGA). Most small business owners prefer to use a Certified Public Accountant (CPA) because of the experience level this professional is required to have. The majority of CPAs have earned a college degree, and all have passed a rigorous national test covering business law, auditing, taxes, and accounting. Accountants who are not CPAs may still have the accounting and tax expertise needed for your operation. Only you can decide what's right for your business.

Choosing an accountant who meets the needs of your company is one of the most important decisions you will make as an entrepreneur. This professional will perhaps become the most significant adviser of your business; his or her advice will greatly impact its success or failure. Do your homework before deciding. Your selection could save a lot of money and, ultimately, your business.

Tunde Dada recalls using an accountant who he thought had his best interests at heart, but whose lack of professionalism cost his Orange, New Jersey-based business over $12,000. "My first accountant started out okay, but there was a time in which he just disappeared," says Dada, whose namesake retail store sells African-inspired housewares, collectibles, jewelry, clothing, hair products, greeting cards, and over 3,000 book titles. "I depended on him to do my payroll, but he was missing for about a month. I could not reach him, so we failed to pay our payroll taxes on time. At that time, I did not know how expensive the fines were for missing the deadline, but the following year we ended up having to pay over $12,000 in penalties. After that experience, my advice to business owners is that, when you're looking for an accountant, you have to make sure that you can trust the individual to be there when you need him. Make sure that you get somebody who is consistent."

Trust is a major factor when choosing an accountant. However, you should weigh several other criteria when making your final selection:

- *Personality.* You will have to work closely with your accountant to prepare your financial statements, income tax returns, and other documents involved in the bookkeeping process. Make sure that you are comfortable with this person and that your personalities do not clash. If they do, you could be setting yourself up for potential problems.

- *Expertise.* Does the accountant you want to work with specialize in businesses the size of yours, or does he or she have expertise working only with larger clients? The accountant you hire must be able to meet the needs of *your* business and address the problems unique to *your* operation.

- *Notoriety.* Is the accountant well known and respected in the local business community? Has he or she received positive recommendations from your business colleagues? Ask yourself these two important questions as you interview candidates. The professional connections that an accountant has with members of the community can be beneficial to your operation. For example, if the accountant you hire has close ties with area bank managers, he or she could make the loan process a lot easier for you if you need to borrow money.

- *Services provided.* Not every accounting firm will offer the same types of services. Some firms may specialize in preparing income tax returns; others may focus more on developing financial statements and preparing annual audit reports. You must find an accounting firm that will provide the services needed to effectively operate your business. You should also make sure that your accountant is easily accessible. He or she should never be too busy to address your business problems. Your accountant should be willing to return phone calls promptly or at least have a member of his or her staff initiate a return call if he or she is otherwise engaged.

- *Additional staff.* What if the principal CPA is not available to assist you at a particular time? Are there other experienced personnel on staff who could address your problems and work out solutions? When deciding which accountant to hire, make sure that he or she has skilled workers who can meet your needs if your accountant is unavailable.

During the interview process, you should discuss billing rates. At any level, accounting services are not cheap, and each accounting firm's fee scale may be different. Large, nationally known firms may charge a high rate—anywhere from $100 to $200 per hour. Smaller firms might impose an hourly rate ranging from $25 to $50 per hour. If you only want a bookkeeper, not an accountant, you should be able to find one for less than $25 per hour.

Whatever accounting firm you choose, make sure you understand the rates and the payment process *before* services are rendered. Discuss the penalties the accountant is willing to shoulder if errors occur. Ask the accountant of your choice to perform an initial diagnostic review of your business financials, as a way of gauging the amount of work that will need to be done and the estimated cost.

An accountant is a critical person for your new business, so don't wait until your income tax or payroll tax deadline approaches to solicit his or her services. Find an accountant during the early stages of your business. Make this one of your short-term goals, as we discussed in Chapter 1. Keep in mind that the worst time to try and find an accountant available is during "the tax season," from January through April.

Work closely with the accountant you bring on board. Don't give him or her stacks of statements to sort out. You will only drive up your accounting costs because the accountant will have to spend extra time organizing your records before the actual number crunching can begin. Keep track of your day-to-day transactions yourself, and prepare a preliminary general ledger (which we will discuss later in this chapter) that your accountant can use to accurately prepare your financial statements and/or income tax returns. If you do as much of your own bookkeeping as possible, you can decrease your accounting costs and enable your accountant to prepare the necessary documents faster and more efficiently.

BACK TO THE ACCOUNTING BASICS

Think back to your Accounting 101 class in high school. Do you remember anything from the curriculum? If you're like most accounting survivors, you can probably conjure up at least one memory of struggling to balance your debit and credit columns with five minutes left in the class. You may even recall a few definitions from those Monday morning pop quizzes: accrual accounting, double-entry accounting, accounts receivable, and general ledger. Now may be the time to pull out and dust off that old accounting textbook you may have stashed on your top bookshelf. Can't find yours? Don't worry. This chapter will take you through some basic accounting concepts that are the foundation of any record-keeping system.

What Is Accounting?

To a CPA, the answer to this question is easy. But to a new business owner who has devoted most of his or her time to conceiving, developing, and selling a product or service, understanding the accounting process is not so simple. Still, it is imperative that you understand the basic principles or concepts behind an accounting system before you set up your accounting records, tackle your day-to-day transactions, and ready your books for closing at the end of the month, quarter, or year.

Accounting is a process in which financial information is gathered, processed, and summarized into a series of financial statements and reports. Here's how the accounting process works. Every accounting entry you make into your books is derived from a business transaction. For example, it can come from a sales invoice or a customer check. After the business transaction is made, it is recorded in a journal, which is a book or a sheet of paper on which your transactions are listed.

The journals typically used by business owners are: sales and cash receipts journal, cash disbursements journal, and general journal. The sales and cash receipts journal and cash disbursements journal are used to record the chronological, day-to-day transactions of a business (e.g., cash transactions and accounts receivable). A general journal is used to record adjusting and closing entries made at the close of an accounting period, or special transactions that are not listed in one of the other journals. (We will discuss the various types of journals in greater detail later in this chapter.)

At the end of an accounting period, all journal entries are summarized and posted (transferred) to a general ledger, a collection of the balance sheet, income, and expense accounts used to keep the accounting records of a company. When posting is complete, a trial balance is prepared by adding up all of the account balances entered in the general ledger. When totaling the columns, your debit balances should equal your credit balances. If they don't, you must retrace your steps to find the error. In the final step of the accounting process, the information from the trial balance is used to prepare the financial statements (the balance sheet and income statement).

Although it's pretty straightforward, the accounting process can become tricky if you are not familiar with the basics. In addition to learning about the various journals used in accounting, you must distinguish between the two basic types of accounting methods: the cash method and the accrual method.

Cash Method

The cash method of accounting involves recording income only when you receive cash from your customers, and recording expenses only when you write a check for a supplier, vendor, or other creditor. When you use the cash method of accounting, you conduct business according to your real-time cash flow. Say the cash register starts ringing, or a customer hands you a check. At the end of the day, you record this income into your sales and cash receipts journal, and charge it to the period to which it applies. The same procedure would apply to expenses. If you need to pay a supplier for a shipment of materials and you write a check as payment, you record that expense in your cash disbursements journal and charge it to the period to which it applies. The Tax Reform Act of 1986 states that if you operate as a corporation, partnership, or trust, and your gross sales are above $5 million yearly, you cannot use the cash method. However, farming enterprises and sole proprietorships are among the businesses permitted, under the law, to adopt this method of accounting.

Accrual Method

The accrual method of accounting involves recording income when a sale is made, and charging it to the period to which it applies, regardless of whether payment is received at that time. Expenses are also recorded when you receive products or services, even if you will pay for them at a later date. To illustrate, let's say you operate a construction company and you are using the accrual method of accounting. If you build an addition onto an office building but have not received payment for supplies, labor, and other expenses incurred while working on the project site, you record in your books the expenses connected with that project, and you charge them to the period in which they were supposed to be paid, regardless of whether you have received a check from your client.

Choosing Your Accounting Method

The cash method of accounting is easier to use than the accrual method because you don't record income or expenses until a customer actually pays you or you pay a vendor. With the cash method, you record only one transaction. With the accrual method, you may have to record several transactions. For example, if you make a credit transaction, you must record the income at the time the sale is made and then make an entry into your accounts receivable ledger. When payment is actually made, you must record another transaction indicating that the bill was paid. The cash method saves you a few steps.

Another benefit of using the cash method is that it affords you more flexibility in your tax-planning strategies. You can time your expense payments and income receipts so that you can transfer these items from one tax year to the next. Keep in mind, however, that you can only delay income (or payment of expenses) until the following year if you do not actually receive the income (or pay for the expenses) in the present year. For example, if a customer issues you a check in September 1999, but you do not cash it until March 2000, you must still record the check as income received in 1999. To shift this income from 1999 to 2000, you would have to delay billing until 2000.

Despite the advantages of the cash method, most business owners prefer to use the accrual method. As mentioned previously, federal law states that concerns with gross sales above $5 million per year *must* use the accrual method. If your business has inventory, you must also adopt this accounting method for record-keeping purposes, at least for sales and the purchase of inventory for resale.

Single-Entry or Double-Entry Accounting?

Single-entry and double-entry accounting are basic concepts with which you should become familiar. Under a double-entry accounting system, each transaction has two journal entries: a debit and a credit. Debits must always equal credits. With double-entry accounting, all transactions affect at least two accounts: the balance sheet account and the income or expense account.

A single-entry accounting system involves recording only one side of a transaction, rather than dealing with debits *and* credits. For a small business, single-entry accounting is a sensible method to use. However, most entrepreneurs prefer to use double-entry accounting because it helps them find common bookkeeping errors more easily. If debits and credits do not match, you immediately know that a mistake has been made somewhere along the way. You must then find the error and make the correction. Some typical bookkeeping errors are:

- Entering amounts incorrectly.
- Inaccurately copying a figure from one page to the next.
- Forgetting to record a particular transaction.
- Transferring amounts incorrectly.

RECORDING YOUR DAILY TRANSACTIONS

Now that you have taken this chapter's crash course in accounting basics, you can begin recording your daily transactions. The transactions that you should indicate in your books every single day are: cash transactions, sales and revenue transactions, accounts receivable, and accounts payable. At the end of your accounting period (a month or a quarter), all journal entries should be summarized and posted (transferred) to your general ledger.

Logging Your Cash Transactions

No matter what type of business you operate, you will generate a variety of cash transactions, and each one must be recorded somewhere in your books. Here are the destinations for entries of your cash exchanges.

Sales and Cash Receipts Journal

As mentioned earlier, the sales and cash receipts journal is used to record the chronological day-to-day transactions of your business (see Figure 12.1).[1] For example, when cash or checks are issued, the amounts are recorded in this journal under the appropriate headings. The number of columns in a sales and cash receipts journal varies. Depending on the type of business that you

Figure 12.1   Cash Receipts Journal

Jon's Jazzy Designs

Cash Receipts Journal

Date	Explanation	Ref	Cash	Accounts Receivable	Sales	Miscellaneous Amount
1998:						
				$ -	$ -	$-
January 4	Cash sales		2,000	-	2,000	-
January 7	Cash sales		2,000	-	2,000	-
January 12	Cash sales		2,600	-	2,600	-
January 20	Cash sales		2,500	-	2,500	-
January 28	Partial collection	Babson Co.	13,000	13,000	-	-
January 29	Full collection	Carson Bros.	7,800	7,800	-	-
January 30	Cash sales		2,200	-	2,200	-
			$32,100	$20,800	$11,300	$-

operate, you may have specific categories that do not appear on a standard journal form. You can maintain your sales and cash receipts journal manually by entering entries into a journal purchased from an office supply store (most journals cost under $20), or you can use an accounting software package to create and tailor the journal to your specific business needs. (Accounting software is discussed later in this chapter.)

Daily Cash Sheet

This is a reconciliation of the cash you receive or pay out on a daily basis. Every business, especially one that handles large sums of cash (such as a retail store), should prepare a cash sheet at the end of each business day. Many business owners simply count the amount of money left in their registers and skip preparing a cash sheet, but this leaves them unable to discover shortages or overages for that day. By preparing a daily cash sheet, you are able to pinpoint exactly how much money has flowed in and out of your operation on any given day. After cash receipts are received, you should deposit them in your business bank account. (Always maintain separate bank accounts for personal and business finances. You will avoid a lot of headaches and potential tax problems.) After making the deposits, compare the amounts on your daily cash sheet with those on your daily bank deposits. If the two don't match, you need to investigate the problem.

Cash Disbursements Journal

Also called a purchases journal or expense journal, a cash disbursements journal is used to record when money is paid out from your business, whether in cash or by check (see Figure 12.2).[2] Like the sales and cash receipts journal, this register can be maintained manually by using a journal purchased in an office supply store or via a computer accounting program. You can also integrate your cash disbursements journal into your business checkbook so that when a check is written and issued, your expense entry is made into your journal at the same time.

Petty Cash Fund

Many businesses keep a petty cash fund on hand. Often, it's in an old tattered shoebox kept in the bottom drawer of a filing cabinet. It is typically used for emergencies and miscellaneous expenses. The money that goes into and out of a petty cash fund should be recorded accurately. If your business has a cash register and you always keep some dollars available, you will not have to maintain a petty cash fund as long as you keep track of how much money is paid out from the register. If you accept a lot of credit from customers, you

Figure 12.2   Cash Disbursements Journal

Jon's Jazzy Designs

Cash Disbursements Journal

Date	Check #	Explanation	Accounts	Ref	Cash	Other Accounts	Accounts Payable
1998:							
January 3	185	cash payment	Telephone		$ 105	$105	$ -
January 6	186	cash payment	Utilities		75	75	-
January 19	187	cash payment	Tudor		10,000	-	10,000
January 28	188	cash payment	Insurance		200	200	-
January 20					$10,380	$380	$10,000

would be wise to create this type of fund. To make sure that your petty cash does not turn into a hefty expense, use the following guidelines:

1. Begin your petty cash fund by writing a check made payable to "Petty Cash." Then cash the check.

2. Place the money you will use for your petty cash fund into a cash box used specifically and exclusively for that purpose. No other funds should be integrated with the money in that box.

3. When you withdraw any money from your petty cash fund, record how much is being taken out, and for what purpose. For example, if you withdraw $20 to purchase bandages and alcohol from the neighborhood drugstore, specify this on your petty cash list.

4. When the fund is about ready to run dry, add up all of the expenses recorded on the list.

5. Write a check to "Petty Cash" that covers the expenses paid for from the petty cash fund. Cash the check and deposit the money in the petty cash box. You should then have the same amount with which you began.

Bank Reconciliation

This process involves verifying the cash you have in your business checking account by reviewing your monthly bank statement. Bank reconciliation may seem like an inconsequential task, but it is important that you perform this activity to maintain control over your cash procedures, and to discover any inconsistencies in your funds that may be due to employee theft or miscalculation.

The cash balance you list in your books will never match the balance shown on your bank statement. A deposit may have been made after the statement cutoff date, checks may not have cleared the bank, or some bank charges and fees may not have been recorded. After you reconcile your bank statement, you will get a more accurate picture of exactly how much money you have, and you will feel more assured that your books are up-to-date. To prepare your bank reconciliation, use the following steps:

1. *List deposits that have not cleared.* Match the deposits listed on your bank statement with those indicated in your sales and cash receipts journal. On your bank reconciliation, list the deposits that have not cleared the bank.

2. *List checks that have not cleared.* In your cash disbursements journal, indicate which outstanding checks have cleared the bank. On your bank reconciliation, list the checks from the cash disbursements journal that did not clear the bank.

3. *Record bank fees or credits.* Most bank customers can recall looking at a bank statement and noticing a bank charge that they were unaware

of. Look closely at your bank statement for any special fees that may apply. If you have not recorded the charges, do so as though you had known about the fee. Any credits that may be listed on your statement should also be recorded in your books. Post (summarize and transfer) both charges and credits to your general ledger.

4. *"Foot" your general ledger.* Remember, a general ledger is a depot for the bottom-line amounts recorded on the balance sheet and the income and expense accounts. To foot a journal or general ledger, you total the columns in the journal or ledger. As part of your bank reconciliation, you should foot your general ledger to figure out your ending cash balance.

5. *Indicate the bank balance on your reconciliation.* At the top of your bank reconciliation, list the ending balance indicated on your bank statement.

6. *Total the deposits in transit.* Some recent deposits may not have cleared the bank and therefore do not appear on the bank statement, but they are recorded in your sales and cash receipts journal. Add their total to the ending balance listed on your bank statement.

7. *Add up all outstanding checks.* Total your outstanding checks, and put this amount on your bank reconciliation.

8. *Calculate your book balance.* Subtract the total of your outstanding checks (Step 7) from the figure derived in Step 6. This should give you a balance that is equal to the amount listed in your general ledger.

If your bank reconciliation does not equal the balance on your bank statement, an error has been made. Some common mistakes that could cause a bank balance blunder include:

- Bank balance incorrectly recorded.
- Journals added incorrectly.
- Outstanding checks added incorrectly.
- Deposits in transit totaled incorrectly.
- Failure to record a deposit or check.
- Failure to record items that have cleared the bank.

Sizing Up Your Sales and Revenue Transactions

These types of transactions include cash and credit sales and should be recorded in your sales and cash receipts journal, as indicated earlier. Your sales and revenue transactions can come in the following forms.

Sales Invoices

Many businesses will use sales invoices when selling their products or services. If you use this type of document, you will have to post the information from each invoice to an entry in your sales and cash receipts journal. If you issue credit to your customers, you will also have to post entries to your accounts receivable ledger, which we will discuss in greater detail later in this chapter. Every sales invoice should be numbered and should indicate the date of the sale, the price charged, the quantity issued (if applicable), and the payment due date. At the very least, you should prepare two copies of every sales invoice: one for your records and one to issue to the customer. It's not a bad idea to make three copies. This will allow you to keep two for your business records: one to be filed by customer name and the other by invoice number.

Daily Sales Registers/Cash Receipts

If you don't plan to use a cash register, you can record your cash receipts on a daily cash sheet, as previously mentioned, and list your sales on a sales register (a record of your daily sales). At the end of each business day, you total your sales register and daily cash sheet and post the entries to your sales and cash receipts journal.

Cash Register Totals

If you do plan to use a cash register in your business, you can record your sales on the register itself. Most registers available today can distinguish cash sales from credit sales, and can track sales tax. At the end of each business day, you simply print out your cash register totals and post that figure in your sales and cash receipts journal.

Recording Your Accounts Receivable

Accounts receivable represent the money owed to your business by customers. When setting up your bookkeeping system, you should create an accounts receivable ledger account for each customer to whom you extend credit. Here's how the accounts receivable ledger should work. When a customer purchases a product or service from your business, you first record the amount of the sale in your sales and cash receipts journal under the accounts receivable debit and credit columns. At the end of each day, you post the credit sales recorded in the sales and cash receipts journal to each customer's accounts receivable ledger account (in your accounts receivable ledger). By doing this, you will be able to keep track of the total amount that your customers owe and the amount each individual client owes.

At the end of each month, you total all entries made in your sales and cash receipts journal, and post the results to the accounts receivable account in your general ledger. A general ledger is a permanent summary of all of the journals (e.g., your sales and cash receipts journal and your cash disbursements journal) from which your financial statements are created. The general ledger also includes accounts such as cash, accounts receivable, accounts payable, and purchases (see Figure 12.3 for an example of a journal included in a general ledger).[3] When you post the entries of your general ledger, you arrive at the ending balances for each general ledger account.

The accounts receivable account listed in your general ledger is known as your control account. After posting all your entries, the ending balance of your accounts receivable ledger should match the balance in the control account of your general ledger. If it doesn't match, an error has been made.

Accounts receivable accounts will tell you which customers are paying and when. To help initiate timely payments, consider sending a copy of each customer's accounts receivable ledger account with his or her monthly statement, or use the ledger account as the statement. Realize that if you use the accounts receivable ledger account as a customer's statement, you will have to prepare a new accounts receivable ledger sheet every month.

To stay on top of customer payments, you can periodically prepare an accounts receivable aging schedule. This document lists the customers included in your total accounts receivable balance. Most businesses prepare an accounts receivable schedule at the close of each month. This is a handy cash-flow management tool because it will ferret out problem customers and possibly shed light on certain management and/or collection techniques that need improvement. For example, if the nature of your accounts receivable changes from one month to the next, you may be seeing the effect of a change in your credit policy or billing technique. Or, if a large number

Figure 12.3 Accounts Receivable from General Ledger

**Jon's Jazzy Designs
General Ledger**

Accounts Receivable

Date	Ref	Debit	Credit	Balance
1998				
January 31	S1	$90,230	$	$90,230
January 31	S1		20,800	$69,430

of new customers are consistently late with their payments, perhaps you need to tighten your collections policy. With an accounts receivable aging schedule, you can quickly spot problems and devise solutions that will improve your cash flow and make collections easier.

Documenting Your Accounts Payable

Accounts payable represent the money that your business owes to vendors/ suppliers or other creditors. For businesses using the accrual method of accounting, accounts payable are listed in a cash disbursements journal when products or services are purchased, even if payment has not been made.

When documenting accounts payable, you should create a separate accounts payable ledger account for each creditor. When an expense is incurred, it should be recorded in your cash disbursements journal under the debit and credit columns, and, at the end of the business day, posted from the cash disbursements journal to the appropriate accounts payable ledger account or the control account in your accounts payable ledger. At the end of each month, you should total the entries in your cash disbursements journal and post them to the accounts payable account in your general ledger.

Keep in mind that if you use accounting software, the program will automatically do all the posting to your accounts receivable and accounts payable ledger accounts.

CLOSING YOUR BOOKS

When you reach the end of an accounting period, you will have to close your books. At the very least, you should close your books once a year to ready your financial statements for analysis, and to gather the information needed for filing your income tax returns. However, you would be wise to perform this procedure more often, perhaps monthly, particularly if it involves reconciling your bank statements, submitting sales tax reports, sending out customer statements, and issuing payments to vendors.

Here are the steps you should take when closing your books. Perform these steps with your accountant's guidance, to prevent any potential problems.

1. Post (summarize and transfer) to your general ledger accounts all account totals from your sales and cash receipts journal and your cash disbursements journal.
2. Foot (total) your general ledger accounts to determine a preliminary ending balance for each account.
3. Prepare a preliminary trial balance. A trial balance is a worksheet that lists the debit or credit balances for all of your general ledger

accounts. When you create your trial balance, the debits must equal the credits. If they do not, an error has been made.

4. Create adjusting journal entries. You will not be able to close your books without making some adjustments to your entries. Adjusting entries are typically made to account for items that are not recorded in your day-to-day transactions. Many of the changes are straight-forward, but others will require a knowledge of accounting, so have your accountant prepare these entries for you, and make copies to put into your general ledger. Typical adjusting entries are: accrued property taxes, accrued wages payable, inventory depreciation expense, and bad debts. In a traditional accounting system, adjusting entries are listed in a general journal.

5. Foot your general ledger accounts a second time, to reflect the adjusted balance of each general ledger account.

6. Prepare an adjusted trial balance using the adjusted balances of each general ledger account. (Remember, debits must equal credits.)

7. Create your financial statements. After adjusting your entries and uncovering any errors, you and/or your accountant can prepare your balance sheet and income statement. (See Chapter 7 for more details about financial statements.)

8. Segregate your closing entries (the journal entries that you must prepare to set up your general ledger for the next accounting period). To do this, you must clear out all revenue and expense accounts, and transfer your income or loss to the company's equity account.

9. Prepare a postclosing trial balance. After all closing entries have been made, your revenue and expense accounts should have a zero balance. You can then prepare a final trial balance. It will contain only balance sheet accounts; therefore, when you start the next accounting period, your books should be balanced.

OTHER RECORDS TO MAINTAIN

In addition to the records mentioned above, you should hold onto several others. Consult your accountant for a complete list of all the records your business should retain for future reference. As a general practice, every business should preserve its payroll records, its insurance policies (and receipts for premiums paid), and its general business records.

Payroll Records

No matter how many employees you have, you will have to keep all records pertaining to payroll taxes. These include your documentation of income tax withheld, federal unemployment tax, and Social Security deductions. Keep these documents for at least four years after your taxes are due or paid, whichever is later. When preparing your records of income tax withheld, include the following information:

1. Name, address, and Social Security number of each employee.
2. The gross and net amounts and the date of each payment of compensation.
3. The amount of tax withheld from each employee's paycheck.
4. Copies of each employee's W-2 forms.
5. Statements indicating tips (gratuities) received by employees.
6. The total amount of wages subject to withholding in each of your company's pay periods.
7. The dates and amounts of all tax payments made by your company.

Your Federal Unemployment Tax (FUTA) records should list the total amount paid as salaries during a calendar year, the amount that is subject to unemployment tax, and any contributions paid to your state unemployment fund. In your Social Security (FICA) tax records, you should indicate the amount of each employee's paycheck that is subject to FICA tax, and the amounts and dates of actual FICA tax collections.

Insurance Documents

Maintain any records pertaining to your life, auto, health, or disability insurance policies. Within these records, indicate the insurance carrier and agent who issued the policies. Also document any claims you may have filed: the dates, the basis for the claim, and the award (if any). When you update your records to document payment of an insurance premium, include the check number, the date the check was written, and the number of the policy for which it was written. Keep all insurance records indefinitely.

General Business Records

As much as you might like to shred old sales receipts, you should keep them, along with canceled checks, cash register tapes, receiving reports, and customer invoices, for at least six years. Maintain precise records regarding these items. They will be very helpful if you have to address an important legal or tax question.

USING ACCOUNTING SOFTWARE

Because you will need to track your daily transactions yourself, consider automating your bookkeeping system to make your accounting procedures easier. Several accounting software programs are available to support your record-keeping needs. Some programs are written specifically for certain industries, such as construction, retail, and service-oriented businesses. A typical program can track inventory, create a time reporting and billing system, allow updates to inventory at the point of sale, and offer fixed-asset packages.

Alisa K. Bowens, president of Brushworks Unlimited, uses an accounting package called Simply Accounting to keep intact the books for her full-service construction company. "It really helps me calculate my payroll taxes and maintain my inventory list," says Bowens, whose firm supplies roofing, electrical wiring, masonry, and window replacements for a variety of clients, including Yale University School of Medicine and the National Guard.

"Using the software is almost like having an accountant, because the program lets me know where my money is going. When my accountant comes in to check my books, I simply hand him the disk along with the company checkbook so that he can balance the checkbook. He goes over the accounting payroll sheets prepared with Simply Accounting and, in minutes, he is able to calculate the necessary figures," she says.

To find a software package that matches the needs of your business, consult your accountant or talk with someone in your industry. Accounting software is sold at office supply stores, electronics stores, and software outlets. Here are three packages that are popular for automated bookkeeping. You should be able to purchase them for under $200.

1. *Quickbooks (www.quickbooks.com)*. This is a great starter system for new business owners. No accounting knowledge is required. Users need only the ability to click a mouse. Quickbooks provides these features:

   - Calculates sales tax.
   - Tracks records for income tax and payroll.
   - Prints payroll voucher checks.
   - Instantly updates and reconciles checking account balances.
   - Automatically tracks each invoice until payment is made.
   - Calculates finance charges on overdue invoices.
   - Handles cash and credit sales.
   - Writes and prints checks.
   - Provides tax tables through paid subscription.
   - Calculates payroll and earnings deductions.

2. *DacEasy (www.daceasy.com)*. Small business owners find this accounting package easy to use. It manages payroll, order entry, job costing, and point-of-sale data, plus more advanced features for mature businesses. For example, its Sales Assistant feature offers customers extended product or service descriptions at the point of sale.

When a new product or service is entered into the system, the Sales Assistant feature prints, on the invoice, advice about alternative products, replacement suggestions for items that are out of stock, availability notices, and other information.

3. *Peachtree Office Accounting (www.peachtree.com).* As with Quickbooks, you need not have an accounting background to use this software. Peachtree provides a user-friendly step-by-step process for entering transactions such as customer invoices, checks, and business forms. The system automatically calculates math and double-entry accounting. Paying bills is virtually painless because this system calculates the total payment due to each vendor and then creates and prints the checks for you to sign and mail. Payroll is also a snap. The program can print payroll checks just minutes after installation.

When you're shopping for an accounting package, decide how much access you will give your employees. Many business owners restrict or forbid employee access to their accounting records. However, if only certain accounting transactions are proprietary, look for an accounting package that requires the use of passwords.

Keep in mind that your accountant's job will be much easier if you use accounting software. You will hand over a disk rather than a folder full of forms, and the bill you receive for the accountant's services will be proportionally lower.

Whether you decide to use accounting software or not, you must keep your records in a convenient and safe place. The Internal Revenue Service (IRS) may request them years later. Also, as your business grows and changes, they will be valuable reminders of what worked and what didn't. Their history may keep you from repeating an earlier mistake.

CHECKLIST

THINGS TO DO WHEN PREPARING YOUR BOOKS

✓ **Find a reputable accountant.** You may not need an accountant to assist you with your day-to-day business transactions, but you should engage a professional's services at least once a year, to help you prepare your financial statements, income tax returns, and adjusting entries, and to deal with nonroutine bookkeeping chores. Ask business colleagues for referrals, or talk with your banker or attorney about available accounting firms in your area.

✓ **Purchase some accounting software.** Your daily bookkeeping activities can be easily handled by using an accounting software package. Besides maintaining your payroll records, inventory, and point-of-sale purchases, many programs allow you to create and print checks for employees and creditors. Quickbooks, a preferred package among new and existing business owners, requires no prior accounting knowledge.

✓ **Review the accounting basics.** Before you can set up your record-keeping system, you must become familiar with the basic concepts of accounting. Learn the functions of a sales and cash receipts journal and a cash disbursements journal, and be clear about cash versus accrual accounting and single- versus double-entry accounting.

✓ **Record your daily transactions.** Day to day, you will have cash transactions, sales and revenue transactions, accounts receivable, and accounts payable. Each of these activities must be posted to particular journals and ledgers before your books can be closed.

✓ **Close your books.** This process takes place at the end of every accounting period. At a minimum, close your books once a year, prior to filing your income tax returns. If you must collect sales tax, or issue customer statements, or reconcile your bank statements, close your books monthly. Whenever you decide to close your books, get assistance from your accountant.

✓ **Prepare your financial statements.** After all of your entries have been posted to your general ledger, a preliminary trial balance has been prepared, adjusting journal entries have been made, and your general ledger accounts have been footed, you can prepare your balance sheet and income statements—a key step in closing your books.

RESOURCES FOR MORE INFORMATION

ASSOCIATIONS

- *American Accounting Association (AAA),* 5717 Bessie Drive, Sarasota, Florida 34233-2399; 941-921-7747. AAA was founded in 1916 as the American Association of University Instructors in Accounting. It was created to promote and support accounting education, research, and practice. To brush up on your accounting skills before you put your record-keeping system in place, check out a few of the publications, journals, and newsletters produced by this organization. The AAA should be able to recommend a reputable accountant in your area.

- *Service Corps of Retired Executives (SCORE),* 409 Third Street SW, Washington, DC 20062; 1-800-634-0245; www.score.org. This organization can give you advice on how best to maintain your record-keeping system. SCORE can also help you prepare your financial statements and yearly income tax returns. A national organization supported by the U.S. Small Business Administration, SCORE offers a variety of services for new and existing business owners. Bookkeeping is just one of many subjects about which you can gain valuable information. This organization also provides details about licensing procedures, taxes, and business plan writing. SCORE offices are scattered throughout the country. Call to locate the one nearest you.

- *Small Business Administration's Office of Women's Business Ownership,* 409 Third Street, Suite 4400, Washington, DC, 20416; 202-205-6673; www.sba.gov/womeninbusiness. Through a series of Women's Business Ownership Centers, this organization provides expert advice on a number of business-related topics, including finance, management, and technology. By visiting one of the centers or the Online Women's Business Center at www.onlinewbc.com, you will find valuable information about record keeping.

13

THE TAX
MAN COMETH

Tax time. It's the one time of year that virtually all businesspeople wish they could just skip over. But, as the old cliché says, "In life there are two things that are certain—death and taxes." As a new business owner, you will have to pay your fair share of taxes if you want to keep your shingle intact.

Your new business will be obligated to pay or collect several taxes. Others, you will have to pay yourself. A typical roster includes: federal and state income tax, federal unemployment tax, payroll, Social Security, sales, self-employment, and excise taxes. The taxes that apply to your enterprise will depend on several factors: the type of business you own, your legal form of operation (sole proprietorship, partnership, corporation, subchapter S corporation, or limited liability company), whether you hire employees, and whether you use vehicles for your company.

For some entrepreneurs, taxes can be a bitter pill, especially if they have not kept meticulous records documenting their income and expenses (see Chapter 12 for details about how to prepare your books). For entrepreneurs who have a solid bookkeeping system, a good CPA at their side, and a basic awareness of tax law, tax time can become a little less taxing.

The laws governing taxation of business or personal income can be difficult to understand. For this reason, it is important to solicit the help of a CPA or tax adviser who will help you plow through the jargon and prepare your tax returns accurately and on time. However, as with bookkeeping, you should never totally abandon your responsibility to gain basic knowledge about the tax system. Even when you hire a professional to assist you in readying your returns for Uncle Sam, you are still ultimately responsible for seeing that all of your tax obligations are met. If they're not, the government is not going to come after your tax adviser. The government will come after you.

In this chapter, we will discuss some of the basic tax issues that are important to new and existing business owners. We will examine some standard business deductions that you may be able to claim, whether you work in an office high-rise or out of your home. As mentioned previously, not all businesses are subject to the same taxes. We will discuss those that apply to each legal business form and will show you some of the forms you will be required to file when Uncle Sam comes calling for a piece of your new business. Because of space constraints, forms are not included in their entirety here.

As you read this chapter, keep in mind that the information reflects the tax law at the time this book went to press. Congress constantly tinkers with the tax laws, so stay in close touch with your accountant about any changes in the tax laws that could affect your business. When in doubt, you can ask your local Internal Revenue Service (IRS) office for advice. The IRS will be more than happy to tell you what you owe.

TAX PLANNING FOR YOUR BUSINESS

As you now know, becoming a business owner requires a lot of planning. Among other things, you will have to outline how you will advertise your product or service, what prices you will set to attract and retain customers, and where you will hang out your shingle. As the owner, you will take a hands-on approach to each of these tasks. But if you're like most new shopkeepers, your stance will be different when it comes to tax planning. Instead of taking care of your taxes yourself, you will probably pay an accountant or some other tax professional to prepare the forms for you. We recommend enlisting the help of a professional to decipher the language surrounding tax law, credits, and deductions, but we also believe that you should develop a working knowledge of the subject matter yourself. At the very least, you won't look totally lost during discussions with your tax consultant. More important, you will be better able to spot tax advantages and potential tax blunders that pertain to your business.

Tax planning is a process that involves looking at various tax options to determine how you will conduct your business and personal transactions in a way that eliminates or reduces your tax liability. You and your accountant should discuss the strategies that will earn the biggest tax breaks for your business. At the very least, you want to be paying the minimal allowable amount of business tax. You may also find ways to claim available tax credits, lower your tax rate, and control the schedule for when your taxes must be paid.

A number of issues must be considered when you are weighing your tax liability. We will start by discussing how your business's legal form, tax year, accounting method, and inventory valuation process can impact the calculation of your taxes due.

Taxes by Business Form

When defining your tax liabilities, you must consider your legal form of business. How you structure your operation will have direct income tax implications. The Treasury Regulations vary for a sole proprietorship, a partnership, a corporation, a Subchapter S corporation, or a limited liability company. Know exactly what you are entitled to before you start claiming deductions.

Sole Proprietorship

A sole proprietorship is a business that has a single owner. It is the easiest and cheapest legal business form to establish. To be a sole proprietor, you choose a business name, acquire necessary licenses and/or permits, and, if you plan to hire employees, obtain a Federal Employer Identification Number (EIN). The IRS considers a sole proprietorship a "nontaxable" entity, which means that business assets and liabilities are not separate from the business owner; they are considered to belong to the owner. All income and expenses generated by the business are listed on Schedule C, Profit or Loss from Business, or Schedule C-EZ, Net Profit from Business. (See Chapter 4 for examples of these forms.) The net profit or loss that is earned is transferred from Schedule C and listed on the first page of the business owner's Form 1040, U.S. Individual Income Tax Return. No separate tax rate schedule is applied to a sole proprietorship. The tax rate for individuals will be assessed on your earnings from your business. If you decide to operate your company as a sole proprietorship, you will not be obligated to pay any special business income taxes. However, you will be required to remit self-employment taxes on the company's net profits (as calculated on Schedule SE), and payroll taxes for any employees you hire. (Self-employment and payroll taxes are discussed in greater detail later in this chapter.)

As a sole proprietor, you must file and pay your taxes on a yearly basis. If your business uses a calendar year, you must file and make payment by April 15. If it uses a fiscal year, you must file no later than the fifteenth day of the fourth month after the end of your tax year. Whether you operate according to a fiscal year or a calendar year, if you cannot meet the original filing deadline, you are entitled to a four-month extension to file your return. To take advantage of the extension, you must file Form 4868, Application for Automatic Extension of Time to File U.S. Individual Income Tax Return (see Figure 13.1). If your business uses the calendar year, this form should

Figure 13.1   Form 4868, Application for Automatic Extension of Time to File U.S. Individual Income Tax Return

| Form **4868**
Department of the Treasury
Internal Revenue Service | **Application for Automatic Extension of Time
To File U.S. Individual Income Tax Return** | OMB No. 1545-0188
1998 |

General Instructions

Purpose of Form

Use Form 4868 to apply for 4 more months to file **Form 1040EZ, Form 1040A, Form 1040, Form 1040NR-EZ,** or **Form 1040NR.**

To get the extra time you **MUST:**

- Properly estimate your 1998 tax liability using the information available to you,
- Enter your tax liability on line 9 of Form 4868, **AND**
- File Form 4868 by the regular due date of your return.

You are not required to send a payment of the tax you estimate as due. However, see **Interest** and **Late Payment Penalty** on page 3. Any remittance you send with your application for extension will be treated as a payment of tax.

You do not have to explain why you are asking for the extension. We will contact you only if your request is denied.

Do not file Form 4868 if you want the IRS to figure your tax or you are under a court order to file your return by the regular due date.

If you need an additional extension, see **If You Need Additional Time** on this page.

Note: *Generally, an extension of time to file your 1998 calendar year income tax return also extends the time to file a gift or generation-skipping transfer (GST) tax return (Form 709 or 709-A) for 1998. Special rules apply if the donor dies during the year in which the gifts were made. See the Instructions for Form 709.*

Out of the Country

If you already had 2 extra months to file because you were a U.S. citizen or resident and were out of the country, use this form to obtain an additional 2 months to file. Write "Taxpayer Abroad" across the top of Form 4868. "Out of the country" means either **(a)** you live outside the United States and Puerto Rico **and** your main place of work is outside the United States and Puerto Rico, **or (b)** you are in military or naval service outside the United States and Puerto Rico.

When To File Form 4868

File Form 4868 by April 15, 1999. Fiscal year taxpayers, file Form 4868 by the regular due date of the return.

If you had 2 extra months to file your return because you were out of the country, file Form 4868 by June 15, 1999, for a 1998 calendar year return.

How To Send In Your Payment

- When sending a payment with Form 4868, use the addresses in the middle column under **Where To File** on page 2.
- Make your check or money order payable to the "United States Treasury." Do not send cash.
- Write your social security number, daytime phone number, and "1998 Form 4868" on the front of your check or money order.
- Do not staple or attach your payment to the form.

If You Need Additional Time

If the automatic 4-month extension (until August 16, 1999, for most calendar year taxpayers) does not give you enough time, you can ask for additional time later. But you will have to give a good reason, and it must be approved by the IRS. To ask for the additional time, you must **either:**

1. File **Form 2688,** Application for Additional Extension of Time To File U.S. Individual Income Tax Return, or

2. Explain your reason in a letter. Mail it to the address in the right column under **Where To File** on page 2.

File Form 4868 **before** you file Form 2688 or write a letter asking for more time. Only in cases of undue hardship will the IRS approve your request for an additional extension without receiving Form 4868 first. Ask early for this extra time. Then, you can still file your return on time if your request is not approved.

For Privacy Act and Paperwork Reduction Act Notice, see page 4.   Cat. No. 13141W   Form **4868** (1998)

▼ DETACH HERE ▼

| Form **4868**
Department of the Treasury
Internal Revenue Service | **Application for Automatic Extension of Time
To File U.S. Individual Income Tax Return**
For calendar year 1998, or other tax year beginning   ,1998, ending   ,19 | OMB No. 1545-0188
1998 |

Part I Identification	**Part III** Individual Income Tax
1 Your name(s) (see instructions)	**4** Total tax liability on your income tax return for 1998 $ _____
	5 Total 1998 payments . . . . _____
Address (see instructions)	**6** **Balance.** Subtract 5 from 4 . . . . _____
City, town or post office, state, and ZIP code	**Part IV** Gift/GST Tax—If you are **not filing** a gift or GST tax return, go to Part V now. See the instructions.
2 Your social security number **3** Spouse's social security no.	**7** Your gift or GST tax payment. . . $ _____ **8** **Your spouse's** gift/GST tax payment . _____
Part II Complete ONLY If Filing Gift/GST Tax Return	**Part V** Total
This form also extends the time for filing a gift or generation-skipping transfer (GST) tax return if you file a calendar (not fiscal) year income tax return. Check below **only** if requesting a gift or GST tax return extension, and enter your tax payment(s) in Part IV:	**9** **Total liability.** Add lines 6, 7, and 8 $ _____ **10** Amount you are paying. . . . . ▶ _____
Yourself ▶ ☐ Spouse ▶ ☐	If line 10 is less than line 9, you may be liable for interest and penalties. See page 3.

be submitted by April 15, along with the money you calculate you owe in taxes. The extension applies only to the physical filing of your return, not to payment of taxes. You may have until August 15 to send in your completed income tax form, but you must make a best-guess payment by April 15 or risk accumulating penalties and/or interest on overdue taxes. If you still cannot file your return by August 15, you can request an additional two-month extension by filing, before August 15, Form 2688, Application for Additional Extension of Time to File U.S. Individual Income Tax Return (see Figure 13.2). This extension is not automatic. You must not assume that the IRS will grant you the additional time. If the IRS does grant it, you must file your return by October 15. The filing dates for fiscal-year taxpayers under the four- and two-month extensions would be: the fifteenth day of the fourth month after the original due date, and the fifteenth day of the second month after the automatic four-month extension date.

Partnership

A partnership is a business entity that has two or more business owners who share management responsibilities, profits, and all liability—tax or otherwise. There are two types of partnership: general partnership and limited partnership. Like a sole proprietorship, a partnership is not considered a taxable entity; no separate partnership income tax is levied. All of the profits or losses generated by the partnership "pass through" to each partner's personal income and are taxed at the personal rate. The partnership is required to report its income or loss by filing Form 1065, U.S. Partnership Return of Income, using Schedule K-1 (see Chapter 4). Any taxes due are paid individually by the partners. Keep in mind that if your business has more than one owner, the IRS will tax your company as a partnership unless you incorporate under state law or elect to be taxed as a corporation by filing Form 8832. Partnerships must file their returns annually. The due date is April 15, but partnerships are entitled to a three-month extension. To file for this extension, you must submit Form 8736, Application for Automatic Extension of Time to File U.S. Return for a Partnership, by April 15 (see Figure 13.3). Your return would then be due on July 15. Remember: Extensions apply only to the filing of your return, not to the payment of your taxes. You can obtain an additional three-month extension by filing Form 8800, Application for Additional Extension of Time to File U.S. Return for a Partnership (see Figure 13.4). Your request must reach the IRS by July 15. If the extension is granted, you have until October 15 to file your return. These deadlines apply to businesses operating on a calendar-year basis. If you are a fiscal-year taxpayer, your original deadline would be the fifteenth day of the fourth month after the end of your partnership tax year. The deadline for your automatic three-month extension would be the fifteenth day of the third month after the original due date for your return. If you need three additional months to file, you have

Figure 13.2   Form 2688, Application for Additional Extension of
Time to File U.S. Individual Income Tax Return

Form **2688**	**Application for Additional Extension of Time To File** **U.S. Individual Income Tax Return** ▶ See instructions on back. ▶ You MUST complete all items that apply to you.	OMB No. 1545-0066 19**98**
Department of the Treasury Internal Revenue Service		

Please type or print.	Your first name and initial	Last name	Your social security number
File by the due date for filing your return.	If a joint return, spouse's first name and initial	Last name	Spouse's social security number

Home address (number and street)

City, town or post office, state, and ZIP code

Please fill in the Return Label at the bottom of this page.

1 I request an extension of time until .... , 19.......... , to file Form 1040EZ, Form 1040A, Form 1040, Form 1040NR-EZ, or Form 1040NR for the calendar year 1998, or other tax year ending .... , 19... .

2 Explain why you need an extension. You must give an adequate explanation ▶ ....
....
....
....
....

3 Have you filed Form 4868 to request an automatic extension of time to file for this tax year? . . . . ☐ **Yes** ☐ **No**
If you checked "No," we will grant your extension only for undue hardship. Fully explain the hardship in item 2. Attach any information you have that helps explain the hardship.

If you expect to have to file a gift or generation-skipping transfer (GST) tax return, complete line 4.

4 If you or your spouse plan to file a gift or GST tax return (Form 709 or 709-A) for 1998, generally } **Yourself** . . ▶ ☐
due by April 15, 1999, see the instructions and check here . . . . } **Spouse** . . ▶ ☐

Signature and Verification

Under penalties of perjury, I declare that I have examined this form, including accompanying schedules and statements, and to the best of my knowledge and belief, it is true, correct, and complete; and, if prepared by someone other than the taxpayer, that I am authorized to prepare this form.

Signature of taxpayer ▶ _____ Date ▶ _____

Signature of spouse ▶ _____ Date ▶ _____
(If filing jointly, BOTH must sign even if only one had income.)

Signature of preparer
other than taxpayer ▶ _____ Date ▶ _____

Please fill in the **Return Label** below with your name, address, and social security number. The IRS will complete the **Notice to Applicant** and return it to you. If you want it sent to another address or to an agent acting for you, enter the other address and add the agent's name.

(Do not detach)

Notice to Applicant **To Be Completed by the IRS**	☐ We **HAVE** approved your application. ☐ We **HAVE NOT** approved your application. However, we have granted a 10-day grace period to .... This grace period is considered a valid extension of time for elections otherwise required to be made on a timely return. ☐ We **HAVE NOT** approved your application. After considering the information you provided in item 2 above, we cannot grant your request for an extension of time to file. We are not granting a 10-day grace period. ☐ We cannot consider your application because it was filed after the due date of your return. ☐ Other..

_____   _____
Director   Date

Return Label (Please type or print) (Agents: Always include taxpayer's name.)

Taxpayer's name (and agent's name, if applicable). If a joint return, also give spouse's name.	Taxpayer's social security number
Number and street (include suite, room, or apt. no.) or P.O. box number	Spouse's social security number
City, town or post office, state, and ZIP code	

For Privacy Act and Paperwork Reduction Act Notice, see back of form.   Cat. No. 11958F   Form **2688** (1998)

Figure 13.3   Form 8736, Application for Automatic Extension of
Time to File U.S. Return for a Partnership, REMIC, or for Certain Trusts

Form **8736** (Rev. October 1998) Department of the Treasury Internal Revenue Service	**Application for Automatic Extension of Time To File U.S. Return for a Partnership, REMIC, or for Certain Trusts** ▶ File a separate application for each return.	OMB No. 1545-1054

Please type or print. File by the due date for filing the return for which an extension is requested. See instructions.	Name	Employer identification number
	Number, street, and room or suite no. If a P.O. box, see instructions.	
	City or town, state, and ZIP code. If a foreign address, enter city, province or state, and country. Follow the country's practice for entering the postal code.	

1   I request an automatic **3-month** extension of time to file (check only one):

☐ Form 1041   ☐ Form 1041-QFT   ☐ Form 1065   ☐ Form 1065-B   ☐ Form 1066

2   If the entity does not have an office or place of business in the United States, check this box . . . . ▶ ☐

3a   For calendar year ...., or other tax year beginning .... , ..., and ending...................... , ...

  b   If this tax year is for less than 12 months, check reason:

     ☐ Initial return   ☐ Final return   ☐ Change in accounting period

4   If this extension is requested for Form 1041, Form 1041-QFT, Form 1065-B, or Form 1066, enter the following amounts:

  a   Tentative total tax from Form 1041, Form 1041-QFT, Form 1065-B, or Form 1066 (see instructions) . $ _____

  b   Refundable credits and estimated tax payments, including any prior year overpayment allowed as a credit, from Form 1041, Form 1041-QFT, or Form 1065-B (see instructions). REMICs, enter -0- . . $ _____

  c   **Balance due.** Subtract line 4b from line 4a. If zero or less, enter -0-. Enclose payment, if any, with Form 8736 (see instructions) . . . . ▶ $ _____

Caution: *Interest will be charged on any tax not paid by the regular due date of Forms 1041, 1041-QFT, 1065-B, and 1066 from the due date until the tax is paid.*

General Instructions

Section references are to the Internal Revenue Code unless otherwise noted.

Purpose of Form

Use Form 8736 to request an automatic 3-month extension of time to file a return for:

• Trusts filing **Form 1041**, U.S. Income Tax Return for Estates and Trusts, or **Form 1041-QFT**, U.S. Income Tax Return for Qualified Funeral Trusts.

• Partnerships filing **Form 1065**, U.S. Partnership Return of Income, or **Form 1065-B**, U.S. Return of Income for Electing Large Partnerships.

• Real estate mortgage investment conduits filing **Form 1066**, U.S. Real Estate Mortgage Investment Conduit (REMIC) Income Tax Return.

If allowed, the automatic extension will extend the due date of the return to the 15th day of the 3rd month following the month in which the regular due date falls. The automatic 3-month extension period includes any 2-month extension granted under Regulations section 1.6081-5 to certain foreign partnerships.

Note: *An estate filing Form 1041 should not file this form. Instead, it should request an extension using Form 2758, Application for*

Extension of Time To File Certain Excise, Income, Information, and Other Returns.

The extension will be allowed if you complete Form 8736 properly, make a proper estimate of the tax on line 4a (if applicable), and file the form on time. We will notify you only if your request for an extension is not allowed.

For most partnerships, trusts, and REMICs, an automatic extension will extend the due date of the return to July 15th of the year following the close of the calendar year.

When To File

File Form 8736 by the regular due date of the return for which an extension is requested (or, in the case of certain foreign partnerships, by the expiration date of any extension of time to file granted under Regulations section 1.6081-5). The regular due date is generally the 15th day of the 4th month following the close of the entity's tax year. However, the regular due date for a partnership in which all partners are nonresident aliens is the 15th day of the 6th month following the close of the partnership's tax year.

Additional Extension of Time To File

If Form 8736 has already been filed but more time is needed, file **Form 8800**, Application

for Additional Extension of Time To File U.S. Return for a Partnership, REMIC, or for Certain Trusts. Except in cases of undue hardship, do not file Form 8800 unless Form 8736 has already been filed. Before an additional extension can be granted, the entity must show reasonable cause for the additional time needed to file.

Ask for the additional extension early so that if it is denied the return can still be filed on time.

Where To File

Except for a charitable or split-interest trust described in section 4947(a), a pooled income fund defined in section 642(c)(5), or a qualified funeral trust, file Form 8736 at the applicable IRS address listed below.

If the entity's principal place of business or principal office or agency is located in	Use the following Internal Revenue Service Center address
New Jersey, New York (New York City and counties of Nassau, Rockland, Suffolk, and Westchester)	Holtsville, NY 00501

(continued on page 2)

Cat. No. 64907Y   Form **8736** (Rev. 10-98)

Figure 13.4   Form 8800, Application for Additional Extension of
Time to File U.S. Return for a Partnership, REMIC, or for Certain Trusts

Form **8800** (Rev. September 1998) Department of the Treasury Internal Revenue Service	**Application for Additional Extension of Time To File** **U.S. Return for a Partnership, REMIC, or for Certain Trusts** ▶ File a separate application for each return.	OMB No. 1545-1057

Please type or print. **File the original and one copy by the due date for filing the return for which an extension is requested. See instructions.**	Name	Employer identification number
	Number, street, and room or suite no. If a P.O. box, see instructions.	
	City or town, state, and ZIP code. If a foreign address, enter city, province or state, and country. Follow the country's practice for entering the postal code.	

1 I request an additional extension of time until .... , ... , to file (check only one):

☐ Form 1041 ☐ Form 1041-QFT ☐ Form 1065 ☐ Form 1065-B ☐ Form 1066

2 If the entity does not have an office or place of business in the United States, check this box . . . . ▶ ☐

3a For calendar year .... , or other tax year beginning .... , ... , and ending .... , ...

b If this tax year is for less than 12 months, check reason: ☐ Initial return   ☐ Final return   ☐ Change in accounting period

4 Explain why the entity needs an extension. All entities filing this form must give an adequate explanation. ....

....

....

....

....

....

....

....

....

....

5 Has the entity filed Form 8736 to request an extension of time to file for this tax year?   ☐ Yes ☐ No
If you checked "No," we will grant an extension only for undue hardship. Fully explain the hardship on line 4.

Signature and Verification

Under penalties of perjury, I declare that I have examined this form, including accompanying schedules and statements, and to the best of my knowledge and belief, it is true, correct, and complete; and that I am authorized to prepare this form.

Signature ▶ _____   Title ▶ _____   Date ▶ _____

File original and one copy. The IRS will show below whether or not your application is approved and will return the copy.

Notice to Applicant—To Be Completed by the IRS.

☐ We **HAVE** approved this application. Please attach this form to the entity's return.

☐ We **HAVE NOT** approved this application.
However, we have granted a 10-day grace period to .... This grace period is considered a valid extension of time for elections otherwise required to be made on a timely return. Please attach this form to the entity's return.

☐ We **HAVE NOT** approved this application. After considering the reasons stated in item 4 above, we cannot grant this request for an extension of time to file. We are not granting a 10-day grace period.

☐ We cannot consider this application because it was filed after the due date of the return for which an extension was requested.

☐ Other: ....

By: _____

Director _____   Date _____

If you want a copy of this form to be returned to an address other than that shown above, please enter the address to which the copy should be sent.

Please Type or Print	Name
	Number, street, and room or suite no. (If a P.O. box, see instructions.)
	City or town, state, and ZIP code. If a foreign address, enter city, province or state, and country. Follow the country's practice for entering the postal code.

For Paperwork Reduction Act Notice, see back of form.   Cat. No. 64938X   Form **8800** (Rev. 9-98)

to submit your return by the fifteenth day of the third month after the automatic extension date.

Corporation

A corporation is perhaps the most preferred business entity among entrepreneurs, but it is also the most complex. Unlike a sole proprietorship, which sustains only one owner, a corporation is owned by several people called shareholders. A corporation offers several benefits, such as perpetual life and limited liability status, but it is considered a separate taxable business entity and is subject to federal and state income taxes. Any income earned by the corporation is taxed at the corporate level and must be recorded on Form 1120, U.S. Corporation Income Tax Return (see Chapter 4). Income paid to shareholders is taxed as dividends, at the shareholder's personal tax-bracket rate. Corporations suffer from double taxation, but not all corporate profits are affected. The corporation can claim deductions for the salaries paid to its operators, as long as the compensation is reasonable. The salaries will not be taxed at the corporate level, but the individuals receiving the salaries will have to pay income tax, and employees, along with the business itself, will have to pay Social Security tax. If you operate as a corporation and will claim a deduction for salaries paid, make sure that the compensation provided is not significantly higher than the industry standards. Overinflated salaries could send up a red flag to the IRS. The deduction may then be refuted on the grounds that the salaries are actually dividends in disguise (and therefore are taxable income). In addition to the corporate tax, you may be subject to an accumulated earnings tax. This tax applies to corporations that, in essence, hold profits earned by shareholders instead of distributing those profits as dividends. Profits earned by shareholders cannot be taxed until they are distributed. However, if your business operates as a corporation, you may not "accumulate" the earnings as a way to reduce your taxable income. If you do, you will be subject to a 39.6 percent accumulated earnings tax, on top of your regular corporate tax. If you use a calendar year, your filing date is March 15. You are entitled to a six-month extension and can request it by filing Form 7004, Application for Automatic Extension of Time to File Corporation Income Tax Return, by March 15 (see Figure 13.5). If the extension is granted, your new deadline would be September 15. If you take advantage of the additional time to file, the taxes you estimate are due must be paid by March 15. You must deposit them at the Federal Reserve Bank serving your area or at an authorized depositary. You should submit payment along with Form 8109, Federal Tax Deposit (FTD) Coupon. You can also use Form 8109-B (Figure 13.6), but only under certain circumstances. Contact your local IRS office for details. If your corporation uses a fiscal year instead of a calendar year, you must file your return by the fifteenth day of the third month after the close of your business's tax year. If you take the automatic six-month extension, your new due date would be the fifteenth day of the sixth month after the original due date for your return.

Figure 13.5   Form 7004, Application for Automatic Extension of
Time to File Corporation Income Tax Return

Form **7004** (Rev. July 1998) Department of the Treasury Internal Revenue Service	**Application for Automatic Extension of Time To File Corporation Income Tax Return**	OMB No. 1545-0233

Name of corporation

Employer identification number

Number, street, and room or suite no. (If a P.O. box or outside the United States, see instructions.)

City or town, state, and ZIP code

Check type of return to be filed:

☐ Form 1120	☐ Form 1120-FSC	☐ Form 1120-ND	☐ Form 1120-REIT	☐ Form 1120-SF
☐ Form 1120-A	☐ Form 1120-H	☐ Form 1120-PC	☐ Form 1120-RIC	
☐ Form 1120-F	☐ Form 1120-L	☐ Form 1120-POL	☐ Form 1120S	

☐ Form 990-C ▶
☐ Form 990-T   **Note:** *Other 990 filers (i.e., Form 990, 990-EZ, 990-BL, 990-PF, and certain filers of Form 990-T (see instructions))* **must** *use Form 2758 to request an extension of time to file.*

Form 1120-F filers: Check here if you do not have an office or place of business in the United States . . . . ▶ ☐

1a I request an automatic 6-month (or, for certain corporations, 3-month) extension of time
until ...., ... , to file the income tax return of the corporation named above for ▶ ☐ calendar
year .... or ▶ ☐ tax year beginning..........................., ..., and ending .... , ...

b If this tax year is for less than 12 months, check reason:
☐ Initial return   ☐ Final return   ☐ Change in accounting period   ☐ Consolidated return to be filed

2 If this application also covers subsidiaries to be included in a consolidated return, complete the following:

Name and address of each member of the affiliated group	Employer identification number	Tax period

3 Tentative tax (see instructions)	**3**	
4 **Credits:**		
a Overpayment credited from prior year. **4a**		
b Estimated tax payments for the tax year **4b**		
c Less refund for the tax year applied for on Form 4466 . . . . . . **4c** ( ) Bal ▶ **4d**		
e Credit for tax paid on undistributed capital gains (Form 2439) . . **4e**		
f Credit for Federal tax on fuels (Form 4136) **4f**		
5 Total. Add lines 4d through 4f	**5**	
6 **Balance due.** Subtract line 5 from line 3. **Deposit this amount electronically or with a Federal Tax Deposit (FTD) Coupon** (see instructions)	**6**	

Signature.—Under penalties of perjury, I declare that I have been authorized by the above-named corporation to make this application, and to the best of my knowledge and belief, the statements made are true, correct, and complete.

_____   _____   _____
(Signature of officer or agent)   (Title)   (Date)

For Paperwork Reduction Act Notice, see instructions.   Cat. No. 13804A   Form **7004** (Rev. 7-98)

Figure 13.6   Form 8109-B, Federal Tax Deposit Coupon

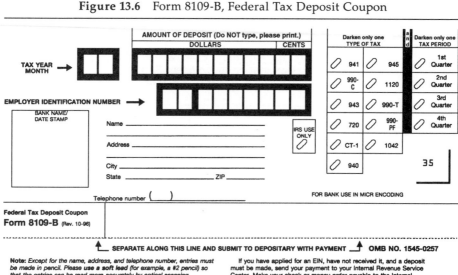

------ ⬆ SEPARATE ALONG THIS LINE AND SUBMIT TO DEPOSITARY WITH PAYMENT ⬆ OMB NO. 1545-0257

Note: *Except for the name, address, and telephone number, entries must be made in pencil. Please use a soft lead (for example, a #2 pencil) so that the entries can be read more accurately by optical scanning equipment. The name, address, and telephone number may be completed other than by hand. You CANNOT use photocopies of the coupons to make your deposits. Do not staple, tape, or fold the coupons.*

Paperwork Reduction Act Notice.—We ask for the information on this form to carry out the Internal Revenue laws of the United States. You are required to give us the information. We need it to ensure that you are complying with these laws and to allow us to figure and collect the right amount of tax.

You are not required to provide the information requested on a form that is subject to the Paperwork Reduction Act unless the form displays a valid OMB control number. Books or records relating to a form or its instructions must be retained as long as their contents may become material in the administration of any Internal Revenue law. Generally, tax returns and return information are confidential, as required by Code section 6103.

The time needed to complete and file this form will vary depending on individual circumstances. The estimated average time is 3 min. If you have comments concerning the accuracy of this time estimate or suggestions for making this form simpler, we would be happy to hear from you. You can write to the Tax Forms Committee, Western Area Distribution Center, Rancho Cordova, CA 95743-0001. **DO NOT** send this form to this address. Instead, see the instructions on the back of this page.

Purpose of Form.—Use Form 8109-B to make a tax deposit **only** in the following two situations:

1. You have not yet received your resupply of preprinted deposit coupons (Form 8109); or

2. You are a new entity and have already been assigned an employer identification number (EIN), but you have not yet received your initial supply of preprinted deposit coupons (Form 8109).

Note: *If you do not receive your resupply of deposit coupons and a deposit is due or you do not receive your initial supply within 5–6 weeks of receipt of your EIN, please call 1-800-829-1040.*

If you have applied for an EIN, have not received it, and a deposit must be made, send your payment to your Internal Revenue Service Center. Make your check or money order payable to the Internal Revenue Service and show on it your name (as shown on **Form SS-4,** Application for Employer Identification Number), address, kind of tax, period covered, and date you applied for an EIN. Also attach an explanation to the deposit. **Do not** use Form 8109-B in this situation. **Do not** use Form 8109-B to deposit delinquent taxes assessed by the IRS. Pay those taxes directly to the IRS. See **Circular E,** Employer's Tax Guide, for information on depositing by Electronic Funds Transfer.

How To Complete the Form.—Enter your name exactly as shown on your return or other IRS correspondence, address, and EIN in the spaces provided. If you are required to file a Form 1120, 990-C, 990-PF (with net investment income), 990-T, or 2438, enter the month in which your tax year ends in the **TAX YEAR MONTH** boxes. For example, if your tax year ends in January, enter 01; if it ends in June, enter 06; if it ends in December, enter 12. Please make your entries for EIN and tax year month (if applicable) in the manner specified in **Amount of Deposit** below. Darken one box each in the TYPE OF TAX and TAX PERIOD columns as explained below.

Amount of Deposit.—Enter the amount of the deposit in the space provided. Enter the amount legibly, forming the characters as shown below:

Hand print money amounts without using dollar signs, commas, a decimal point, or leading zeros. The commas and the decimal point are already shown in the entry area. For example, a deposit of $7,635.22 would be entered like this:

			DOLLARS				CENTS
			7	6	3	5	2 2

If the deposit is for whole dollars only, enter "00" in the **CENTS** boxes.

Types of Tax.—

Form 941	—Withheld income tax and both the employer and employee social security and Medicare taxes from wages and other compensation (includes Forms 941-M, 941-PR, and 941-SS).
Form 945	—Withheld Income Tax From Pensions, Annuities, IRAs, Gambling, Indian Gaming, and Backup Withholding.
Form 990-C	—Farmers' Cooperative Association Income Tax.
Form 943	—Agricultural Withheld Income, Social Security, and Medicare Taxes (includes Form 943-PR).
Form 720	—Excise Tax.
Form CT-1	—Railroad Retirement Taxes.
Form 940	—Federal Unemployment (FUTA) Tax (includes Form 940-EZ and Form 940-PR).
Form 1120	—Corporate Income Tax (includes Form 1120 series of returns and Form 2438).

Form 990-T	—Exempt Organization Business Income Tax.
Form 990-PF	—Excise Tax on Private Foundation Net Investment Income.
Form 1042	—Withholding on Foreign Persons.

Marking the Proper Tax Period.—

Payroll Taxes and Withholding (Forms 941, 940, 943, 945, CT-1, and 1042. See the separate Instructions for Form 1042.)

If your liability was incurred during:

● January 1 through March 31, darken the 1st quarter box
● April 1 through June 30, darken the 2nd quarter box
● July 1 through September 30, darken the 3rd quarter box
● October 1 through December 31, darken the 4th quarter box

Note: *If the liability was incurred during one quarter and deposited in another quarter, darken the box for the quarter in which the tax liability was incurred. For example, if the liability was incurred in March and deposited in April, darken the 1st quarter box.*

(Continued on back of page.)

Department of the Treasury
Internal Revenue Service   Cat. No. 61042S   Form **8109-B** (Rev. 10-96)

Subchapter S Corporation

Generally speaking, a Subchapter S corporation operates as a regular corporation and has basically the same structure (a board of directors, officers, and shareholders). However, it is not taxed twice. Instead, this business entity elects to be taxed similar to a partnership for federal tax purposes. Its income and losses "pass through" the company to the shareholders and are taxed at the shareholder level. If you operate under this legal business form, you will have to file Form 1120S, U.S. Income Tax Return for an S Corporation, on an annual basis. If you use a calendar year, your return is due by March 15. You can apply for an automatic six-month extension by filing Form 7004 by March 15, but you must deposit the amount of your estimated taxes due at a Federal Reserve Bank or an authorized depositary by the original due date or be subject to penalties and interest for overdue taxes. When making your deposit, be sure to include an FTD coupon with your payment. If your S corporation uses a fiscal year, your return is due by the fifteenth day of the third month after the close of your company's tax year. If you apply for the six-month extension as a fiscal year taxpayer, your due date would be the fifteenth day of the sixth month after the original due date for your return.

Limited Liability Company

For federal tax purposes, a limited liability company (LLC) is treated like a partnership. The income and losses generated in an LLC "pass through" to each party's personal income and are taxed at each individual's personal rate. Because an LLC is treated like a partnership, it may be subject to self-employment taxes and (if it hires employees) payroll taxes. If you operate as a limited liability company, your due dates for filing your return are the same as for a partnership, and the same extensions would apply.

No matter which legal form of business you choose, if a due date for filing your returns falls on a Saturday, Sunday, or federal holiday, the date will be pushed back until the next day, as long as that day is not a Saturday, Sunday, or federal holiday. Holidays that are legal within your state will only postpone an original due date if the IRS office where you would file your return is located in that state.

Defining Your Tax Year

A tax year, also called an accounting period, can be either a calendar year or a fiscal year. A fiscal year is a 12-month period that ends on the last day of any month except December. How you define your tax year determines how your taxable income is figured. For example, let's say you open a seasonal business. You keep your books according to a calendar year, but your shop is only open from December 1 through May 31. If you close your books at the end of the calendar year (December 31) and compute your income, your bottom line could be misleading because your tax year would have been split between two seasons. Your apparent profit at the end of your tax year could be smothered by losses when the entire selling season is reviewed. By using a calendar year, you may have difficulty preparing inventory and performing other important tasks during the middle of your season.

Tunde Dada operates his namesake retail shop on a calendar-year basis, but is trying to change it to a fiscal year. Why make the switch? "We do 30 percent of our business in December, so there is a lot going on, leaving us little time to nail down our inventory and everything by the 31st," says Dada. "By using a fiscal year, we could finish our Christmas sales, clean things up, and then do our inventory and plan for the next year," he says.

If you originally choose to use a calendar year, switching over to a fiscal year (or vice versa) is not easy. You may need permission from the IRS. Carefully consider how each tax year will affect your business income, before making a final selection about the type of company you will operate.

Depending on your legal form of business, there are several restrictions on the tax year you can use for federal tax purposes. Sole proprietorships are generally required to use a calendar year as their tax year because, according to the IRS, a sole proprietorship does not exist apart from its owners. It must therefore adopt the same tax year that the owner uses to file his or her individual income tax return (a calendar year).

A partnership or limited liability company must use the same accounting period as the majority of its owners. A Subchapter S corporation must use a calendar year. There are exceptions to these rules, but if you wish to change the status of your tax year, you must show the IRS how it would substantially benefit your business. If you operate a seasonal shop, you may have an easier time persuading the IRS that you need to change your tax year.

Choosing an Accounting Method

As discussed in Chapter 12, there are two methods of accounting: cash and accrual. The cash method of accounting involves recording income only when you receive cash from a customer, and recording expenses only when you write a check to pay a creditor. With the accrual method, income and expenses are recorded at the time they are made, regardless of whether payment is received or issued.

For tax-planning purposes, the cash method of accounting has several advantages that the accrual method does not offer. For example, using the cash method, you can reduce your tax liability by shifting income and expenses from one tax year to the next. In other words, you can collect fees, interest, and other payments in advance, or postpone them until a later date as a way of controlling your income. You can also control your expenses by deferring payment for items such as office supplies or repairs. This cannot be done (at least not without causing a major cash-flow problem) using the accrual method.

On the other hand, if your business handles complex transactions, using the accrual method of accounting is more beneficial. Your expenses are deducted in the year in which the income that relates to those expenses is recorded, regardless of whether payment was made. As a result, your income is leveled out and you avoid the possibility of having to pay higher taxes.

Although both methods have tax advantages, some types of businesses must, according to the law, operate under one method and not the other. For example, according to the Tax Reform Act of 1986, businesses operating as corporations, partnerships, or trusts must use the accrual method of accounting, at least for sales and the purchase of inventory for resale, if their gross sales exceed $5 million a year.

Consult your attorney about which method is best for your business. As with choosing a tax year, once you select a particular accounting method, you may not be able to change it without permission from the IRS.

Valuing Your Inventory

You can deduct the cost of goods sold (the total cost of purchasing products for resale, or the cost of producing or manufacturing goods) when calculating your taxable income. However, to be able to claim this deduction, you must first determine the value of your inventory at the beginning and end of your tax year, as well as the value of goods sold over the course of the year.

For tax purposes, there are two methods you can use to determine your inventory valuation at the beginning and end of your accounting period:

- *Cost method.* Using this method, you value your inventory according to the direct or indirect costs of purchasing or producing it yourself. For example, for products that you manufacture, you may value your inventory based on your labor costs, materials used, and overhead expenses generated during the production process.
- *Market value method.* Also referred to as the "lower of cost" method, this technique allows you to reduce your gross income to reflect any potential decreases in the value of your inventory, such as a drop in market price.

To identify the value of items sold during the year, you can use either the FIFO (first-in, first-out) method, or the LIFO (last-in, first-out) method. The FIFO method represents a general business practice among entrepreneurs: try to sell older items first, to remove them from inventory before they become outdated. If you use this method, the IRS will assume that sales have been generated from the items that have stayed in your inventory the longest. If you use the LIFO method, the IRS will assume that your current purchases are being sold and your older items are still in your inventory.

By choosing LIFO over FIFO, you can save a significant amount in taxes, particularly during a period of increased prices. Why? Because under the FIFO method, the IRS requires that you report as sold the oldest (therefore, cheapest) items, which in turn would require you to report the most taxable income. But if you adopt the LIFO method, the higher costs of goods are applied to your current income, which reduces your profit and, thus, your tax payment. In other words, if you are able to apply higher-priced goods to your current income to drive down your profit, you will be able to reduce your taxes. However, if you apply lower-priced items to your current income, which may barely decrease your profit, you may have to pay higher taxes based on that profit.

Changing your inventory valuation status can help you reduce your tax liability. However, once you adopt one method, you cannot switch to the other unless you have approval from the IRS. You can request the switch by filing Form 970.

Now that you know some of the issues you must consider when conducting your tax-planning strategies, you can begin looking at some specific taxes that your operation may be responsible for collecting and paying. In the sections that follow, we will discuss payroll, state, sales, self-employment, and vehicle taxes.

PAYROLL TAX OBLIGATIONS FOR YOUR BUSINESS

Whether you hire one or a hundred employees for your new business, you will be responsible for withholding taxes from each worker's pay. You will also be obligated to pay certain taxes on the compensation you pay your employees. This combination of taxes, described as payroll tax, includes the following four components:

1. *Federal income tax.* When you pay wages to your employees, you have to withhold income tax from each worker's paycheck. Tax authorities require employers to collect taxes owed by their employees on their wages and other forms of compensation (fringe benefits, gifts, and tips). Withholding allows employees to pay their taxes on a "pay-as-you-go" basis. Although the money withheld represents the amounts owed by your workers, you will ultimately be responsible for collecting the tax and depositing it with the appropriate agencies. The amount you should collect from an employee's paycheck will depend on the length of your payroll period, the employee's marital status, the amount of the employee's wages, and the number of exemptions

the employee claims. A general rule of thumb is: The more withholding exemptions a worker claims, the less tax you will be required to withhold. Your employees can list their exemptions by filling out Form W-4, Employees' Withholding Allowance Certificate (see Figure 13.7). At the time of hire, every employee should fill out this form. On the W-4, employees can claim a withholding exemption for themselves, a spouse, a child (children) or other dependent(s). Your employees may not claim *more* exemptions than they are entitled to, but they can claim fewer exemptions and may even instruct you to withhold additional money from their wages. Don't worry about having to solve algebraic equations to calculate your withholding amounts. The IRS provides easy-to-use tables that indicate the amounts you must collect. There are two types of tables that you can use: (1) wage bracket tables, which categorize computations according to five types of payroll periods (weekly, biweekly, semimonthly, monthly, and daily/miscellaneous), and (2) percentage tables, which cover eight payroll periods (weekly, biweekly, semimonthly, monthly, quarterly, semiannually, annually, and daily/miscellaneous). Both tables can be found in the IRS Publication 15, Circular E: *Employer's Tax Guide.* You can get a free copy of the publication by calling 1-800-TAX-FORM (1-800-829-3676). After figuring your withholding amounts and collecting the necessary taxes, you must file Form 8109 and periodically deposit the money with the Federal Reserve bank serving your area, or with another financial institution authorized to accept federal tax deposits. As mentioned previously, Form 8109 is the Federal Tax Deposit Coupon that you must submit along with your tax payment. When the IRS issues you an Employer Identification Number (EIN), it will also supply you with a stack of deposit coupons, preprinted with your name, address, and EIN. As a new employer, you can also use Form 8109-B, but only if you have been assigned an EIN but have not received your deposit coupons (or a requested refill of coupons). Generally, you will be required to make deposits on a monthly or biweekly basis. Contact your local IRS office to determine which method will apply to your business. When making your deposits, keep in mind that you could be slapped with a penalty if you deposit substantially less than the required amount. However, as long as you do not undercut your deposit by the greater of $100 or 2 percent of the amount you should have deposited, you will not be penalized. You can also be hit with a fine if your deposit arrives late, so be aware of your deadlines and keep track of your bank's daily cut-off times for recording deposits and its holidays schedule.

2. *Social Security and Medicare tax.* According to the Federal Insurance Contributions Act (FICA), every employer must withhold

Figure 13.7   Employee's Withholding Allowance Certificate

Form W-4 (1998)

Purpose. Complete Form W-4 so your employer can withhold the correct Federal income tax from your pay. Because your tax situation may change, you may want to refigure your withholding each year.

Exemption from withholding. *If you are exempt, complete only lines 1, 2, 3, 4, and 7, and sign the form to validate it.* Your exemption for 1998 expires February 16, 1999.

Note: *You cannot claim exemption from withholding if (1) your income exceeds $700 and includes unearned income (e.g., interest and dividends) and (2) another person can claim you as a dependent on their tax return.*

Basic instructions. If you are not exempt, complete the Personal Allowances Worksheet. The worksheets on page 2 adjust your

withholding allowances based on itemized deductions, adjustments to income, or two-earner/two-job situations. Complete all worksheets that apply. They will help you figure the number of withholding allowances you are entitled to claim. However, you may claim fewer allowances.

New—Child tax and higher education credits. For details on adjusting withholding for these and other credits, see **Pub. 919,** Is My Withholding Correct for 1998?

Head of household. Generally, you may claim head of household filing status on your tax return only if you are unmarried and pay more than 50% of the costs of keeping up a home for yourself and your dependent(s) or other qualifying individuals.

Nonwage income. If you have a large amount of nonwage income, such as interest or dividends, you should consider making estimated tax payments using Form 1040-ES. Otherwise, you may owe additional tax.

Two earners/two jobs. If you have a working spouse or more than one job, figure the total number of allowances you are entitled to claim on all jobs using worksheets from only one W-4. Your withholding will usually be most accurate when all allowances are claimed on the W-4 filed for the highest paying job and zero allowances are claimed for the others.

Check your withholding. After your W-4 takes effect, use Pub. 919 to see how the dollar amount you are having withheld compares to your estimated total annual tax. Get Pub. 919 especially if you used the Two-Earner/Two-Job Worksheet and your earnings exceed $150,000 (Single) or $200,000 (Married). To order Pub. 919, call 1-800-829-3676. Check your telephone directory for the IRS assistance number for further help.

Sign this form. Form W-4 is not valid unless you sign it.

Personal Allowances Worksheet

A   Enter "1" for **yourself** if no one else can claim you as a dependent . . . .   **A** _____

B   Enter "1" if:
- You are single and have only one job; or
- You are married, have only one job, and your spouse does not work; or
- Your wages from a second job or your spouse's wages (or the total of both) are $1,000 or less.

. . **B** _____

C   Enter "1" for your **spouse.** But, you may choose to enter -0- if you are married and have either a working spouse or more than one job. (This may help you avoid having too little tax withheld.). . . . .   **C** _____

D   Enter number of **dependents** (other than your spouse or yourself) you will claim on your tax return . . . .   **D** _____

E   Enter "1" if you will file as **head of household** on your tax return (see conditions under **Head of household** above)   **E** _____

F   Enter "1" if you have at least $1,500 of **child or dependent care expenses** for which you plan to claim a credit   . .   **F** _____

G   New—**Child Tax Credit:**   • If your total income will be between $16,500 and $47,000 ($21,000 and $60,000 if married), enter "1" for each eligible child.   • If your total income will be between $47,000 and $80,000 ($60,000 and $115,000 if married), enter "1" if you have two or three eligible children, or enter "2" if you have four or more . . . .   **G** _____

H   Add lines A through G and enter total here. **Note:** This amount may be different from the number of exemptions you claim on your return. ▶   **H** _____

For accuracy, complete all worksheets that apply.
- If you plan to **itemize or claim adjustments to income** and want to reduce your withholding, see the Deductions and Adjustments Worksheet on page 2.
- If you are **single, have more than one job,** and your combined earnings from all jobs exceed $32,000 OR if you are **married** and have a **working spouse or more than one job,** and the combined earnings from all jobs exceed $55,000, see the Two-Earner/Two-Job Worksheet on page 2 to avoid having too little tax withheld.
- If **neither** of the above situations applies, **stop here** and enter the number from line H on line 5 of Form W-4 below.

- - - - - - - - - - - -   **Cut here and give the certificate to your employer. Keep the top part for your records.**   - - - - - - - - - -

---

Form **W-4**	**Employee's Withholding Allowance Certificate**	OMB No. 1545-0010
Department of the Treasury Internal Revenue Service	▶ **For Privacy Act and Paperwork Reduction Act Notice, see page 2.**	19**98**

1 Type or print your first name and middle initial Last name		**2** Your social security number

Home address (number and street or rural route)

3   ☐ Single   ☐ Married   ☐ Married, but withhold at higher Single rate.
Note: *If married, but legally separated, or spouse is a nonresident alien, check the Single box.*

City or town, state, and ZIP code

4   If your last name differs from that on your social security card, check here and call 1-800-772-1213 for a new card . . . . . ▶ ☐

5   Total number of allowances you are claiming (from line H above or from the worksheets on page 2 if they apply) . .   **5** _____

6   Additional amount, if any, you want withheld from each paycheck . . . .   **6** $ _____

7   I claim exemption from withholding for 1998, and I certify that I meet **BOTH** of the following conditions for exemption:
- Last year I had a right to a refund of **ALL** Federal income tax withheld because I had **NO** tax liability **AND**
- This year I expect a refund of **ALL** Federal income tax withheld because I expect to have **NO** tax liability.

If you meet both conditions, enter "EXEMPT" here . . . . ▶   **7** _____

Under penalties of perjury, I certify that I am entitled to the number of withholding allowances claimed on this certificate or entitled to claim exempt status.

Employee's signature ▶ _____   Date ▶ _____ , 19____

8   Employer's name and address (Employer: Complete 8 and 10 only if sending to the IRS) | **9**   Office code (optional) | **10**   Employer identification number

Cat. No. 10220Q

Social Security and Medicare taxes from the wages paid to employees. This law also requires that the employer pay his or her share of these taxes. The employer's contribution must match the amount he or she is required to withhold from employees' wages. Currently, the Social Security tax rate is 6.2 percent for wages up to $68,400 (the dollar limit is adjusted annually and was current at the time this book went to press). The Medicare tax rate is 1.45 percent and has no dollar limit. In other words, as an employer, you must continue to withhold and pay Medicare taxes regardless of how much you compensate your employees. To calculate your FICA withholdings and how much you are required to pay, simply multiply an employee's gross wage by the applicable tax rate. As with federal income taxes, you must periodically deposit your FICA taxes with a Federal Reserve Bank or other authorized financial institution. The same forms, frequency of deposits, and late payment penalties apply.

3. *Unemployment tax.* You must pay federal and state unemployment tax to fund an unemployment system that supports, for up to 26 weeks, workers who have lost their jobs through no fault of their own. According to the Federal Unemployment Tax Act (FUTA), employers are required to pay payroll tax based on the wages that they issue their employees. However, they cannot withhold the money from their workers' pay; the business must pay the taxes itself. The FUTA tax rate is 6.2 percent for wages through $7,000. You will have to pay this tax if, during the current or preceding calendar year, your business meets either of the following criteria: (1) wages paid to your employees in any calendar quarter amounted to at least $1,500, and (2) you employ at least one worker on any given day in each of 20 calendar weeks (a calendar week is a period of seven successive days, beginning with Sunday). FUTA taxes must be deposited every quarter, but if your tax liability is $100 or less, you can add it to your next quarter's FUTA taxes, rather than depositing it. Generally, if you are required to pay federal unemployment tax, you must also remit state unemployment tax. You can compute the taxes you owe your state by multiplying the wages you pay each employee by your state's tax rate on compensation. State unemployment tax rates are individually assigned to each employer every year. Check with your local IRS office for the rate that applies to your business.

4. *State and local income taxes.* Most states impose a personal income tax, which you will probably have to withhold from your employees' wages. The only states that do not charge a personal income tax are Alaska, Florida, Nevada, New Hampshire, South Dakota, Tennessee, Texas, Washington, and Wyoming. In addition to state income tax,

you may be required to withhold local income tax from your workers' wages, depending on where your business is located. If you employ a worker from a state in which your business does not have a work site, you may be required to withhold that state's income tax percentage from your employee's wages. For example, if your company is headquartered in Florida but you hire some employees who live in Georgia, you may be subject to Florida and Georgia state taxes, depending on the rules of the state where you are conducting business and those of the states whose residents you have hired. State income tax rules usually do not reach beyond the state's borders, so if you do not physically set up shop in a particular state, you are not held by that state's income withholding tax liabilities.

Like all other income tax returns, your payroll tax returns must be filed on time and on current forms. To pay federal income and FICA tax, you must file Form 941, Employer's Quarterly Federal Tax Return (see Figure 13.8). The deadline is the last day of the first month after a quarter ends. You are entitled to an automatic 10-day extension, provided that you've been making timely federal deposits during the quarter.

To file your FUTA taxes, you must submit Form 940, Employer's Annual Federal Unemployment Tax Return (see Figure 13.9) The deadline for filing this annual return is January 31, but you can take an automatic 10-day extension if needed.

In addition to filing your payroll tax returns, you are obligated to provide documentation to your employees indicating how much you paid them in taxable compensation, and the amounts withheld from their wages for federal and state income taxes and for FICA taxes. This information should be supplied on Form W-2, Wage and Tax Statement (see Figure 13.10). You are required to submit this form to each employee by January 31 of the year following the calendar year in which their wages were taxed. Copies of the W-2 forms must be sent to the Social Security Administration (SSA) by the end of February (that same year). When you send the W-2 copies, you must include Form W-3, Transmittal of Wage and Tax Statements (see Figure 13.11). If you need to make a correction on any W-2, you must use Form W-2c, Corrected Wage and Tax Statement (see Figure 13.12). If you neglect to submit a W-2 for each employee, or if those you issue are incorrect, you will face a $50 fine for each statement that should have been issued or was prepared in error.

If you hire independent contractors, you will have to file a Form 1099-MISC, Miscellaneous Income, for any contractor to whom you have paid at least $600 in wages (see Figure 13.13). This form must be issued to each of your independent contractors by January 31, and copies must be forwarded to the IRS by February 28.

Figure 13.8   Form 941, Employer's Quarterly Federal Tax Return

Form **941**
(Rev. July 1998)

Department of the Treasury
Internal Revenue Service   (O)

Employer's Quarterly Federal Tax Return

▶ See separate instructions for information on completing this return.

Please type or print.

Enter state code for state in which deposits were made ONLY if different from state in address to the right ▶ (see page 3 of instructions).

Name (as distinguished from trade name)

Trade name, if any

Address (number and street)

Date quarter ended

Employer identification number

City, state, and ZIP code

OMB No. 1545-0029

T	
FF	
FD	
FP	
I	
T	

If address is different from prior return, check here ▶

IRS Use

1 1 1 1 1 1 1 1 1 1   2   3 3 3 3 3 3 3   4 4 4   5 5 5

6   7   8 8 8 8 8 8 8   9 9 9 9   10 10 10 10 10 10 10 10 10 10

If you do not have to file returns in the future, check here ▶ ☐ and enter date final wages paid ▶

If you are a seasonal employer, see **Seasonal employers** on page 1 of the instructions and check here ▶

1	Number of employees in the pay period that includes March 12th . ▶	1		
2	Total wages and tips, plus other compensation	**2**		
3	Total income tax withheld from wages, tips, and sick pay	**3**		
4	Adjustment of withheld income tax for preceding quarters of calendar year	**4**		
5	Adjusted total of income tax withheld (line 3 as adjusted by line 4—see instructions)	**5**		

6	Taxable social security wages	**6a**		× 12.4% (.124) =	**6b**	
	Taxable social security tips	**6c**		× 12.4% (.124) =	**6d**	
7	Taxable Medicare wages and tips . . .	**7a**		× 2.9% (.029) =	**7b**	

8	Total social security and Medicare taxes (add lines 6b, 6d, and 7b). Check here if wages are not subject to social security and/or Medicare tax . . . . ▶ ☐	**8**		
9	Adjustment of social security and Medicare taxes (see instructions for required explanation) Sick Pay $ _____ ± Fractions of Cents $ _____ ± Other $ _____ =	**9**		
10	Adjusted total of social security and Medicare taxes (line 8 as adjusted by line 9—see instructions)	**10**		
11	**Total taxes** (add lines 5 and 10)	**11**		
12	Advance earned income credit (EIC) payments made to employees	**12**		
13	Net taxes (subtract line 12 from line 11). **This should equal line 17, column (d) below (or line D of Schedule B (Form 941))**	**13**		
14	Total deposits for quarter, including overpayment applied from a prior quarter	**14**		
15	**Balance due** (subtract line 14 from line 13). See instructions	**15**		
16	**Overpayment.** If line 14 is more than line 13, enter excess here ▶ $ _____			

and check if to be: ☐ Applied to next return   **OR**   ☐ Refunded.

● **All filers:** If line 13 is less than $1,000, you need not complete line 17 or Schedule B (Form 941).

● **Semiweekly schedule depositors:** Complete Schedule B (Form 941) and check here . . . . ▶ ☐

● **Monthly schedule depositors:** Complete line 17, columns (a) through (d), and check here . . . . ▶ ☐

17	Monthly Summary of Federal Tax Liability. Do not complete if you were a semiweekly schedule depositor.			
	(a) First month liability	**(b) Second month liability**	**(c) Third month liability**	**(d) Total liability for quarter**

Sign Here

Under penalties of perjury, I declare that I have examined this return, including accompanying schedules and statements, and to the best of my knowledge and belief, it is true, correct, and complete.

Signature ▶   Print Your Name and Title ▶   Date ▶

For Privacy Act and Paperwork Reduction Act Notice, see page 4 of separate instructions.   Cat. No. 17001Z   Form **941** (Rev. 7-98)

Figure 13.9 Form 940, Employer's Annual Federal
Unemployment (FUTA) Tax Return

Form **940**	**Employer's Annual Federal Unemployment (FUTA) Tax Return**	OMB No. 1545-0028
Department of the Treasury Internal Revenue Service (O)	▶ **See separate instructions for information on completing this return.**	19**98**

			T	
⌐ Name (as distinguished from trade name)		Calendar year ⌐	FF	
			FD	
Trade name, if any			FP	
			I	
Address and ZIP code		Employer identification number	T	
⌐_____		_____⌐		

A Are you required to pay unemployment contributions to only one state? (If "No," skip questions B and C.) .   ☐ **Yes** ☐ **No**

B Did you pay all state unemployment contributions by February 1, 1999? ((1) If you deposited your total FUTA tax when due, check "Yes" if you paid all state unemployment contributions by February 10. (2) If a 0% experience rate is granted, check "Yes." (3) If "No," skip question C.) . . . .   ☐ **Yes** ☐ **No**

C Were all wages that were taxable for FUTA tax also taxable for your state's unemployment tax? . . . .   ☐ **Yes** ☐ **No**

If you answered "No" to any of these questions, you must file Form 940. If you answered "Yes" to all the questions, you may file Form 940-EZ, which is a simplified version of Form 940. (Successor employers see **Special credit for successor employers** on page 3 of the instructions.) You can get Form 940-EZ by calling 1-800-TAX-FORM (1-800-829-3676) or from the IRS's Internet Web Site at **www.irs.ustreas.gov.**

If you will not have to file returns in the future, check here, and complete and sign the return . . . . ▶ ☐
If this is an Amended Return, check here . . . . ▶ ☐

Part I **Computation of Taxable Wages**				
1	Total payments (including payments shown on lines 2 and 3) during the calendar year for services of employees		**1**	
2	Exempt payments. (Explain all exempt payments, attaching additional sheets if necessary.) ▶	**2**		
3	Payments for services of more than $7,000. Enter only amounts over the first $7,000 paid to each employee. Do not include any exempt payments from line 2. The $7,000 amount is the Federal wage base. Your state wage base may be different. **Do not use your state wage limitation** .	**3**		
4	Total exempt payments (add lines 2 and 3)		**4**	
5	**Total taxable wages** (subtract line 4 from line 1) . . . . ▶		**5**	

Be sure to complete both sides of this return, and sign in the space provided on the back.
For Privacy Act and Paperwork Reduction Act Notice, see separate instructions.   Cat. No. 11234O   Form **940** (1998)

DETACH HERE

Form **940-V**	**Form 940 Payment Voucher**	OMB No. 1545-0028
Department of the Treasury Internal Revenue Service	**Use this voucher only when making a payment with your return.**	19**98**

Complete boxes 1, 2, 3, and 4. Do not send cash, and do not staple your payment to this voucher. Make your check or money order payable to the "United States Treasury". Be sure to enter your employer identification number, "Form 940", and "1998" on your payment.

1 Enter the amount of the payment you are making	**2** Enter the first four letters of your last name (business name if partnership or corporation)	**3** Enter your employer identification number
▶ $		

Instructions for Box 2	**4** Enter your business name (individual name for sole proprietors)
—Individuals (sole proprietors, trusts, and estates)— Enter the first four letters of your last name.	Enter your address
—Corporations and partnerships—Enter the first four characters of your business name (omit "The" if followed by more than one word).	Enter your city, state, and ZIP code

Figure 13.10   Form W-2, Wage and Tax Statement

a Control number **22222**	Void ☐	For Official Use Only ▶ OMB No. 1545-0008	
b Employer identification number		1 Wages, tips, other compensation	2 Federal income tax withheld
c Employer's name, address, and ZIP code		3 Social security wages	4 Social security tax withheld
		5 Medicare wages and tips	6 Medicare tax withheld
		7 Social security tips	8 Allocated tips
d Employee's social security number		9 Advance EIC payment	10 Dependent care benefits
e Employee's name (first, middle initial, last)		11 Nonqualified plans	12 Benefits included in box 1
		13 See instrs. for box 13	14 Other
		15 Statutory employee ☐ Deceased ☐ Pension plan ☐ Legal rep. ☐ Deferred compensation ☐	
f Employee's address and ZIP code			

16 State Employer's state I.D. no.	17 State wages, tips, etc.	18 State income tax	19 Locality name	20 Local wages, tips, etc.	21 Local income tax

Form **W-2** Wage and Tax Statement **1998**

Copy A For Social Security Administration—Send this entire page with Form W-3 to the Social Security Administration; photocopies are **Not** acceptable.

Cat. No. 10134D

Department of the Treasury—Internal Revenue Service
For Privacy Act and Paperwork Reduction Act Notice, see separate instructions.

Do NOT Cut, Staple, or Separate Forms on This Page   Do NOT Cut, Staple, or Separate Forms on This Page

a Control number **22222**	Void ☐	For Official Use Only ▶ OMB No. 1545-0008	
b Employer identification number		1 Wages, tips, other compensation	2 Federal income tax withheld
c Employer's name, address, and ZIP code		3 Social security wages	4 Social security tax withheld
		5 Medicare wages and tips	6 Medicare tax withheld
		7 Social security tips	8 Allocated tips
d Employee's social security number		9 Advance EIC payment	10 Dependent care benefits
e Employee's name (first, middle initial, last)		11 Nonqualified plans	12 Benefits included in box 1
		13 See instrs. for box 13	14 Other
		15 Statutory employee ☐ Deceased ☐ Pension plan ☐ Legal rep. ☐ Deferred compensation ☐	
f Employee's address and ZIP code			

16 State Employer's state I.D. no.	17 State wages, tips, etc.	18 State income tax	19 Locality name	20 Local wages, tips, etc.	21 Local income tax

Form **W-2** Wage and Tax Statement **1998**

Copy A For Social Security Administration—Send this entire page with Form W-3 to the Social Security Administration; photocopies are **Not** acceptable.

Cat. No. 10134D

Department of the Treasury—Internal Revenue Service
For Privacy Act and Paperwork Reduction Act Notice, see separate instructions.

Figure 13.11 Form W-3, Transmittal of Wage and Tax Statements

DO NOT STAPLE

a Control number	33333	For Official Use Only ▶ OMB No. 1545-0008

b Kind of Payer ▶ 941 ☐ Military ☐ 943 ☐ CT-1 ☐ Hshld. emp. ☐ Medicare govt. emp. ☐	1 Wages, tips, other compensation	2 Federal income tax withheld
	3 Social security wages	4 Social security tax withheld
c Total number of Forms W-2 / d Establishment number	5 Medicare wages and tips	6 Medicare tax withheld
e Employer identification number	7 Social security tips	8 Allocated tips
f Employer's name	9 Advance EIC payments	10 Dependent care benefits
	11 Nonqualified plans	12 Deferred compensation
	13	
g Employer's address and ZIP code	14	
h Other EIN used this year	15 Income tax withheld by third-party payer	
i Employer's state I.D. No.		

Contact person	Telephone number	Fax number	E-mail address
	( )	( )	

Under penalties of perjury, I declare that I have examined this return and accompanying documents, and, to the best of my knowledge and belief, they are true, correct, and complete.

Signature ▶ Title ▶ Date ▶

Form **W-3 Transmittal of Wage and Tax Statements 1998** Department of the Treasury Internal Revenue Service

Send this entire page with the entire Copy A page of Forms W-2 to the Social Security Administration. Photocopies are NOT acceptable. **DO NOT SEND ANY REMITTANCE (cash, checks, money orders, etc.) WITH FORMS W-2 AND W-3.**

Change To Note

New boxes. At the bottom of the form above the signature area, boxes were added to enter the name of a contact person and that person's phone or fax number and e-mail address. This data may be used by the SSA if more information is needed during processing.

Need Help?

For information about the information reporting call site, bulletin board services, substitute forms, and how to get forms and publications, see the **1998 Instructions for Form W-2.**

Where To File

Send the entire first page of this form with the entire Copy A page of Forms W-2 to:

Social Security Administration
Data Operations Center
Wilkes-Barre, PA 18769-0001

Note: *If you use "Certified Mail" to file, change the ZIP code to "18769-0002." Also see* ***Shipping and Mailing*** *on page 2 for additional information. If you use an IRS approved private delivery service, add "ATTN: W-2 PROCESS, 1150 E. Mountain Dr." to the address and change the ZIP code to "18702-7997." See Circular E for a list of IRS approved private delivery services.*

For Privacy Act and Paperwork Reduction Act Notice, see the 1998 Instructions for Form W-2.

Detach From Stub Before Mailing to SSA. Note: Self Duplicating; Carbon Paper Not Required.

★ U.S. GOVERNMENT PRINTING OFFICE 1997 419-114

Figure 13.12 Form W-2c, Corrected Wage and Tax Statement

Form W-2c (Rev. 7-97)　　**Corrected Wage and Tax Statement**

Figure 13.13　Form 1099-MISC, Miscellaneous Income

```
9595        ☐ VOID    ☐ CORRECTED
```

PAYER'S name, street address, city, state, ZIP code, and telephone no.	1 Rents $	OMB No. 1545-0115	
	2 Royalties $	1998	**Miscellaneous Income**
	3 Other income $	Form **1099-MISC**	

PAYER'S Federal identification number	RECIPIENT'S identification number	4 Federal income tax withheld $	5 Fishing boat proceeds $	**Copy A**
RECIPIENT'S name		6 Medical and health care payments $	7 Nonemployee compensation $	**For Internal Revenue Service Center**
Street address (including apt. no.)		8 Substitute payments in lieu of dividends or interest $	9 Payer made direct sales of $5,000 or more of consumer products to a buyer (recipient) for resale ▶ ☐	**File with Form 1096.** For Paperwork Reduction Act Notice and instructions for completing this form, see the
City, state, and ZIP code		10 Crop insurance proceeds $	11 State income tax withheld $	
Account number (optional)	2nd TIN Not. ☐	12 State/Payer's state number	13 $	**1998 Instructions for Forms 1099, 1098, 5498, and W-2G.**

Form **1099-MISC**　　Cat. No. 14425J　　Department of the Treasury - Internal Revenue Service

Do NOT Cut or Separate Forms on This Page

```
9595        ☐ VOID    ☐ CORRECTED
```

PAYER'S name, street address, city, state, ZIP code, and telephone no.	1 Rents $	OMB No. 1545-0115	
	2 Royalties $	1998	**Miscellaneous Income**
	3 Other income $	Form **1099-MISC**	

PAYER'S Federal identification number	RECIPIENT'S identification number	4 Federal income tax withheld $	5 Fishing boat proceeds $	**Copy A**
RECIPIENT'S name		6 Medical and health care payments $	7 Nonemployee compensation $	**For Internal Revenue Service Center**
Street address (including apt. no.)		8 Substitute payments in lieu of dividends or interest $	9 Payer made direct sales of $5,000 or more of consumer products to a buyer (recipient) for resale ▶ ☐	**File with Form 1096.** For Paperwork Reduction Act Notice and instructions for completing this form, see the
City, state, and ZIP code		10 Crop insurance proceeds $	11 State income tax withheld $	
Account number (optional)	2nd TIN Not. ☐	12 State/Payer's state number	13 $	**1998 Instructions for Forms 1099, 1098, 5498, and W-2G.**

Form **1099-MISC**　　Cat. No. 14425J　　Department of the Treasury - Internal Revenue Service

Do NOT Cut or Separate Forms on This Page

```
9595        ☐ VOID    ☐ CORRECTED
```

PAYER'S name, street address, city, state, ZIP code, and telephone no.	1 Rents $	OMB No. 1545-0115	
	2 Royalties $	1998	**Miscellaneous Income**
	3 Other income $	Form **1099-MISC**	

PAYER'S Federal identification number	RECIPIENT'S identification number	4 Federal income tax withheld $	5 Fishing boat proceeds $	**Copy A**
RECIPIENT'S name		6 Medical and health care payments $	7 Nonemployee compensation $	**For Internal Revenue Service Center**
Street address (including apt. no.)		8 Substitute payments in lieu of dividends or interest $	9 Payer made direct sales of $5,000 or more of consumer products to a buyer (recipient) for resale ▶ ☐	**File with Form 1096.** For Paperwork Reduction Act Notice and instructions for completing this form, see the
City, state, and ZIP code		10 Crop insurance proceeds $	11 State income tax withheld $	
Account number (optional)	2nd TIN Not. ☐	12 State/Payer's state number	13 $	**1998 Instructions for Forms 1099, 1098, 5498, and W-2G.**

Form **1099-MISC**　　Cat. No. 14425J　　Department of the Treasury - Internal Revenue Service

Defining Your Taxable Workers

If you have employees, you will almost certainly have to withhold payroll tax from their wages. But before you ready your bank slips for the required deposits, consider whether all those whom you are compensating are considered taxable workers.

As an employer, you are obligated to withhold and pay taxes on any worker's wages, if that worker is considered an employee. According to the common-law rules set by the IRS, a worker is considered an employee if the employer has control over where, when, and how an employee performs his or her work, as well as the results of the work. If the employer does not have control over these aspects, the worker is considered an independent contractor and no payroll taxes must be collected and paid by the employer. The independent contractor would be responsible for paying his or her own taxes.

Some business owners think that if they simply get a worker to sign an agreement classifying the worker as an independent contractor, they will relinquish their payroll tax obligations. This is a misconception. You could be fined thousands of dollars in penalties if one of your workers is classified as an independent contractor when he or she is actually an employee.

It can be difficult to distinguish an employee from an independent contractor. To make the classification process a bit easier, the IRS maintains a 20-factor test to gauge whether independent contractors are truly independent or are regular employees in disguise. If you are unsure about how to define your employees, review the IRS test (see Table 13.1).

For added protection, you can request an IRS ruling by filing Form SS-8, Determination of Employee Work Status for Purposes of Federal Employment Taxes and Income Tax Withholding (see Figure 13.14). With this

Table 13.1   The IRS 20-Factor Test

Determining whether a worker is a regular employee or an independent contractor is not always easy. In some cases, there may appear to be a fine line between the two. However, to eliminate any shades of grey and assign payroll obligations with the right party, the Internal Revenue Code has administered a multi-factor test to help you determine individual worker status. Generally speaking, if you find that any of your workers can be considered an employee according to at least 10 of the following factors, then that individual should be treated as an employee, not an independent contractor.

1. *Set working hours.* Employees typically have a set number of hours that they must work. Independent contractors establish their own work schedules.
2. *Method of payment.* Employees are usually paid by the hour, week, or month. Independent contractors are issued a flat-fee for services rendered.
3. *Profit or loss.* The greater the risk that your workers can make either a profit or loss in performing a service, the more likely that they are independent contractors.

(continued)

Table 13.1   *(continued)*

4. *Supply of tools and materials.* If you supply workers with tools, equipment, and other materials to perform their job, these workers are most likely employees. Independent contractors tend to furnish their own supplies.

5. *Instructions.* Workers who must adhere to oral or written instructions about where, when, and how they should perform their work are typically employees, not independent contractors.

6. *Work performed on premises.* Employees must work on the premises of the business or at a designated place set by the employer. Independent contractors usually perform their work at their own place of business.

7. *Multiple clients.* The more customers for which your workers provide services simultaneously, the more likely they are to be independent contractors.

8. *Right to fire.* An employee can be terminated by an employer at any time. You can only discharge an independent contractor according to the terms of your agreement with that individual.

9. *Right to quit.* A worker that can quit at any given time without suffering any liability to the employer is an employee. A worker that must complete work that he or she agreed to do because of a written agreement is an independent contractor.

10. *Training.* The more training that workers receive from an employer, the more likely they are employees. Typically independent contractors do not require training since they already come equipped with a special set of skills and experience to perform their services.

11. *Sequence of work.* If the order or sequence of work is set for workers, most likely they are employees.

12. *Hiring assistants.* Independent contractors are in charge of hiring, supervising, and paying their own assistants. Employees are not, unless under the direction of their employer.

13. *Investment in equipment or facilities.* The greater your workers' investment in the equipment and facilities that they use, the more likely they are independent contractors.

14. *Full-time work required.* Employees can be called to work full-time or make themselves available at the request of an employer. Independent contractors typically work whenever and for whomever they please.

15. *Continuing relationship.* The longer a worker performs a job for you, the more likely they're employees. Independent contractors tend to perform one job and then move onto the next.

16. *Offering services to the public.* Independent contractors can make their services available to the general public. Employees can only offer their services to their employers.

17. *Expenses.* If you pay your workers' business and travel expenses, most likely these workers are employees. Independent contractors are responsible for their own overhead expenses.

18. *Performing services personally.* Employees cannot get someone else to do their jobs for them. Independent contractors, however, can use another individual's services to fulfill their contract.

19. *Integration into business.* The greater the importance of your workers' services to the success of your business, the more likely these workers are employees.

20. *Oral or written reports.* Workers who are required to submit regular oral or written reports about their progress are considered employees rather than independent contractors.

Figure 13.14 Form SS-8, Determination of Employee Work Status for Purposes of Federal Employment Taxes and Income Tax Withholding

Form **SS-8** (Rev. June 1997) Department of the Treasury Internal Revenue Service	**Determination of Employee Work Status for Purposes of Federal Employment Taxes and Income Tax Withholding**	OMB No. 1545-0004

Paperwork Reduction Act Notice

We ask for the information on this form to carry out the Internal Revenue laws of the United States. You are required to give us the information. We need it to ensure that you are complying with these laws and to allow us to figure and collect the right amount of tax.

You are not required to provide the information requested on a form that is subject to the Paperwork Reduction Act unless the form displays a valid OMB control number. Books or records relating to a form or its instructions must be retained as long as their contents may become material in the administration of any Internal Revenue law. Generally, tax returns and return information are confidential, as required by Code section 6103.

The time needed to complete and file this form will vary depending on individual circumstances. The estimated average time is: **Recordkeeping,** 34 hr., 55 min.; **Learning about the law or the form,** 12 min.; and **Preparing and sending the form to the IRS,** 46 min. If you have comments concerning the accuracy of these time estimates or suggestions for making this form simpler, we would be happy to hear from you. You can write to the Tax Forms Committee, Western Area Distribution Center, Rancho Cordova, CA 95743-0001. **DO NOT** send the tax form to this address. Instead, see **General Information** for where to file.

Purpose

Employers and workers file Form SS-8 to get a determination as to whether a worker is an employee for purposes of Federal employment taxes and income tax withholding.

General Information

Complete this form carefully. If the firm is completing the form, complete it for **ONE** individual who is representative of the class of workers whose status is in question. If you want a written determination for more than one class of workers, complete a separate Form SS-8 for one worker

from each class whose status is typical of that class. A written determination for any worker will apply to other workers of the same class if the facts are not materially different from those of the worker whose status was ruled upon.

Caution: Form SS-8 is **not** a claim for refund of social security and Medicare taxes or Federal income tax withholding. Also, a determination that an individual is an employee does not necessarily reduce any current or prior tax liability. A worker must file his or her income tax return even if a determination has not been made by the due date of the return.

Where to file.—In the list below, find the state where your legal residence, principal place of business, office, or agency is located. Send Form SS-8 to the address listed for your location.

Location:	Send to:
Alaska, Arizona, Arkansas, California, Colorado, Hawaii, Idaho, Illinois, Iowa, Kansas, Minnesota, Missouri, Montana, Nebraska, Nevada, New Mexico, North Dakota, Oklahoma, Oregon, South Dakota, Texas, Utah, Washington, Wisconsin, Wyoming	Internal Revenue Service SS-8 Determinations P.O. Box 1231, Stop 4106 AUSC Austin, TX 78767
Alabama, Connecticut, Delaware, District of Columbia, Florida, Georgia, Indiana, Kentucky, Louisiana, Maine, Maryland, Massachusetts, Michigan, Mississippi, New Hampshire, New Jersey, New York, North Carolina, Ohio, Pennsylvania, Rhode Island, South Carolina, Tennessee, Vermont, Virginia, West Virginia, All other locations not listed	Internal Revenue Service SS-8 Determinations Two Lakemont Road Newport, VT 05855-1555
American Samoa, Guam, Puerto Rico, U.S. Virgin Islands	Internal Revenue Service Mercantile Plaza 2 Avenue Ponce de Leon San Juan, Puerto Rico 00918

Name of firm (or person) for whom the worker performed services	Name of worker
Address of firm (include street address, apt. or suite no., city, state, and ZIP code)	Address of worker (include street address, apt. or suite no., city, state, and ZIP code)

Trade name	Telephone number (include area code) ( )	Worker's social security number

Telephone number (include area code) ( )	Firm's employer identification number	

Check type of firm for which the work relationship is in question:

☐ Individual   ☐ Partnership   ☐ Corporation   ☐ Other (specify) ▶ ....

Important Information Needed To Process Your Request

This form is being completed by: ☐ Firm   ☐ Worker

If this form is being completed by the worker, the IRS **must** have your permission to disclose your name to the firm.

Do you object to disclosing your name and the information on this form to the firm? . . . .   ☐ Yes   ☐ No

If you answer "Yes," the IRS cannot act on your request. **Do not complete the rest of this form unless the IRS asks for it.**

Under section 6110 of the Internal Revenue Code, the information on this form and related file documents will be open to the public if any ruling or determination is made. However, names, addresses, and taxpayer identification numbers will be removed before the information is made public.

Is there any other information you want removed? . . . .   ☐ Yes   ☐ No

If you check "Yes," we cannot process your request unless you submit a copy of this form and copies of all supporting documents showing, in brackets, the information you want removed. Attach a separate statement showing which specific exemption of section 6110(c) applies to each bracketed part.

Cat. No. 16106T	Form **SS-8** (Rev. 6-97)

(continued)

Figure 13.14   *(continued)*

Form SS-8 (Rev. 6-97)   Page **2**

*This form is designed to cover many work activities, so some of the questions may not apply to you. **You must answer ALL items or mark them "Unknown" or "Does not apply."** If you need more space, attach another sheet.*

Total number of workers in this class. (Attach names and addresses. If more than 10 workers, list only 10.) ▶ _____

This information is about services performed by the worker from _____ to _____
(month, day, year)   (month, day, year)

Is the worker still performing services for the firm? . . . . ☐ **Yes**   ☐ **No**

- If "No," what was the date of termination? ▶ _____
(month, day, year)

1a Describe the firm's business ....

b Describe the work done by the worker ....

....

2a If the work is done under a written agreement between the firm and the worker, attach a copy.

b If the agreement is not in writing, describe the terms and conditions of the work arrangement ....

....

....

c If the actual working arrangement differs in any way from the agreement, explain the differences and why they occur ....

....

....

3a Is the worker given training by the firm? . . . . ☐ **Yes**   ☐ **No**
- If "Yes," what kind? ....
- How often? ....

b Is the worker given instructions in the way the work is to be done (exclusive of actual training in 3a)? . ☐ **Yes**   ☐ **No**
- If "Yes," give specific examples ....

c Attach samples of any written instructions or procedures.

d Does the firm have the right to change the methods used by the worker or direct that person on how to
do the work? . . . . ☐ **Yes**   ☐ **No**
- Explain your answer ....

....

e Does the operation of the firm's business require that the worker be supervised or controlled in the
performance of the service? . . . . ☐ **Yes**   ☐ **No**
- Explain your answer ....

....

4a The firm engages the worker:
☐ To perform and complete a particular job only
☐ To work at a job for an indefinite period of time
☐ Other (explain) ....

b Is the worker required to follow a routine or a schedule established by the firm? . . . . ☐ **Yes**   ☐ **No**
- If "Yes," what is the routine or schedule? ....

....

c Does the worker report to the firm or its representative?. . . . . ☐ **Yes**   ☐ **No**
- If "Yes," how often? ....
- For what purpose? ....
- In what manner (in person, in writing, by telephone, etc.)? ....
- Attach copies of any report forms used in reporting to the firm.

d Does the worker furnish a time record to the firm? . . . . ☐ **Yes**   ☐ **No**
- If "Yes," attach copies of time records.

5a State the kind and value of tools, equipment, supplies, and materials furnished by:
- The firm ....

....

- The worker ....

b What expenses are incurred by the worker in the performance of services for the firm? ....

....

c Does the firm reimburse the worker for any expenses? . . . . ☐ **Yes**   ☐ **No**
- If "Yes," specify the reimbursed expenses ....

Figure 13.14   *(continued)*

Form SS-8 (Rev. 6-97)   Page **3**

6a Will the worker perform the services personally? . . . . ☐ **Yes** ☐ **No**

b Does the worker have helpers? . . . . ☐ **Yes** ☐ **No**
   - If "Yes," who hires the helpers? ☐ **Firm** ☐ **Worker**
   - If the helpers are hired by the worker, is the firm's approval necessary? . . . . ☐ **Yes** ☐ **No**
   - Who pays the helpers?   ☐ **Firm** ☐ **Worker**
   - If the worker pays the helpers, does the firm repay the worker? . . . . ☐ **Yes** ☐ **No**
   - Are social security and Medicare taxes and Federal income tax withheld from the helpers' pay? . . ☐ **Yes** ☐ **No**
   - If "Yes," who reports and pays these taxes?   ☐ **Firm**   ☐ **Worker**
   - Who reports the helpers' earnings to the Internal Revenue Service? ☐ **Firm** ☐ **Worker**
   - What services do the helpers perform? ....

7 At what location are the services performed? ☐ **Firm's** ☐ **Worker's** ☐ **Other** (specify) ....

8a Type of pay worker receives:
   ☐ **Salary**   ☐ **Commission** ☐ **Hourly wage**   ☐ **Piecework** ☐ **Lump sum**   ☐ **Other** (specify) ....

b Does the firm guarantee a minimum amount of pay to the worker? . . . . ☐ **Yes** ☐ **No**

c Does the firm allow the worker a drawing account or advances against pay? . . . . ☐ **Yes** ☐ **No**
   - If "Yes," is the worker paid such advances on a regular basis? . . . . ☐ **Yes** ☐ **No**

d How does the worker repay such advances? ....

9a Is the worker eligible for a pension, bonus, paid vacations, sick pay, etc.? . . . . ☐ **Yes** ☐ **No**
   - If "Yes," specify ....

b Does the firm carry worker's compensation insurance on the worker? . . . . ☐ **Yes** ☐ **No**

c Does the firm withhold social security and Medicare taxes from amounts paid the worker? . . . . . ☐ **Yes** ☐ **No**

d Does the firm withhold Federal income tax from amounts paid the worker? . . . . ☐ **Yes** ☐ **No**

e How does the firm report the worker's earnings to the Internal Revenue Service?
   ☐ **Form W-2** ☐ **Form 1099-MISC**   ☐ **Does not report** ☐ **Other** (specify) ....
   - Attach a copy.

f Does the firm bond the worker? . . . . ☐ **Yes** ☐ **No**

10a Approximately how many hours a day does the worker perform services for the firm? ....

b Does the firm set hours of work for the worker? . . . . ☐ **Yes** ☐ **No**
   - If "Yes," what are the worker's set hours? _____ a.m./p.m. to _____ a.m./p.m. (Circle whether a.m. or p.m.)

c Does the worker perform similar services for others? . . . . ☐ **Yes** ☐ **No** ☐ **Unknown**
   - If "Yes," are these services performed on a daily basis for other firms? . . . . . ☐ **Yes** ☐ **No** ☐ **Unknown**
   - Percentage of time spent in performing these services for:
     This firm .... % Other firms .... %   ☐ **Unknown**
   - Does the firm have priority on the worker's time? . . . . ☐ **Yes** ☐ **No**
   - If "No," explain ....

d Is the worker prohibited from competing with the firm either while performing services or during any later
   period? . . . . ☐ **Yes** ☐ **No**

11a Can the firm discharge the worker at any time without incurring a liability? . . . . ☐ **Yes** ☐ **No**
   - If "No," explain ....

b Can the worker terminate the services at any time without incurring a liability? . . . . ☐ **Yes** ☐ **No**
   - If "No," explain ....

12a Does the worker perform services for the firm under:
   ☐ **The firm's business name**   ☐ **The worker's own business name**   ☐ **Other** (specify) ....

b Does the worker advertise or maintain a business listing in the telephone directory, a trade
   journal, etc.? . . . . ☐ **Yes** ☐ **No** ☐ **Unknown**
   - If "Yes," specify ....

c Does the worker represent himself or herself to the public as being in business to perform
   the same or similar services? . . . . ☐ **Yes** ☐ **No** ☐ **Unknown**
   - If "Yes," how? ....

d Does the worker have his or her own shop or office? . . . . ☐ **Yes** ☐ **No** ☐ **Unknown**
   - If "Yes," where? ....

e Does the firm represent the worker as an employee of the firm to its customers? . . . . ☐ **Yes** ☐ **No**
   - If "No," how is the worker represented? ....

f How did the firm learn of the worker's services? ....

13 Is a license necessary for the work? . . . . ☐ **Yes** ☐ **No** ☐ **Unknown**
   - If "Yes," what kind of license is required? ....
   - Who issues the license? ....
   - Who pays the license fee?

(continued)

Figure 13.14   *(continued)*

Form SS-8 (Rev. 6-97)   Page **4**

14 Does the worker have a financial investment in a business related to the services
performed? . . . . ☐ Yes   ☐ No   ☐ Unknown
    • If "Yes," specify and give amount of the investment ....

15 Can the worker incur a loss in the performance of the service for the firm? . . . . ☐ Yes   ☐ No
    • If "Yes," how? ....

16a Has any other government agency ruled on the status of the firm's workers? . . . . ☐ Yes   ☐ No
    • If "Yes," attach a copy of the ruling.

  b Is the same issue being considered by any IRS office in connection with the audit of the worker's tax
return or the firm's tax return, or has it been considered recently? . . . . ☐ Yes   ☐ No
    • If "Yes," for which year(s)? ....

17 Does the worker assemble or process a product at home or away from the firm's place of business? ☐ Yes   ☐ No
    • If "Yes," who furnishes materials or goods used by the worker? ☐ Firm   ☐ Worker   ☐ Other
    • Is the worker furnished a pattern or given instructions to follow in making the product? . . . . . ☐ Yes   ☐ No
    • Is the worker required to return the finished product to the firm or to someone designated by the firm? ☐ Yes   ☐ No

18 Attach a detailed explanation of any other reason why you believe the worker is an employee or an independent contractor.

Answer items 19a through o only if the worker is a salesperson or provides a service directly to customers.

19a Are leads to prospective customers furnished by the firm? . . . . ☐ Yes   ☐ No   ☐ Does not apply
  b Is the worker required to pursue or report on leads? . . . . ☐ Yes   ☐ No   ☐ Does not apply
  c Is the worker required to adhere to prices, terms, and conditions of sale established by the firm? . . ☐ Yes   ☐ No
  d Are orders submitted to and subject to approval by the firm? . . . . ☐ Yes   ☐ No
  e Is the worker expected to attend sales meetings? . . . . ☐ Yes   ☐ No
    • If "Yes," is the worker subject to any kind of penalty for failing to attend? . . . . ☐ Yes   ☐ No
  f Does the firm assign a specific territory to the worker? . . . . ☐ Yes   ☐ No
  g Whom does the customer pay?   ☐ Firm   ☐ Worker
    • If worker, does the worker remit the total amount to the firm? . . . . ☐ Yes   ☐ No
  h Does the worker sell a consumer product in a home or establishment other than a permanent retail
establishment? . . . . ☐ Yes   ☐ No
  i List the products and/or services distributed by the worker, such as meat, vegetables, fruit, bakery products, beverages (other
than milk), or laundry or dry cleaning services. If more than one type of product and/or service is distributed, specify the
principal one ....
  j Did the firm or another person assign the route or territory and a list of customers to the worker? . . ☐ Yes   ☐ No
    • If "Yes," enter the name and job title of the person who made the assignment ....
  k Did the worker pay the firm or person for the privilege of serving customers on the route or in the territory? ☐ Yes   ☐ No
    • If "Yes," how much did the worker pay (not including any amount paid for a truck or racks, etc.)? $ ....
    • What factors were considered in determining the value of the route or territory? ....
  l How are new customers obtained by the worker? Explain fully, showing whether the new customers called the firm for service,
were solicited by the worker, or both ....
  m Does the worker sell life insurance? . . . . ☐ Yes   ☐ No
    • If "Yes," is the selling of life insurance or annuity contracts for the firm the worker's entire business
activity? . . . . ☐ Yes   ☐ No
    • If "No," list the other business activities and the amount of time spent on them ....
  n Does the worker sell other types of insurance for the firm? . . . . ☐ Yes   ☐ No
    • If "Yes," state the percentage of the worker's total working time spent in selling other types of insurance .... %
    • At the time the contract was entered into between the firm and the worker, was it their intention that the worker sell life
insurance for the firm: ☐ on a full-time basis   ☐ on a part-time basis
    • State the manner in which the intention was expressed ....
  o Is the worker a traveling or city salesperson? . . . . ☐ Yes   ☐ No
    • If "Yes," from whom does the worker principally solicit orders for the firm? ....
    • If the worker solicits orders from wholesalers, retailers, contractors, or operators of hotels, restaurants, or other similar
establishments, specify the percentage of the worker's time spent in the solicitation .... %
    • Is the merchandise purchased by the customers for resale or for use in their business operations? If used by the customers
in their business operations, describe the merchandise and state whether it is equipment installed on their premises or a
consumable supply

Under penalties of perjury, I declare that I have examined this request, including accompanying documents, and to the best of my knowledge and belief, the facts
presented are true, correct, and complete.

Signature ►   Title ►   Date ►

If the firm is completing this form, an officer or member of the firm must sign it. If the worker is completing this form, the worker must sign it. If the worker wants a
written determination about services performed for two or more firms, a separate form must be completed and signed for each firm. Additional copies of this form may
be obtained by calling 1-800-TAX-FORM (1-800-829-3676).

♲ *Printed on recycled paper*   *U.S. Government Printing Office: 1998 - 432-190/80020

four-page form, you must also submit information about the person for whom you are requesting the ruling. For example, you must include a copy of any agreement you may have with the worker, a description of the services that will be provided, the amount of compensation, and details about the level of direction or supervision you will have over the work. If you are requesting an IRS ruling on a worker's status, have a tax professional review the form before you submit it.

The tax law does provide a "safe haven" rule that could help you define your workers. According to this rule, if an individual has not been consistently treated as an employee for any period after 1977, and the employer has filed all the required federal tax returns and information forms (Form 1099-MISC), and has a valid reason for not treating the individual as an employee, the individual will most likely not be reclassified as an employee. However, if you have treated a worker as an employee after 1977 and then try to convert that worker to an independent contractor, you will not be protected by the safe haven rule. Even if your workers do not meet the requirements for the safe haven rule, they are not automatically designated as employees. If any of your workers fail the safe haven test, apply the IRS 20-factor test.

Normally, you will be required to withhold and pay payroll taxes only for workers classified as employees. However, for some individuals who would otherwise be considered independent contractors, you will have certain payroll tax obligations if you decide to use their services. These workers are called "statutory employees" and include the following:

- Life insurance agents who generally work for one insurance company.
- Commissioned drivers who deliver specific products such as beverages (except milk), fruit, meat, and vegetables. These individuals operate their own truck (or a truck owned by others for whom they are performing a service), make wholesale or retail sales, and are paid commissions on their sales.
- Traveling or regional salespeople who work full-time and take orders from customers who are contractors, wholesalers, retailers, or restaurant operators.
- Homeworkers who perform work for you on a contract basis in their own home or the homes of others. For example, an individual who performs word processing work for you in his or her home would be considered a "statutory employee."

If you use a statutory employee in your place of business, you will not be required to withhold federal income tax from that person's wages. However, you will still be responsible for collecting and paying FICA taxes. A worker can only be considered a statutory employee if that worker is not designated a regular employee under common-law rules set by the IRS.

Another type of worker may bring you some payroll tax breaks: a family member. If you decide to bring your mom, dad, or offspring into your business and your family member is considered a regular employee, you will be responsible for withholding federal income taxes from that person's wages. However, as long as you do not run your business as a corporation or partnership, you will not have to collect and pay some FICA taxes and federal and state unemployment taxes.

For example, if your hire your children, you will not have to withhold and pay Social Security taxes until they reach age 18. You will also be excused from paying FUTA taxes until each child reaches age 21. If you hire a spouse or your parents, you will not be responsible for paying FUTA taxes. However, you will have to withhold and pay FICA taxes for them. Unfortunately, if you hire a sibling or a second-degree relative such as an aunt or uncle, you will receive no payroll tax breaks. You will have to withhold and pay the same taxes for these workers as you would for others who are not related to you.

Identifying Taxable Wages and Compensation

After you have identified who your taxable workers are, you can determine what portion of their compensation is taxable. According to federal and state payroll tax laws, taxable compensation is defined as an employee's wages. This can include straight salary, commissions, gifts, or fringe benefits. If you transfer anything of value to an employee as a way to compensate for services rendered, that "payment" is considered to be a taxable wage.

There is an exception to almost every rule. Here are some methods of compensation from which you may not always be required to withhold and pay some or all of the payroll taxes.

Reimbursements for Business Expenses
Some business owners will reimburse employees who incur expenses for business travel and other purposes related to their jobs. You may be free from withholding and paying payroll taxes on reimbursed business expenses if the compensation is reasonable and necessary to the operation of your company. Each expense must meet the IRS rules for standard business deductions. (We will discuss business deductions later in this chapter.) However, unless the reimbursements are made under an "accountable plan," they will be subject to payroll taxes. An accountable plan is one that provides advances and reimbursements for deductible business expenses that employees generate as a result of working for your business. For reimbursements to qualify under an accountable plan, an employee must document all expenses within a reasonable amount of time. For example, if one of your employees takes a business trip and wants to be reimbursed for meals, he or she must supply receipts soon after returning to the office. The employee must also return all

unused portions of an advance or excess reimbursements within a reasonable amount of time.

Tips

Tips are payments that customers make without being forced or pressured to do so. If you operate a business in which your employees receive cash tips of $20 or more in a calendar month and the employees report the tips to you by the tenth day of the month following the month in which the money was received, the tips are considered taxable wages. You must withhold income taxes and FICA taxes on the tips, and pay your share of FICA and FUTA taxes as well. To report tips, your employees must file Form 4070, Employee's Report of Tips to Employer, and Form 4070-A, Employee's Daily Record of Tips and Report to Employer. To make sure that your employees file correctly, you may want to provide them with a copy of Publication 1244, which outlines tip reporting requirements. Special tip reporting and disbursement rules apply to large food and beverage businesses. According to the IRS, if you operate in a trade or business where tipping is customary (this does not include fast-food restaurants and cafeteria-style eateries) and where you employed more than 10 workers on any given business day during the previous calendar year, you must distribute at least 8 percent of your gross sales to employees as tips, if your employees do not report at least this much. You will not have to withhold or pay taxes on the tip allocations; however, you will be required to report this information to the IRS by filing Form 8027, Employer's Annual Information Return of Tip Income and Allocated Tips (Figure 13.15). If you operate more than one food and beverage business, you will have to include Form 8027-T, Transmittal of Employer's Annual Information Return of Tip Income and Allocated Tips, with Form 8027. You will also have to provide information about your tip allocations to your employees on their W-2 forms. Form 8027 must be filed on or before the last day of February of the year following the calendar year for which the return was made. If you are not sure whether your business is considered a large food and beverage company, consult your accountant or call your local IRS office for a ruling. Also, determining whether you have 10 or more employees is not as simple as counting heads. The process you must use involves calculating employee hours as a determinant of the number of workers that you actually have. Check your figures with your tax professional before releasing them.

Gifts and Prizes

Any gifts you give to employees are considered taxable wages for payroll purposes unless you can prove that a gift was not related to the operation of your business. For example, if you give one of your workers a wedding gift, this would not be considered a taxable wage. Christmas gifts of little value, such as a fruit cake or a turkey, are also exempt, but cash is not. Most prizes and awards are also taxable wages, but if you give away an item that

Figure 13.15 Form 8027, Employer's Annual Information
Return of Tip Income and Allocated Tips

Form **8027**	**Employer's Annual Information Return of Tip Income and Allocated Tips**	OMB No. 1545-0714
Department of the Treasury Internal Revenue Service	▶ See Separate Instructions.	1998

Use IRS label. Make any necessary changes. Otherwise, please type or print.

Name of establishment

Number and street (See instructions.)

City or town, state, and ZIP code

Employer identification number

Type of establishment (check only one box)
- [ ] 1 Evening meals only
- [ ] 2 Evening and other meals
- [ ] 3 Meals other than evening meals
- [ ] 4 Alcoholic beverages

Employer's name

Establishment number (See instructions.)

Number and street (P.O. box, if applicable.) | Apt. or suite no.

City, state, and ZIP code (If a foreign address, enter city, province or state, postal code, and country.)

Check the box if applicable: Final Return [ ]   Amended Return [ ]

1 Total charged tips for 1998 . . . . **1**

2 Total charged receipts (other than nonallocable receipts) showing charged tips **2**

3 Total amount of service charges of less than 10% paid as wages to employees **3**

4a Total tips reported by indirectly tipped employees **4a**

b Total tips reported by directly tipped employees **4b**
   Note: *Complete the Employer's Optional Worksheet for Tipped Employees on page 4 of the instructions to determine potential unreported tips of your employees.*

c Total tips reported (Add lines 4a and 4b.) **4c**

5 Gross receipts from food or beverage operations (other than nonallocable receipts). . . **5**

6 Multiply line 5 by 8% (.08) or the lower rate shown here ▶ _____ granted by the district director. Attach a copy of the district director's determination letter to this return . **6**
   Note: *If you have allocated tips using other than the calendar year (semimonthly, biweekly, quarterly, etc.), put an "X" on line 6 and enter the amount of allocated tips from your records on line 7.*

7 Allocation of tips. If line 6 is more than line 4c, enter the excess here **7**
   This amount must be allocated as tips to tipped employees working in this establishment. Check the box below that shows the method used for the allocation. (Show the portion, if any, attributable to each employee in box 8 of the employee's Form W-2.)
   a Allocation based on hours-worked method (See instructions for restriction.) . . . [ ]
      Note: *If you checked line 7a, enter the average number of employee hours worked per business day during the payroll period. (See instructions.)* _____
   b Allocation based on gross receipts method . . . . [ ]
   c Allocation based on good-faith agreement (Attach copy of agreement.) . . . . . [ ]

8 Enter the total number of directly tipped employees at this establishment during 1998 ▶

Under penalties of perjury, I declare that I have examined this return, including accompanying schedules and statements, and to the best of my knowledge and belief, it is true, correct, and complete.

Signature ▶   Title ▶   Date ▶

For Privacy Act and Paperwork Reduction Act Notice, see page 4 of the separate instructions.   Cat. No. 49989U   Form **8027** (1998)

*U.S. Government Printing Office: 1998 — 455-238/80115   ⊛ *Printed on recycled paper*

is valued at less than $400, you will not be required to withhold and pay payroll taxes on it.

Benefits

There are several benefits for which you will not have to meet payroll tax obligations, as long as you adhere to certain rules. Here are some of the benefits that are generally exempt from FICA and FUTA taxes:

1. Employer contributions to pension and retirement plans, including SIMPLE (Savings Incentive Match Plan for Employees), SEP (Simplified Employee Pension plan), and profit sharing. Employees' contributions to a 401(k) or SIMPLE plan are subject to FICA and FUTA taxes, but not federal income tax.

2. Property or services that you supply to an employee when that employee would have been able to claim a deduction for it, had he or she purchased it personally (e.g., a company car, or safety equipment).

3. Health plan payments, including insurance premiums and payment for medical expenses.

4. Premiums from workers' compensation.

5. Some employee discounts on your products or services.

6. Reimbursements for moving expenses or parking privileges.

7. Group-term life insurance premiums on policies up to $50,000 per employee.

Loans and Cash Advances

If you provide an employee with an advance to pay for certain items to be used during the course of business activity, you will not be subject to payroll taxes on the advance if the money is allotted for a deductible business expense and if the employee substantiates the expenditure (e.g., by providing a detailed expense report, or a sales receipt). Advances are also considered nontaxable wages if employees are required to repay whatever money is loaned.

STATE INCOME TAXES

Staying on top of your federal income tax obligations is difficult enough without having to worry about meeting your state income tax responsibilities as well. Nevertheless, you must become familiar with your state tax system and the laws that could affect your business.

Because states do not impose the same types of taxes or filing requirements, it is important to contact the appropriate government agency in your area for specific information regarding which taxes apply to your business, the deadlines for filing, and the required forms. You should be able to contact your Department of Revenue, Department of Taxation, State Tax Commission, or a similar agency for assistance.

Among the taxes you may find yourself responsible for withholding and/or paying are: business income tax, personal income tax, sales tax, and franchise tax.

SALES TAX

If you conduct business in Alaska, Delaware, Montana, New Hampshire, or Oregon, you will not have to pay sales tax (although some cities and boroughs throughout Alaska impose their own local sales taxes). However, if you set up shop in any of the other 45 states and generate sales that are subject to sales tax, you will be required to register to collect the tax, physically gather the money, and then remit it to the appropriate agency.

To register to collect sales tax, you must apply for a sales permit, license, or certificate of registration for your business. Contact your state tax department for the proper forms. After you receive your permit, you must display it in your company.

To collect sales tax, you must calculate the amount at the time of each sale. Most business owners will use a cash register or computer that automatically calculates the sales tax as purchases are being made. Sales tax bracket tables are available from your state tax department, but, to save time, your best bet is to have your cash register do the math for you. After sales tax is collected, you must report and pay the tax to the appropriate agency. Each state has its own filing requirements and deadlines; most states require that you file a tax return and submit the sales tax monthly.

SELF-EMPLOYMENT TAX

If you operate your business as a sole proprietorship, partnership, or limited liability company, and you earn at least $400 per year from your business, you will have to pay self-employment taxes. These taxes resemble FICA taxes; they consist of a Social Security tax of 12.4 percent for wages up to $68,400, and a Medicare tax of 2.9 percent with no dollar limit. The taxes are imposed on your net self-employment income and must be reported on Schedule SE of Form 1040.

As a sole proprietor, partner, or member of a limited liability company, you will not be paid a salary; therefore, you will not have to withhold income taxes from the money that you take from your business. However, you will be required to estimate your tax liability every year and make quarterly estimated tax payments after filing Form 1040 SE.

TAXES ON VEHICLES

If you purchase a vehicle for your business, you will have to contend with a number of tax consequences. Depending on the type of car you purchase, you could be exposed to the following excise taxes:

- *Luxury tax.* If you purchase a car priced over $36,000, you will be hit with what is known as a luxury tax—currently a 6 percent excise tax that is imposed on any part of the sales price of a new car over this amount; it was 7 percent in 1998. This tax is expected to decrease one percentage point each year until arriving at 3 percent in 2002. Not every type of vehicle is subject to this duty, so check the details with your tax accountant or attorney.
- *Gas guzzler tax.* This tax is levied on new cars that do not meet federal fuel economy standards. Although the tax is imposed on the vehicle manufacturer, it becomes a part of the retail price, so you end up paying it.

Along with these charges, you could be entitled to a few tax breaks if (1) you purchase an electric vehicle, (2) the car you buy is identified as a "clean-fuel" automobile, or (3) you own a diesel vehicle. The IRS will allow you to claim a deduction from your gross income for a portion of the cost of your car if it is powered by clean-burning fuels such as natural gas or hydrogen, or fuels that consist of at least 85 percent alcohol, ethanol, ether, or methanol. This deduction applies to "clean-fuel" vehicles put into circulation after June 30, 1993, and before January 1, 2005. If you decide to purchase a vehicle for your business, bear in mind that you need not use it strictly for business in order to take advantage of these tax breaks. (We will discuss vehicle deductions in greater detail later in this chapter.)

YOUR BASIC BUSINESS DEDUCTIONS

Meeting your tax obligations can be bitter, but business owners get some relief in the form of deductions. According to federal income tax law, you are permitted to reduce your taxable business income if certain expenses and other costs are generated during the course of a year. However, you can't claim a deduction for every item you buy for your business. IRS rules state that you can claim a business deduction for expenses only if the expenses are "ordinary and necessary" for the operation of your company. Unless the costs you incur for a particular item or service are commonly accepted in business or are helpful to your business, you will not be able to claim a deduction for them.

Opening a new business requires significant costs, but, in general, you will not be able to deduct any of your start-up expenses under the standard business deduction rules. However, you can elect to amortize or deduct your costs over a period of at least 60 days, as long as the costs would be eligible for a deduction if incurred by an existing operation. Some amortized costs of starting a business include salaries, consultant fees, advertising, and travel before the business gets off the ground. Some costs that don't qualify for the election, but are usually incurred when starting a new business, include partnership and incorporation organizational expenses.

Business Travel Expenses

Travel expenses are among the most common business deductions. To claim this deduction, you must keep adequate records that substantiate your travel expenses *and* meet the following criteria:

1. *The expenses must be related to an existing business.* If you incur travel expenses in trying to get your business off the ground, you will not be able to claim a deduction. Travel expenses are only deductible in relation to existing concerns. The costs must be "ordinary and necessary" to the business and cannot be extravagant in any way. You will not be penalized if you choose to fly first class rather than coach, but if you choose to stay in a penthouse suite at the Waldorf-Astoria and order room service three times a day, every day, during a three-week business trip, the IRS may question your request for a deduction.

2. *The expense must be generated away from home.* You may be permitted to deduct travel expenses only if the trip is long enough, or far enough away, that you are unable to travel to and from the destination without having to stop for rest or sleep, and the trip is away from the general area of your principal place of business. If you conduct business in several locations, you must determine your principal place of business by considering the amount of time you spend working at each location, the type of business activity that takes place at each site, and the amount of income generated at each place.

If you take a trip and engage in both personal and business activities, you can deduct the travel expenses generated to and from the destination, as long as the trip is primarily related to business. If you plan to take a personal trip and then conduct a little business on the side, you will not be able to claim a travel expense deduction. When determining the purpose of a trip, you must consider the amount of time you will spend on business versus personal activities. If the former outweighs the latter, you will be able to claim a deduction.

Here are some of the travel expenses you may be able to deduct:

- *Cost of meals.* You can deduct 50 percent of your meal expenses. Transportation employees, bus drivers, merchant mariners, and truck drivers are among those permitted to deduct 55 percent of their meal costs. (We will discuss meal deductions in greater detail later in this chapter.)
- *Local transportation costs.* You can deduct the cost of taxi fare between the airport or other transportation facility and your hotel, or from one place of business to another.
- *Costs of using a vehicle*—payment for gas, parking, tolls, or repairs.
- *Airline, bus, and train fare.*
- *Hotel accommodations.*
- *Cleaning and laundry costs.*
- *Telephone and fax expenses.*
- *Computer rental fees.*

You can also deduct expenses incurred when traveling to and from a convention, as long as you can prove that the convention is directly related to your business and will benefit your operation. If the convention will be held overseas, the rules become much stricter. The IRS works hard to prevent individuals from claiming deductions for personal vacations disguised as business trips abroad. For an overseas travel expense to cut the mustard with the IRS, you must provide a valid reason for holding the meeting outside as opposed to within the United States. For example, if the majority of the attendees will come from the country where the convention will be held, the deduction probably will not be questioned.

Any expenses related to foreign travel and incurred purely for business purposes can be deducted. Any charge that smacks of personal expense will not qualify for a deduction.

Meals and Entertainment Expenses

As a new business owner, you may have to entertain clients, suppliers, customers, and other business colleagues with whom you will associate. If so, you can claim a 50 percent business deduction for your meals and entertainment expenses.

To claim deductions, your expenses must be closely related to the operation of your business. The IRS maintains two tests to gauge whether your meals and entertainment expenses qualify:

1. *"Directly related" test.* Your expenses will qualify for a deduction under this test if the entertainment takes place in a setting that is

clearly designated for business purposes (e.g., a convention hall). Entertainment expenses that are generated at nightclubs, sporting events, theaters, cocktail parties, or other social gatherings are not considered directly related to business activity and generally do not qualify for a deduction.

2. *"Associated-with" test.* Your meals and entertainment expenses will qualify under this test if they occur immediately before or after a business discussion and are associated with business conduct. When using this test, keep in mind that the facts and circumstances of each case will be considered. For example, if you have a meal right before or after a conference, you can claim the deduction, but if a meal does not precede or follow your tête-a-tête, several factors will be reviewed to gauge whether you can still claim the deduction (the place and time of the meal, and the reasons for it not occurring on the same day as the business discussion).

If you dine alone, you can claim a meal deduction only during an overnight business trip or a journey that is so long that it would require you to sleep or rest before departing. Rather than deducting half of your actual meal costs, you can elect to deduct half of the Standard Meal Allowance (SMA), which is $30 per day for most locations in the United States. For areas known to have higher costs of living, a higher SMA is accepted. For a complete list of rates, visit or call your local IRS office and obtain a copy of Publication 1542, *Per Diem Rates for Travel Within the Continental United States,* or visit the U.S. Office of Governmentwide Policy Web site at http://www .policyworks.gov (click on "Per Diem Rates").

When you calculate your meal expenses, keep in mind that you cannot deduct this cost as an entertainment expense if you have designated it as a travel expense.

Employee Benefits and Compensation

A host of benefits can be deducted as business expenses if you provide them to your employees. They include: premiums for health and life insurance policies, pension plans, travel expenses, meals and hotel accommodations, relocation expenses, and other fringe benefits. Remember, for payroll tax purposes, some types of benefits (e.g., health insurance and group term life insurance up to $50,000) are not subject to FICA taxes and federal income tax withholding. As an employer, you are not required to pay FICA or federal unemployment tax on the costs of providing these benefits, but you can still claim deductions for these expenses.

You can claim a deduction for the wages, salaries, bonuses, commissions, and other forms of compensation you give your employees, as long as the compensation is "ordinary and necessary" and represents a reasonable amount of pay based on the service that the employee provides. To qualify for the deduction, the employee must be paid or the compensation must have been incurred in the year in which the deduction is claimed. If compensation is a noncash item, the amount you can deduct must be equal to the fair market value of the property that is provided as a form of payment.

Depending on your legal form of business, you may or may not be able to claim a deduction on wages and salaries. If you operate your business as a sole proprietorship, you may deduct wages paid to your employees but not wages paid to yourself. A sole proprietor is not considered an employee of the business, so the salary he or she draws from the company is not a deductible expense. If you operate as a corporation, you may claim your salary as a deduction as long as it is reasonable and coincides with industry standards. However, if your salary and that of other owners/employees is noticeably high and your company has paid out little or no dividends to shareholders for a long period of time, the IRS may regard your salaries as dividends in disguise and will then disallow or reject your salary deduction. For corporations, other situations may red-flag salary deductions, so consult your accountant or tax professional for more information.

Vehicle Expenses and Reimbursements

Depending on the type of business that you operate, you may require the use of a car, truck, or van. To perform their work, your employees may have to operate a company-owned vehicle or use their own cars. Whatever the circumstances, you will probably reimburse your employees for expenses incurred in using an automobile.

Whether these reimbursed expenses are deductible will hinge on whether they occur under an accountable plan, as mentioned previously. If you use a vehicle exclusively for business purposes, you can deduct the entire cost of operating the vehicle. But if you sometimes use your car for business and drive it for personal reasons the remainder of the time, you will have to allocate a percentage of your automobile expenses to your business and the rest to personal use.

According to the IRS, vehicle usage can be defined in these three categories:

1. *Business use.* Business use is typically defined as travel between two business-related destinations, one of which can be your principal place of business. Basic travel expenses include travel from one client site to another, from one job to another, or from your business site to a site where you pick up items or perform a task that will benefit your operation.

2. *Commuting/travel.* The costs you incur traveling from your home to your principal place of business are not deductible. However, if you travel between your home and a site that is not your regular workplace, the expense is deductible. If you do not have a principal place of business, you can still deduct your travel expenses if you commute to a temporary site that is outside of the area where you normally work. Your commuting expenses may be partially deductible if you have to haul heavy equipment or tools to and from work.

3. *Personal use.* The IRS identifies use of a vehicle for personal activities. For example, if you use your car to go to the supermarket, beauty salon, or mall, you cannot deduct those travel costs as business-related expenses.

To compute your vehicle deduction, you can use one of two methods:

1. *Standard mileage rate method.* To use this method, you must multiply the number of business miles traveled in a given year by the standard mileage rate, which for 1998 was 32.5 cents per mile. Therefore, it is important that you, and any employees who will use a vehicle to perform work, keep a written record of the number of miles traveled for business purposes, and calculate the business use percentage. To determine your business use percentage, add up the total number of miles and the business-related miles driven in a given year. Divide the number of business-related miles by the total number of miles to arrive at the percentage used for business purposes. This method is easy to use, but it is not available to everyone. For example, expenses incurred in connection with vehicles that are used for hire, such as taxis or leased vehicles, cannot be calculated this way. If you want to use the standard mileage rate method, you must do so during your first year in operation. Once you adopt it, you must use the straight-line method of depreciation. Also, when using this method, the deduction will include an amount for depreciation, and you cannot claim additional depreciation. (We will discuss depreciation in greater detail later in this chapter.) As your business grows and matures, you can switch from the standard mileage rate method to the actual cost method.

2. *Actual cost method.* To determine your deduction under this method, you must keep track of the actual costs of operating your vehicle throughout the year. These costs are likely to include: gas, parking, tolls, insurance, tires and supplies, repairs and maintenance, and depreciation (if you own the car, truck, or van). The cost of the vehicle is not a deductible expense nor are any expenses incurred for extensive repairs that will prolong the useful life of the vehicle or increase

its value. However, you can claim deductions on these items through depreciation deductions over a number of years, after the car is placed in service.

In most cases, you will have to claim your vehicle deduction expenses by filing Form 4562, Depreciation and Amortization (see Figure 13.16). However, if you are self-employed, you will have to use Schedule C or Schedule C-EZ of Form 1040. If you are claiming the standard mileage rate and are not required to file Form 4562, you will have to fill out Part IV of Schedule C or Part III of Schedule C-EZ.

Depreciation

As a new business owner, you will probably acquire several pieces of equipment, machines, furniture, cars, and other capital assets to be used in your company. You probably will not be able to deduct the total cost of these items in the year that you acquire them. However, you can claim depreciation deductions, based on their original cost, over several years of their useful life.

Straight-line depreciation is the most widely used method of depreciating new equipment. Under this method, equipment loses can equal part of its total value each year of its life. You will be required to use another method, Modified Accelerated Cost Recovery System (MACRS), to calculate depreciation if your property was put into service after 1986 and if you will not claim a deduction for the full cost of the equipment. MACRS categorizes business assets into separate groups and indicates the time period over which the materials can be depreciated. For example, if you own a car, a truck, or computer equipment, you can depreciate these items over a five-year life. Some intangible items, such as trademarks and patents, cannot be depreciated using MACRS.

After you classify the asset you want to depreciate, you can use a special table produced by the IRS to determine the item's *tax basis* (the maximum amount of depreciation you can claim on a business asset). Typically, the tax basis of an item is equal to the item's purchase price, minus any discounts that are applied, plus any delivery charges, installation fees, and sales tax. Let's say you buy a piece of equipment priced at $5,000. If you pay 6 percent in sales tax and $300 in installation fees, the tax basis for that item would be $5,600.

To obtain copies of the depreciation deduction charts, call 1-800-TAX-FORM and request a copy of Publication 946, *How to Depreciate Property.* You can also view the charts by visiting the IRS Web site at www.irs.ustreas.gov.

Not every asset you acquire can be depreciated. That would be too generous. Among the assets for which you can claim depreciation deductions are: real estate, cars, office furniture, machines, computers, buildings, and

Figure 13.16   Form 4562, Depreciation and Amortization

Form **4562**	**Depreciation and Amortization** (Including Information on Listed Property)	OMB No. 1545-0172
Department of the Treasury Internal Revenue Service (99)	▶ See separate instructions. ▶ Attach this form to your return.	19**98** Attachment Sequence No. **67**
Name(s) shown on return	Business or activity to which this form relates	Identifying number

Part I   Election To Expense Certain Tangible Property (Section 179) (Note: *If you have any* ™*listed property,* *complete Part V before you complete Part I.*)

1	Maximum dollar limitation. If an enterprise zone business, see page 2 of the instructions . .	**1**	$18,500
2	Total cost of section 179 property placed in service. See page 2 of the instructions	**2**	
3	Threshold cost of section 179 property before reduction in limitation	**3**	$200,000
4	Reduction in limitation. Subtract line 3 from line 2. If zero or less, enter -0-	**4**	
5	Dollar limitation for tax year. Subtract line 4 from line 1. If zero or less, enter -0-. If married filing separately, see page 2 of the instructions	**5**	

(a) Description of property	**(b)** Cost (business use only)	**(c)** Elected cost
6		

7	Listed property. Enter amount from line 27.	**7**	
8	Total elected cost of section 179 property. Add amounts in column (c), lines 6 and 7 . . .	**8**	
9	Tentative deduction. Enter the smaller of line 5 or line 8	**9**	
10	Carryover of disallowed deduction from 1997. See page 3 of the instructions	**10**	
11	Business income limitation. Enter the smaller of business income (not less than zero) or line 5 (see instructions)	**11**	
12	Section 179 expense deduction. Add lines 9 and 10, but do not enter more than line 11 . .	**12**	
13	Carryover of disallowed deduction to 1999. Add lines 9 and 10, less line 12 ▶	**13**	

Note: *Do not use Part II or Part III below for listed property (automobiles, certain other vehicles, cellular telephones, certain computers, or property used for entertainment, recreation, or amusement). Instead, use Part V for listed property.*

Part II   MACRS Depreciation For Assets Placed in Service ONLY During Your 1998 Tax Year (Do Not Include Listed Property.)

Section A–General Asset Account Election

14	If you are making the election under section 168(i)(4) to group any assets placed in service during the tax year into one or more general asset accounts, check this box. See page 3 of the instructions . . . . ▶	☐

Section B–General Depreciation System (GDS)   (See page 3 of the instructions.)

(a) Classification of property	**(b)** Month and year placed in service	**(c)** Basis for depreciation (business/investment use only–see instructions)	**(d)** Recovery period	**(e)** Convention	**(f)** Method	**(g)** Depreciation deduction
15a 3-year property						
b 5-year property						
c 7-year property						
d 10-year property						
e 15-year property						
f 20-year property						
g 25-year property			25 yrs.		S/L	
h Residential rental property			27.5 yrs.	MM	S/L	
			27.5 yrs.	MM	S/L	
i Nonresidential real property			39 yrs.	MM	S/L	
				MM	S/L	

Section C–Alternative Depreciation System (ADS)   (See page 5 of the instructions.)

16a Class life					S/L	
b 12-year			12 yrs.		S/L	
c 40-year			40 yrs.	MM	S/L	

Part III   Other Depreciation (Do Not Include Listed Property.) (See page 6 of the instructions.)

17	GDS and ADS deductions for assets placed in service in tax years beginning before 1998	**17**	
18	Property subject to section 168(f)(1) election	**18**	
19	ACRS and other depreciation	**19**	

Part IV   Summary (See page 6 of the instructions.)

20	Listed property. Enter amount from line 26.	**20**	
21	**Total.** Add deductions on line 12, lines 15 and 16 in column (g), and lines 17 through 20. Enter here and on the appropriate lines of your return. Partnerships and S corporations–see instructions . .	**21**	
22	For assets shown above and placed in service during the current year, enter the portion of the basis attributable to section 263A costs	**22**	

For Paperwork Reduction Act Notice, see the separate instructions.	Cat. No. 12906N	Form **4562** (1998)

improvements (but not repairs) to property. (If you lease equipment, you will not be able to depreciate it; however, you can deduct your lease payments, which can translate into a bigger tax advantage for your business.)

Items you cannot depreciate include inventory and personal assets such as a home or vehicle used exclusively for personal activities. If you will split the use of either of these items between personal and business activities, you will be able to depreciate only the percentage of use that is for business purposes.

Depreciation deductions begin in the tax year in which you place an asset in service. You cannot claim a depreciation deduction on a piece of equipment unless you begin to use it productively before the end of the tax year in which you will file for the deduction.

As mentioned previously, usually you cannot claim a business deduction for the entire cost of a capital asset during the year in which you purchase it. However, a special tax provision, called an expensing election, allows small businesses to claim a deduction in the first year, up to a specified dollar limit. To qualify for this election, the asset must be tangible, used more than 50 percent for business, and new rather than renovated. For example, if you purchased a car in 1998, the maximum dollar amount that you could have written off under the expensing election would have been $3,160, provided your car met all the expensing election guidelines.

The dollar limits used for assets eligible to be expensed are not fixed. They change periodically to reflect inflation, so, before claiming your deduction, you should consult your tax adviser about the most current depreciation guidelines and the method of depreciation that must be used.

Whatever depreciation method you use, you must cease claiming deductions when the total amount of those deductions is equal to the original cost of the asset, or when you stop using the item in your business.

Business Gifts

You can deduct only $25 for business gifts given to clients or customers. Any amount that exceeds this dollar limit cannot be deducted, so if you plan to give your customers a $75 item at Christmas, you will be allowed to deduct only $25. This limit does not include incidental costs such as gift wrapping, insurance, mailing costs, or jewelry engraving.

If you plan to give food-related items as gifts and the recipients will probably not consume them for a period of several days or even weeks, treat them as a gift expense, not a meal expense. You will have difficulty justifying a meal expense if the meal does not occur immediately before or after a particular event.

If you have a choice of treating a gift as a gift expense or an entertainment expense, it will be more advantageous to claim it as a entertainment expense, particularly if it costs over $50. You can claim a 50 percent deduction on your entertainment expenses, so if you plan to give a $200 theater ticket as a gift to a certain client, you can deduct more ($100 instead of $25) by treating the ticket as an entertainment expense.

THE HOME OFFICE DEDUCTION

The deductions we've discussed thus far have been those that you can claim if you operate your business in a place other than your home. If you decide to set up shop in your humble abode, a number of deductions are available, but you must first qualify for the deductions according to guidelines set by the IRS.

To be eligible for the home office deduction, your home office must be used regularly and exclusively for business and must meet at least *one* of the following criteria:

- It must be your principal place of business.
- It must be used to meet with customers or clients, in person, during the normal course of business activity.
- If you use a separate structure that is detached from your home, it must be used only for your business or trade.

The space you have allotted for your business need not be a traditional office. You can set up a lab, a showroom, or a storage facility, but the space you so designate must be used regularly, not just occasionally, for that purpose.

In the past, satisfying the "principal place of business" criteria has been difficult. Many home-based business owners have disagreed with the IRS over where their principal place of business is located. In 1999, the introduction of a new tax law revamped the definition. A home office now qualifies as the principal place of business if it meets the following criteria:

1. The office is used by the taxpayer (home-based business owner) to conduct administrative or management activities of a business or trade.
2. The taxpayer maintains no other fixed location to conduct a substantial amount of management activities and administrative functions of his or her trade or business.

If you determine that you can qualify for a home office deduction, you must then calculate how much of a deduction you can obtain. Perhaps the biggest factor that will affect the size of your deduction is the percentage of your home that you use for business. To calculate the percentage of business use, you can use:

- The "square footage method," which involves dividing the square footage of the space used for your business by the total square footage of the house; or
- The "rooms used method," in which you divide the number of rooms used for your business by the total number of rooms in the house. (If you use this method, the rooms in your home must be roughly the same size.)

If you operate a home day care center, you will not have to use either method to calculate your business use percentage. According to IRS tax rules, if you operate a home day care business, you can count whatever portion of your home you regularly use to operate your business, even if the same space is also used for personal activity. If you use your kitchen to prepare the children's lunches, or your bedrooms for their naps, these areas can be included as part of your business. Still, unlike most home-based business owners, you will have to prorate your expenses according to the number of hours the day care center is actually open.

Here is a breakdown of some of the home office deductions you can claim:

- *Rent or mortgage interest.* If you rent your home, you can deduct your rental payments as part of the home office deduction. If you are a homeowner, you can deduct a portion of your real estate taxes and your qualified mortgage interest (but not the principal) payments on your home. You can also claim a depreciation deduction on the purchase price of the house. To calculate your deduction, multiply your total yearly payments (in rent or mortgage interest) by your business use percentage. The mortgage interest you deduct can include interest on a second mortgage or home equity loan, but a maximum dollar limit is imposed. You can claim a deduction on mortgage interest payments up to $1 million used to buy, build, or improve your property, and up to $100,000 for home equity loans. Consult your tax adviser for more information regarding these dollar limits, or request a copy of Publication 936, *Home Mortgage Interest Deduction*, from your local IRS office.
- *Insurance.* You can deduct the business percentage of your homeowner's or renter's insurance, but do not include the cost of business insurance or home office policy riders in the amount. These costs are fully deductible as ordinary business expenses and are not covered under the home office deduction. You can calculate your insurance deduction by multiplying the total cost of your policy by your business use percentage.
- *Utilities.* You can deduct the business percentage of payments you make for utilities, such as heat and electricity, as well as for general

home services (trash collection, cleaning, and security services). However, if you pay for a utility that you do not use for your business at all, you cannot deduct any portion of that expense.

- *Telephone.* Because your telephone bill is considered a "direct" business expense, it is not a part of the home office deduction. You cannot deduct the cost of basic telephone use on the first telephone line that you install for your business. However, you can deduct the expenses you incur when making local or long-distance business-related calls. You can also deduct the cost of installing a second telephone line in your home office, if that line will be used exclusively for business.

- *Repairs and decorating.* Costs that you incur for the benefit of your business are considered "direct" home office expenses and are fully deductible. For example, if you repaint a bedroom that you use as your office, or repair wood paneling in your office, these expenses are deductible. You can also deduct a portion of the expenses that benefit your entire home (e.g., if you patch your roof or repair leaky pipes in the basement). These are called "indirect" home office expenses. However, if the expenses benefit only the personal-use part of your home, they are not deductible. For example, if you install a hot tub in your house, you will not be able to write off this expense. It is often difficult to distinguish between what constitutes a repair and what constitutes an improvement for tax purposes. According to the IRS, a repair is something that supports the efficient operation of your home, but does not add value to your home (e.g., patching walls or painting ceilings). As previously mentioned, these expenses are deductible. On the other hand, an improvement is something that clearly adds value to your home or extends its useful life (e.g., installing a new roof or a central air-conditioning system). Capital improvements must be added to your tax basis and depreciated.

- *Casualty losses.* If your home office is damaged or destroyed by flood, fire, theft, an earthquake, vandalism, or a hurricane, you may be able to include some of the loss as part of your home office deduction. If the loss applies only to your home office, it will be considered a "direct" expense that is fully deductible. However, if it applies to the entire home, you will be able to deduct only a portion of the loss as a business expense, using your business use percentage as a basis. If a loss affects only the personal part of your home, you will not be entitled to deduct any of the loss amount as a business expense, but you can claim it as a personal expense. To claim a casualty loss, you must file a claim for any insurance that you have on the property. You will be able to deduct only the portion of the loss that is *not* covered by your insurance policy.

- *Depreciation.* If you own your home and have set up shop there, you cannot directly deduct any part of the purchase price, the fair rental value of the home, or the principal payments made on the mortgage. You can, however, recover some costs through depreciation deductions based on your business use percentage. But before you can calculate your depreciation amount, you must first determine the *tax basis* of your home: the cost of the house (including closing costs, settlement fees, legal fees, and title insurance, but excluding the land on which it stands), plus the cost of permanent improvements, minus casualty losses deducted in previous tax years. By multiplying this amount by your business use percentage, you will arrive at the amount you can depreciate. After you calculate the tax basis of the depreciable amount of your home, you must multiply that number by a fraction defined by the IRS and based on the month and year when you purchased your home. The result determines the number of years over which you can depreciate the property. You can find the fraction tables in Publication 534, *Depreciation*.

After computing your home office deduction, you must file the appropriate forms. If you are self-employed, you must file Form 8829, Expenses for Business Use of Your Home (see Figure 13.17) and then transfer the total to Schedule C of Form 1040.

CLAIMING AVAILABLE TAX CREDITS

In addition to standard business deductions, you can claim a number of available tax credits. Because tax credits are subtracted directly from your tax bill, they are typically more advantageous to your business than deductions, which are subtracted from the income on which your tax bill is based.

Claiming a tax credit is not easy. The allowable situations are very limited, and the rules that you must follow to the letter in order to qualify are very complex. Many tax credits apply only to certain industries, such as the energy industry or the restaurant industry, so unless your business operates in one of the specified fields, tax credits may be useless.

Currently, tax credits are targeted to encourage business owners to take action in ways they might not normally consider because a situation seems undesirable or unprofitable. Many tax credits are aimed to benefit low-income people, the environment, and the disadvantaged. Among the tax credits that you may want to consider claiming are:

- *Empowerment Zone Employment Credit.* Federal empowerment zones are located in Philadelphia, New York, Chicago, Detroit, Atlanta, Baltimore, Los Angeles, and various other cities across the country. If you operate your business in an empowerment zone and you hire workers who live within the zone, you can claim a tax credit for 20 percent of the first $15,000 of wages paid to *each* of your employees.

Figure 13.17   Form 8829, Expenses for Business Use of Your Home

Form **8829**	**Expenses for Business Use of Your Home**	OMB No. 1545-1266
Department of the Treasury Internal Revenue Service (99)	▶ File only with Schedule C (Form 1040). Use a separate Form 8829 for each home you used for business during the year. ▶ See separate instructions.	**1998** Attachment Sequence No. **66**

Name(s) of proprietor(s)   Your social security number

Part I   Part of Your Home Used for Business

1	Area used regularly and exclusively for business, regularly for day care, or for storage of inventory or product samples. See instructions	**1**	
2	Total area of home	**2**	
3	Divide line 1 by line 2. Enter the result as a percentage	**3**	%

- **For day-care facilities not used exclusively for business, also complete lines 4±6.**
- **All others, skip lines 4±6 and enter the amount from line 3 on line 7.**

4	Multiply days used for day care during year by hours used per day .	**4**	hr.
5	Total hours available for use during the year (365 days × 24 hours). See instructions	**5**	8,760 hr.
6	Divide line 4 by line 5. Enter the result as a decimal amount . . .	**6**	.
7	Business percentage. For day-care facilities not used exclusively for business, multiply line 6 by line 3 (enter the result as a percentage). All others, enter the amount from line 3 . . . . ▶	**7**	%

Part II   Figure Your Allowable Deduction

8	Enter the amount from Schedule C, line 29, **plus** any net gain or (loss) derived from the business use of your home and shown on Schedule D or Form 4797. If more than one place of business, see instructions		**8**	
	See instructions for columns (a) and (b) before completing lines 9±20.	**(a)** Direct expenses	**(b)** Indirect expenses	
9	Casualty losses. See instructions	**9**		
10	Deductible mortgage interest. See instructions .	**10**		
11	Real estate taxes. See instructions	**11**		
12	Add lines 9, 10, and 11.	**12**		
13	Multiply line 12, column (b) by line 7		**13**	
14	Add line 12, column (a) and line 13			**14**
15	Subtract line 14 from line 8. If zero or less, enter -0- .			**15**
16	Excess mortgage interest. See instructions . .	**16**		
17	Insurance	**17**		
18	Repairs and maintenance	**18**		
19	Utilities	**19**		
20	Other expenses. See instructions	**20**		
21	Add lines 16 through 20	**21**		
22	Multiply line 21, column (b) by line 7		**22**	
23	Carryover of operating expenses from 1997 Form 8829, line 41 . .		**23**	
24	Add line 21 in column (a), line 22, and line 23			**24**
25	Allowable operating expenses. Enter the **smaller** of line 15 or line 24			**25**
26	Limit on excess casualty losses and depreciation. Subtract line 25 from line 15			**26**
27	Excess casualty losses. See instructions		**27**	
28	Depreciation of your home from Part III below		**28**	
29	Carryover of excess casualty losses and depreciation from 1997 Form 8829, line 42		**29**	
30	Add lines 27 through 29			**30**
31	Allowable excess casualty losses and depreciation. Enter the **smaller** of line 26 or line 30 . .			**31**
32	Add lines 14, 25, and 31			**32**
33	Casualty loss portion, if any, from lines 14 and 31. Carry amount to **Form 4684**, Section B .			**33**
34	Allowable expenses for business use of your home. Subtract line 33 from line 32. Enter here and on Schedule C, line 30. If your home was used for more than one business, see instructions ▶			**34**

Part III   Depreciation of Your Home

35	Enter the **smaller** of your home's adjusted basis or its fair market value. See instructions . .	**35**	
36	Value of land included on line 35	**36**	
37	Basis of building. Subtract line 36 from line 35	**37**	
38	Business basis of building. Multiply line 37 by line 7	**38**	
39	Depreciation percentage. See instructions	**39**	%
40	Depreciation allowable. Multiply line 38 by line 39. Enter here and on line 28 above. See instructions	**40**	

Part IV   Carryover of Unallowed Expenses to 1999

41	Operating expenses. Subtract line 25 from line 24. If less than zero, enter -0-	**41**	
42	Excess casualty losses and depreciation. Subtract line 31 from line 30. If less than zero, enter -0- .	**42**	

For Paperwork Reduction Act Notice, see page 3 of separate instructions.   Cat. No. 13232M   Form **8829** (1998)

Your employees can work part-time or full-time. You cannot claim a credit on wages paid to workers who work less than 90 days (unless the person was fired for misconduct or became disabled), who are related to you, or who own 5 percent (or more) of your business. To file for this credit, you must fill out Form 8848, Empowerment Zone Employment Credit.

- *Credit for Contributions to Community Development Corporations.* This credit is intended to encourage business owners to give long-term loans or gifts to particular organizations that provide employment and other business opportunities to low-income people. If you make a contribution to a community development corporation, you can claim a tax credit for 5 percent of the amount you contribute, for each of ten tax years starting with the year in which your contribution is made. To file for this credit, you must submit Form 8847, Credit for Contributions to Selected Community Development Corporations (see Figure 13.18).

- *Disabled Access Credit.* According to the Americans with Disabilities Act of 1990, businesses that are open to the public must be set up in a fashion that allows access to disabled persons who want to visit the facility. Under the law, business owners must remove any physical barriers that hinder access, and, when making renovations, must include facilities that allow the disabled to safely move about. In an effort to get smaller businesses to comply with the law, the government issues a tax credit for 50 percent of eligible expenses that exceed $250 but do not go over $10,250. This tax credit covers the cost of removing physical barriers during renovations (but not new construction), and the expense of using equipment or facilities to make services available to blind, deaf, and otherwise disabled customers. This tax credit is only available to small businesses (those with $1 million or less in gross receipts and fewer than 30 full-time workers). To claim this tax credit, you must file Form 8826, Disabled Access Credit (see Figure 13.19).

AVOIDING AN IRS AUDIT

Preparing your taxes may be the most challenging task you encounter as a new business owner. The language surrounding tax filing, deductions, and tax credits can be confusing. To keep the IRS at bay, always consult your tax adviser or accountant before filing any forms or returns.

Start and maintain a complete set of well-annotated books in which you document your income, losses, gains, expenses, and other amounts that will yield useful information for your tax preparer. Keep all records that substantiate the information listed on your tax returns for at least four years. The

Figure 13.18   Form 8847, Credit for Contributions to Selected
Community Development Corporations

Form **8847**	**Credit for Contributions to Selected Community Development Corporations**	OMB No. 1545-1416
Department of the Treasury Internal Revenue Service	▶ **Attach to your return.**	**1998** Attachment Sequence No. **100**
Name(s) shown on return		Identifying number

Part I   Current Year Credit

1	Total qualified community development corporation (CDC) contributions from attached Schedule(s) A (Form 8847).	**1**	
2	Current year CDC credit. Multiply line 1 by 5% (.05)	**2**	
3	CDC credits from flow-through entities:		

	If you are a—	Then enter total of current year CDC credit(s) from—		
	a Shareholder	Schedule K-1 (Form 1120S), lines 12d, 12e, or 13	} . . .	**3**
	b Partner	Schedule K-1 (Form 1065), lines 12c, 12d, or 13		

4	**Total current year CDC credit.** Add lines 2 and 3	**4**	

Part II   Tax Liability Limit (See **Who Must File Form 3800** to find out if you complete Part II or file Form 3800.)

5 Regular tax before credits:
- Individuals. Enter amount from Form 1040, line 40 . . . .
- Corporations. Enter amount from Form 1120, Schedule J, line 3 (or Form 1120-A, Part I, line 1)
- Other filers. Enter regular tax before credits from your return . . . .   } . .   **5**

6a	Credit for child and dependent care expenses (Form 2441, line 9) .	**6a**
b	Credit for the elderly or the disabled (Schedule R (Form 1040), line 20)	**6b**
c	Child tax credit (Form 1040, line 43)	**6c**
d	Education credits (Form 8863, line 18).	**6d**
e	Mortgage interest credit (Form 8396, line 11)	**6e**
f	Adoption credit (Form 8839, line 14)	**6f**
g	District of Columbia first-time homebuyer credit (Form 8859, line 11) .	**6g**
h	Foreign tax credit.	**6h**
i	Possessions tax credit (Form 5735, line 17 or 27)	**6i**
j	Credit for fuel from a nonconventional source	**6j**
k	Qualified electric vehicle credit (Form 8834, line 19)	**6k**

l	Add lines 6a through 6k	**6l**	
7	Net regular tax. Subtract line 6l from line 5	**7**	
8	Alternative minimum tax:		

- Individuals. Enter amount from Form 6251, line 28 . . . .
- Corporations. Enter amount from Form 4626, line 15 . . . .   } **8**
- Estates and trusts. Enter amount from Form 1041, Schedule I, line 39 . . . .

9	Net income tax. Add lines 7 and 8	**9**	
10	Tentative minimum tax (see instructions):		

- Individuals. Enter amount from Form 6251, line 26 . . . . .
- Corporations. Enter amount from Form 4626, line 13. . . . .   } **10**
- Estates and trusts. Enter amount from Form 1041, Schedule I, line 37 . . . .

11	If line 7 is more than $25,000, enter 25% (.25) of the excess (see instructions)	**11**	
12	Enter the greater of line 10 or line 11	**12**	
13	Subtract line 12 from line 9. If zero or less, enter -0-.	**13**	
14	**CDC credit allowed for current year.** Enter the **smaller** of line 4 or line 13 here and on Form 1040, line 47; Form 1120, Schedule J, line 4d; Form 1120-A, Part I, line 2a; Form 1041, Schedule G, line 2c; or the applicable line of your return	**14**	

General Instructions

Section references are to the Internal Revenue Code unless otherwise noted.

Purpose of Form

Use Form 8847 to claim the credit for qualified contributions made to selected community development corporations (CDCs).

The credit is part of the general business credit and is figured under the provisions of section 13311 of the Revenue Reconciliation Act of 1993.

For Paperwork Reduction Act Notice, see back of form.   Cat. No. 16149K   Form **8847** (1998)

Figure 13.19 Form 8826, Disabled Access Credit

Form **8826**	**Disabled Access Credit**	OMB No. 1545-1205
Department of the Treasury Internal Revenue Service	▶ **Attach to your return.**	**1998** Attachment Sequence No. **86**
Name(s) shown on return		Identifying number

Part I Current Year Credit

1	Total eligible access expenditures	**1**	
2	Minimum amount	**2**	$ 250 00
3	Subtract line 2 from line 1 (if less than zero, enter -0-)	**3**	
4	Maximum amount	**4**	$10,000 00
5	Enter smaller of line 3 or line 4	**5**	
6	Current year credit. Multiply line 5 by 50% (.50)	**6**	

7 Disabled access credits from flow-through entities:

	If you are a—	Then enter total of current year disabled access credit(s) from—			
a	Shareholder	Schedule K-1 (Form 1120S), lines 12d, 12e, or 13	}	. . .	**7**
b	Partner	Schedule K-1 (Form 1065), lines 12c, 12d, or 13			

8	Total current year disabled access credit. Add lines 6 and 7, but do not enter more than $5,000 .	**8**

Part II Tax Liability Limit (See **Who Must File Form 3800** to find out if you complete Part II or file Form 3800.)

9 Regular tax before credits:
- Individuals. Enter amount from Form 1040, line 40 . . . . }
- Corporations. Enter amount from Form 1120, Schedule J, line 3 (or Form 1120-A, Part I, line 1) } . . | **9** |
- Other filers. Enter regular tax before credits from your return . . . . }

10a	Credit for child and dependent care expenses (Form 2441, line 9) .	**10a**	
b	Credit for the elderly or the disabled (Schedule R (Form 1040), line 20)	**10b**	
c	Child tax credit (Form 1040, line 43)	**10c**	
d	Education credits (Form 8863, line 18)	**10d**	
e	Mortgage interest credit (Form 8396, line 11)	**10e**	
f	Adoption credit (Form 8839, line 14)	**10f**	
g	District of Columbia first-time homebuyer credit (Form 8859, line 11) .	**10g**	
h	Foreign tax credit	**10h**	
i	Possessions tax credit (Form 5735, line 17 or 27)	**10i**	
j	Credit for fuel from a nonconventional source	**10j**	
k	Qualified electric vehicle credit (Form 8834, line 19)	**10k**	
l	Add lines 10a through 10k	**10l**	
11	Net regular tax. Subtract line 10l from line 9	**11**	

12 Alternative minimum tax:
- Individuals. Enter amount from Form 6251, line 28 . . . . }
- Corporations. Enter amount from Form 4626, line 15 . . . . } . . . | **12** |
- Estates and trusts. Enter amount from Form 1041, Schedule I, line 39 . . . }

13	Net income tax. Add lines 11 and 12	**13**

14 Tentative minimum tax (see instructions):
- Individuals. Enter amount from Form 6251, line 26 . . . . . }
- Corporations. Enter amount from Form 4626, line 13 . . . . . } **14**
- Estates and trusts. Enter amount from Form 1041, Schedule I, line 37 . . . . }

15	If line 11 is more than $25,000, enter 25% (.25) of the excess (see instructions) **15**	
16	Enter the greater of line 14 or line 15	**16**
17	Subtract line 16 from line 13. If zero or less, enter -0-	**17**
18	**Disabled access credit allowed for current year.** Enter the **smaller** of line 8 or line 17 here and on Form 1040, line 47; Form 1120, Schedule J, line 4d; Form 1120-A, line 2a; Form 1041, Schedule G, line 2c; or the applicable line of your return	**18**

General Instructions

Section references are to the Internal Revenue Code.

Purpose of Form

Eligible small businesses use Form 8826 to claim the disabled access credit. This credit is part of the general business credit.

A partnership or S corporation that is an eligible small business completes Part I of the form to figure the credit to pass through to its partners or shareholders. Electing large partnerships, include this credit in "general credits."

For Paperwork Reduction Act Notice, see back of form.   Cat. No. 12774N   Form **8826** (1998)

IRS may challenge a return up to three years after filing, so make room for your records, keep them in a safe and convenient place, and make sure they are readily accessible to any future reviewer.

Document all your business deduction expenses. Collect and save receipts or canceled checks. They are probably the best proof that an expense was actually incurred, if the IRS questions a deduction you have claimed. During an audit, if you do not have a record of a certain expense but it is obvious that you must have generated the cost, the IRS will simply estimate the amount of the expense and allow a deduction. However, written documentation is always preferred.

As previously mentioned, proof via written records is required for you to claim deductions for travel, business gifts, transportation, and meals and entertainment expenses, so gather up all your receipts, find an accordion-pocket folder, an empty filing cabinet, a shoe box, or other protective container, and preserve them carefully. Trust us: you'll need them.

CHECKLIST

FACTORS TO CONSIDER WHEN SUITING
UP FOR UNCLE SAM

✓ **Your business form.** The types of taxes you will be required to withhold and/or pay will depend on whether you operate as a sole proprietorship, partnership, corporation, Subchapter S corporation, or limited liability company. Your legal business form will also determine which tax forms you need to file and when you need to file them. Sole proprietorships and partnerships are considered nontaxable business entities for tax purposes. They require no separate filing for business income. The profits (or losses) pass through to the sole proprietor, or to each partner, as personal income, and they are taxed at their personal rates. Each of these entities is required to pay self-employment taxes and payroll taxes on the wages of their employees, and each must file Form 1040 (Schedule C or Schedule C-EZ) or Form 1065, Schedule K-1. Corporations, which must file Form 1120 each year, are subject to a corporate income tax. Stockholders are taxed on the dividends they receive. Subchapter S corporations are similar to regular corporations, but they are spared the corporate income tax. They are treated as partnerships for tax purposes, as are limited liability companies.

✓ **Your tax year.** Your decision to operate using a calendar year or a fiscal year will help determine how your business income is computed. Seasonal businesses are among those that may find it more beneficial to use a fiscal year and avoid splitting their season in half. Some businesses, however, will have no choice when it comes to choosing a tax year. For example, sole proprietorships must define their tax year as a calendar year.

✓ **Your accounting method.** The accounting method you choose—cash or accrual—will affect your tax liability. The cash method allows you to reduce your taxes by shifting income and expenses from one year to the next. The accrual method is beneficial to businesses with complex transactions because expenses are deducted in the year in which the income to which they relate is reported. By leveling out your income, you avoid paying higher taxes.

(continued)

CHECKLIST *(continued)*

✓ **The value of your inventory.** If your business manufactures products or purchases goods for resale, you can deduct the cost of goods sold from your revenues when calculating your taxable income. However, before you can claim your deduction, you must determine the value of your inventory at the beginning of the year, during the course of the year, and at the end of the year. You can determine your inventory's value using the cost method, which looks at the direct or indirect costs of purchasing the materials, or the market value method, which allows you to minimize your gross income to mirror a decreased value in inventory.

✓ **Tax obligations.** The types of taxes you will be required to withhold and/or pay are: payroll, which includes federal income tax withholding, Social Security and Medicare taxes (FICA), federal and state unemployment taxes (FUTA), and state and local income tax; self-employment taxes; sales tax; state income tax; and taxes on vehicles.

✓ **Available deductions.** Whether you operate your business in a high-rise office building or out of the basement of your home, you can claim several deductions to ease your tax burden. If you operate your business outside of the home, some of the deductions you can claim include: expenses for travel, meals, and entertainment; business gifts; depreciation; benefits and compensation; and vehicle use. Home-based business owners can claim a home office deduction if their home office is their principal place of business. Expenses for utilities, rental payments or mortgage interest, repairs, casualty losses, and insurance are allowable deductions.

✓ **Access to tax credits.** You can claim numerous tax credits to decrease your tax bill while you help to improve the community, support low-income individuals, or aid the disabled. Among these tax credits are: the empowerment zone employment credit, credit for contributions to community development corporations, and disabled access credit. Tax credits generally benefit the disadvantaged and are targeted toward small business owners.

✓ **Substantiation of records.** Business owners are required to keep records of all materials supporting items listed on their tax returns. Document all your expenses in case a business deduction is called into question. Keep records for expenses such as travel, meals and entertainment, and vehicle use.

RESOURCES FOR MORE INFORMATION

ASSOCIATIONS

- *Internal Revenue Service (IRS),* 1111 Constitution Avenue NW, Washington, DC 20224; 1-800-829-1040; www.irs.ustreas.gov. The IRS offers one-stop shopping for your tax needs. It provides extensive information about the types of taxes your business may be subject to, all the forms you may be required to submit to claim a deduction, and a host of publications that can assist you in your tax-planning strategies.

14

BUYING A BUSINESS

Jill Patton was working as a computer consultant in the real estate industry when she decided to turn her hobby of making gift baskets into an entrepreneurial endeavor. But unlike many people who envision building a company from the ground up, Patton decided to buy her way into the American dream. "The reason why I decided to buy a business is because the groundwork had already been laid by the previous owner," says Patton, owner of Essentially Chocolate and the Basket Gallery, a mail-order enterprise that specializes in gourmet gift baskets packed full of imported chocolates, coffees, cookies, and fresh fruit.

"I thought I'd be able to reach my goal faster by adding on to what they had already created as opposed to starting from scratch, so when I saw the business advertised in the business opportunities section of the *Washington Post*, I jumped at the chance."

Patton purchased the first half of her company, the Basket Gallery, in 1992, for $15,000. By borrowing $5,000 from credit cards, she acquired the store's inventory and soon began taking orders. Patton says most of the sales were coming in over the phone, so, in 1994, she transformed the retail operation into a mail-order business. In 1995, Patton purchased the second half of her business, Essentially Chocolate, using a $50,000 Small Business Administration-guaranteed loan. That same year she merged the two companies to form Essentially Chocolate and the Basket Gallery, and moved the entire operation into a 3,000-square-foot facility in Rockville, Maryland. Today, the company's clients include Marriott Corporation,

PricewaterhouseCoopers, Ernst & Young, and Hilton Hotels, and its sales are a half-million dollars.

Patton is one of many successful entrepreneurs who have started their own businesses by buying a company. Many people who want to experience ownership without the hassles of launching a new venture buy a going concern. That strategy can reduce the risk of ownership and increase the chances of success, but the process of acquisition is not without its own challenges. Acquiring an existing firm takes time, careful preparation, and the trained eye of a professional who can separate the wheat from the chaff.

In this chapter, we will discuss the process of buying a business, and will outline some of the advantages and disadvantages. Some aspects of buying a business resemble starting one from scratch. For example, before you even search the newspaper for "For Sale" opportunities or approach a business broker about buying a firm, you must determine your reasons for wanting to become a business owner. Then you must evaluate whether you have what it takes to succeed in the world of entrepreneurship (analyze your strengths and weaknesses) and decide what type of business you want to own.

After conducting these preliminaries, you can begin your search for a business that matches your talents and your tastes. Like Jill Patton, you can search the daily newspaper for an appealing buy. However, there are many other ways to find a business that's right for you. We will examine some of the sources of information about existing companies, and will show you how to investigate a business, negotiate and finance its purchase, and close the deal.

GETTING A HEAD START

One of the primary reasons people choose to acquire a business rather than start one from scratch is that acquisition gives them a head start on ownership. Buying a business reduces both the amount of time it takes to become an entrepreneur and the risk involved.

Statistics indicate that half of all new businesses fail within their first four years of operation. Some falter because of mismanagement of finances. Others close their doors because of undercapitalization or the owner's inexperience. Whatever the reasons, many businesses are gone before their first anniversary. For people who want to start their own companies with a greater chance of survival, acquisition seems to be the way to go.

Advantages of Buying a Business

There are many advantages to buying a business. Those that are most common are described here.

Established Customer/Supplier Base

For a new business, attracting and retaining customers can be very expensive. First, market research is needed to identify the customer base. Next, advertising and other marketing techniques that will grab attention and guarantee dollars must be introduced. In contrast, the purchase of an existing concern delivers a client base that is already loyal because the company provides the products or services that its customers need. You need not shell out additional dollars to bring customers through the door, and you inherit a ready-made vendor/supplier list. Finding vendors who are reliable and trustworthy, and who carry the types of products you need, can take a damaging amount of time. If you purchase a business, none of that effort may be required.

Immediate Cash Flow

One of the biggest concerns of any new business owner is cash flow (the movement of money into and out of your business). As a new entrepreneur, your cash flow will not be steady during the first few years of operation. But as the purchaser of an established firm, you have existing inventory and accounts receivable, and they can generate cash flow from the very first day you take over the business.

Existing Reputation

If you start a business from scratch, it will take some time for you to make a name for yourself. You may want to be known for having the fastest lube facility in the county. Or maybe you want your ice cream parlor to win blue ribbons for serving the tastiest low-fat smoothies in the area. Whatever your goal for building a solid reputation, you will have to wait patiently as customers, vendors, and other business colleagues get to know you and your business. However, if you purchase an existing company, its reputation is already in place. If that reputation is untarnished, you immediately profit. If it has some dents and scratches, you can meet customers' curiosity and complaints with innovations, energy and courtesy, and the unspoken message that the new broom is sweeping clean.

Existing Inventory

When you take over an existing business, you inherit the inventory. You will want to evaluate it and add to it, but you can pursue those activities at a reasonable pace, and your inventory expenditures will be far lower than if you were launching a new business.

Ready-Made Staff

One of the most valuable assets you will obtain when you buy a business is the staff. The employees know the business inside-out, so you will save the considerable money and time you would have spent training new recruits. Experienced employees may be able to show you some important ropes in a few areas. Having a ready-made staff spares you the arduous task of recruitment at a time when you have a host of other concerns. You will be able to devote more time to selling your product or service.

Reduced Cost

Depending on the type of business you want to buy and how you structure the deal, you may be able to purchase a business for far less money than it would cost to build one from the ground up. Also, your financial projections and the previous owner's records (budget, business plan, and financial statements) will combine to provide you with realistic and achievable goals.

Recognized Market Positioning

An existing concern has already defined how to position its product or service. It has created a marketing communications campaign (via advertising, promotions, and/or public relations) and has set the prices for its product or service. As a "second-generation" entrepreneur, you inherit these important aspects of building a successful business.

Current Operating Systems

Anyone who starts a new business becomes responsible for creating a number of tools that will aid the operation: employee payroll, accounting procedures, inventory tracking systems, and sales and marketing campaigns. Existing businesses have these operating systems securely in place. They may require some fine-tuning or tweaking to match your specific standards as a new owner, but the building phase was completed long before your purchase.

Ease in Financing

Most financial lending institutions feel more comfortable lending money to a buyer of an existing business, rather than a start-up, because the existing business has an established credit record, in addition to a solid customer base, experienced personnel, a known market position, and positive cash flow. All of these elements are attractive to bankers, venture capitalists, and other lenders whom you may want to tap for funds to close your deal. Also, when you seek financing to support an existing business, you are not subject to the same security and guarantee requirements that would be demanded if you were starting the business from ground zero. You may only have to put up the assets of the business as collateral to secure financing for the buy.

Disadvantages of Buying a Business

Obsolete Equipment

You may inherit a roomful of equipment and tools when you buy a business, but much of your inheritance may prove useless. To effectively run the business and continue competing in the marketplace, you may have to update obsolete inventory and equipment, which will translate into increased costs for you.

Cost

Cost can be a benefit of buying a business, but it can also be a drawback. Depending on the type of business you buy and how you structure the deal, you could end up paying a probitively high price for an existing concern, particularly if the economy is good and the seller feels that the company's revenue and reputation warrant the high price tag.

Personality Conflicts with Staff

Having a ready-made staff at your disposal can be advantageous, but if you are unable to work with the current personnel, it could spell trouble for your operation. As the new owner, your personality may clash with those of current managers and other staff members. Some employees may resent your having taken over the business reins, and may be hard to manage.

Outdated Receivables

Not every business that posts a "For Sale" sign is in great condition. Some businesses may have a wad of uncollectible receivables that you will have to handle if you decide to purchase. Dealing with outdated accounts receivable can affect your immediate cash flow and, ultimately, your business. When purchasing a business, try to structure the deal so that you are reimbursed for uncollectible receivables. Or, look for another company that is for sale and has fewer unpaying customers.

Inherent Problems

The due diligence process, which we will discuss later in this chapter, is critical if you are thinking about buying an existing business. It should uncover any potential problems, but there is still a chance that something may fall through the cracks. Many inherent problems may not be noticeable until after you close the deal and begin operating as the new owner. For example, you may discover that the financial records you reviewed to gauge the viability of the business do not match actual performance. Or maybe you realize that a key employee—the person who supposedly knew the operation well—knows nothing at all. Whether you decide to start a business or buy one, there's little chance that everything will go off without a hitch. Be prepared for the unexpected, and have a resolution plan in place just in case.

New Competition

When buying a business, you may find that the seller is trying to unload this company so that he or she can open another one around the corner. Is the seller planning to compete with you? If you decide to acquire a business, have the seller sign a "noncompete" agreement—a promise that he or she will not open a similar type of business within a stated area for a specified period of time. (Noncompete clauses are described in greater detail later in this chapter.)

HOW AND WHERE TO FIND A BUSINESS TO BUY

After weighing the advantages and disadvantages, identify your reasons for wanting to buy a business, then ask yourself what type of enterprise you would like to purchase. Are you looking for a service or retail operation, a distribution company, or a manufacturing plant? A variety of enterprises go up for sale every day. You can buy an office supply store, athletic gym, marketing firm, toy store, hair salon, restaurant—you name it. You can also buy into a franchise, a category that includes operations ranging from shoe repair shops or ice cream parlors or cleaning services. (We will discuss franchising in Chapter 15.)

In addition to considering the type of business you want to buy, you should determine where you would like the business to be located (the city versus the suburbs). Also, define the makeup of the industry you intend to enter. Is it viable and expanding, or is it oversaturated or stagnating in growth? Do enough research on the industry to know how your venture might fare.

As long as you have the right amount of capital, you can buy whatever business is available. But be sure you have the skills and qualities required to make it a success.

As discussed in Chapter 1, successful business owners are those who have leadership skills, business experience, strong management and interpersonal skills, a competitive attitude, self-confidence, and an unflappable disposition. If you do not have what it takes to be a successful entrepreneur, you should rethink your decision to buy a business. The company will not run itself; you must have some knowledge of what is required for ownership. Conduct an honest appraisal of what you can and cannot do before buying an existing firm (see Chapter 1 for a detailed discussion about evaluating your strengths and weaknesses). If you are confident that you have the right tools, set the purchase in motion.

If you know the type of business you would like to buy, you may want to contact industry and trade associations for a list of business opportunities. Check the *Encyclopedia of Associations*, published by Gale Research Inc., for an association that serves the industry in which you are interested. You should be able to find this publication in your local library. Call the association you select, and ask to speak with a consultant about finding leads on businesses for sale.

An association is not the only resource for finding an enterprise that piques your interest. Here are some other places to look.

Newspapers

The classified section of your daily newspaper is a great place to start your search. The Sunday editions of most national and local papers list businesses for sale in their classified ad section. *The Wall Street Journal* is one of several publications that maintain special sections on "Business Opportunities" or lists of companies for sale.

Internet

A number of Web sites list businesses for sale. By using one of the major search engines (AltaVista, InfoSeek, or Excite), you can find sites addressed to business buyers. Check out two URLs during your search: (1) www .bizbuysell.com, which allows you to search by company type, geographic area, or business broker, and (2) www.vrbusinessbrokers.com, which posts thousands of businesses and franchises for sale.

Trade and Business Publications

A variety of trade and specialized magazines publish classified ad sections, usually on the back pages. However, beware of "get-rich-quick" business opportunities such as multilevel marketing schemes and vague work-at-home offers. Carefully read any listing before pursuing the sale.

A Business Broker

Working with a business broker is probably your best route to finding a business to buy. Professional brokers deal exclusively in finding enterprises for interested buyers, and they are trained to distinguish the money pits from the money makers. Here are some services that a broker performs to help make your business shopping spree a success:

1. *Screens potential candidates.* One of the major benefits of using a broker is that, before proceeding with any negotiations, he or she will evaluate businesses for sale, to determine whether they have any major problems. If you go it alone, you may miss flaws that the trained eye of a business broker will spot after minimal investigation. Compared to newspapers or monthly trade magazines, a business broker can offer you a wider selection of listings in your price range and preferred industry.

2. *Defines your needs.* A good business broker works with you to focus your interests and define the size and type of enterprise you want to buy. He or she also helps you identify your own strengths and weaknesses, and matches them against the businesses that are for sale.

3. *Prepares paperwork.* Business brokers know all the procedures required to secure permits, licenses, financial records, tax returns, and other documents handled during the negotiation process and at the close of the sale. Their experience in handling such documents

can reduce the amount of time you must spend on purchasing your company.

4. *Negotiates the sale.* During the negotiation process, you will be most thankful that you decided to use a business broker. Known for their gift of gab, these professionals are able to finesse a deal that is attractive to both the buyer and the seller. Business brokers are experts at keeping tempers at bay during the negotiation process, and they have license to say things or ask questions that you could not broach (at least not without killing the deal) if you were negotiating the sale on your own. A business broker might tell the seller that the price is too high and suggest what would have to be done to salvage the deal.

Using a broker has advantages, but this level of assistance is not cheap. Brokers' fees range between 5 and 10 percent of the final price of the sale. Be sure to deal with a business broker, not a real estate broker. The latter may have a business broker license and a record of a few business sales, but may be less effective in closing the kind of deal you hope to net. Buying a business is very different from buying real estate. Stay with the person who is the specialist in acquisitions of businesses—the business broker.

If you encounter a seller who is using a business broker, always go through the broker. Never approach the seller directly about the business. Not every seller will use a "go-between" to find a buyer for his or her company. If you find a seller who is self-representing, you, the seller, and your attorney and/or accountant can begin negotiations, but just be prepared for a long negotiation process. Without a broker to finesse the deal, a process that might normally take several weeks may stretch out over several months.

To find a business broker, you can research the *Corporate Finance Directory,* which lists brokers and investment bankers. You should be able to find this book in your local library. You can also search the BizBuySell Web site at www.bizbuysell.com or contact the International Business Brokers Association at 703-437-7464.

Local Chamber of Commerce

If you are looking to buy a business in a particular area, the local chamber of commerce should be able to assist you. Many chapters keep files of businesses that are for sale in their geographic area, and can play a matchmaker role for buyers and sellers. In addition to this service, chambers of commerce can provide you with information about local business communities.

Outside Professionals

Attorneys, accountants, bankers, and insurance professionals deal with small businesses daily and may be good resources for finding a business to buy. They may receive advance notice before a sale is publicized and may even be able to put in a good word for you with the seller. Bankers are particularly important contacts because they usually keep records of companies that are up for sale.

Other Business Owners

As a last resort, you can try contacting business owners in your area. There's a chance they may have a friend or client who is looking for a buyer. Most small business owners will be more than happy to help you in your search or will point you in the right direction if they are unable to provide assistance.

To begin your search, you need not wait to see a listing of businesses for sale. If you see a company that you would like, call the owner and ask whether he or she is interested in selling. This is an unconventional approach, but you may hit pay dirt with it. The owner may be interested in selling but reluctant to publicize the sale for fear of alarming employees and long-time customers. Or, you might reach a seller just days before he or she was ready to run an advertisement. Either way, you will have an advantage over other prospective buyers.

When searching for your future enterprise, take your time. You're not likely to find exactly what you want when you want it. A successful search can take several months, so be patient. Whichever method you choose, always consult with your attorney and accountant before making a final decision about which company to pursue.

INVESTIGATING THE BUSINESS

After you find a business that you would like to purchase, begin investigating its history and its current status. By thoroughly researching the business, you will be able to uncover any existing problems that could sway your decision to buy.

You will not be able to conduct an in-depth evaluation of the business until you've decided to go through with the acquisition, but basic financial and credit information is publicly available. Also, you can do some preliminary legwork to determine whether the company is worth pursuing.

Start by simply asking the seller the most important question: Why is the business up for sale? An owner might have many reasons for wanting to bail out. If the seller has been in business for a long time, he or she may be ready to retire. If the firm is family-owned, personal differences among the family members, or the death of an owner, may be the reason for the sale. Or, the owner might simply be tired of running the company.

When Jill Patton purchased her second shop, Essentially Chocolate, she discovered that the owner wanted to sell for lifestyle reasons. "He was running the business for 15 years and was basically burnt out. Plus he loved to travel overseas but could not just pick up and go whenever he wanted to with the kind of company that he had, so he decided to put his business on the market," she says.

These types of motives for a business sale are obvious and not a cause for concern. Other reasons are not so obvious, and should be cause for alarm. A primary reason for selling a business is: the business is failing. An owner may want to bail out because of a bad management structure, impending competition, a negative cash flow, or a stagnant economy. Few sellers will tell you that the business is undercapitalized and that's why they have chosen to sell. Hire a business broker to help you get to the heart of the matter. An experienced broker will either know the real reasons for a business sale or will be able to get a straight answer for you. Still, it is important for you to gain the seller's and the broker's confidence and to show that you have a genuine interest in purchasing the business. In return, you can expect them to be forthright with you.

Even if the seller's motives are clear, you still need to dig deeper (perform due diligence) to make sure there are no hidden problems, financial or otherwise. To gauge the financial health of the company, ask how much seller financing the owner is willing to provide for the purchase. If the owner offers to help you finance the acquisition, chances are the business is standing on solid ground. (We will discuss seller financing later in this chapter.)

Besides the motive for the sale, find out the price of the business. The owner will set the price, but you and your broker can negotiate the terms and possibly get a lower price than was originally quoted. Besides the initial down payment, you will need money to cover the expenses for rental fees, utilities, supplies, a business license and/or permits, additional inventory that may be needed, equipment and fixtures (if needed), and other operating expenses.

Factors to Consider When Evaluating a Business

Several factors dictate the price of a company that is for sale. These include, but are not limited to, the following list.

Condition of the Business
If the company and the facility are in good shape (the books are complete and accurate, and the building looks brand new), the seller will be more inclined to ask for a price that may be higher than the fair market price. If plaster is falling around your ears and the books are in shambles, you can use these conditions as leverage to negotiate a lower price.

Profit History
If the company's cash flow has been steady and positive and the business has earned a profit every year, the seller has leverage to ask for more money because he or she is handing over a financially stable company.

Profit Potential

If the market that the business serves is growing at a steady rate each year, the company stands to make more money. The seller will then be more apt to ask for a higher purchase price.

Market Position

If the demand for the company's product or service is increasing, the asking price is likely to increase as well. However, if inventory is moving off the shelves slowly, customers are coming in dribs and drabs, and the overall demand is lackluster, the buyer can negotiate a lower price.

Economic Conditions

When the economy is good, the market is a seller's market. Owners assume buyers have more money to spend because the financial health of the country has improved: therefore, they do not hesitate to ask for a fair (or higher) market price.

Company Reputation

If the business is well known and respected, the price of goodwill can be very high. Buyers won't spend thousands of dollars for a company that no one likes. Talk to customers about the business. Ask whether they are happy with the product or service that is provided. Gather surrounding business owners' evaluations, but take whatever they say with a grain of salt. An owner may be displeased with the seller for personal reasons that have no bearing on how the business is actually operated.

Approach the company's vendors and suppliers to see whether the seller has a reputation for paying bills on time or is consistently late. This is particularly important because the company's accounts payable records may affect your ability to obtain financing for the purchase. If you approach a vendor before making an agreement to actually purchase the company, you may get a cold shoulder. Sensitive information that involves financial records is kept closed until a letter of intent is signed. Nevertheless, give it a try. Some vendors may at least be willing to give you rank, file, and serial number information.

Location

Location is an important aspect to consider. *How* important it is depends on the type of business you are looking to buy. If you want to purchase a retail store, you will want the business to be situated in an area that is exposed to heavy foot and/or vehicular traffic. If you plan to buy a manufacturing business, nearness to major highways and transportation facilities will make deliveries of your product easier. Whichever business you choose, its location will affect the purchase price. Businesses located in heavily populated areas may be greater in price than those situated in ghost towns. (See Chapter 5 for more information on choosing a location.)

When surveying a location, note whether the surrounding area is undergoing any changes that could impact the business. Are any new competitors planning to open up shop? Are developers laying the foundation for a new office building or condominiums? Any of these changes could positively or negatively affect the business you plan to buy, so pay particular attention to what's going on in the area.

Signing a Letter of Intent

If you still want to buy the business after conducting your preliminary research, you will have to sign a letter of intent, which is a nonbinding agreement between you and the seller. It will state that you intend to purchase the business. The letter is usually drafted by an attorney after the buyer and seller have reached a general agreement about the price and terms of the sale. The letter outlines the conditions of the purchase, the ways to get financing, and the due diligence process (the procedure a buyer performs to check out the financial health and other aspects of the business). This document also prohibits the seller from taking offers from other interested buyers.

When a letter of intent is created, the buyer usually makes a deposit on the purchase price. Because the document is nonbinding, the buyer can get the deposit back if, for any reason, negotiations cease and the deal falls through. Once the letter is signed, it can be issued to third parties such as bankers and other financiers as evidence of the intent to purchase. The letter also gives you permission to contact the seller's lawyer, accountant, banker, and other professionals whom you would approach during your due diligence process.

In addition to a letter of intent, you may be required to sign a confidentiality agreement—a promise not to use, for purposes outside of making a sound buying decision, any of the information that you obtain.

Performing Due Diligence

As mentioned above, due diligence is a process that involves investigating the seller and the business itself before finalizing the deal. During this period, you are permitted access to the company's financial records, facility, employees, suppliers, and other aspects of the business. It is important that you involve your accountant, attorney, and banker in this fact-finding mission; they will be able to keep your emotions at bay and prevent you from making rash decisions. Like buying a house, buying a business can be a very emotional experience. It is easy to get so wrapped up in the excitement of the purchase that you want to move full-speed ahead without taking notice of some warning signs along the way. Perhaps no one knows this danger more than Vern Crosby.

For five years, Crosby was head of marketing for a service-based business in Maryland. Then the principal owners, who were experiencing problems, announced that they wanted to bail out. They made Crosby an offer to buy the company. He knew the market well. In fact, after coming on board in 1991, he had helped the company's sales climb from $1 million to nearly $15 million in 1996. He had made no secret of wanting a piece of the business, and when the offer was made, he jumped at the opportunity.

Like any interested buyer, Crosby began investigating the company. He checked out the firm's customers and vendors and learned that the company was not paying its suppliers on time. The principal owners shifted the blame for delays to accounts receivable, but Crosby took their response as a sign to dig deeper. He discovered that the owners were funneling money into several ventures in an attempt to diversify, but were doing so unsuccessfully. "There was so much commingling of dollars, robbing Peter to pay Paul," says Crosby. "It was a nightmare once you got into it."

Despite these red flags, Crosby proceeded. Even after his advisers warned him not to go through with the purchase, Crosby still moved forward. "I had on my Lee Iacocca hat, and just knew I could turn this company around," he remembers. But when he approached the banks about financing, he realized the deal was going to fall through. After checking the firm's books, the bank discovered that the tax debt was more than $1 million (with late fees and penalties) instead of the $250,000 originally stated. Needless to say, that ended the deal—and Crosby's dream of purchasing this business.

Down but not out, Crosby took the lessons he learned in this fallout and applied them to the successful purchase of two other companies: Excell Management and Outsource Inc. He enlisted the help of an attorney, hired an accountant, and retained an acquisitions attorney to deal with the company's valuations.[1]

Following are several items you should review before putting your John Hancock on any purchasing agreement. Consult your attorney, accountant, and banker for specifics concerning all the documents and areas you should evaluate.

Financial Statements

These are perhaps the most important documents you will need to review. They include the company's income statements, balance sheets, and cash flow statements for the past five years. Take a good look at the company's bookkeeping system and the records maintained there. Match all of these documents against the firm's tax returns. Enlist the help of an accountant who is familiar with the type of business you are planning to buy. Ask him or her to review the sales and operating ratios of the company. Match these against the industry standards, which can be found in annual publications produced by Dun & Bradstreet, and similar agencies. When reviewing the company's income statement, analyze the monthly gross sales, profit, salaries, advertising costs, and utilities and miscellaneous expenses. Careful review of the income statement is important because this document often includes a lot of fat that can be trimmed. By honing in on the fixed and variable expenses, you will get a better picture of those factors that will impact the profitability of the company.

Tax Records
Review the company's tax returns for the past five years. This examination will help you determine the firm's actual net worth. Often, business owners will draw a fine line between company and personal expenses. For example, they might take a personal trip and write it off as a fully deductible business expense, when they only made one business phone call from the beach in Tahiti. Or, an owner may purchase products that he or she uses for personal use and charge them to the business. You and your accountant must analyze the company's tax returns to decipher the actual profitability of the business.

Contracts/Lease Agreements and Other Legal Documents
The types of contracts and lease agreements you should look over include: equipment and machinery leases, purchase agreements, subcontractor/independent contractor agreements, sales contracts, business employee agreements, distribution agreements, and real estate leases. You will need to review these legal documents to determine the amount of obligation the business has to certain parties. For real estate and equipment leases, you will have to specifically find out whether the property is transferable, and the terms and length of the lease. You don't want to close the deal to buy a retail store, for example, only to find out that the lease for the space ends in two weeks and you will have to move. The other legal documents you need to read include articles of incorporation, fictitious business name statements, registered trademarks, patents, and copyrights. If the business you plan to purchase has intellectual property, you should have an intellectual property attorney review the forms.

Organizational Documents
No matter what type of business you decide to buy, it will have to operate under one of the six legal forms of business: (1) a sole proprietorship, (2) a general partnership, (3) a corporation, (4) a Subchapter S corporation, (5) a limited liability company, or (6) a limited partnership. The documents you should study to determine how the company is structured and capitalized include partnership and shareholder agreements, articles of incorporation, and business certificates. If the company is a corporation, in what state is it incorporated? Make sure that individuals who claim to have title to the company's assets and authority to proceed with the transaction do in fact have those powers. For a corporation, the secretary or the board of directors

should be able to provide you with a certificate that confirms this information. If the business you want to buy is not a corporation, you will have to get confirmation from the owner's attorney and other outside parties.

Sales Records

These are important indicators of current business activity. Sales will be an item in the company's financial statements, but look at them separately for the past three months (or longer). If you intend to purchase a product-oriented business, break down sales according to credit and cash, and group products into different categories. This will give you a better sense of what sells and what does not—and when. It will also alert you to certain business cycles. Match any seasonal changes or patterns that the business experiences with the norms for the industry.

Accounts Receivable

It is important that you check the accounts receivable records to determine whether you are buying a business that has trustworthy, paying customers or one that has unreliable and delinquent clients. The longer a receivable is outstanding, the lower is its value and the slimmer are your chances of collecting on the account. When reviewing the accounts receivable, break them down into 30, 60, and 90 days overdue, and beyond 90 days. Make a list of the top ten accounts (these are most likely to be your bread-and-butter accounts), and evaluate their creditworthiness. If you find that some of the accounts are outstanding past 60 or 90 days but the majority of clients are creditworthy, don't scrap your plans to buy the business. After becoming the owner, you can simply tighten the credit collections policy, which should turn things around fast.

Accounts Payable

As with accounts receivable, group the accounts payable into 30, 60, and 90 days, and beyond 90 days. Reviewing these records will give you a good indication of the company's cash flow. It will also tell you whether the company has been paying its bills on time, and what accounts are in arrears. If you purchase a business that has been consistently late in paying vendors and other creditors, you may find it difficult to do business with these individuals after you assume ownership.

Inventory

This includes all products that are intended to be sold to customers. When reviewing the inventory, check its age, quality, and condition. Calculate how much inventory is currently available, and how much existed at the end of the previous fiscal year. To make sure that you are getting items that you can actually use if you assume control of the company, have the inventory appraised. If the value of the items does not line up with the products you would like to offer for resale, or if they are obsolete with respect to current market demand, you can leverage this situation to negotiate a lower purchase price.

Facility and Equipment

Survey the build-out of the facility. What (if any) leasehold improvements have been made, and what changes to the structure will you have to make to satisfy your needs? Make sure the building is in good condition outside and inside, and that there are no leaky pipes or faulty electric wires. You may want to spend some time (perhaps a few days) milling around the building to make sure there are no hidden problems. Everything may appear to be in top condition, but unless you spend some time walking around the building at different times of the day and in different weather conditions, you may not be able to uncover potential problems. Any equipment and other tangible assets that the company owns should be listed by name and model number and evaluated for its current condition, market value when purchased, and current market value. Find out whether the equipment has been purchased or leased. If you are acquiring leased equipment, you will need to know the terms and length of the lease and, consequently, the company's obligations.

All Liabilities

You will definitely need an attorney and accountant to review the company's liabilities—property liens, pending lawsuits, unpaid taxes, and unpaid bills. Your attorney and accountant should be able to determine the costs and legal ramifications involved in settling outstanding liabilities. Contact your local Better Business Bureau for information regarding current or past complaints filed against the company, or search local court records for any charges filed before state or federal commissions.

Customer and Supplier Base

Obtain a complete customer list from the seller. Determine which customers are first-time buyers. Find out how many customers were lost during the past year, and which customers are most loyal. Identify which merchandise is most popular among certain customers. Contact the customers on the list and ask them what they like or dislike about the company. Ask whether they would continue to patronize the company under new ownership. Look at the business's customer service policy, especially how it handles returns and complaints. This may be an area that, if improved, will bring in more customers.

Management Structure

An owner's rapport with his or her employees is critical. When reviewing the management structure, study the management practices as well as the company's organizational chart, and determine where certain levels of authority lie. Review the employee wage scale, and find out how long each employee has worked within the establishment. Talk with the employees. What do they like and dislike about the company? The workers will appreciate your valuing their opinion, and your approach may persuade some valuable employees not to quit. By speaking with the workers, you may identify some truly necessary changes and create a more productive environment. Gather information about employee benefits: health, life, disability, and accident insurance; paid vacations; sick leave; retirement plans; and profit sharing. Bring in your attorney to examine any lawsuits that may have been filed by an employee against the company.

Price Points

Examine the pricing schedule for all products or services, and match it against industry standards. When was the last price increase, and what was the percentage of the increase? Consider the number and amounts of discounts that have been allowed. By checking the price points, you may find that the company's prices are too high or too low. If so, you will have to make changes that fall in line with the industry and with what the customers are willing to pay.

Marketing Campaigns

Every company has a way of reaching its customers, whether through advertising, public relations, or promotions. What techniques is the business you want to buy using to attract consumers? Obtain copies of the company's sales literature and other printed materials, to gain a clear sense of how the company is presenting itself. Define the advertising and other marketing communications costs.

Insurance

Review the insurance policies held by the business, and the amounts of the premiums. If you plan to buy a manufacturing business, make sure the owner has obtained product liability insurance. This is extremely important because it will protect you if a customer becomes ill or injured—or worse—from using your product. (See Chapter 6 for a complete discussion of business insurance.) Many companies do not have the right kind or right amount of insurance to protect them if disaster strikes. If you find that the business you want to buy is underinsured, you may have to obtain additional coverage or place a "rider" on an existing policy to shield you from catastrophe.

History of Market and Industry

Examine the industry and the market to determine whether sales are increasing, or decreasing, or have leveled off. Reviewing the history of the market that the business serves is important because it will indicate how the firm might fare in the future. If sales have been decreasing year after year for the type of business you want to buy, you may want to rethink your decision.

As you are conducting your investigation, bear in mind that the seller will also want to perform some due diligence. In other words, the seller may want to investigate your credit report, reputation, management experience, and vision or goals for the company. This profile becomes particularly important if the owner wants to assume employment within the business after handing it over to you. (We will discuss some after-sale roles of the seller later in this chapter.)

Conducting a Business Appraisal

As part of your due diligence, you may want to have the business appraised. The seller will determine the asking price, but, by appraising the business, you will be able to determine whether the company is actually worth the price the seller is requesting. You will also know whether you are being taken for a ride.

To conduct a business appraisal, you will need a *business* appraiser, not a real estate or equipment appraiser. Many people lump all three together, but they are actually three different disciplines. Make sure a business appraiser reviews the company you want to buy.

A business appraiser will have a specific professional designation following his or her name. Some professed business appraisers offer great expertise in valuing a company and have no letters after their name, but the designation indicates solid appraisal experience and, probably, greater peace of mind for you. The designations you should look for include: CBA (Certified Business Appraiser); CVA (Certified Valuation Analyst); ASA (Accredited Senior Appraiser); and CPA/ABV (Certified Public Accountant Accredited in Business Valuation).

The cost of using a business appraiser varies according to the type of appraisal you request—oral or written. An oral appraisal can cost between $200 and $300. A written appraisal may run from $2,500 to $5,000. A business appraiser who conducts an oral valuation may need two to four hours to gather preliminary data, and as many as six hours to actually complete the valuation. A business appraiser who performs a written valuation will usually take 20 to 50 hours to complete the task, and may create a written report exceeding 100 pages.

To find a business appraiser, you can contact the American Society of Appraisers or the Institute of Business Appraisers (both are listed at the end of this chapter). As with any professional, when searching for a business appraiser, look at his or her credentials, conduct an interview, and go over all costs before agreeing to any fee. Before the appraiser begins the valuation, he or she will require that you sign an appraisal agreement or engagement letter. This document basically spells out the independent nature of the appraisal so that buyers or sellers are not inclined to think that the appraiser's assessment was based on anything other than facts.

MAKING THE BUY

When you have finished playing private eye by looking into all aspects of the company, you are ready to begin negotiations. You may think that you need to be hard-nosed and tough in order get a good deal. You don't. In fact, the best way to get a deal that is favorable for both you and the seller is to be friendly. You have to sell yourself as well as your ideas, to convince the owner to hand over the business. If he or she doesn't like you, there probably will be no deal.

When negotiating the sale, you, your broker, and the seller should discuss the purchase price, how the price was determined, and any information uncovered in the due diligence process that you would like to use as leverage to reduce the asking price. If you negotiate without a broker present, document all discussions in a memorandum that outlines the points addressed during your meeting and any agreements made. You and the seller should each have a copy of any written memoranda. You might find this procedure a bit tedious, but in the event that the seller gets a touch of amnesia and denies having quoted a price that the two of you agreed on just two days earlier, you will have written proof that will ease future negotiations.

When negotiating the terms of the sale, keep in mind that you're not likely to get everything you want and the seller is not likely to get everything he or she wants. Successful negotiations require compromise, and your broker plays a big part in massaging the terms so that they are acceptable to both parties. If you come across a seller who is unwilling to budge on price or any other terms of the sale (e.g., he or she refuses to release certain financial documents), take it as an indication that you need to move on.

Financing the Purchase by Using Seller Financing

When a fair price for the business has been established, you must figure out how you will finance the buy. Securing capital for acquisition is not unlike raising money for your own growing concern: you can use debt or equity financing to obtain the funds that you need (see Chapter 8). Many buyers take advantage of seller financing.

Seller financing is a process in which the seller of a business allows the buyer to make a down payment on the purchase price and to carry a promissory note for the outstanding balance. In short, the seller plays the role of banker. This financing technique is normally used when a company has difficulty attracting conventional lenders, when the purchase price is so large that a cash sale would be nearly impossible, or when the price is too small to attract a venture capitalist. As discussed in Chapter 8, venture capitalists typically deal with firms that have more than $2 million in revenue.

The terms of seller financing depend on the circumstances. Most sellers will finance from one third to two thirds of the sale price for a period of five to seven years, with an interest rate that is at or below prime bank rates. By offering seller financing, sellers are able to attract more interested buyers and speed up the selling process. Still, some owners are uncomfortable offering selling financing and will not do so unless they are familiar with the buyer's business reputation. This funding technique gives a clear indication that the seller has confidence in the company's future profit potential.

To obtain seller financing, you will have to put up the business assets as collateral or security for the loan. Some sellers may require additional security, such as a home mortgage or a security agreement based on real estate and personal property that you own. Depending on the seller, you may also have to offer a personal guarantee of the loan, just as you would if you were to borrow money from a neighborhood bank. In most circumstances, however, the company's assets will suffice unless the seller has reason to believe that your creditworthiness is highly questionable.

Seller financing offers many advantages over conventional lending. Some of these benefits are described below.

Speedier Sale

When the seller acts as the banker, the deal can be handled much faster. On average, banks take from 30 to 120 days to approve and close out a loan. Many acquisitions loans are not even granted. A seller is much more likely to grant a loan request and push the papers through as quickly as possible. He or she wants to sell a business, not tie up an interested buyer in a whole lot of unnecessary red tape.

Flexible Terms

When using seller financing, the buyer can adjust his or her payment schedule, loan period, interest rates, and other terms a lot easier than if he or she were to do business with a neighborhood bank. The buyer is also subject to a less stringent credit review.

Reduced Price

If the buyer agrees to assume the existing debts or liabilities of the business, he or she can use this as a bargaining chip to negotiate a lower purchase price. Keep in mind, however, that the seller may remain personally liable for those debts. If the seller has signed a contract or committed a personal guarantee for outstanding debt, he or she cannot escape that debt by simply selling the business. Unless the creditors agree to substitute the new owner for the former owner, the seller is not likely to allow the buyer to assume the debts in exchange for a lower purchase price because the seller will still remain obligated to pay his or her debt.

Gradual Buyout or Earnout

A buyout is an arrangement between a buyer and a seller that allows the buyer to purchase pieces of the business over a period of time. For example, the buyer may purchase the business name and a few tangible assets up front, but then lease equipment and other property, with the intention of engaging in a buyout of these materials at a later date. Under seller-assisted financing, the seller may also offer an earnout. In this arrangement, a portion of the purchase price hinges on the future success of the business. An earnout is typically used when there is a disagreement between the buyer and seller over how much the company is actually worth. A minimum price is established, and goals (expressed as percentages of gross sales or revenues) are set, indicating how much a seller stands to make if the business is a success. For example, an earnout arrangement might state that the seller is entitled to 2 percent of all gross sales between $5 and $6 million, and 3 percent of all sales over $6 million, during the first four years after the sale is made. If you use an earnout under your seller-assisted financing arrangement, be sure to place a cap on the total earnout payments, or you could end up giving away the business you just purchased.

Financing by Leveraged Buyout

Another way to finance your purchase is through a leveraged buyout (LBO). Unlike seller financing, when using a leveraged buyout, the buyer puts very little of his or her own money into the business. Instead of issuing a down payment on the purchase price, with the seller financing the rest, the buyer secures a loan from a bank or other investment firm to finance the purchase. In short, a leveraged buyout involves lining up outside lenders and persuading them to invest in a company that you want to buy.

LBO financing can include money pooled from different sources, including a bank, a venture capital firm, or a commercial finance company. LBOs are not for every type of company. They are best suited for mature companies that generate a cash surplus, have little debt, and market well-known product lines. If you plan to use a leveraged buyout to finance your acquisition, you will have to make provision for an investor's exit if he or she wants to withdraw at some future date.

PREPARING YOUR PURCHASING AGREEMENTS

You will have to sign a number of written agreements and documents before the deal is finalized, and you may want to consider some special arrangements before closing the sale.

Becoming a business owner is no easy task. Even more challenging is the responsibility for operating the company after all the papers are signed and the lawyers fees are paid. To that end, when they buy a business, many new owners arrange for the previous owner to remain on board to help with the transition and contribute his or her expertise.

If the seller decides to offer seller financing or to engage in an earnout, he or she will already remain tied to the business for some time after handing over the keys. However, there are other ways in which you can maintain a connection with the seller. Two options are especially common.

Creating a Consulting Arrangement with the Seller

A consulting arrangement involves commissioning a seller to provide business advice for a specified period of time. Like a doctor, the seller is essentially "on call" to handle problems as they arise, if the buyer is unable to develop a solution. Among sellers, consulting agreements are used more often than employment agreements because they create an atmosphere in which the seller does not feel he or she is taking a step backward. The seller is paid even if he or she is not called upon for help. The terms of the contract spell out how long the seller's services will be needed, and at what rate. In addition to having a ready-made hot line, the buyer benefits through tax advantages. The payments made to the seller are deductible as a business expense. The IRS may question the arrangement, so make sure that you have an agreement in writing and that the seller's fee falls in line with the market rate.

Offering Employment to the Seller

Not every seller will be willing to become an employee of a business he or she once owned, but, for those whose egos may be able to handle the arrangement, engaging in an employment contract can be a short-term solution that works well for both parties. The seller may want to finish a project that he or she started. By staying on as an employee, the seller will be able to reach that goal. Or, the new owner may feel shaky about certain aspects of the company and will be more at ease by having the seller show him or her the ropes (at least for a while). Employment contracts are typically used among family-owned businesses as part of a succession plan. The retiring founder stays on board as an employee to smooth the transition of ownership to a son or a daughter.

If the seller turns down an offer of consultation or employment, make sure that he or she at least signs a noncompete agreement. As previously discussed, this contractual agreement is a promise by the seller that he or she will not set up a similar business in the same geographic area for a specified period of time. The document may also specify that the seller will not use any customer lists, trade secrets, or business processes taken from his former company. Noncompete agreements are used in about 80 percent of all business sales.

The last agreement you will need to sign is the purchase agreement. This document, usually crafted by the buyer's lawyer, indicates the date on which the transfer of business ownership and all other possessions of the company will take place. It also states when the seller will receive payment. Depending on the nature of the purchase, this document can run several hundred pages in length. Review it carefully with your attorney and be sure you understand all of its provisions. After you and the seller agree on the language of the agreement, you can sign by the "X," and get ready for the closing.

PREPARING TO CLOSE

Closing. It's what every buyer looks forward to from the very first day he or she lays eyes on a particular business and says, "I've got to have that." Closing is the period in which all necessary documents are signed by all parties, checks and company keys are exchanged, and ownership and title are transferred.

Depending on the nature and culture of the deal, closing can take place when all parties meet to sign the final documents in the presence of one another and their respective attorneys, or it can happen through an escrow agent. An escrow agent gathers all signed documents forwarded by the individual parties over a matter of weeks, and, when all the forms are accounted for, releases payment to the seller, at which time the deal is officially closed.

Before you close your deal, make sure you've dotted your I's and crossed your T's. Be certain that you have made this important decision with your head and not just your heart. Review all the terms of the agreement, the liabilities you agreed to assume, and the special provisions one last time. Walk through the facility again, to make sure that no equipment is broken and that inventory and other items are in their rightful place. If, after doing this last bit of due diligence, you find that everything is satisfactory, pat yourself on the back and get ready to get down to business. You're an entrepreneur. Congratulations!

CHECKLIST

STEPS TO BUYING A BUSINESS

✓ **Consider the advantages and disadvantages.** Buying a business has its benefits and its drawbacks. Some of the advantages include quick cash flow, easier financing, an existing customer base, and a ready-made staff. However, by purchasing an existing concern, you may have to deal with obsolete equipment, personality conflicts among staff members, and uncollectible receivables. Before you decide to buy, consider what you have to gain and lose through acquisition.

✓ **Identify the type of business you want to buy.** You will find a number of businesses for sale. Ask yourself what type you would like to own. Retail store? Distribution company? Manufacturing plant? Mail order business? By identifying what industry you like and what type of firm you can operate successfully, you will make a smarter choice in your search for a perfect business fit.

✓ **Conduct an appraisal of your skills and talents.** You may find a business that you absolutely love, but unless you have the skills and experience to run the company, you will not be successful. Identify your strengths and weaknesses, and match them against the qualities of a successful business owner. Entrepreneurs are people who have strong leadership, management, and organizational skills. They are also competitive, self-confident, and energetic.

✓ **Search for a business to purchase.** Finding a business that is right for you can be as easy as looking in the Sunday newspaper. You can search for an enterprise in a number of ways: scour the classified ads in your local daily or the "Business Opportunities" section of a trade publication; take your search into cyberspace and enlist a major search engine to find businesses for sale; or commission a business broker to do the legwork for you.

✓ **Investigate the company.** Researching a company you want to buy is perhaps the most important step in the entire acquisition process. By thoroughly investigating the business, you will uncover existing problems within the firm. By conducting an in-depth investigation called "due diligence," you will be able to examine the company's financial records, tax returns, organizational documents, contracts and leases, financial statements, and other documents. During this procedure, you will also be able to speak with customers, vendors, and current employees. The information you gather will help you make a smart buying decision.

(continued)

CHECKLIST *(continued)*

✓ **Negotiate the sale.** Grab your business broker for this session. Negotiating the sale of a business can be a very time-consuming and complex task. It can take several months, depending on the nature of the deal. Your negotiations should involve discussions about the asking price, as well as any questionable information uncovered during the due diligence process. Realize, when you enter negotiations, that you will not get everything you want and the seller will not get everything he or she wants. Negotiations involve compromises, so be prepared to bend just a little.

✓ **Finance the buy.** Financing the purchase of a business is not unlike funding a growing company that you own. You can choose to use debt or equity financing. Many buyers, particularly first-time buyers, opt for seller financing. In this financing technique, the seller requires that the buyer make an initial down payment and then finances the rest of the purchase price over a specified period (usually five to seven years) at an interest rate that is at or below a prime bank rate. Sellers who offer seller financing typically agree to finance one third to two thirds of the sale price.

✓ **Close the sale.** Closing is the period in which all parties sign the necessary documents and exchange keys and cash. Closing can take place via an escrow agent, or all parties can sign the sale agreement in the presence of each other and their respective attorneys. Before closing the deal, reread the purchasing agreement, to make sure you understand all of the language, and walk through the facility a final time, to make sure all equipment and materials are in place.

RESOURCES FOR MORE INFORMATION

ASSOCIATIONS

- *American Society of Appraisers (ASA)*, 555 Herndon Parkway, Suite 125 Herndon, VA 20170; 703-478-2228; www.appraisers.org. If you are looking for a business appraiser, contact the ASA. This organization has over 55 years experience and is the only major appraisal agency that represents all appraisal disciplines: business valuation, real property, personal property, and machinery.

- *Association of Small Business Development Centers*, 3108 Columbia Pike, Suite 300, Arlington, VA 22204; 703-271-8700; www.asbdc-us.org. The Association offers a partnership program that brings together government, higher education, private enterprise, and local nonprofit economic development organizations to provide support for small businesses. Through it, small business owners can receive information about a variety of issues, including business plan writing, human resources development, financing, and acquisitions.

- *The Institute of Business Appraisers (IBA)*, P.O. Box 1447, Boynton Beach, FL 33425; 561-732-3202; www.instbusapp.org. The IBA was founded in 1978. It focuses exclusively on the appraisal of closely held businesses. Members are provided technical assistance, access to a database of private transactions, and a bibliographic file of business valuations. This organization will also help you find a business appraiser to value a company you are looking to buy.

- *International Business Brokers Association, Inc. (IBBA)*, 11250 Roger Bacon Drive, Suite 8, Reston, VA 20190; 703-437-7464; www.ibba.org. IBBA is an organization that can help you buy or sell a business. It is the largest international nonprofit association devoted exclusively to supporting individuals involved in business brokerage, mergers, and acquisitions. This organization also provides a number of educational programs and networking activities to educate buyers and sellers about acquisitions.

- *National Black Chamber of Commerce (NBCC)*, 2000 L Street NW, Suite 200, Washington, DC 20036; 202-416-1622; www.nbcc-e-train.org. NBCC is an umbrella organization for hundreds of affiliates nationwide. The organization supports new and existing business owners by providing information on topics such as start-up financing, procurement, advertising, acquisitions, and management.

(continued)

RESOURCES FOR MORE INFORMATION *(continued)*

- *Service Corps of Retired Executives (SCORE),* 409 Third Street SW, Washington, DC 20024; 800-634-0245; www.score.org. SCORE is a nonprofit volunteer association that advises business owners on a number of issues, including how to start and grow an enterprise and how to buy and sell a business. The organization holds a number of workshops, including one titled "Buying a Business," which, led by a member of the business brokerage community, provides information on how to evaluate a business and determine its true worth.

15

FRANCHISING

When most people think of franchises, they immediately envision a Big Mac, crispy golden french fries, and a chocolate shake. McDonald's is one of the most popular and successful franchises in the nation, but several others have carved out a place in their industries as well: Jackson Hewitt, Heel Quick!, Coverall, Lawn Doctor, Dunkin' Donuts, Blockbuster, CruiseOne, Molly Maid, and Baskin-Robbins, to name a few. All types of businesses have been franchised. According to the International Franchise Association, there are more than 600,000 American franchises, and they generate $1 trillion in sales.

John Daniels and Valerie Daniels-Carter are two of the most successful African American franchisees in the nation. Owners of V & J Foods Inc., in Milwaukee, Wisconsin, the brother-and-sister team owns a string of Burger King outlets in Detroit and Milwaukee. In 1997, they carved out an even bigger piece of the franchising pie by purchasing 61 Pizza Hut franchises in Rochester and Syracuse, New York. Together, the franchises have earned V & J Foods $70 million in sales and a slot on the *B.E.* Industrial/Service 100, an annual listing of the nation's largest black-owned businesses, published by *Black Enterprise* magazine. And these savvy entrepreneurs are not the only ones who have found success through franchising.

Jonathan and Beverly Chandler are also establishing themselves in this booming industry. The Chandlers became franchisees in 1996, when they purchased Padgett Business Services, an accounting and tax services franchise. The husband-and-wife team operated a home-based accounting company for eight years prior to entering the franchise industry. But when they had to move from Alabama to Memphis, Tennessee, to care for Jonathan's elderly parents, the Chandlers had to shut down their company. The move was sudden; they did not have the time needed to rebuild the business nor enough marketing expertise to research a new market. They decided to purchase a franchise in the same field. To raise the $35,000 in start-up costs, the two secured a loan from an independent banker and began operating Padgett from their new home. During the first eight months in operation in Tennessee, the Chandlers earned $20,000 in revenues. In 1998, their business generated nearly $50,000.

As one of the reasons they like franchises, the Chandlers cite the support services that they provide. "We take advantage of Padgett's marketing tools to get clients," says Beverly Chandler. "They have a nine-week program that allows a client to get acquainted with us and our business. We do one thing each of those nine weeks—make an initial cold call, send a thank-you card, make follow-up calls, and send additional information. Then, in the ninth week, we do a site visit. By that time, people fully understand the service that we provide and, as a result, we get appointments."

Jonathan Chandler adds: "We also use marketing data; that helps us speak the language of a diversity of businesses such as florists, beauty salons, and restaurants."[1]

Ongoing support is one of the main reasons why aspiring entrepreneurs choose to purchase a franchise rather than start a business from scratch. But it is not the only motivator. Many people who want to become business owners buy a franchise because franchises have a higher success rate than start-ups. Statistics indicate that less than 20 percent of all franchises fail whereas half of all start-ups close their doors during the first four years of operation.

Reduced risk does make franchising an attractive option for ownership, but purchasing a franchise is not a guarantee of success. To be a successful franchisee, you must have the knowledge, skills, drive, competitiveness, and attitude to make it work. Granted, the franchisor gives you the right to sell a well-known product or service that it has designed, but the franchisor will not run the business for you while you cool your heels and collect the cash. When operating a franchise, you have to take the same hands-on approach that you would have if you were building a business from the ground up.

In this chapter, we will discuss the process of purchasing a franchise and the advantages and disadvantages of pursuing this type of venture. The steps you will have to take to buy a franchise are not unlike those required to buy a going concern. For example, before plunking down any money, you must first determine your reasons for wanting to become an entrepreneur and outline your goals. Not everyone is cut out to operate a franchise. Many people who decide to go into business for themselves do so because they want the freedom to run their own shop according to their rules and vision. But when you're operating a franchise, you do not have license to call all the shots. You must follow specific guidelines (and pay certain ongoing fees) in order to operate this type of venture. If you are a person who enjoys total autonomy, franchising is not for you.

In addition to conducting a personal appraisal, you must search for a franchise that matches your talents and your tastes. There are a number of places you can look to find a franchise; we will examine some resources that will help you find a franchise that's right for you. We will also show you how to investigate this business opportunity and identify ways to finance your new venture.

WHAT IS FRANCHISING?

Franchises first became popular in the United States in the 1960s, but the concept was born well over 100 years ago. Franchising began in the 1840s in Germany, when major ale brewing companies gave certain taverns the exclusive right to sell their ale. In 1851, the Singer Sewing Machine Company issued distribution franchises for its sewing machines, and in the 1880s, many cities granted monopoly franchises to streetcar, electric, gas, water, and sewage companies. These events triggered franchising as we know it today.

What exactly is a franchise and why are franchises so popular? A franchise is a contractual arrangement in which the owner of a business concept (the franchisor) gives a businessperson (the franchisee) the right to own and operate a business based on that concept. As a franchisee, you buy the right to sell a trademarked product or service designed by the franchisor. For the privilege of using the product or service, the franchisee is required to pay a franchise fee plus start-up costs, ongoing royalty fees, and operating expenses (inventory, rent, build-out, and so on). In return, the franchisor provides assistance with choosing a location for the franchise and developing the site. The franchisor may also offer job training, and advice on marketing, management, personnel, and finance issues. Some franchisors issue monthly newsletters, hold frequent workshops and seminars catering to the needs of franchisees, and maintain a toll-free 800 number for technical assistance. The assistance that is available will depend on the type of franchise you select. The exact services that a franchisor provides for each franchise are described in the Uniform Franchise Offering Circular (UFOC), which we will discuss later in this chapter.

As mentioned earlier, thousands of franchises are scattered across the nation. More than likely, a handful can be found in your own neighborhood. All franchises fall into one of the following three categories:

1. *Business format franchise.* This is the most popular and best known type of franchise. A business format franchise provides the franchisee with a complete package of tools and materials for operating

a business. Often called a turnkey package, this type of franchise gives the franchisee the right to use the company name, products, internal systems, quality assurance standards, marketing and advertising techniques, operational procedures, and facility design. Examples of business format franchises are: fast-food restaurants and convenience stores.

2. *Product and trade-name franchise.* This type of franchise involves the distribution of a product through a dealer. For example, a Saturn dealership would be a product and trade-name franchise because it sells products produced by the franchisor. Although the franchisee is limited to selling only the products included in this type of arrangement, the franchisee does enjoy the recognition and notoriety that accompany the franchise name and history. The franchisee may also receive financial, managerial, and marketing support from the franchisor.

3. *Affiliate or conversion franchise.* This franchise is generally used by a group of independent entrepreneurs who operate in a segmented industry. To create more visibility for themselves, these business owners pool their monetary resources, advertising contacts, and marketing expertise to form a franchise network. The group is not required to use the franchise name in order to conduct business. However, to identify their outlet, many will take on the trade name as well as their own.

No matter which type of franchise you choose to purchase, you will experience several advantages and disadvantages. Let's look at each in turn.

Advantages of Buying a Franchise

Name Recognition
One of the greatest challenges when starting a new business is development of name recognition. Customers have no idea what your new business is like, or what types of products or services you provide, so getting them to come through your doors can be difficult at first. But when you purchase a franchise, you are buying an established name with a proven record of success. As a result, you are able to attract customers and generate sales immediately, which translates into a cash flow for your business.

Financial Support
There are a number of ways to obtain the capital necessary to purchase a franchise. You can secure a bank loan, ask family or friends, or contact the Small Business Administration (SBA) about a guaranteed loan. Lending institutions tend to look more favorably on franchises than on start-ups, so, as

a potential franchisee, you may receive a warmer welcome from your neighborhood bank when you ask for financing. Most franchisors will assist you in finding the funds that you need to make the purchase. Some may even provide financing themselves by covering some of the costs of the initial franchise fee, equipment purchases, leasehold improvements, and land acquisition (if necessary).

Reduced Risk

You will assume less risk when purchasing a franchise because franchises are established businesses with proven success. Many of the errors you might make as the owner of a start-up are eliminated when you purchase a franchise, because the franchisor has already ironed out the wrinkles. Most franchise owners plunk down their money, manage the operation, and watch the profits roll in. Less than 20 percent of all franchises fail.

National and Local Advertising Assistance

One of the greatest expenses you will incur as a new business owner is advertising. As a franchisee, you cut some of these costs and increase your level of exposure at the same time. The types of advertising used will depend on the franchisor and its size, but many have budgets big enough to create glitzy ad campaigns with widespread visibility. (Look at what Taco Bell and McDonald's have done over the years.) As a franchisee, you would benefit from this publicity.

Reduced Cost on Equipment/Other Materials

Franchisors have major purchasing power. They can buy items in bulk at much cheaper prices than individual business owners can negotiate. As a franchisee, you will have low costs for equipment and inventory.

Site Selection

Some franchises belong in certain locales. A franchisor knows where an ice cream parlor, burger joint, lawn care service, residential cleaning company, or tax preparation service will generate the most sales. To that end, most franchisors will help you choose a site that will showcase your business. You may also receive help in developing your facility.

Job Training

One of the main reasons entrepreneurs purchase franchises is to take advantage of the training that is provided. The amount of training offered will depend on the type of franchise that you purchase and how much you know about the franchisor's products or services. For example, if you have 20 years' experience in preparing income tax returns and you purchase a Triple Check Income Tax Service franchise, chances are you will not need much training. As part of the training, most franchisors will offer marketing and management support. Others even supply employee training.

Use of Operations Manual

One of the biggest challenges in starting a new business is finding the right people to operate it. You may find workers who have the experience and skills to do the job, but you will probably have to offer some kind of training to fully introduce them to your business operations and culture. When purchasing a franchise, the job training is made easier because of the operations manual provided by the franchisor. This manual offers helpful information for your own training as well as that of the individuals you hire to help run your business.

Disadvantages of Buying a Franchise

High Cost

Purchasing a franchise can be a budget breaker. The costs vary according to the type of franchise that you buy; however, you can spend well over $100,000 to get your franchise off the ground and running smoothly. You will incur a number of costs as a franchisee. You must pay an up-front franchise fee for the privilege of using the franchisor's name and established format and system. The fee can range from $5,000 to $50,000 or more. In addition, you must pay the start-up costs. Like the franchise fee, they vary from $2,000 to $2 million, depending on the type of franchise that you buy. (Start-up costs for a McDonald's franchise range from $400,000 to $600,000, as opposed to Travel Network costs, which are $1,000 to $15,000.) In most cases, franchisees must pay ongoing royalty fees to the franchisor whether they earn a significant income or not, and regardless of whether the franchisor delivers promised support. These fees are based on a percentage of your weekly or monthly gross income. They can range between 2 percent and 15 percent, depending on the franchise. Like other business owners, franchisees must meet typical operating costs such as rent, inventory, leasehold improvements, utilities, insurance, employees' salaries, and equipment. But unlike entrepreneurs who have started a business from scratch, franchisees may have to contribute a percentage of their income to a national advertising fund. Paying into this fund helps to increase the visibility of each franchise, but it can also drain needed money from your business. You have no control over how your contribution is spent. It may, in fact, go toward attracting more franchise owners in your region.

Loss of Control

Most people decide to open their own shop because it gives them the opportunity to be their own boss. When you purchase a franchise, you are required to operate your business according to a set of guidelines set forth by the franchisor and outlined in the franchise agreement. You become more a manager than a boss. You do not call the shots. If you think that you can purchase a Baskin-Robbins and add to your menu a recipe that your great-great-grandmother used when you were a kid, think again. Besides dictating the types of products and services that you are permitted to sell, franchisors control a number of other day-to-day decisions as part of their effort to maintain uniformity among their outlets. Here are some of the control factors:

1. *Facility design and appearance.* To ensure that customers receive the same quality of products or services in each outlet, franchisors will often require that their facilities maintain a specific design and appearance. Some franchisors will also require periodic renovations and seasonal changes. These modifications can increase your operating costs considerably but must be adhered to.

2. *Method of operation.* Franchisors may require that you operate your franchise in a particular manner. For example, they may dictate your hours of operation, use of employee uniforms, preapproved signage, kinds of advertising, and supplies and vendors. All of the required methods of operation are spelled out in the franchise agreement, which we will discuss later in this chapter.

3. *Geographic sales area.* Franchisors can restrict the areas or territories in which you are permitted to operate. This rule is often imposed to keep one franchisee from competing with another for the same customers, but it can be a hindrance to your business if your location is not lucrative or if you would like to purchase additional franchises in other parts of your city or state.

4. *Franchise location.* Even if you find a spot that would be ideal for your franchise, you may not be able to use it. Most franchisors preapprove the sites for their franchises. For most franchisees, this is an advantage because the franchisor has expertise in choosing profitable locations. But if you are adamant about using a particular corner lot with a huge parking lot and the franchisor rejects your choice, the two of you could find yourselves at an impasse.

Binding Agreement

Every franchisee has to sign a franchise agreement. This document is the foundation on which your franchise is built because it clearly outlines the obligations of both the franchisee and franchisor, as well as all fees that must be paid. The agreement is binding and quite restrictive. Franchisees must follow all the guidelines stated in the agreement or risk forfeiting their rights to operate the franchise.

Share in Problems of the Parent Company

Just as a franchisee experiences the successes of the franchisor, he or she also has to bear the failures. As a franchisee, you buy the name, the product, and the image of a larger company. Therefore, you cannot separate yourself from the parent company in good times *or* bad times.

Is Franchising Right for You?

Like any investment, purchasing a franchise has its perks and pitfalls. You must weigh the advantages and disadvantages to determine whether franchising is the right type of business for you. As mentioned previously, not everyone is capable of operating a franchise. Determine whether you have what it takes to be a franchisee *before* investing your hard-earned dollars.

Whether you purchase a franchise, buy an existing firm, or start a business from scratch, one of the biggest mistakes that you can make is to rush your decision. Entrepreneurship is not something you should take lightly. Before jumping into it (or into any venture), outline your reasons for wanting to become a business owner (see Chapter 1). Is it because of a wish for financial freedom, a chance to pursue an idea that you've always dreamed about, or an opportunity to make lots of money? Identifying your goals will help you determine whether franchising is right for you. For example, if your goal is to operate a business for a short period of time—let's say five years—you will not want to purchase a franchise. Franchising is a long-term relationship between the franchisee and the franchisor. It is not uncommon for some franchisors to lock franchisees in for 20 years, so unless you plan to be in it for the long haul, look for another form of ownership.

In addition to your business goals, review your skills and abilities. As discussed in Chapter 1, successful and savvy entrepreneurs possess certain qualities: a competitive attitude, self-confidence, and strong leadership and managerial skills. Even though training is provided for most franchisees, having these attributes will make it easier for you to operate your outlet.

Lastly, go back over your budget. How much can you afford to spend? To purchase a franchise, you will need money for the franchise fee, start-up costs, ongoing royalty payments, advertising fees, and operating expenses. The total can quickly run into six figures, so if you can spare only $50,000 for your entrepreneurial endeavor, consider starting a small business from scratch or acquiring an existing firm. If after assessing your skills and your budget, you find that you are franchise material, you can then begin your search.

FINDING A FRANCHISE

When Kathy Burton decided to leave her job at H&R Block to purchase a franchise in 1994, she didn't have to look very far to find one that was right for her. "The general manager at H&R Block had moved to Jackson Hewitt, and she invited me to come over with her and work," says Burton, who worked at H&R Block for eight years before becoming a franchisee.

Burton worked with her former general manager for one tax season at Jackson Hewitt Tax Services, in Houston, Texas. That experience convinced Burton that she could make a comfortable living in the franchise industry. But, like most people who start their own businesses or buy an existing company, Burton did not have the capital to make the purchase. "I was worried how I was going to buy a franchise. After tax season ended, there were very few positions that were available, so I had to go on unemployment. Fortunately, I found a job and was able to pay the $25,000 franchise fee up front. The franchisor helped me with the start-up costs by allowing me to buy everything on credit. I repaid the loan that tax season."

Today, Burton owns and operates five Jackson Hewitt franchises. Her revenues in 1998 reached $375,000.

Where to Look for Franchise Opportunities

Like Burton, you can find a franchise by simply looking at your own environs. Perhaps a former coworker, a family member, or a friend has recently purchased a franchise. If you want to buy a franchise and you know exactly what kind you would like to acquire, you can approach the franchisor directly or contact a franchisee who may be interested in selling his or her outlet. There are several ways to find a franchise that matches your talents, your tastes, and your pocketbook. Here are some of the resources you should check.

Newspaper
Most newspapers maintain, in their classified ads, a list of franchises and other businesses for sale. *The Wall Street Journal* has an entire section dedicated to "Business Opportunities." Compare the list over a period of weeks to get a sense of what franchises are bought quickly (the ads disappear).

World Wide Web
When looking for any business to buy, whether a franchise or an existing concern, the Internet is a valuable resource. Use a major search engine, such as AltaVista or Excite, to find franchises for sale, or visit Web sites dedicated to the franchise industry. Among the latter are the International Franchise Association (IFA) site (www.franchise.org) and the American Association of Franchisees & Dealers (AAFD) site (www.aafd.org). When visiting the IFA Web site, you can view the association's annual *Franchise Opportunities Guide Online*, which allows you to search for a franchise by category, investment range, and location. You can order a printed copy of the entire *Guide* by contacting the IFA office at 202-628-8000.

Business Brokers

These professionals match buyers with sellers. They can help you find a franchise that matches your criteria. A business broker can preselect franchises for you, prescreen them to determine whether there are any inherent problems, and negotiate the sale. The drawback to using a broker is that, in addition to the sale price, you must pay the broker's fee, but the experience a broker brings to an acquisition is invaluable. (See Chapter 14 for a complete discussion on how to find and use business brokers effectively.)

Franchise Expositions

By attending a franchise exposition or trade show, you are afforded the opportunity to talk to many franchisors and industry experts in one location. These shows usually have workshops and seminars that educate potential franchisees about the industry and explore the advantages and disadvantages of purchasing a franchise. Attending a franchise exposition can put you in a candyland of ideas, but don't let yourself be persuaded into making any binding decisions. Before attending one of these shows, conduct a preliminary review of the type of franchise that best suits your investment range and business goals. An exhibiting franchisor may try to tell you how much you can afford or insist that you cannot pass up this "once-in-a-lifetime" offer. Don't be persuaded by such hard-sell tactics. Always keep in mind how much money you can comfortably part with, and what type of franchise you think you could operate comfortably for the next 20 years.

An exhibitor may also try to persuade you that a particular opportunity is perfect for you, but only you can make that decision. You know what you like and what skills you will be able to bring to a franchise. As you tour the trade show floor, do some comparison shopping for an opportunity that meets your criteria. Don't just take brochures and packets of information from each table. Ask questions and take detailed notes. How long has the franchisor been in business? How many franchised outlets are currently in existence? Where are they located? Discuss all fees and costs that apply to purchasing the franchise. Some franchisors may offer earnings *estimates* to potential buyers to indicate how well current franchisees are doing. If an exhibitor makes any such claims, ask for a written substantiation, as required by rules set forth by the Federal Trade Commission.

To find scheduled franchise expositions, search the Trade Show Central Web site at www.tscentral.com, or check with your local chamber of commerce for a list of upcoming shows.

Business Publications

Several business-related magazines list franchises for sale or provide general information about the industry in feature articles. Since 1987, *Black Enterprise* has provided a comprehensive list of franchise companies that offer the best opportunities for African American business owners. Many of the lists have categorized the most affordable franchises for small entrepreneurs, and the best home-based franchises for black business owners. Throughout the year, the magazine publishes feature articles about the franchising industry and highlights individuals who have found success with these types of ventures.

Factors to Consider When Evaluating Franchise Opportunities

When conducting your search, always keep your abilities and business goals in mind. Don't just consider a Taco Bell franchise because you like to make and eat tacos, or a Century 21 franchise because you love to look at expensive homes. Neither of these franchises may be a strong fit for you. Whatever choice you make, it should be based on hard facts. These are the elements that should determine your selection.

Competition
No matter what type of franchise you choose to buy, you will have to deal with competition. It may not be next door to your outlet, but it could very well be in the same geographic area. When scouting a franchise, consider the level of local and national competition. Find out how many franchised and company-owned outlets the franchisor has in the area where you are hoping to set up shop. Determine what types of products or services those franchises offer. Are they similar to what you want to sell? Are they offered at the same price or a higher or lower price?

Name Recognition
Potential business owners often purchase franchises because they have a well-known and respected brand name; in fact, name recognition is often considered the biggest benefit of buying a franchise. But be aware that not every franchise will have mass appeal. Is the franchise you have your eye on widely recognized? Does it have a registered trademark? If you have never heard of a particular franchise, determine how long the franchisor has been in operation and whether the company has a reputation for selling quality products and services. If customers have filed complaints against a franchise that interests you, thoroughly investigate the grievances before making a final decision on a purchase.

Demand for Product or Service
If consumers do not want or need a particular product or service, they are not likely to become customers for your business even if you are the nicest person to walk the planet and offer superior service. To attract consumers, there must be a demand for the items you sell. To that end, when searching for a franchise, consider the demand for the types of goods or services that your outlet would provide. Is the demand seasonal, temporary, or long-lasting?

For example, if you choose to operate a Lawn Doctor franchise in a northern region, you are not likely to generate brisk business year-round. Most of your business will be conducted during the spring and summer. If you would prefer to operate a franchise that allows the potential for a steady cash flow 365 days a year, don't choose a seasonal franchise.

Support Services

Training is another advantage to purchasing a franchise. When shopping for an outlet, determine what training (if any) will be provided, and match that against the training provided for other workers in the industry that the franchise serves. Identify the franchisor's experience and background skills, and find out how long the franchisor has managed a franchised system. Proper training cannot come from someone who does not have the necessary knowledge.

Potential Growth

Like any other business owner, you will want to grow your franchise and achieve greater success and more profits. But if you grow too quickly, you could grow yourself right out of business. To what extent is the franchisor able to provide promised support services and other training? Consider the franchisor's growth plans, and examine the amount of financial resources and staff it has available to effectively support its successful franchisees.

INVESTIGATING THE FRANCHISE

When you have selected a franchise that you feel you can comfortably operate, your next major step is to investigate the franchisor. But before you begin your detective work, familiarize yourself with the laws that regulate the franchising industry. They will help you make a smarter and more informed decision.

Franchise Laws

The majority of franchises are legitimate operations, but there is always a possibility that con artists are preying on innocent people who want to become business owners but lack the savvy to spot a scam when they see one. To protect against that possibility, states and the federal government have instituted disclosure regulations that govern the franchising industry and protect potential entrepreneurs from financial ruin.

The most important protection for potential franchisees comes from the Federal Trade Commission (FTC) Franchising and Business Opportunity Ventures Trade Regulation Rules. Known as "the FTC rules," these regulations were instituted in 1979. They require that franchisors provide franchisees with full disclosure of all the information that they need to make an informed and rational decision about whether to purchase a franchise. The information is supplied in a document called the Uniform Franchise Offering Circular (UFOC). Franchisors are obligated, under law, to present a UFOC to the prospective franchisee during the first meeting at which the possibility of purchasing a franchise is discussed or at least ten business days before the franchisee signs any documents or makes any payments. Under the FTC rules, the franchisor must also supply completed contracts (the franchise agreement) covering all details of the franchising arrangement at least five days before the franchisee signs any forms or issues any money. Later in this chapter, we will discuss the various components of a standard UFOC and some items you can expect to see in your franchise agreement. If a franchisor fails to supply a UFOC to a potential franchisee, the franchisor could be subject to a $10,000 fine, plus damages.

The FTC does not require that franchisors register with the Commission in order to conduct business, but several states do impose registration rules: franchisors must sign up with a municipality before offering franchises for sale. In some states, franchise requirements are stricter than those enforced by the FTC. At press time, 13 states required registration: California, Hawaii, Illinois, Indiana, Maryland, Minnesota, New York, North Dakota, Rhode Island, South Dakota, Virginia, Washington, and Wisconsin.

If, during your search for a franchise or even after investing thousands of dollars, you find that a franchisor has violated the law, act quickly. Contact the FTC, your state district attorney, or a consumer protection agency in your area. Besides protecting you from unscrupulous sellers, the legal system allows you recourse in the courts.

Information Included in the Uniform Franchise Offering Circular (UFOC)

Think of the UFOC as your own personalized tour through a franchise you want to buy. This disclosure document provides a detailed account of what you can expect when purchasing a franchise; everything from the franchise fee to services provided and the grounds on which your arrangement can be terminated. The terms outlined in this document are uniform and nonnegotiable.

The details provided in the UFOC must comply with the FTC rules. Read the document and then have your attorney or accountant verify your understanding of its content. Too often, franchisees simply glance over portions of the document and sign by the "X" without raising questions or asking for clarification. Read the UFOC from beginning to end. If necessary, read it two or three times to make sure you understand *all* of the terms that are presented. Your due diligence in comprehending the document will help you avoid problems in the future.

The UFOC contains 23 items of information about a franchise. Here are just a few of the points you can expect to find when poring over this document.

Franchise Background

This is the first section you will find in the UFOC. It provides a brief history of the franchise and includes such information as when the company was founded, when it actually began operations, and the date it started franchising. If the company is incorporated, the date of incorporation is given. The background section of the UFOC is very important because it alerts the franchisee to the franchisor's level of experience. If the franchisor has been in business for 35 years and has been franchising for the past 15, you will probably do well by purchasing that franchise. If the franchisor launched the company only three years ago and has franchised for just one year, you should exercise caution. More than likely, this franchisor has little experience in the industry and may not be able to serve your needs.

Franchise Fees and Royalties

This section outlines in full detail the cost of the franchise fee and the royalties franchisees are expected to pay. As previously mentioned, franchise fees vary according to the size and type of the franchise, but can range from $5,000 to $50,000 or more. Royalties, generally paid on a monthly basis, are a percentage of your gross income and can run as high as 15 percent. Contributions to an advertising fund, if required by the franchisor, can siphon off an additional 5 percent of your gross income. When considering the costs of purchasing a franchise, remember that the franchise fee does not include the costs involved in actually operating the outlet. Rent, inventory, salaries, and equipment are separate expenses.

Resumes of Company Executives and Directors

This portion of the document identifies the executives of the franchise and briefly explains their background and experience. Pay attention to their general business background as well as their expertise in the franchise industry. You may find that a director of the company has extensive skills in general business functions, but no particular expertise in operating a franchise—or vice versa. Determine what's most important to you and your needs as a franchisee, when reviewing these credentials.

Litigation History

The last thing you will want to learn after plunking down several thousand dollars to purchase a franchise is that the franchisor was involved in a series of class action suits filed by franchisees. Carefully study this section of the UFOC. It will indicate any major civil, criminal, or bankruptcy actions that the company has been involved in, and any felonies, fraud, or violation of franchise law that particular executives have committed. Lawsuits are not uncommon these days. Because a franchisor has experienced litigation in the past, you should not conclude that there are huge problems with the company. On the other hand, if several claims have been filed against the franchisor, it could indicate lapses in living up to the promised support, or serious discontent among franchisees who are unhappy with the arrangement. If the franchisor has experienced lawsuits, investigate the reasons and the outcomes.

Terms of the Franchise Agreement
The franchise agreement is a separate document, but the terms of the agreement are mentioned in the UFOC as well. The franchise agreement is for a limited time, and there is no guarantee that you will be able to renew it. Most franchisors offer terms of 5 to 10 years (some offer 20 years) with an option to renew when the contract expires. However, it is not uncommon to find deals of 5 to 10 years in which the franchisor does not offer an option to renew. Some franchisors provide the renewal option but charge a higher franchise fee, impose new sales and design restrictions, and require an increased royalty payment if the franchisee wants to continue operating the outlet. Renewal of your contract does not guarantee that you will enjoy the terms of the original deal, so be prepared for changes.

Start-Up Costs
This section is separate from the discussion of franchise fees and royalties. In this part of the UFOC, you will find information about the costs you will incur to actually operate the franchise. It lists expenses such as rent, equipment, inventory, leasehold improvements, insurance, employee salaries and benefits, and business licenses and permits. Estimate your operating costs for the first year in operation, and compare the total with what other franchisees actually doled out during their first year in business. Ask your accountant to help you evaluate your costs.

Grounds for Termination
A franchisor can end your franchise agreement if you fail to pay required royalties, violate standard operating procedures, or allow your location to deteriorate in appearance and value. This part of the UFOC outlines all the conditions under which the franchisor can terminate your franchise agreement before it actually expires. A franchisee may not end the agreement under any circumstances, but, under certain circumstances, you can sell or assign your franchise to another person. If you follow the guidelines set forth by the franchisor, pay your royalties on time, and maintain a safe and clean environment for your employees and your customers, you will not have to fear termination. However, if you go against any of the franchisor's rules, the franchisor could use noncompliance as a reason to give you your walking papers. The franchisor may find a better franchisee to operate the location or simply reacquire the outlet. Provisions in the UFOC permit termination

based on certain conditions, but several states make it very difficult for a franchisor to fire a franchisee before the agreement is supposed to end.

Earnings Claims

The FTC requires that if a franchisor makes claims regarding the amount of sales a potential franchisee can make, the franchisor must provide a written substantiation of those claims. For this reason, few franchisors indicate projected sales. In this section, you will find information about earnings potential. As you review this information, keep in mind that each franchisee is different. The success of one franchisee does not automatically guarantee that you will succeed. When poring over the numbers, consider the following factors:

1. *Average incomes.* A franchisor will often provide an average income of its franchise system. This offers little indication of how each individual franchisee is doing, or what costs and profits he or she is experiencing. By quoting an average income of, say, $100,000 for the entire system, the franchisor could be misleading franchisees about how well their particular outlet will succeed. Average numbers may make the franchise look more successful than it actually is.

2. *Geographic area.* How much a franchise will earn will vary according to where it is located. A residential cleaning franchise in Beverly Hills, California, might generate more income than the same franchise on the South Side of Chicago. If the UFOC lists the income of a particular franchise, always ask where the outlet is located.

3. *Franchisee's background.* Each franchisee brings his or her own talents and skills to a franchise and a difference in background or experience may affect how well each operates the business. Therefore, no two franchisees will realize the same financial success. Keep this in mind as you review the earnings claims.

4. *Sample size.* The sample size the franchisor uses to gauge potential sales may not reflect the entire franchise system. For example, if a franchisor lists yearly earnings of $75,000 but only a few franchisees generate this level of revenue for a particular year, it will not be representative of the actual amount earned by the outlets. Always ask how many franchisees were included in the sample size to arrive at the figure listed.

5. *Gross sales.* As with average incomes, some franchisors may only indicate gross sales, which offer little information about costs and profits. A franchisee who has high gross sales may actually be losing money because of the high cost of overhead and other expenses. Be careful about using gross sales as a measuring rod for what you might earn.

The best way to find out about a franchise's actual finances is to talk with current franchisees about their financial status. (We will discuss how you can conduct an interview with existing franchisees later in this chapter.)

Territory Rights

As much as you might like to have a 10- or 12-block radius all to yourself, you are not entitled to dominate a particular geographic area or territory when purchasing a franchise. Most UFOCs will state that it is not the policy of the franchisor to permit another franchise to move into the same neighborhood, but this doesn't mean you won't find a similar outfit a stone's throw away.

Required Purchases

If you plan to purchase a product-oriented franchise, the UFOC will indicate that you must buy goods from preapproved suppliers and vendors. It will also indicate the types of products or services you are permitted to offer.

Franchisor's Obligations

After reading about all of the fees and restrictions placed on the shoulders of the franchisee, you may be wondering what you get out of this whole arrangement. Well, there are certain obligations that the franchisor has to meet. They generally include an offer of training, site selection, and continuing support in the form of advertising, marketing, and management. When reviewing this section of the UFOC, keep in mind that it will list only general responsibilities on the part of the franchisor. To get a detailed account of how the franchisor can lend a helping hand, obtain a copy of the franchisor's operating manual and meet with the personnel who actually provide the assistance that is described.

Financial Information

The UFOC provides three years' audited financial statements, including the franchisor's balance sheet and income statement for the most recent fiscal year. You can study these documents to gauge the financial health of the franchise. Always consult your attorney or accountant when reviewing this part of the disclosure document. He or she can help you pinpoint whether the franchisor has steady growth and what percentage of profits is being reinvested in the company to provide support to the franchisees. Dialogue with current franchisees about their income and expenses. It's the best way to get the most accurate information. You can also talk with industry experts and others operating the type of business you hope to purchase.

Franchisee Contact List

This is one of the most important areas of the UFOC because it is probably the most effective way for you to substantiate the franchisor's claims. In this section are the names, telephone numbers, and addresses of current and former franchisees. Contact as many people on the list as possible, and ask them about their experiences with the franchise you anticipate purchasing.

Conducting a Franchisor or Franchisee Interview

The interview process is an important part of your investigative efforts. After you obtain the UFOC from the franchisor and review it in detail, you should formally meet with the franchisor to begin negotiations. Concurrently, you should contact current and/or past franchisees to gauge the viability of the franchise arrangement.

When you meet with the franchisor, you will be dealing with the franchise owner, a franchise broker, or another salesperson representing the parent company. The franchisor will expect you to present information detailing your financial status, your background, and your business experience. Be prepared to ask questions of your own. This is the perfect time to raise questions and to clarify terms and projections found in the UFOC. Don't be shy!

Here are some questions you may want to ask the franchisor:

- Will the franchisee be required to provide working capital in addition to the franchise and royalty fees? If so, how much?
- Does the parent company have plans to expand in the near future? Has it identified the new locations it expects to reach?
- Have any franchises gone bankrupt or been terminated? (If so, find out how many and the reasons for the failures.)
- What types of financing does the franchisor offer, if any?
- Have any franchisees filed suit against the franchisor? If so, how were the grievances settled?
- What are the current prices for the products and supplies the franchisor orders for its outlet?

Franchisors should be forthright in their descriptions of their obligations and of what you are required to do. If you come across a franchisor who skirts the issues, asks for deposits to hold a franchise, or is unwilling to hand over a franchise contact list, move on to the next. You may be looking at a con artist who is just waiting to rob you of your money.

As we have stated, you should interview current and former franchisees who are willing to talk with you. Keep in mind that even the persons named on the franchisee contact list are not obligated to talk with you. To encourage them to describe their experiences, emphasize that the entire discussion will be kept confidential. If they adamantly refuse to speak with you, it could be a sign that they are unhappy with the present

arrangement or are not experiencing the financial success they had anticipated. If you come across an uncooperative franchisee, move on to the next.
Eventually, you should find someone who is willing to give you the information you need.

Here is a list of questions you should ask when conducting your franchisee interviews:

- How long has the franchisee operated the outlet?
- What were the initial start-up costs?
- Were there any hidden or unexpected costs?
- Does the franchise have a good location?
- Did the franchisor provide training? If so, was it helpful?
- How long did it take for the franchisee to earn a profit?
- What regular operating costs does the franchisee have?
- What experience did the franchisee bring to the enterprise?
- What support services does the franchisor offer?
- What are the annual income and expenses? (Compare these figures
  with any earnings claims the franchisor has made.)
- Did the franchisor provide logos, signage, and other equipment at no
  additional cost, or was the franchisee responsible for acquiring them?
- Is the franchisee afforded any control, or are regulations tightly
  enforced?
- Have there been any problems with product supply?
- How was the purchase financed?
- How many hours does the franchisee work in an average week?
- Does the franchisee belong to a franchise owner's association?
- Would the franchisee consider purchasing another unit of this
  franchise?

Besides reviewing the UFOC and conducting interviews with the franchisor and franchisees, perform a credit check on the franchisor and check
any references the franchisor may provide. Banks on the reference list
should be able to give you a Dun & Bradstreet report detailing the financial
status of the franchisor. You should also contact the Better Business Bureau
to see whether any recent complaints have been filed against the parent
company.

The Franchise Agreement

The franchise agreement is a binding contract between the franchisor
and the franchisee. You must sign that contract when making the purchase.

It spells out the operating procedures of the franchise and indicates the obligations of both parties.

No two franchise agreements are alike because this contract is fashioned to suit each situation. However, here are some basic issues that are covered in most of these documents:

Fees
The agreement will state the amount of the franchise fee and the royalty fee. It will also indicate how, and how often, the franchisor will collect these fees.

Location Provisions
The franchisor has the right to preapprove sites and, if it so chooses, enter a lease arrangement. This means that your franchise agreement could be tied to a specific leased location.

Franchisor Obligations
Most franchisors will assist you with site selection and development. They will also help you acquire equipment and inventory.

Operating Manual Requirements
The franchisor will require that you comply with the company's operating manual and run the outlet using the systems, supplies, and other products requested by the company. Although the franchisor can dictate the types of vendors that you can use, it cannot require you to buy products from a particular supplier if you can obtain the same items at a lower price elsewhere. This has been a sticky point for franchisors over the years and has resulted in many closing their doors.

Signage Requirements
The types of signs you may and may not use will be listed.

Training
The agreement will indicate that the franchisor must offer you assistance during the early stages of your franchise, and that you must complete a training program.

Advertising Obligations
Franchisors typically want to review and approve whatever promotional materials, packaging, and ad copy you use, to make sure that it upholds the image of the entire franchise. If you must contribute to an advertising fund, the amount of your gross income that you will be required to donate will be indicated in this section of the franchise agreement.

Maintenance and Repairs
The agreement will spell out the upkeep that is required for your facility, both internally and externally.

Bookkeeping Provisions

Most franchisors will require that you adhere to certain accounting and record-keeping procedures and that you maintain such documents as weekly sales reports and monthly profit-and-loss reports. It is important that you follow this requirement to the letter. The franchisor has the right to send a company representative to check your books and verify that you are recording your business activities correctly. If errors are found, you could face early termination.

Release of Financial Statements

The franchisor will require that you present annual financial statements prepared and audited by a CPA.

Quality Assurance Standards

The more labor-intensive your franchise, the stricter these guidelines will become. The bottom line is that the franchisor wants to maintain uniformity across its entire franchise system. You will be required to perform certain procedures (outlined in the franchise agreement) that allow each outlet to look and feel the same.

Modification Requirements

The franchisor has the right to change the concept, but you cannot perform modifications at will. Prior approval must be given before any adjustments to the franchise are made.

Terms of the Franchise Arrangement

The franchise agreement will indicate how long you can operate the franchise and what options are available when the initial period ends. The terms will vary according to each franchisee–franchisor relationship, but most franchisors will match the terms of the agreement with the terms of the facility lease. In other words, if the franchisor has entered a 10-year lease for the outlet, the terms of the agreement will be for 10 years as well. After the term expires, most franchisees will have an option to renew. However, the franchisor can opt to sell to another potential candidate or buy back the property.

Cause for Termination

There is a possibility that your franchise agreement will end early. As previously mentioned, you can be terminated if you fail to follow required operating procedures or if your franchise goes bankrupt. The franchise agreement will list the conditions under which you can be fired. It will also indicate the course of action if you are found to be in default, and will specify the amount of time you will have to correct an action against you. For example, if your facility is found to be unclean or unsafe, the franchisor may give you 30 days to correct the deficiency. If you do not comply within this time, your contract could be terminated.

Definition of Franchisee

The agreement will indicate that the term "franchisee" includes you and any persons who will succeed you.

The franchise agreement will include a number of issues other than those mentioned above, so make sure you review the entire document with your attorney and accountant before signing on the dotted line.

FINANCING YOUR FRANCHISE

One of the most difficult tasks for any entrepreneur is to obtain financing. Potential franchisees will often look toward the franchisor for financial assistance. Some franchisors will not provide funding, but most may be willing either to carry the entire amount needed or to finance a percentage (anywhere from 15 to 25 percent) of the start-up costs. The loans may be structured so that the franchisee pays minimal interest, no principal, and a balloon payment several years after setting up shop. Or, the franchisee can be required to begin repaying the loan after the first year in operation. In addition to assisting with start-up expenses, the franchisor may make arrangements with leasing companies that enable the franchisee to obtain equipment at a reduced rate.

After you determine how much financing the franchisor will be willing to provide, you can look toward outside funding. Make a list of all sources from which you may be able to obtain additional capital: family and friends, commercial finance companies, traditional banks, the Small Business Administration, and investor angels. See Chapter 8 for a complete discussion on how to ready your business for debt and equity financing.

After your investigations are complete and you have your financing locked down, all that's left to do is sign. But before you do, go over the language of the UFOC and franchise agreement one last time. If everything checks out, grab your welcome mat, your keys, and start ringing your cash register.

CHECKLIST

THINGS TO DO WHEN BUYING A FRANCHISE

✓ **Identify the types of franchises that are available.** There are three basic types of franchises: (1) product and trade-name franchises (such as gas stations) which involve the distribution of a product through dealers; (2) business format franchises, which offer a turnkey package to the franchisee in the form of trade names, operating procedures, quality assurance standards, facility design, and management support; and (3) affiliate or conversion franchises, which group independent entrepreneurs operating in a segmented industry into a franchise network for the purpose of gaining greater visibility.

✓ **Weigh the advantages and disadvantages.** Purchasing a franchise has several advantages. They include reduced risk, name recognition, and site selection. There are also numerous drawbacks: high cost, loss of control, and required purchases. Before you plunk down any money, weigh both sides and match the perks and pitfalls against your needs and business goals.

✓ **Assess your skills and business goals.** It's not enough to purchase a fast-food franchise because you like french fries or a cleaning company because you're a neat freak. You must consider what talents and experience you are able to bring to the enterprise and identify whether they will benefit the franchise you are looking to buy. In addition to assessing your skills, consider your business goals. Franchising is not for everyone. Loss of control is a major disadvantage. If you are the type of person who wants to own his or her own business so that you can call the shots, you will not want to purchase a franchise.

✓ **Take a look at your budget.** Purchasing a franchise can be very expensive. In addition to the up-front franchise fee, you must shell out money for start-up costs (rent, equipment, utilities, and leasehold improvements), monthly royalty payments, and advertising fees. Depending on the franchise you buy, you can spend anywhere from $5,000 to $50,000 or more in franchise fees and $2,000 to $2 million in start-up costs. If you can only comfortably part with $30,000 to realize your entrepreneurial dream, you may want to choose a different road to ownership.

(continued)

CHECKLIST *(continued)*

✓ **Search for a franchise.** You can find a franchise in a number of places. Most newspapers list franchises (and other businesses for sale) in their classified ads. Consider searching the Internet, contacting a business broker to conduct a search for you, or attending a franchise exposition and talking one-on-one with franchisors about the industry and the advantages and disadvantages of becoming a franchisee.

✓ **Investigate the opportunity.** After you choose a franchise that interests you, conduct an investigation of the franchisor. This includes reviewing the Uniform Franchise Offering Circular (UFOC), a disclosure document that every franchisor is obligated to provide to potential franchisees at least ten business days prior to a franchisee's signing contracts or delivering payment. As part of your research process, conduct interviews with the franchisor and current and/or former franchisees.

✓ **Obtain financing for your venture.** You can finance your franchise in several ways. Most franchisees immediately look toward the franchisor for funding. Some franchisors will finance all the start-up costs. Others will cover 15 to 25 percent of the costs. In the event the franchisor does not offer financial assistance, you should consider approaching family or friends, a commercial finance company, a traditional bank, an investor angel, or the Small Business Administration.

✓ **Review your franchise agreement.** The franchise agreement is the foundation on which your franchise is built. It outlines all operating procedures and spells out the obligations of the franchisor and franchisee. Consult your attorney and/or accountant when reviewing this document, and make sure you understand all of the terms and the language before signing on the dotted line.

RESOURCES FOR MORE INFORMATION

ASSOCIATIONS

- *American Association of Franchisees and Dealers (AAFD)*, P.O. Box 81887, San Diego, CA 92138-1887; 1-800-733-9858; www.aafd.org. This is a national nonprofit trade association that supports the interests of franchisees throughout the United States and represents their rights. The association offers information on how to buy a franchise and provides several publications that highlight the franchising industry.

- *The American Franchise Association (AFA)*, 53 West Jackson Boulevard, Suite 205, Chicago, IL 60604; 312-431-0545; www.infonews.com/franchise/afa. This organization represents and protects the interests of small business franchises. It publishes the *AFA Quarterly*, a newsletter that provides up-to-date details about the franchising industry, and information about the organization's annual convention. AFA also provides franchisees no-cost referrals to reputable franchise attorneys and other business experts.

- *Federal Trade Commission (FTC)*, Room 130, Washington, DC 20580; 202-326-2222; www.ftc.gov. The Federal Trade Commission is a consumer protection agency that maintains regional offices throughout the United States. It can provide you with information regarding franchise law, and will help you seek recourse if you find that a franchisor has violated any federal regulations. The FTC also offers reports, speeches, testimonies, trade regulation rules, consumer and business brochures, and other general information for consumers.

- *Franchise Finance Corporation of America (FFCA)*, 17207 North Perimeter Drive, Scottsdale, AZ 85255-5402; 602-585-4500; www.ffca.com. This specialty retail finance company provides capital for the restaurant, automotive, and service parts industries and for convenience stores. Some of the custom financing solutions it provides include leasing alternatives, equipment loans, and acquisition financing.

(continued)

RESOURCES FOR MORE INFORMATION *(continued)*

- *The International Franchise Association (IFA),* 1350 New York Avenue NW, Suite 900, Washington, DC 20005-4709; 202-628-8000; www.franchise.org. IFA, founded in 1960, supports franchisors, franchisees, and suppliers by providing expert advice and resources for members of the franchising industry. This association provides publications and video and audio cassettes on franchising and issues the *Franchise Opportunities Guide* in printed form and online. This text lists thousands of franchises along with their franchisee fees, start-up costs, and other operational aspects.

- *International Franchise Capital (IFC),* 3900 5th Avenue, Suite 340, San Diego, CA 92103; 619-260-6000; www.franchiseloan.com. This company maintains an aggressive franchise lending program for franchises of all sizes. It approves loans for as little as $200,000 and has virtually no limit on the loan size. No personal guarantees or outside collateral is required to qualify.

NOTES

Chapter 1: Being Your Own Boss: Are You Ready?

1. Cassandra Hayes, "Go For It," *Black Enterprise* (February 1997), p. 82.
2. Hersch Doby, "Snapshot of a Decade," *Black Enterprise* (March 1998), p. 97.

Chapter 3: Market Research 101

1. Marketing Research Association, *What is Marketing and Opinion Research?* 1344 Silas Deane Highway; Suite 306; Rocky Hill, CT 06067-0230.

Chapter 4: Making Your Business Legal

1. Roz Ayres Williams, "Partners for Profit," *Black Enterprise* (January 1998), pp. 78–79.
2. Williams, "Partners for Profit," p. 80.

Chapter 5: Location, Location, Location

1. Wendy Beech, "Look Before You Lease," *Black Enterprise* (November 1997), p. 110.
2. "How a Small Business Incubator Can Nurture Your Start-Up Company." Information and lists in this section are from National Business Incubation Association (Athens, Ohio). Reprinted with permission.

Chapter 6: Insurance and Licenses

1. Sean Mooney, *Insuring Your Business* (New York: Insurance Information Institute Press, 1992).
2. Sean Mooney, *Insuring Your Business* (New York: Insurance Information Institute Press, 1992), p. 49.

Chapter 7: Creating a Winning Business Plan

1. Facts and descriptions of Just Chairs and Gilda & Amir's Salon, Inc. are from Carolyn Brown, "The Do's & Don'ts of Writing a Winning Business Plan," *Black Enterprise* (April 1996). See especially pp. 114 and 122.
2. David Rhine, National Advisor on Family Wealth Planning, BDO Seidman, LLP, Accounts and Consultants, New York, 1998.
3. David Rhine, National Advisor on Family Wealth Planning, BDO Seidman, LLP, Accounts and Consultants, New York, 1998.
4. Roz Ayres-Williams, "Making Sure You Go the Distance," *Black Enterprise* (April 1998), p. 23.
5. Tariq Muhammad, "Plan Write from the Start," *Black Enterprise* (November 1997), p. 42.

Chapter 8: Financing Your Start-Up

1. Karen Gutloff, "Five Alternative Ways to Finance Your Business," *Black Enterprise* (March 1998), p. 82.

2. Information on ACE-Net and The Capital Network taken from page 84 of the article by Karen Gutloff, cited earlier.
3. The Commercial Barter Industry Fact Sheet, International Reciprocal Trade Association, Chicago, IL.
4. Carolyn Brown, "Bartering for Business," *Black Enterprise* (April 1996), p. 36.
5. See page 82 of the article by Karen Gutloff, cited earlier.

Chapter 9: Advertising Your Business

1. Online Women's Business Center, "Advertising Myths," www.onlinewbc.org /docs/market/mk_adv_myths.html (June 1997).
2. Karen Gutloff, "Show and Sell," *Black Enterprise* (July 1998), p. 106.
3. Karen Gutloff, (cited earlier), p. 110.

Chapter 10: Cyberpreneur

1. Tariq Muhammad and Cheryl Coward, "The Black Digerati," *Black Enterprise* (March 1998), p. 49.
2. Bevolyn Williams-Harold, "Riding the Tech Wave," *Black Enterprise* (March 1998), p. 22.
3. Patrick Henry Bass, "Riding the Information Superhighway," *Black Enterprise* (March 1996), p. 86.
4. Cheryl Coward, "Calling All Geeks," *Black Enterprise* (November 1997), p. 39.
5. Tariq K. Muhammad, "Search by Location," *Black Enterprise* (August 1997), p. 42.
6. Carolyn Brown, "Open Your Own Shopping Mall—Online," *Black Enterprise* (July 1998), p. 34.
7. Deidra-Ann Parrish, "Set Up Shop on the Web," *Black Enterprise* (August 1998), p. 36.

Chapter 11: Pricing Your Product or Service

1. Online Women's Business Center, "Pricing—Understanding Costs and Pricing for Profit," www.onlinewbc.org/docs/market/mk_4ps_pricing.html (July 1997).

Chapter 12: Bookkeeping for Your Business

1. David Rhine, National Advisor on Family Wealth Planning, BDO Seidman, LLP, Accountants and Consultants, New York (1998).
2. David Rhine, National Advisor on Family Wealth Planning, BDO Seidman, LLP, Accountants and Consultants, New York (1998).
3. David Rhine, National Advisor on Family Wealth Planning, BDO Seidman, LLP, Accountants and Consultants, New York (1998).

Chapter 14: Buying a Business

1. Joyce Jones, "Shopping for an Enterprise," *Black Enterprise* (September 1998), pp. 78, 82, 83.

Chapter 15: Franchising

1 Gerda Gallop, "15 Franchises You Can Run from Your Home," *Black Enterprise* (September 1998), p. 60.

INDEX

New from the leading source of African American business news and information

BLACK ENTERPRISE FOR

teens

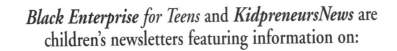

Teaching children to think big while they're still small

Black Enterprise for Teens and *KidpreneursNews* are children's newsletters featuring information on:

- Entrepreneurship
- Investing and money management
- Financial responsibility
- African American History
- Money making ideas

To receive further information, please call toll free: **1-877-KidPren** or visit the Kidpreneurs web pages at **www.blackenterprise.com**